PILGRIMAGE to CRETE

W. E. Welbourne

Copyright © 2019 by W.E. Welbourne.

ISBN-10:   1645504603
ISBN-13:   9781645504603

All rights reserved. No part of this book may be reproduced or transmitted in any form or by any means, electronic or mechanical, including photocopying, recording, or by any information storage and retrieval system, without permission in writing from the copyright owner.

NIV – New International Version
Scripture taken from the Holy Bible, NEW INTERNATIONAL VERSION®. Copyright © 1973, 1978, 1984, 2011 by Biblica, Inc. All rights reserved worldwide. Used by permission. NEW INTERNATIONAL VERSION® and NIV® are registered trademarks of Biblica, Inc. Use of either trademark for the offering of goods or services requires the prior written consent of Biblica US, Inc

CONTENTS

INTRODUCTION v

Chapter 1   THE GREEK ODYSSEY 1

Chapter 2   THE MEDITERRANEAN 28

Chapter 3   THE HOLY LAND 66

Chapter 4   THE AEGEAN 100

Chapter 5   TURKISH DELIGHT 134

Chapter 6   THE DANUBE 152

Chapter 7   THE CZECH REPUBLIC 193

MAPS

Pilgrimage Route 235

German Prisoners of War Camp Locations 236

Sketch Map of Mahrisch Trubau Camp 237

INTRODUCTION

At the outset of the Second World War on September 1, 1939, young Aussie 'diggers' are rushed to assist Britain in its hour of need… to the nearest European war zone in the Middle East and North Africa. My Uncle Arthur, young 'Arty', is one of these – a sapper with 6 years militia training as an army engineer. The ANZAC forces sweep through Libya, from Egypt to Benghazi, defeating superior numbers of heavily armed Italians… the first Allied land victory of the war.

Ill-equipped and lacking promised supplies, the ANZACs are then inappropriately redirected from North Africa to Greece to help the Greeks face the overwhelming German advance. Retreating to Crete, Arty is captured in the Battle of Crete and becomes a POW.

Years later in 2014 I embark on a pilgrimage to trace my uncle's wartime footsteps.

I am born in Newcastle, Australia, on June 27, 1939, barely two months before the outbreak of the war. My childhood memories of the conflict are limited. I am too young to know that I have an uncle overseas fighting against the Nazi. He is my mother's brother, Arthur. Eventually, I have a dim notion that our soldiers are somewhere fighting some bad soldiers. I vaguely recall a patriotic gathering of our extended family and friends at my grandmother's house. There are some soldiers there, so I ask my grandmother to let me sing to everyone. I proudly sing, *'There'll always be an England and England shall be free… Red, White and Blue, What does it mean to you?'*

My mother, Jean Esme (nee Dawson), born April 4, 1919, would sometimes take me to visit my Uncle 'Pop' Smith who lost a leg while fighting overseas in France during in the Great War. He and his wife Emma are without children, so during the Great Depression years my grandmother, Ivy Dawson, reluctantly allows her older sister Emma to raise my mother for a short time. However, Emma wants to keep my mother as her own child.

Mum's parents, Edward known as 'Ted' and Ivy Dawson, struggle through the depression years of the mid 1920s and 30s. They cannot afford rent so my Pa Dawson obtains a miners permit and takes the family to live in a bush humpy near Cessnock on the outskirts of Newcastle. About ten years later they rent an old wooden bungalow in Whiteman's Lane in Waratah, an industrial inner suburb of Newcastle. Suddenly, without warning, my mother is returned, unceremoniously, to her family fold as a 14 year old teenager when Emma gives birth to a son. My mother has lived in the relative comfort of her Aunt Emma's place in comparison to her four siblings who have spent much of their early upbringing living in the bush shack.

Naturally, my mother regards herself as the 'black sheep' of her family. But she makes the adjustment and is well accepted into the family fold upon her return. She has an older brother Arthur, an older sister Clare, a younger sister Dorothy and a younger brother Edward, also called Ted.

Her father remains unemployed and receives 'Susso', a sustenance welfare payment during the Great Depression. Arthur delivers milk twice a day 1.00 am to 7.30 am and 1.00 pm to 3.30 pm for 25 shillings a week and free milk, less than half the average wage at the time. Clare has an office job at the Co-op Store. My mother and sister Dorothy find work as domestics. Teddy is still at school and has been selected to represent the district rugby schoolboy team at the inter-State level.

Growing up in the 1940s I sense that my dad, Sydney or 'Sid' Welbourne, has an important job making steel at the Steel Works. He is sometimes dressed in a soldier's uniform. Eventually, I find out that he is a Lieutenant in the Militia, involved in training to protect the home front against the Japanese. In June 1942 there is a great kerfuffle when a midget Jap submarine fires a shell which just misses the BHP steel works. Mum would sometimes grumble about 'Pig Iron Bob', our former Prime Minister, Robert Gordon Menzies, for wanting to sell pig iron to the Japanese war machine. Our wharfies protest and refuse to load the pig iron onto ships bound for Japan, fearing the Japs would turn it into weapons.

I live through the wartime episode without ever knowing that the war has finished. I eventually realise that the soldiers must have stopped fighting when I am introduced to my Uncle Arthur for the first time. He is interested in me because he has been away for six years and has never seen me. He has returned home from the war and is regarded as a hero. He is a POW who has escaped from the Germans three times. On the other hand, Arthur's younger brother, my Uncle Ted, I know well because he plays rugby league which is a proud tradition in the family. I let them down in this regard, but I will redeem myself in later years by winning NSW 400 m hurdles title in 1962 and a selection on the Empire Games squad.

My dad is the son of a country policeman and is raised in country towns until he comes to Newcastle during the Depression years leading up to the war. He does not engage in sport but is a tough, wiry bushman type who loves the outdoor life of fishing and hunting for rabbits. Australia's rabbit plague provides opportunities for him in his teenage years to earn good money during the Depression. His goal is to shoot and skin 100 rabbits a day on his uncle's New England sheep property at Glen Innes. Dad remains close to his two brothers and three sisters so this means interesting holidays to Sydney, Lismore and the Gold Coast to catch up with my other cousins.

After the war there are too many strikes at the steel works by workers looking for pay increases. Dad does not have a bar of it so he packs us off to Queensland to camp on the waterfront near the Southport jetty on the Gold Coast. His brother-in-law, Howard Waters, lives in Ipswich where he has a flourishing business selling ice-creams, well before Mr Whippy comes along. He sets Dad up selling ice-creams on the coast. For my young sister Gloria and me, this idyllic lifestyle could have lasted forever. But twelve months later a cyclone comes along and flattens most of the tents in the camping ground, except ours. My mother's pleas to return south to our house in Newcastle prevail, despite Dad having just put down a deposit of five pounds to buy a 2 acre Gold Coast weekender for a mere 100 pounds. I cannot imagine what it would be worth today.

Dad settles into a steady job as a train driver until he retires. Our family increases when another four siblings, a brother and three extra sisters, arrive after our return to Newcastle. There is a ten year gap from Gloria and me to the next three, Adrian, Leonie and Susan. Then there is another gap of ten years to Cathy, a happy mistake.

Our parents take us regularly to visit our grandparents, Ma and Pa Dawson, of a Sunday evening. Here the gathering of our extended clan of uncles, aunts and cousins would eat, drink and be merry. Most likely at tea, there is the round table discussion of the local Waratah football match involving my Uncle Ted who plays hooker. Dad may tell a risqué joke especially for grandma and out of earshot of us kids. He may have to explain it a second time to my Aunty Clare so she can get the gist of it. Inevitably she will blush and go, 'Oooh… Sid!' and let out chuckle. Clare meets her boyfriend, my Uncle Frank, at a dance during the Depression, but keeps him waiting for 50 years before tying the knot in 1984. One evening Dad brings along his 'fart' machine, a rubber band and wire affair. Sitting on a padded chair he would occasionally let one rip and cause laughter, especially when Arthur's wife Jean, not in on the act, announces, "I smell burning rubber!"

A hearty sing-song around the piano usually follows as my cousin Judy belts out a few old favourites such as *'On Top of Old Smokey'* and *'You Are My Sunshine'*. A half-serious game of cards often takes place with the grown-ups. They mainly play 500 or Rummy, but we kids have a variety of favourites, including Snap, 31, and Poker. Eventually, a cup of tea and supper comes along. Aunty Clare magically produces Sao biscuits with tomato and cheese and also my favourite-- a double cream filled sponge cake smothered with passion fruit icing.

I am raised as a protected species, shielded from the war and raised as a baby boomer. My mother is especially protective and often will warn me against any men who wear yellow socks. However, fortunately, I never come across any, neither at Sunday school nor the Boy Scouts. I simply wonder what on earth she is talking about. Nor do I come across any yellow sock people after leaving school aged 14 to work as a clerk in the wool packing firm of Grazcos, where a diet of rough language is the order of the day. It is not until I enter teachers college in 1962, engaged to be married at the age of 23 that the penny drops. I am at ASOPA, the Australian School of Pacific Administration, in the Sydney suburb of Mosman, attending a lecture by well-known anthropologist Ruth Finke. Our intake of 56 students is being prepared to teach in the Australian Territories of Papua and New Guinea. Her lecture touches on a tribe of natives that practise sodomy. I look the word up later and suddenly a yellow sock flashbulb sets my brain alight. But really, can this perversion occur in our civilised society? I dismiss the thought, thinking it is a crude sexual ritual practiced in some uncivilized native cultures.

My posting to Rabaul as a Cadet Education Officer in November 1963 has a profound effect upon my views of the world. One cannot help to notice how determined the Japanese war machine must have been in attempting to add New Guinea, the second largest island in the world, to its Pacific Empire. In 1942 the Japanese war plans include the invasion and occupation of the Australian Territories of Papua and New Guinea.

Rabaul, located on the northern tip of the Gazelle Peninsula on the island of New Britain, is under the Japanese radar to become a permanent base to protect their conquests in in the South-West Pacific. At the time, Rabaul is probably the only township in the world located on a caldera, inside the rim of a huge extinct volcano. The beautiful Rabaul Harbour is formed following a volcanic eruption in the fifteenth century which created a circular rim of smaller smoking mountains around a deep water caldera with an opening to the sea called Blanche Bay. This is the site chosen for the first Japanese landing in New Guinea.

Soon after midnight, on January 23, 1942, the Japanese attack in overwhelming numbers at six points around the harbour. The small Australian Lark Force under the command of Colonel J. J. Scanlan consists of 1397 men. Outnumbered, they scatter in all directions when Scanlan gives his famous order, 'Every man for himself'. Remnants of the Lark Force manage to escape by staggering through jungle and plantations to the south coast of the island where they are rescued by small craft and taken to Samaria, Port Moresby or Cairns. A Patrol Officer turned Coastwatcher, Ian Downs, helps one group of 156 soldiers, under the command of Major Owen, to escape to Jacquinot Bay on the south coast. Here they cram onto the 31 metre *Laurabada*, commanded by Patrol Officer, Lt Ivan Champion. Leaving on April 9, 1942, they escape detection and arrive three days later in Port Moresby from where they are shipped aboard the *Macdhui* to Cairns and Townsville.

These are the lucky ones. Others die from sheer exhaustion or illness in the jungle. Some 800 soldiers surrender or are captured. Of these more than 150 are brutally bayonetted to death at Tol and Waitavolo Plantations. On June 22, 1942, some 849 half-starved military prisoners and about 200 civilians are marched from the prison compound in Rabaul and boarded on the steamer *Montevideo Maru,* bound for Japan. On July 1, 1943 the ship is sunk by the US submarine *Sturgeon* off Luzon in the South China Sea. Not one prisoner survives.

The Japanese soon convert Rabaul into a major naval base for launching her attacks on Papua and New Guinea and also to support its drawn-out land and sea battles in Guadalcanal. Japan's two major sea battles emanating from Rabaul end disastrously for their southern advance towards Port Moresby in Papua and the Australian mainland. Japan's defeats in *The Battle of the Coral Sea* in 1942 and *The Battle of the Bismarck Sea* in 1943 effectively destroy its naval supremacy in the Pacific.

Rabaul Harbour becomes a graveyard of wrecked Japanese ships. Salvage operations for tons of scrap metals are still in progress when our squad of teachers arrive in November, 1963. Today Rabaul is well-known as a wreck-diver's paradise. Even if you are not a diver, Rabaul offers visitors its magnificent scenery and a fascinating history. My wife Pam and I fly into Rabaul on a DC 3 aircraft which lands on the wartime Lakunai airstrip. A strong smell of sulpha fumes from the nearby active Matupit volcano is evident upon our arrival. The fumes act like a big mosquito repellent for the area and also help my wife's asthmatic condition during our seven years there.

Clearly seen from the air on the approach to the town are the rusting hulls of the remaining wartime shipping wrecks in Simpson Harbour, like an open museum of the tragedy. This blot on the tropical paradise leaves me begging the question of why mankind finds it necessary to beat the hell out of one another. Years later I am still searching for answers. But greed and lust for power, often combined with exalted narcissism, have a lot to answer for in this selfish disregard of humanity. What is the purpose of such futile and senseless actions that causes so much death and destruction to society?

History helps to explain man's shortcomings and achievements. In my case it explains why my mother's ancestors are convicts transported from England to Australia in the 1829 and 1834. It explains why my father's ancestors choose an assisted immigration passage from England to Newcastle in 1856 to help build the nation's first railway. History helps to explain the combination of factors of why England joins the Allied forces against the Axis powers in the Second World War.

During our time in Papua New Guinea from 1963 to 1975, I witness history in the making as the two territories continue their path towards Independence. Since the war, the Territories of Papua and New Guinea have been jointly administered and are being prepared for nationhood. In 1971 I am posted to Port Moresby in Papua to a research position in the Land Settlement Section of the Lands Department. In the lead up to Independence I am appointed Secretary to the Commission of Inquiry into Land Matters, 1972-73. Land problems have to be sorted out as part of the nation building process before Independence. I am able to travel to all parts of the country and witness the wartime recovery, a quarter of a century later. I witness the initiatives being made in industry, forestry and agricultural development. In 1974 I am invited to be the Chief Executive Officer to PNG's Independence Planning Committee. On September 16, 1975 Independence is achieved when both territories amalgamate to become the nation of Papua New Guinea, also called 'PNG'.

During our annual leave from PNG we ritually fly home to reconnect, face-to-face, with our family connections. Our two sons, Tony and Andrew, are born in Rabaul and our two daughters, Julie-Anne and Angelique, follow during our stay in PNG. Our days in PNG are over when, for family reasons, it is necessary to return to Australia soon after Independence. Our boys are ready for high school and both girls were ill, particularly Julie-Anne who requires chemo therapy. I return to teaching, accepting a position in the Junior School at Brisbane Boys' College. I am still an active athlete, so part of my duties includes the role as Sports Master. One of the joys of the Junior School is the annual camping trip made available for senior primary students. We would travel to iconic places in Australia, such as Ayers Rock, The Barrier Reef, Cape York and Tasmania. These busy years last until 1998 when I retire to nurse my wife who eventually succumbs to asthma.

I remember a distinguished family gathering in the summer of January 23, 1993, for the marriage of our son Commander Tony Welbourne to Paulina Butler in St Mark's Chapel at HMAS Cerberus Naval Base, a training establishment at Crib Point on the Mornington Peninsula. A snapshot is taken of my dad proudly seated with my four most senior aunts and uncles. Wartime hero Uncle Arthur Dawson is with his wife Jean (nee Kent) and his sister, my Aunty Clare (nee Dawson), and her husband Frank Dennett at the opposite end (See photo). My mother, Jean Esme (nee Dawson) is not included because she dies of arthritis and stroke in January 1990 at the relatively young age of 70. Within a decade the three men in the photo, all in their eighties, have passed on: my dad 'Sid' in December 1997, Arthur in April 2000 and Frank in October 2002.

The men are smiling, displaying contentment, in this moment of happiness. But they have witnessed the scourge of war in their youth. My dad first meets Arthur when he joins the same militia training unit at Waratah in the lead up to the war. Arthur joins in 1933, aged 19, when war is brewing. Hitler is causing trouble in Europe and it seems obvious to Arthur that another World War is in the making. My dad joins the unit in 1936 when he comes down to Newcastle from Lismore in the Northern Tablelands of NSW. Arthur introduces him to his sister Jean and in 1938 they marry. Strange as it seems, maybe I owe my life to Hitler, because militia training brings Dad and Arthur together.

Their Militia Unit is the headquarters of the First Field Company of Engineers that teaches skills other than just weapons and their uses. Arthur is hooked on being a Sapper and he joins the queue as soon as enlistments open when England declares war on Germany, December 3, 1939. Arthur realizes the dangers of being killed or maimed, but he is determined to return in one piece. My dad tries a couple of times to enlist, but his job making steel is deemed too important and debars him from active service overseas. When not making steel, dad is required to spend time at training camps, preparing recruits for service on the homefront or overseas.

Arthur can consider himself lucky to return after six long years in the theatre of war. On January 10, 1940 he sails on the *Orcades* to Egypt in the first convoy. The ANZAC troops take part in the successful Western desert Campaign that sweeps through Libya, from Egypt to Bengasi, defeating superior numbers of heavily armed Italians in the first allied land victory of WW II. In 1941, the battle-hardened ANZACs are redirected from North Africa to Greece in a hazardous effort to assist the Greeks against the Germans. The Greek campaign ends in disaster. Our ill-equipped troops face the overwhelming German advance and are forced to evacuate to Crete in April, 1941.

Two months later Arthur is captured on Crete following the successful but costly invasion by German paratroopers. The Royal Navy manages to evacuate around 10,000 allied soldiers from Crete to Egypt, but they do not have enough ships to take the remaining troops. Arthur becomes a POW on June 1, 1941. He is herded with other prisoners onto a train heading to German through Greece.

As a POW, Arthur escapes three times. Two attempts are made in Greece and result in his recapture. His successful third escape is from a German POW working party at Mahrisch Trubau in Czechoslovakia when Central Europe is in turmoil during the closing stages of WW II. The Germans are too busy protecting themselves from the Allied advance to worry about escapees.

Arthur never forgets the kindness and courage of the Greek family who rescues and supports him for three weeks following his first escape from a train bound for Stalag 8B POW camp in Germany. The humble Antoniadou family feeds Arthur sour milk and a kind of porridge which helps cure his dysentery. Following the war his gratitude widens into a deep lasting friendship, conducted by correspondence, twice a year at least. Imagine his joy in 1991 when at the age of 75 he gets his chance to return to the tiny village of Pefkodassos in northern Greece to meet his Greek rescuers. The occasion is during the 6th Division Veteran's tour of Greece and Crete marking the fiftieth year of the battle.

I begin to learn of my uncle's war exploits after I return from my time in PNG. He seems content to get up early to do his newspaper run. But etched in his mind are the vivid memories of his family's struggles during the Depression and the story of his wartime exploits and mateship. In his late 70's he buys a second-hand typewriter to write from memory his story, predominately for family consumption. He makes two carbon copies of his remarkable war service, amounting to 462 pages under the title of *'A Sapper's Story'* by T.A. Dawson. I am privileged to have a copy. The original copy is available in the research department of the Australian War Memorial. Arthur thinks about calling his book, *'Five Bob a Day Bloody Murderers'*, because that is all the soldiers are paid during their warfare training.

I am troubled to know why Arthur and my father are willing to fight for their king and country. A simple answer is provided by Sergeant Reg Jobber who writes a forward to Arthur's book – *'I, along with Arthur and many more mates from the Militia, joined the Army when England declared war. We felt it was our duty to do so.'* Was this Declaration for Australia's 'Mother Country' a just cause to make them feel so duty bound? Surely, human nature suggests that Blind Faith in leadership is wrong if that leadership aims to conquer without just cause. How many times in history have leaders sent their sons to war in order to uphold their own power or to subdue, invade and take from others? In the animal kingdom, the Law of the Jungle presumes that the strongest survive. Unfortunately, for the same reason, the animal law applies to human beings whose activity is not regulated by the laws or ethics of civilization. And so it was on the eve of 1939.

During the 1930s it seems clear that Hitler and his Nazi party are acting like an unruly mob of school bullies in the playground which is Europe and subsequently the whole world. Diplomacy has failed so England and its Allies are left with no option other than to use force to defend themselves. The catastrophic consequences result in deaths of over 60 million people, the deadliest military conflict in history.

A century after the start of First World War (1914-18) I am motivated to visit the conflict zones of Gallipoli and to follow my uncle's wartime exploits from the time of his capture in the Battle of Crete in June 1941 until his final escape from a German work camp in Czechoslovakia in 1945. Modern day travel makes it possible to visit not only the more recent wartime scenes of Central Europe, but also to visit the classical civilizations to discover the history, art and cultures of the Mediterranean.

Accompanying me on my journey is Avril who is born in England a year before me. Unlike me, she has vivid wartime memories of the conflict from her childhood. She is sent to the countryside to escape the bombing and remembers time spent in air raid shelters. During the war her family survives on wartime rations and Avril thinks the gravy bits of dripping soaked in bread are a real treat. In 1950 Avril's parents decide to join the queue leaving war-ravaged England, thinking that Australia offers better opportunities for their two daughters.

In the years after the Second World War Australia feels isolated and the popular belief is that Australia must 'populate or perish'. An ambitious post-war reconstruction program is established, aimed at increasing Australia's population by 1 percent per annum. The Government of Australia establishes the Assisted Passage Migration Scheme to subsidize British citizens willing to migrate under the program. The colloquial term 'Ten Pound Poms' is used to describe these migrants. For Avril's parents the effect of war has brought about their decision to migrate.

Leaving school friends behind is a tough social adjustment for Avril who is about to enter her teens. But survive she does. Avril meets me at an old time dance and joins me on this historic journey which begins in Greece at the small village of Pefkodassos where Arthur recuperated following his first escape.

We journey to Crete to the tiny fishing cove at Sfakia where Arthur was captured. We then continue to the Holy Land where Australian troops disembarked before entering Egypt to begin the Western Desert Campaign. We visit ancient sites in Turkey before arriving at ANZAC Cove in Gallipoli. In Central Europe we follow the Danube from Budapest to Nuremburg where Nazi war criminals were brought to trial after the war. We travel to Prague in the Czech Republic where our guide Radek takes us to the township of Moravska Trebova. He has located the site of the POW German work camp, now occupied by modern housing. We are introduced to the town mayor, Milos Izak, who is interested in a sketch map which pinpoints the village locations and prison quarters where Arthur and his mates stayed. The map entitled 'Mahrisch Trubau and District', the German name of the town, is drawn from memory by Norm Shute after returning home.

This book crams in a history of heroes, conquerors and misfits throughout its pages, a good title for the book. However, I am inspired to write about why we made this journey which follows my uncle's wartime footsteps. Our pilgrimage centres on the aftermath of Arthur's capture in the Battle of Crete and that is why the book receives its title.

A 1993 family photo shows Arthur, coat in hand, seated between his wife Jean and brother-in-law Sydney. Arthur's sister Clare and her husband Frank are on Jean's right.

Sweetheart Jean Kent, Arthur's future wife.

Preparing for war, Arthur farewells his mother.

The fruits of the Middle East. Arthur enjoys a bunch of grapes with his digger mates whilst on leave in Palestine.

Arthur at home in Newcastle with his parents, final leave, Christmas 1939.

George Antoniadou and Arthur reunion, Pefkodassos 1991.

Young Arthur with parents, 'Ted' and Ivy Dawson, and his sister Clare.

In 1991, 50 years since the Battle of Crete, Arthur Dawson returns to Greece to meet his 'Greek Family', George and Rachel Antoniadou and grandchild Rafael

CHAPTER 1

THE GREEK ODYSSEY

Day 1
Wednesday March 12, 2014.

Melbourne to Thessaloniki

At 5.00 pm we are farewelled by our eldest sons from Avril's abode -- Avril's Russell and my Tony, still dressed in his navy gear and on his way home from the naval base at HMAS Cerberus. The 5.00 pm traffic flows freely and we arrive at Eager Beaver Airport Parking by 6.30 pm as arranged. We have ample time to catch our Emirate Flight 407 due to depart at 10.30 pm for Dubai, connecting to Athens. I have already completed our online boarding passes and all we have to do is check in our two medium size suit cases. We are actually the first in line when the check-in lines open at 7.30 pm. We do some duty free shopping for Grand Marnier and Glenfiddich whiskey. Our long haul A 380 jet flight is delayed for nearly an hour but we make good time to Dubai, almost a 12,000 km straight line across the Indian Ocean from Melbourne. The jet flies at 40,000 feet which would clear Mt Everest by 10,000 feet. The outside temperature reaches - 50 C. We kill the 14 hour flight time by watching from the extensive range of the latest on-flight movies.

Dubai is a cool 24 C at 6.30 am touchdown. Our connecting flight from Dubai to Athens allows us 3 hours before boarding. The airport is so extensive that a busy rail train is needed to transport connecting passengers to their various destinations. You are then taken by lifts to another floor where you walk several blocks past the glittering duty free shops. I have a heavy backpack and I'm thankful to find moving escalators to assist us to Gateway A 19, about a kilometre away from the lifts. We think about buying a MacCafe coffee. They say we can use Euro but we will get change in local currency. At 4 Euro for each coffee we pass on it, and pocket our 10 Euro.

The hike to our flight connection from Gateway A19 becomes a marathon. The real purpose of going up to the Tinsel Town of Duty Free shops is to entice you to buy overpriced stuff before you are sent back down to ground level. Two hours later we are directed to move through a door and down 4 levels of electronic stairs to the ground floor where a bus is waiting. It transports us through a maze of roadways to our plane which is parked among others on the tarmac about 5 kilometres away. Here we wait 10 minutes before climbing an outside stair ladder of our connecting Flight EK 105 to Athens. Here we are stuffed inside for an hour in the desert sun while we wait for two or three other busloads of passengers to join us. Once the full complement of about 200 passengers are on board, we are ready to make the 4 hour 50 minutes flight to Athens. We leave the dusty haze of Dubai behind as we climb above the Red Sea and the North African desert.

Athens is a picture of cultivated green hills as we approach the airport. A couple of small islands are seen in the vivid blue of the Aegean Sea. We arrive at 1.30 pm Greek time. Athens airport is easy to negotiate by comparison to Dubai and the Duty Free is nowhere near as ostentatious. We have over 3 hours to kill before our domestic flight departs to Thessaloniki at 5.30 pm. We relax in a lounge and enjoy a crisp bun filled with juicy tomato, cheese, lettuce and ham. Our Flight A3 124 takes only half an hour to reach the northern and second largest city in Greece. We need to pass through a security conscious check-in before boarding. Avril walks through a body scan forgetting she has her tiny pill box in her pocket. The miniscule container is placed in one of the big security boxes to go through the main screen. Nothing is left to chance; it could be an explosive item! I too have to remove my leather belt and empty my trouser pockets of tissues and a plastic comb.

Aegean Airways is one of the top domestic companies operating in Greece. There is a power charger on hand in the airport lounge. I make use of it to charge up my computer as we wait for our flight. Avril is dressed only in a light top and slacks and says she is feeling a little cold. I have dispensed with my coat but I notice that 99 per cent of the awaiting passengers all have coats.

Our flight arrives in Thessaloniki on time at 6.35 pm, just as the sun, a huge red glow, is setting in the distant hills. The temperature is probably a pleasant 15 C. Fine weather in the low 20's is expected over the next couple of days. We quickly pass through immigration and head for Hertz Rental Cars to check our prior arrangements. Fortunately we are first in a busy line. The attendant takes our details and he quizzes my request for a GPS. He thought a map might do. We then wait outside the terminal for the Hertz mini bus to take us to our small black 120 Hyundai.

Our car is manual drive and we have trouble fitting our luggage in. I have never driven a left hand vehicle before and this will be a real test. Avril goes to hop in but realizes she is on the wrong side. I go to use the indicators and find the rear windscreen wipers are on. I go to put on the GPS and our attendant says I will not need it to find our hotel. 'Just follow the dual lane straight road into the city as far as you can go, and then take the roundabout. You are then in the main street. You can't miss the Electra Palace Hotel. It is the main building.' WRONG – it sounds simple enough, but it's now nightfall and city is packed like sardines with the locals scampering in all directions.

The traffic is a mingle of motor scooters, small cars, large busses and taxis, all jockeying for positions like a dodgem cars at a circus. There isn't a sign of our hotel. Not knowing where we are, we search for a place to pull over in order to connect to the GPS. It directs us to our destination in front of a busy square which is blocked for use by pedestrians. So we circle again and again for more than an hour and we finally guess that the hotel has no parking facilities. In the process I side swipe an awkwardly parked car with its nose sticking out. Later we use tissues to wipe the white paint streak from the side panels of our little black Hyundai.

Too exhausted to continue we stumble across a 24 hour parking site down a narrow alley and we walk to the hotel. Reception confirms that they have no parking facilities, but they provide vouchers to be used at nearby private parking. Fortunately the site where we parked is one of their sites available at 16 Euros per day. At last we have arrived after a day and a half of travel. We brew a cup of tea, take a hot shower and sink into a proper bed.

Day 2…
Friday March 14, 2014.
Thessaloniki to Pefkodassos

I wake at 6.00 am to the welcoming sunlight of a delightful spring day in northern Greece. I make a morning cuppa and prepare to travel up to Pefkodassos, a small village near the northern Greek border. This is where my uncle, Arthur Dawson, spends 3 weeks while on the run from the Germans as an escaped POW in 1941. Arthur is captured at Sfakia on Crete on June 1, 1941. He escapes his capture by jumping out of a train in Greece and he finds support from the humble Antoniadou family of Pefkodassos.

This is his recall of events: *'The Germans put me on a train heading for Germany. We were jam-packed together, herded like horses or cattle. The train was full of dysentery; just about everyone on board had it. Packed in as we were, with no toilets and no washing facilities, you can imagine how disgusting we were.'*

The train chugs slowly north across the broad Macedonian plain and into the foothills on the Yugoslav border. At this point, Arthur finds an opportunity to escape. He explains: *'Some blokes managed to open a hole in the floor. It was risky but I decided anything would be better than being a prisoner of war. I slipped through the hole, and watched the train go away.'*

Arthur is lucky. Others who try similar methods of escaping are caught under the wheels.

With neither map nor compass, Arthur staggers across unfamiliar country alone. Weak from dysentery and exhaustion he collapses in a field near the small Greek village of Pefkodassos. *'I had only gone a mile or two when I collapsed in the field, not far from this little village. The next thing I knew, I was being cared for by this Greek family. I couldn't speak their language. They couldn't speak mine. It didn't matter to me.'*

The head of the Antoniadou family finds Arthur unconscious in a patch of melons. At an enormous risk to himself and his family, Mr Antoniadou carries Arthur back to the safety of his home. Arthur stays there for three weeks until his health is restored. They feed him on sour milk and a kind of porridge, which helps cure his dysentery. During his recuperation he works in the fields dressed up like a Greek peasant.

Arthur never forgets the Antoniadou kindness and over the years he keeps in touch by writing to them after the war. Fifty years later in 1991, he and two of his army mates are able to visit the village during a trip to Greece made by veterans from the 2/3rd Field Engineer Company. The old man of the family and his wife are now dead. But Arthur is able to enjoy a reunion with their daughter Rachel, 15 at the time of Arthur's escape, and her then-boyfriend, George, whom she later marries. Arthur dies in 2002 but the Greek family continue writing to his wife Jean and his sister Clare who live in retirement villages in Newcastle.

On this lovely spring day I hope that my trip to Pefkodassos will allow me the privilege to meet the Antoniadou family. Avril's navigation and the GPS guide me through the tight morning traffic to the highway leading north. Here the speed limit is 120 km per hour. Many cars ignore the limit and glide past me as I head towards Arthur's village. At midday we turn off the highway onto the road that leads to Pefkodassos. Twenty minutes later we come to a cluster of probably three hundred homes and a few shops. I choose to stop at a small fruit and drink store at the top of the hill. A young woman walks out and I ask if she could help me find Arthur's Greek family. I show her a newspaper photo of Arthur's visit in 1991. She immediately is overwhelmed with excitement. She is Alexandra who is the daughter of Rachel's cousin. She wants us to meet Rachel.

We reverse a short way down the hill and stop at a small brick cottage with a second floor. In an instant Alexandra rouses the family and what follows is something akin to the Second Coming as the Antoniadou family emerge to greet us. The 88 year old Rachel (Rahil in Greek) is first on the scene and plants kisses on Avril and me. She is quickly followed by her son George (Junior) who is the spitting image of his father George Senior who died 5 years ago. By good fortune Arthur met Rachel's husband in the 1991 reunion.

Plastic chairs appear and we are invited to sit in the perfect spring sunshine. We are introduced to Marie who is married to the 55 year old George junior. They introduce us to their son Rafael, a well-built young man who is all smiles. He is an IT economist but is unemployed, given the constraints of the Greek economy. I cannot imagine how his qualifications would help him find employment in a small village. His brother has had to move to Europe's economic powerhouse, Germany, to find work. George Jnr and Marie's daughter, Sophia, is also there and she helps to organise our chairs and prepare cups of coffee which we later take inside.

George Jnr dashes about in the background taking photos. Later he slips away to copy these onto a flash drive which he gives me before we leave. He comes up to me and says, 'You are my Brother.' He cannot be generous enough. He gives me two bottles of wine and two batteries for my camera when mine are spent from taking too many photos. We transfer inside and the young daughter of Sophia appears. She is Maria, a slim attractive nurse on her fortnightly leave from Athens where she tests blood of haemophiliacs. She explains in perfect English that she returns home every fortnight to stay with the family. She misses her husband who is a road construction worker and they rarely have time together. She says her monthly wage of 1200 Euro was reduced to 700 Euro following Greece's Economic squeeze which almost bankrupted their economy. Half of her wage goes on rental accommodation in Athens.

We are encouraged to stay on for lunch. Sophia sneaks away and returns with chicken pieces and meat balls and chips. We all eat around a small table and enjoy lively conversation. Maria interprets in English. I notice that Avril and I are the only ones with chicken and Rachel and George have a couple of meat balls. They also have a rice mix of vegetables. Rafael has nothing to eat and I query his abstinence. They are Orthodox Greeks and it is the period of fasting during Lent.

Rachel sits next to me and is still overwhelmed by our visit. Maria tells me that she had tears of joy when we arrived. Rachel later hands me a photo keepsake of her in her younger days when she visited Russia. I wonder why she would visit Russia. Apparently, over the years, Greek families would settle in various parts of Europe. Indeed many Greek families have settled in Australia. At home in Melbourne is the largest Greek community of any city outside of Greece – over 150,000 Greeks call Melbourne home. Some of Rachel's ancestors settle in Turkey and Russia. The First World War changes everything. After the war in 1921, a transmigration swap scheme forces Greeks living in Turkey to be returned to Greece as refugees. Rachel's ancestors settle near the Bulgarian border in Pefkodassos and live off the land. Rachel still has family connections living in Russia and she used to visit them. This is no longer possible because of her age.

After lunch we visit the old house where Arthur stayed during his escape. It is very run down and only a short walk away. George Jnr's brother, wife and family now occupy the ramshackle home. Chooks roam about an extensively fenced backyard, protected by an angry chained dog which growls its annoyance at our visit. We are shown where Arthur and a couple of his mates slept on the floor while on the run. There is an escape doorway in another room which allows them to slip away in the event of a visit from the Nazis.

At 4.00 pm it is time to leave, but not before keepsake gifts are bestowed upon us. Marie involves herself with fine tapestry and has two large scenes on display in the living room. She hands Avril a handcrafted woollen carry bag and Sophie presents Avril with a pair of ear rings. Their generosity is overwhelming. George Junior hugs me and tells me again that we are brothers. He gives me a small keepsake to remind me of this bond. More hugs and kisses send us on our way.

In little more than an hour we reach Thessaloniki. The city traffic is then a crawl, but we manage to find our car park at our first attempt. We make a cuppa and later decide to mingle with the ceaseless trample of feet in the outside city square. We squeeze inside one of the many bars for a light snack and drink. The hot chocolate and strawberry dessert pie is too rich for Avril to complete. I fare better with a cool beer and a slice of tangerine pie. We then return to check our itinerary and find that no provision has been made for our overnight accommodation on Saturday. We sort this out with the concierge and finally retire to bed about 11.15 pm.

Day 3
Saturday March 15, 2014.

Thessaloniki

'Beware the ides of March.' Today is the anniversary of that fateful day of the assassination of Julius Caesar in 44 BC. Surely, we have nothing to fear. We wake at 7.15 am to a glorious sunny day. We relax and later in the morning we join the throngs that crowd the bars and restaurants of the city. At 10.30 am we take a walk along the waterfront to visit the White Tower which Maria recommended to us. This tower was built in the fifteenth century after the fall of Thessaloniki to the Ottomans in 1430. At its location there had been an older tower belonging to Thessaloniki's Byzantine fortifications.

Over the years the tower has had various names: the Lion Tower in the sixteenth century and the Tower of Kalamaria in the eighteenth. In the nineteenth century it becomes the Tower of the Janissaries when the garrison of Janissaries are stationed there. Then it is known as the Tower of Blood when it becomes a prison and place for the execution of convicts. Later in the nineteenth century those condemned to death are slaughtered on its terrace and their blood is used to dye its walls red. A cannon shot from the western part of the city signifies that the death sentence has been carried out. In 1883, on the orders of Sultan Abdul Hamid II, the Tower is painted white and given the name 'White Tower'. A convict, Nathan Guiledi, whitewashes the Tower in exchange for his freedom. It has remained with its current name since then.

The busy bars spill out onto the pavement. To avoid jostling crowd we cross the road to the sea-walk and parklands which recently have undergone a makeover. Now opened to the public, the modern extensions form an attractive 3.5 kilometre walkway. A half hour stroll eventually leads us to the Tower which is now a museum. There is a small entrance fee of 4 Euro. We are offered headphones to explain the exhibits which have Greek captions. The Tower is circular with a height of 34 metres and a diameter of almost 22 metres. It consists of a ground floor entrance and six upper stories, built of stone, brick and plaster. A glorious panoramic view of the city and the harbour is obtained from the battlements at the rooftop. One has to climb the circular stairwell to get there. But you take your time and visit the historic exhibits at each level. At the third level I take a shortcut to another exhibit by slipping through a low narrow archway. Avril also tries but forgets to duck her head. She thinks and feels that *'The Ides of March'* truly have arrived.

Around 2.00 pm we return to the ever busy main square outside our hotel. We find a comfortable nook in one of the street bars and order a cool Heineken beer. The waiter serves water and a small bowl of tasty crisps. We now sit back and admire the activity in the square and the lovely view of the blue Aegean Sea.

It is such a nice setting that we return again at 7.30 pm in the evening for coffee and a plate of toasted sandwiches. Back at the hotel we have our dessert by sharing a banana and a plum we swiped from the breakfast table this morning. We make a cuppa tea and we finish off the chocolates left on our bed by our room attendant. We catch up on the World News and crash to bed at 11.15 pm.

Day 4
Sunday March 16, 2014.

Thessaloniki to Larissa

I arise at 6.08 am to prepare a cuppa and quickly shower. Today we begin a self-drive for 6 days around northern Greece. We will be heading south to Larissa, about 247 kilometres away. We are in the hotel restaurant having breakfast by 7.30 am. The view from the top floor affords a splendid view of the Aegean. A couple of Greek flags are fluttering from nearby buildings and pigeons are enjoying a fly past. Three or four ships are at anchor in the harbour. Bright sunlight streams in through the window beside our breakfast table. We settle the hotel account for an extra day at 140 Euro and then drag our suitcases and backpacks to the car park about 400 metres away. Sunday morning traffic in Thessaloniki is light, so we manage to escape the city without too much hassle.

We head to Vergina, the first capital of Macedonia. Acres of peach trees are in full bloom, painting a pink landscape as we make our way to this ancient centre situated in the foothills of snow-covered mountain peaks. Fresh snowy water flows into a river crossing where we stop to take in the scene. From a spring fed water fountain I fill our water bottle. Arriving at Vergina, we stop near the sleepy main centre which has a pub and few shops. Greek dwellings here are moderate square brick constructions and most have fruit trees growing in their gardens. One has a magnificent pink magnolia, so we park our car near it and walk to the pub. Seated around tables under the verandah and inside are about six groups of middle aged men chatting contentedly and playing cards. We order espresso which tastes like mud and we are quickly on our way.

Next we head to Dion about an hour away. The country road network leads us through more orchards and some freshly planted fields of wheat. Dion is perched in the foothills below the mountain range. Outside the township a few walking groups are enjoying their Sunday outing. We notice a road sign that points to an old monastery, so we decide to follow it into the mountains. It twists and winds its way up the heavily forested mountain slope. About 7 kilometres on we stop outside a rest area where several cars are parked. The large modern building complex is a restaurant and accommodation centre which offers a grand view of the coastline. This is a perfect place to have lunch as it is now 1.15 pm. We climb the stairs and sit ourselves down to take in the panoramic view of the mountain scenery and the coastal townships. Avril orders a welcome cup of black tea and a chicken souvlaki and I have coffee and a burger.

We are informed that the monastery is a further 7 kilometres away. It is hidden deep within the mountain ridges. We arrive about 2.30 pm and I am in awe of its crumbling features. A sign in the car park says it is St Dionysus of Olympos. Some of the structure is still standing but much its thick walls are fractured. A warning sign cautions visitors. We enter the grounds and a sign tells its story:

> The Holy Monastery of Saint Dionysios of Olympos having been characterized as a historical scheduled monument, was erected by Saint Dionysios himself in 1542. During its long history the holy monastery has been plundered several times and has undergone many disasters, the most important of which was its complete destruction in 1943 by the German troops. From then on, for a period of more than 60 years, this monastery has been in ruins. Recently the construction works of the catholicon (the principal church in the monastery complex) were completed. However, for its general completion among other things the following scheduled works are still to be done. Therefore we ask for your love and care: 1. Construction of the doors and windows 2. Installation of central heating 3. Construction of a woodcarved iconostasis (the screen separating the nave from the sanctuary, usually decorated with a number of icons) 4. Construction of pews 5. Purchase of chandeliers, church vessels etc.

An archway leads us into the inner sanctum where some progress has been made to the reconstruction. A couple of bearded priests dressed in long black robes are busily moving about the site, opening up construction sheds and talking to a layman. Avril and I keep exploring and enter a doorway leading to the partially restored worship area. It is an oasis of splendour among the ruins and a hopeful sign of the eventual full restoration. Shameful acts of mankind brought about its destruction; inspired hopes are working to restore its former glory.

We push on towards our destination at Larissa which is still over a 100 kilometres away. It doesn't seem much effort if you pay the toll to travel the motorways which allow speeds of 130 km per hour. But you wouldn't see much. I press AVOID on the GPS. So now we find ourselves in goat country, travelling a twisted route high into the mountains. The variety of scenery is magnificent to witness. We climb slowly around the twisted S-shaped bends, higher and higher through forested slopes which allow occasional glimpses of the coast. We stop to allow a herd of wild goats to cross our path. Eventually we reach a high undulating plain with farms and a backdrop of snow-topped mountains. We stop near a farm gateway to admire the scene. Time slips by quickly and we need to move on through farmlands carrying livestock of cattle, sheep and goat herds. We crawl slowly past some cattle crossing the narrow sealed roadway. Farm dogs snap at our intrusion.

About 15 km out from Larissa we come to the main coastal roads leading to the busy township. It is now 6.00 pm and I am very much weary from driving all those twists and turns. Fortunately I remember to go anti clockwise on the multiple entry roundabout leading into the main street. A little further on my GPS tells me to turn into what is really pedestrian thoroughfare. I see another car parked there so I do likewise. Avril hops out and asks someone the whereabouts of the Divani Larissa Palace. He points and says, 'It is just down there.' She goes inside and the receptionist says that she has been expecting us.

The receptionist waits outside and directs me to a section where I can park temporarily. This allows us time to remove our suit cases. The destination of the car park requires me to drive around the corner of the pedestrian mall through rows of tables and chairs filled with local Greeks enjoying a late afternoon sundowner. An electronic key allows us to park our car inside, all for 10 Euro. To complete our day we need a drink, a refreshing Heineken beer in the hotel restaurant. We have a light meal of minestrone soup for Avril and toasted sandwiches for me. We watch some news on TV and retire in need of a good rest at 11.00 pm.

Day 5
Monday March 17, 2014.

Larissa to Ioannina

I wake at 6.10 am after a sound sleep. The air is cool and crisp outside when Avril opens the door to our balcony on the fifth floor. The bright morning sunlight offers a splendid panoramic view of the city and of the snow-capped mountains in the distant central range. Today we will drive 212 kilometres to Ioannina where we will overnight at the Du Lac Hotel. At 10.00 am we collect our car and set the GPS for the mystical Meteora, an easy drive about 100 km away. Midway into the journey the GPS goes crazy near new road constructions. I realize that it is directing us to enter an exit ramp of a new freeway. I overrule 'Floss', the name I bestow upon the female communicator of my GPS, and eventually negotiate a way through the maze of road works.

Gigantic boulders of barren rock face seem to leap out of the flat terrain as we approach Meteora. The typical Greek homes, dual storey pastel concrete blocks, are dwarfed by the rock towers. The road climbs steeply towards the rocks as we bypass the town centre. We are now in need of a coffee and we stop at the oddly named Arsenis Guest House, Restaurant and Tavern, which has a commanding view of the town and the rocks. The impressive guest house seems deserted, but an old Greek lady emerges to summon us inside and she makes us welcome. We sit in a comfortable couch beside a small coffee table in the reception area while she prepares us coffee and biscuits. A cosy fire is burning in the far corner but I doubt it would provide much heat to the large open area with its spread of dining tables and chairs, all empty of guests. Later the owner appears and says he hopes to attract foreign tourists. I suggest he should think about changing the name.

I notice on display some booklets and pamphlets which explain Meteora's sacred rocks and their history. Apparently the wildness and inaccessibility of the terrain make Meteora the ideal refuge of men fleeing from the path of various invaders who, over the centuries, push their way into Thessaly. The untenanted rocks provide safe eyries for those hermits. Here they dwell in awe and privation, hoping to achieve lives of Christian perfection. In the beginning these hermits live solitary lives, praying alone in rudimentary chapels. In the course of time they see advantage in joining spiritual forces and sharing a more fully Christian life together in small monasteries called sketes. No one knows exactly when Meteora is first settled, but, according to one tradition, the first hermit is Barnabas who, between 950 and 970 AD, founded the ancient skete of the Holy Ghost.

The first hermits scaled the rocks of Meteora by means of a sort of scaffolding lashed to a series of timbers wedged into crevices. These contraptions are replaced later by enormously long ladders. A visitor with no head for heights could be hauled up in a net, involving half an hour of giddy twirling at the end of a creaking rope that threatened to plunge the terrified passenger hundreds of feet to his death.

Over the centuries this community of monasteries is richly endowed by the leading Christian families of Greece and are granted many privileges. At the height their prosperity in the 17th century the monastic community houses a very large number of monks and hermits. Subsequently their fortunes begin to decline. Today, only the monasteries of the Transfiguration, Barlaam, St Nicholas Anapavsas, Rousanou, the Holy trinity and St Stephen are still in use. The rest have disappeared.

Our road continues to scale the rocky slopes to a lookout where we obtain an awe inspiring view of the monasteries. A friendly middle aged Greek man approaches us as we marvel at the site. He seems pleased that we are from Australia and are touring his country. He has friends in Melbourne where about 300,000 Greeks live, making it the largest Greek community outside of Greece. He and his travelling mate are from Athens and they offer to take photos of us against the impressive backdrop of monasteries, now drenched in the bright morning sunlight. He cannot be kind enough and hands me a small book that contains information on all the monasteries at Meteora. In front of us about a kilometre away we clearly see two large monasteries perched on two of the giant boulders. He suggests that we visit the second one where two coaches and several cars are parked. It is the Holy Monastery of the Transfiguration of Jesus or the Great Meteoron. It was founded in the middle of the 14th century by Holy Athanasios the Meteorite (first owner and organiser of the Monastic coenobium) at the largest rock (Wide Rock).

We find a good parking position in front of the monastery. Fortunately we do not have to be hauled up by a basket attached to a rope. In 1922 steps were hewn out of the rock and now visitors can climb easily and safely. We observe a steady stream of visitors that seem like ants as they climb and descend the steps. Avril is apprehensive at first. I remind her that last year she managed Machu Picchu easily enough. We have little difficulty and find the visit a wonderful experience. The monastery contains a remarkable collection of historic manuscripts, icons and holy heirlooms. There are two rooms containing portraits of historic figures in Greek history. One has models of Greek soldiers dressed in past uniforms and the weaponry of the time. We are impressed with the large 'trapeza' or dining hall which explains the daily life of a monk.

By now it is 3.00 pm and we need to press on to our destination at Ioannina still 140 km away. It seems easy enough if we are to arrive by 6.00 pm, but by pressing Avoid Toll Roads on our GPS we could end up in the sticks. We are on our way after having a quick bite of left over stale bread and a banana, courtesy of yesterday's breakfast table. The road leading out of Meteoro winds through mountainous country with small townships, living on the edge so to speak. We are about to enter a freeway when our trusty GPS directs us onto a secondary road that snakes high into pine forest country. It seems to continue forever, eventually taking us onto a small 600 m dirt track and past a saw mill. This brings us to a better road that leads into high alpine country at the roof of the central mountain range of Greece. At the snowline we stop to chuck a couple of snow balls at one another before proceeding.

Time is of the essence – still over 100 kilometres to our destination. The road passes through snow fields and we see hikers from nearby ski hamlets enjoying a late afternoon walk. We think that there is Buckley's chance of arriving in Ioannina by 6.00 pm. However, suddenly our GPS leads us onto a magnificent freshly sealed highway down the mountain slopes. We whizz through several road tunnels carved though the mountains, at speeds of up to 130 km per hour, faster than I have ever driven, especially in a little black Hyundai. Even so, others pass me as if I'm standing still. Avril does a great job of warning me when it's time to slow down, which is often, and when I'm too close to kerbs, edges and trucks and cars etc., or when traffic lights are about to change colour. We finally get to Ioannina by 6.00 pm in peak hour traffic.

The city is well spread and I have not put the address of our hotel into the GPS. We conveniently park and find that we have gone too far. I have to backtrack through a maze of smaller streets, bustling traffic and numerous traffic lights. Finally at 6.30 pm the GPS directs us to our overnight stay at Du Lac Hotel. It is situated within an expanse of parklands with ample parking outside. We stagger over and find the complex consists of three buildings: a conference centre which is closed, a private apartment section which is locked and the main hotel with many cars parked outside. We enter the reception area of the latter, after trying the other two, and are made welcome. At last we have arrived.

We waste no time ordering a large Heineken and a meal in the restaurant. Avril has a delicious mushroom and sun dried tomato risotto and I have chicken with cucumber pasta and yoghurt. We dine in a private dining room in the quiet ambience of chandeliers and soft music. We agree the food is excellent as we make our way back to retire for the evening.

Day 6
Tuesday March 18, 2014.

Ioannina to Kastoria

It is almost daybreak when I arise at 5.55 am. We sort out our gear and at 7.45 am we take breakfast at a table overlooking the hotel's substantial swimming pool. It looks inviting in the bright sunlight, but the water would be quite cool. There is not a cloud in the clear blue sky. We comment favourably to reception when checking out at 10.00 am. One of the receptionists says, 'It is an honour for us to receive English visitors.'

We are in no hurry today because our next stop is only 167 kilometres away at Kastoria, regarded as one of the most beautiful towns in Greece with its lake surrounded by mountains. There is time to take a walk outside before we leave. Nearby is an avenue of cherry blossom trees, contrasting with the cheerful backdrop of snow-capped mountains. The gardens of the hotel are a picture of colourful black faced yellow pansies and potted shrubs in full bloom. Two gardeners are watering and attending them with loving care. The gardens lead us to the swimming pool which we saw through the window during breakfast.

In such wonderful spring weather our drive to Limneon Resort Kastoria should be easy. In fact we find ourselves backtracking through all those road tunnels, over the mountains and snow again. We flash through the tunnels and the new roadwork leading to the ski hamlets. Then we pass a snowy section before descending along a twisting forest road on the other side of the range. At this point I notice that our petrol gauge indicates that we are down to less than a quarter. There is little sign of habitation in this area and I anxiously await any sign of a village hamlet or small town where there is a service station. Suddenly I spot a very small sign on a forest pine tree saying, 'GAS 2 KM.'

Avril and I count down the metres and sure enough, around a bend in the road, a small hamlet appears with a corner store containing two bowsers. An elderly Greek lady, who cannot speak a word of English, emerges. There is much friendly incomprehensible talk and smiles and somehow we manage the refuelling by using lots of sign language. By this time it is midday and we search the forest road for a place to have a cuppa. We pull up at a roadside restaurant, but it is rundown and deserted. A signpost suggests refreshments are available down a side road a bit further on. We search it out and find a narrow street containing some Greek homes of good standard and a shop with a few cars parked in front, including one of the local police. Lots of chattering by middle-aged Greek men seated around tables is halted suddenly as we enter the restaurant. One of the men, using limited broken English, acts as interpreter to help the friendly old lady at the counter to take our order. We end up with two cups of chai, a delicious brew of herbal tea, with a slice of lemon. This plus two chocolate wafers like Kit Kats cost only 3 Euros. The men continue on chatting and drinking as we enjoy our order, seated on bar stools at the counter. They stop chatting again to wave a friendly goodbye as we leave.

Half an hour later the land becomes undulating with small patches of freshly cultivated fields of wheat and grasses. To the side of the road I notice an ancient arch bridge over a running steam of melted snow. I have to stop to check it out. The old road leading to the bridge now serves as a pleasant rest stop for picnics. We pass an old stone fountain that continually releases clear water from the mountain stream. I stop near the arch bridge and walk over it to the other side to take a picture. The old road continues on through dry scrub and over a low steep ridge seemingly to nowhere. I can only wonder for what purpose this lovely old bridge once served.

Soon after at about 1.30 pm our GPS leads us onto a new dual lane freeway allowing speeds of 130 km per hour. I must admit I hit the 140 mark at one stage and hardly knew it. In no time at all we have left the quiet scene at the mountain stream and checked into the Limneon Resort Kastoria by 2.45 pm. Given all the driving since we arrived in Greece, we now enjoy an afternoon nap before taking a 3 km walk down the busy main drag in front of the lake. At 6.30 pm we have an early dinner in the huge comfortable bar and restaurant. We are seated by a window overlooking the shimmering lights of the night view across the lake. We order two Heineken beers to go with the meal – lamb and eggplant with crusted parmesan for Avril and grilled turkey slices and salad with an orange olive dressing for me.

Day 7
Wednesday March 19, 2014.

Kastoria

At 6.20 am it is still dawn and the mountains around Lake Kastoria are peaceful silhouettes awaiting the first glimpses of sunlight. We are in no hurry as we have a full day to explore the beautiful township of Kastoria. We take breakfast at 8.00 am and then drive a short distance to the prehistoric lake settlement area at Dispilio. The lake settlement of 5000 BC was randomly discovered here, proving that Kastoria was inhabited during Neolithic times. At the excavation site the first Greek Eco museum has been created. It contains a model display village with huts on wooden platforms in the reedy foreshore of the lake. This morning we are the first and only visitors viewing this interesting site. The curator opens up each of the half a dozen circular clay structures built on land and on wooden stakes in the lake. Each replica hut, about the size of a kitchen or small hotel room, contains domestic utensils and tools of the era. Researchers estimate that approximately 3000 people once resided in the area, in typical huts built on the shores and on the lake.

Some of the artefacts discovered at the site are housed in a museum workshop building opposite the replica Neolithic settlement. We visit the workshop and meet a young Greek curator who says it is work in progress. He ushers us inside to a large room containing artefacts from the dig. The archaeological dig began in 1938 by the Professor of Archaeology at the University of Athens, Mr Keramopoulos.

The curator explains that the prehistoric dwellings were constructed mainly of wood and clay. Several ruins were found buried in mud as the lake receded. The foundations of the dwellings were wooden posts which supported the raised huts on wooden bases. He shows us a post which was discovered in its preserved state in the lake. He says the inhabitants would have felt a measure of safety above the shallow waters because they were surrounded by dense forests in which lived many wild animals. The area provided plenty of food. The inhabitants raised livestock, were farmers, fishermen and hunters. They built their huts on dry land near the shore as well as over the water. They also used wooden boats carved from whole tree trunks.

In the museum are tools made of stone -- fishing weights, blades and arrow points. Other tools are of bone (digging implements for agriculture) and clay (missiles for slingshots). We see clay pots that they used for cooking their food and large clay jars used for preserving the leftover food. Broken pieces of pottery have been carefully pieced together like a jigsaw puzzle.

The curator explains that the daily life of these Neolithic people was not only about work. They made their lives enjoyable by making various small idols out of clay and playing melodies on flutes made of bone. He shows us one of the small bone flutes and jewellery made of clay, bone, stones and shells. They could also write. He shows us a wooden tablet bearing inscribed markings. These markings are also found on various clay pots and other objects. The markings have not yet been decoded, but they are early examples of an advanced civilization.

At 11.00 am we drive around the lake towards the busy township of Kastoria, 5 kilometres away. From across the lake we can see its pastel painted buildings reflected in the water. The scene presents a photo opportunity so we stop to take the picture. Nearby is a Greek man selling packets of dried food. He takes an interest in us and offers to take our photo. He then offers me a plastic cup and pours what I think is water. But he only pours a small sample and I try it. Boom! Boom! It sure is fire water. We thank him and move on, hoping I will not be arrested.

We join the tight traffic squeeze of Kastoria. Many drivers double park leaving their hazard lights on. There is barely a centimetre to spare as you negotiate oncoming vehicles. Avril almost has heart failure. Eventually we squeeze through the tangle and park at a quiet spot by the foreshore. We watch a fisherman in a small boat come ashore accompanied by a flotilla of pelicans closing in behind him. He tosses some of his catch to them and there is a flurry of activity as they jockey for the scraps.

We proceed further around the lake to view a couple of old Byzantine churches. In Kastoria and the surrounding areas there are more than 70 of these churches. Further down, the road becomes almost a footpath. A tape has been placed across the road barring further progress, so we turn back to the city. I decide to do a bit more investigating in town centre, but it's a nightmare. I escape the traffic snarl again through an almost blocked narrow alley. Somehow I end up at the narrow lakeside road again, only further down. A car approaches me and I have to reverse into a tiny space to allow it through. Then I come to a parked work truck and it is impossible to fit through. My outside mirror touches the rear end of the truck. He obliges by inching forward. That's it! It is time to get back to base for a coffee. But where are we? In another narrow alley a school teacher blows a whistle so her mob of children can move over to allow me to pass. Our little black Hyundai desperately searches for a way out, hopefully to find the sanctuary of our hotel where our BP levels can return to normal!

Tomorrow involves a big day of travelling some 341 kilometres to Edessa, Pella and Kavala. We spend time in the afternoon checking the map and sorting out our gear so we can make an early start. Tonight we dine at 7.00 pm, much earlier than the locals. We share a Greek salad and for mains Avril has creamy pasta Papadelle; I settle for a dish of chicken, tomato, mushroom and zucchini with a melted cheese of very great elasticity. We catch up on CNN world news events which have not improved since we left a week ago – problems continue in Crimea and the Malaysian plane is still missing. Avril repacks her suitcase and we retire early around 11.00 pm.

Day 8
Thursday March 20, 2014.

Kastoria to Kavala

We arise at 6.10 am to another glorious spring day. At 8.20 am we head off into the foothills of the snowy peaks around Kastoria. It is a pleasant morning about 16 C and 45 minutes later we arrive at an attractive Greek village called Lechovo. The Greek homes here are well maintained and cling tightly to the mountain slope. A few of the locals are up and about, enjoying the sunshine and freshness of the morning. We park in the small square outside an impressive church which has a large cherry tree in front. This is a Kodak moment. We are being watched by an elderly Greek lady from the second floor of her balcony. Another is walking down a narrow alley towards the square. A few Greek men are chatting on a seat near a small supermarket where we stop to buy water and a chocolate bar. They are curious to know where we are from and nod their approval when I mention Australia.

Further on, in the valley floor, we come across a delightful scene of orchards in full bloom. We miss a turn on the main road into Edessa and come to another small village holding a market day. We have to crawl past locals spilling over the roadway. We can almost touch the stalls filled with a huge variety of fresh fruits and vegetables. 'Floss', the nickname of our trusty GPS navigator, gets us back on track and an hour later we reach our first stop, Edessa. The area is known for its waterfalls and the old Byzantine Bridge of Kourpi. The large township is a maze of darting traffic. Suddenly 'Floss' announces 'destination' in the middle of the city. We find ourselves caught up in thick traffic in the narrow main street which has multiple entries.

Escaping the city I search vainly for the landmarks, the waterfalls and the old bridge of Kourpi. Somehow we end up at a dead end in a sports field near a stream of rushing water. We then search higher up in a little hillside suburb where we find ourselves caught in a labyrinth of laneways barely wide enough for two small cars. 'Floss' pours out instructions and seems annoyed with us. Forsaking Edessa, we push on to Pella to see the mosaics at its famous archaeological site.

Pella becomes an important seaside centre of the ancient world when the capital of the Macedonia kingdom is moved from Aigai. Pella's location ensures better trade and communication connections with the rest of the Greek world, both via sea routes and the inland open plain. Continuous habitation of the area dates from the Early Bronze Age, as confirmed by the discovery of cemeteries of the Early and Middle Bronze Age (3rd millennium BC) and of the Iron Age (9th c. BC to 5th c. BC). The presence of pottery from the same periods has been found throughout the greater area, confirming the existence of older settlements. The Macedonian capital succeeded on the same site.

We arrive at midday and find the ancient site of Pella resembling a disorganised jumble of rocks. No wonder! We find out that in the 4th century, at the height of its power, a huge earth quake destroys the city. It struggles on, but barbarian attacks eventually cause its abandonment. We take a walk around the complex. These old rocks are being painstakingly arranged to show the layout of the old city. A few workmen at the site are busy with the restoration process. We are impressed at the efforts to showplace the ancient city in its original plan dating back to the last quarter of the 4th century BC.

The layout of ancient Pella extends over an area of about 400 hectares. The impressive city contains rectangular building blocks separated by roads between 6 and 9 metres wide. It is the most fully-developed historic city of the Greek world, stretching over an area extending 2.5 km North-South and about 1.5 km East-West. Some of its main roads are wider than others, paved and surrounded by sidewalks and colonnades. Beneath the roadbeds lay dense, well-organized water and drainage networks. Rock-hewn tunnels once carried water down from mountain springs. Fountains, wells and cisterns in public and private buildings testify to a high standard of living enjoyed by residents.

Private residential areas, ranging from 150 sq. m. to 3000 sq. m in size, feature central peri-style courtyards of Doric and Ionic architectural elements. There are banqueting rooms with floors decorated elaborately in natural mosaic tesserae, wall paintings, household shrines, private apartments and hygiene spaces – all suggesting an economically and culturally-flourishing city.

Near the restorations is the Pella Museum which was designed by architect Kostas Skroumpellos and completed in 2009. The modern complex is located at the foot of a hill in the northeast part of the archaeological site, where once the palace stood. A video explains the high level of sophistication reached in times we call antiquity. They may not have had electricity or motorized transportation, but they enjoyed a vigorous and progressive lifestyle. Today the modern city of Pella is built on a plain adjacent to the archaeological site. Over the centuries silt carried down from the mountains built-up, causing the former trading port, nowadays, to be located 20 kilometres in from the coast.

Archaeological digs have unearthed a wealth of information which is on display in four thematic exhibits. We tour the exhibits accompanied by a personal guide. The first theme concerns the daily life of Pella's inhabitants. Set in the floor are beautiful detailed mosaics from the Houses of Dionysus and of the Abduction of Helen. Around the walls are show-cases exhibiting articles that depict the day-to-day functions of rooms in the ancient residences; on display are many articles of usage in the daily lives of their residents: their furnishings, their clothing, personal adornment, ritual pieces used at household shrines, as well as examples of objects used in exercise, education, occupations and amusements.

A second theme shows the public life in Pella, particularly in administration and commerce. We see clay seals for public documents, inscriptions, monumental sculpture and lots of silver and bronze coins, including some discovered in mint-like condition. On display are vases for storing and transporting wine and oil etc., many with seals on their handles, indicative of commercial exchange. We are puzzled why most of the storage jars are pointed at the base. Our guide explains that the merchant ships stuck them in sand to prevent them moving during sea journeys.

A third theme displays the mosaic floors and the discoveries unearthed from Pella's sanctuaries, with information about gods worshipped there. It explains the functions of religious buildings, particularly the sanctuaries of Darron, the Mother of Gods, and Aphrodite, the Thesmophorion (The Thesmophoria was an ancient fertility festival for women commemorating the loss of Demeter's daughter).

The fourth thematic exhibit shows the findings from the city's cemeteries. Two burials are on display together with their contents, one in a clay pithos of the Bronze Age and the other in a restored cist grave of the 5th century BC. Display cases also exhibit the contents from Pella's cemeteries in the Bronze and Iron Age (9th-6th c. BC), the Classical (5th-4th c. BC) and Hellenistic periods (3rd-2nd c. BC). These provide an insight into the daily lives of the inhabitants: social structures, funeral customs, the language of residents (i.e., Doric Greek) and their accomplishments in numerous artistic fields.

At 2.30 pm we have to leave this wonderful site and press on to our destination at Kavala which is 180 kilometres away. The road heads to the outskirts of Thessaloniki before swinging north and following the coastline. Picturesque seaside townships hug the coastal stretches on the right. We find ourselves on a super modern highway and zooming along at speeds of 130 km per hour. For this privilege we encounter two toll gates which catch us unawares. We scramble to find the modest fee of 2.4 Euros. We haven't had a bite to eat since breakfast so Avril peels the two bananas we nicked from the breakfast table this morning – an interesting eating challenge at 130 km per hour.

Twenty kilometres out of Kavala we pull into a roadhouse for a welcome coffee and a delicious cake. We have covered 150 km in not much more than one and a half hours and now time is on our side. But where is our hotel? The GPS did not allow me to program the address of our hotel. From the top of the rise leading into Kavala the traffic is pressing. Avril urges me pull over in one of the hillside parking areas about 3 km from the centre of the city to admire the breathtaking view. The city of Kavala is like an amphitheatre of multi storey pastel brick and terracotta roofed buildings overlooking the serene Aegean Sea. We choose a perfect site to pull over to soak in the magnificent vista.

My GPS allows me to press places nearby and to my amazement we are merely 350 m away from our two night stay at Egnatia Hotel, just a little further down the slope. The hotel takes its name from the ancient roadway, Via Egnatia, which passed through the nearby ancient city of Philippi in the 1st c. BC.

Later in the evening, from our position in the dining room, we capture a grand view of the illuminated city below. We order pasta meals: colourful veges and chicken with wine for Avril; seafood and spaghetti with Heineken beer for me. The ambience of the occasion is wonderful after the long drive from Kastoria. I switch on the TV which immediately causes Avril to fall fast asleep on the large sofa. I press on till after 11.00 pm.

Day 9
Friday March 21, 2014.
Kavala-Krinides-Kavala

At 6.20 am my body clock awakens me, 10 minutes later than usual. Outside another fine spring day looms with clear skies and a predicted 18 C. This is the final day of the self-drive tour before we return to Athens early tomorrow morning. At 9.00 am we call into reception to order tomorrow's take-away breakfast for 2.00 am. We hope to be at the airport before 5.00 am to return our Hertz rental car and to catch the 6.40 am Aegean Flight 101 to Athens.

At 10.30 am we take a short drive to Krinides to see the ancient Theatre of Philippi. Krinides is a small quiet township next to the archaeological site. We pass through the town's shops and up a hill to some old Greek homes with big backyards for chooks and a few fruit trees. This is where 'Floss' announces, 'You have reached your destination.' I scratch my head and return to the shops to inquire from a local shopkeeper. She is a Greek-speaking Dutch woman who recognizes the word 'Theatre of Philippi'. Her English is limited. An elderly Greek man approaches who wants to help us. Much head nodding and waving of hands follows but it is incomprehensible. We guess that he wants us to follow him. He hops in his old farm Ute and drives straight ahead, a little more than a kilometre. He stops and, with much hand waving and aplomb, he indicates that we have arrived at the site. He gestures for us to park our car in the wide cobblestone car park outside the entrance of the complex. This is typical Greek hospitality – they are friendly and fun-loving, except perhaps for their driving habits!

We walk past a huge café which contains enough chairs and tables, inside and out, to cater for several coachloads of visitors. The parkland site has shaded areas with amenities and a souvenir shop. A group of young American students is just ahead of us as we purchase our tickets to enter the site. The senior rate is 3 Euros per person, which allows you to visit the museum as well. In front of us is the impressive Theatre of Philippi which was probably built by King Philip II in the middle of the 4th c. BC. In the 2nd and 3rd c. AD, it was considerably modified and extended to accommodate the requirements of the spectacles of the Roman Period.

The ancient city of Philippi was built on the fringes of the marshes that occupy the south-east part of the plain of Drama. The first settlers are colonists from Thasos who are aware of the rich sources of precious metals, timber and agricultural products in the region and therefore they found the colony of Krenides in 360 BC. The new colony is soon threatened by the Thracians and in 356 BC they seek the aid of Philip II, king of Macedonia. Discerning the economic and strategic importance of the city, Philip captures and fortifies it, and gives it his name: Philippi.

A sign at the Theatre explains important historical facts relating the city:

The city prospered greatly in the Hellenistic period (3rd, 2nd c. BC) when it acquired its fortification walls, theatre, public buildings and private residences. The fact that the Via Egnatia passed through Philippi in the 1st c. BC made the city much more important and transformed it into a major centre of the region.

In 42 BC, the Battle of Philippi, fought on the two low hills outside the west walls of the city, changed its character completely after its victory. Octavian converted Philippi into a Roman colony (Colonia Augusta Julio Philiooenis). The city expanded and developed into an economic, administrative and artistic centre.

However, another important event was to change the personality of the city once again: the visit of St Paul the Apostle, who founded the first Christian church on European soil here in AD 49/50. The *predomination of the new religion and the transfer of the capital of the Roman Empire to Constantinople lent Philippi considerable lustre and reputation in the early Christian period (4th-6th c. AD); the Octagon complex was built on the site of the Roman buildings, with the cathedral dedicated to St Paul and three magnificent basilicas.*

The city began to be abandoned in the early 7th c. AD, as a result of major earthquakes and the Slav raids. It survived in the Byzantine period as a fort, but was finally completely desolated after the Turkish conquest in the late 14th c.

Excavations here were commenced by the French School of Archaeology in 1914. The finds from the excavation are now housed in the Archaeological Museum of Philippi which was built in the 1960s on the outskirts of the archaeological site. Avril and I visit the museum after an inspection of the Theatre and other extensive restorations on site. The exhibits in the museum are housed in two levels and contain the most exquisite examples from the discoveries made at this important historic site.

At 1.30 pm we need a coffee at the park before returning to our hotel. Then we head back to prepare for our departure early in the morning to Thessaloniki. At 4.30 pm we visit the downstairs bar for an early sundowner. The young Greek waiter, Elena, serves Avril an iced coffee and suggests I try a Greek beer instead of a Heineken. She is interested in our travels and the fact that the main reason for my visit to Northern Greece was to visit a Greek family at Pefkodassos who rescued my uncle during the war. I ask Elena what the name of the village means. 'Greek for 'Kodassos' is a forest and 'Pef' is a kind of tree,' she replies.

We need to allow enough time to drive 160 km to Thessaloniki airport, so we skip dinner and eat our left-over fruit, a chocolate bar and sweet wafer biscuit. We more or less cat nap a couple of hours till 1.15 am before checking out at 2 am.

Day 10
Saturday March 22, 2014.

Kavala-Thessaloniki-Athens

At 2.00 am a pleasant young lady at Reception hands us our packed breakfasts which we plan to eat at the airport. I organize 'Floss' to guide us to the Airport Makadonia at Thessaloniki. Hopefully we have enough time up our sleeves to hand in the car and relax. The dual lane super highway is a fairyland of lights which guide me safely at speeds of 130 k per hour. At that early hour of the morning we have the freeway to ourselves, except for half a dozen slow moving trucks. We arrive well ahead of schedule and return our car into the Hertz yard at 4.00 am. There is not a soul in sight to receive our car and we wonder what to do. The airport is still a kilometre away. Avril reads the fine print of our contract which states we need to return the vehicle at the time arranged. I cannot remember arranging any fixed time. We can't just sit there so I drive to the airport entrance to deposit Avril and the luggage. She stands guard while I check the Hertz desk inside. It is deserted like all the other rental desks, but I note there is a 'drop key' hole in the desk. So with Avril guarding our gear I return our vehicle to the car park, missing it on my first attempt because I didn't go far enough. I 'toot' Avril and I receive a puzzled stare as I drive by to attempt a second run. This time I am successful. I run back and drop the keys into the drop hole in the downstairs area. I then climb the stairs to the top level and Avril is relieved to see me when I call out to her. We can now relax and munch on an apple from our breakfast box. It is 5.00 am, still over an hour and a half to wait before our flight at 6.40 am.

The airport becomes a hive of activity as passengers suddenly pour in to catch early flights. Our flight has 200 passengers and the air hostesses are flat out to provide us with drinks and a croissant during the 40 minute flight. A friendly taxi driver is there to transport us to our hotel in the centre of Athens, 30 km by freeway. The King George is a luxury hotel opposite the main Constitution Square with stairs leading to Parliament House. The Receptionist informs us that a big peaceful demonstration is planned later in the afternoon. It is for racial harmony and is a worldwide event held annually. I am thinking, 'I wonder how many Russians will be shaking hands with the Ukrainians?'

Our hotel porter escorts us to our room on the fourth floor and another porter is following carrying the Greek flag. He plants the flag on our balcony as if to announce our arrival. But in reality all of the balconies at this level sport Greek flags. We overlook the historic square where the demonstration will take place. Fortunately I have rested well and had a soak in the bath before the demonstration begins. It is accompanied by drums and a heavy metal band.

Upon arrival I manage to sleep for almost three hours before stirring at midday. I am no sooner awake than Mia, our cruise assistant, phones to welcome us. She has a desk set up downstairs to welcome guests joining the *Aegean Odyssey* cruise ship. We wander down for a chat and to hand in our excursion choices for the month long cruise of the Eastern Mediterranean which will take us to Sicily, Crete, Israel, the Greek Islands and Turkey. Here we also meet Annette and Graham from the Gold Coast. They have been here for a week, touring with a small group around southern Greece.

For lunch we eat a bit more of the breakfast basket, a bun and jam. At 1.30 pm it is time to take a walk in the square below and to join the hordes in the crowded central avenue. A young woman approaches me and says she is homeless and wants money. I ignore her and tell Avril to watch her purse. Street merchants mingle about tempting you to buy balloons, flowers, food, lottery tickets etc. We jostle our way along the pedestrian mall that leads to the old church of St Paul. Amazingly, among the thick of the pedestrian ant heap, we spot Annette and George walking in the opposite direction. There is any number of street cafes crammed with people relaxing in sunny spring weather. We also need a cappuccino and manage to squeeze ourselves into one of the bars. We return to our hotel via a different route which is relatively quiet. No sooner than we return than the demonstration begins. It is nothing more than a gigantic din and an opportunity for hundreds to let their hair down to enjoy loud music. It's a big bang for world racial harmony.

Tonight we arrange to dine on the 7th floor at 7.00 pm. A magnificent view of the Acropolis, all lit up, provides ambience to the occasion, except for the rousing music and singing from the world harmony group still going strong in the square. A special menu of Greek cuisine is available for cruise members for 47 Euro per person. It proves a grand banquet. Avril chooses the Green salad which is like a Greek salad with grapes, orange and grape fruit. I choose the Santorini salad, a mix of tomatoes, herbs, croutons and greens. We both choose the marinated chicken and roasted potatoes. This comes with olives and cheeses and breads, wine and coffee. Dessert is a selection of Greek pastries and ice cream. We come away quite replete, though we did not meet any other passengers scheduled for our cruise.

Day 11
Sunday March 23, 2014.

Athens

This morning I arise at 5.30 am, ready for an early breakfast and excursions to the Acropolis and the Cycladic museum. Avril and I arrive for breakfast at the scheduled time, only to find the restaurant full of early arrivals from our cruise. I'm surprised to find that I must skip my usual choice of fried eggs because they vanish quickly, as does the scrambled eggs. There is not enough time to wait for a further lot to appear. So I choose a large serving of healthy fruits instead.

We look forward to the refreshing spring day as we board the coach and meet Antonis, our guide. The Sunday morning traffic is light and at 9.00 am our coach arrives outside the Acropolis museum which is situated across the road from the base of the Acropolis. Our excursion is due to begin at the museum before climbing the flat hill of Athens famous landmark. This is reversed when Antonis finds that the museum opens an hour later on Sundays. This ends up being a better arrangement because, by the time we finish touring the Parthenon temples, the place is crawling with tourists.

Antonis outlines some history of the site before we commence our climb. He poses the rhetorical question of why the first settlers chose to build here when Athens is a city of hills. He says it offered safety and was steep enough to defend. It was flat for building and contained water. It was also far enough from the sea to prevent pirate raids. Later the inhabitants came down and settled around the Acropolis. The Parthenon became the dwelling place of Greek Gods and the most important God was Athena after which the city of Athens is named. The Agora or market place became the civic centre of the city.

Antonis says, 'Athena is considered a virgin and therefore equal to man.' A lady in our group brings a chuckle when she mutters, 'So that's where I went wrong.'

The Acropolis looks stunning up close. Antonis walks us slowly to the top, cautioning us to be careful of the slippery marble sections. He directs us to take note of the Grand Monument situated on top of a steep hill nearby called Philopappous Hill which overlooks Athens. He says that Athens was once the centre of learning like Oxford and Cambridge. People from all parts of the ancient world came here for education. One student, who was accepted as a citizen of Athens, was so grateful for the financial support of his grandfather that he built the monument. He loved his grandfather, hence the name, Philopappous.

Antonis directs our attention to the Greek columns. There are two types to note: the shorter and simpler Doric columns have no base and a capital (the top, or crown) made of a circle topped by a square. The shaft is plain and has 20 sides. The Parthenon is the most famous example of the ancient Doric buildings. The taller Ionic columns have a large base structure looking like a set of stacked rings and a capital with scroll relief etchings. The Temple of Athena, near the Parthenon, is one of the most famous Ionic buildings in the world. Both column types have flutes, which are lines carved into them from top to bottom. Interestingly, the shafts of each column have a little bulge to make them look straight to your eye, even from a distance.

The top of the Acropolis provides a stunning view of the city as far as the port of Piraeus. This cradle of civilization seems to speak to the heavens. Tourists crowd around the Parthenon and the famous Temples of Athena and Poseidon. Antonis arranges a set time to allow us to mingle and to meet with him later near the entrance. The great archaeological treasures are a privilege to see. They have suffered over the centuries as vandals have wrecked or stolen their treasures. But the ongoing process of restoration is now well advanced for us to marvel at this wonder of antiquity. Many of the important statues and artefacts are now preserved and displayed in the Acropolis Museum.

Antonis is waiting at the Acropolis exit to take us to the museum which opened to the public only three years ago. While we wait, we chat with Lorraine and her husband David from Washington DC. Lorraine is a retired and formerly strict secondary school teacher of English. Her surname is Montesary but the kids called her 'Montescary'. She says, 'The students had the coronaries, but I didn't.'

The Acropolis Museum is an impressive structure covering four floors. You gain entry by walking across a long glass floor that has been built across a section of the old city. Once inside Antonis guides us through the important exhibits on each of the four levels. He shows us a heavy block of stone called Athena's Box where people would pay a tribute by placing one drachma into a hole at the top. It is quite a resourceful piggy bank because in her times a drachma was a day's wage, probably equivalent to 80 Euros today.

Antonis explains the story of two interesting pediments or friezes of small statues, one depicts the birth of Athena and the other tells of her struggle for power against another powerful adversary, the God Poseidon. The Gods agreed to allow the citizens to vote and campaigned for support. This is seen as the beginnings of democracy. Athena won because she offered the life giving olive tree. Poseidon, a sea God, tried to win the struggle by offering water, but it was salty. We thank Antonis for his excellent guidance during our morning tour. One could easily spend the whole day here.

Our excursion schedule provides for an afternoon visit to the Museum of Cycladic Art. This museum was founded in 1986 to house a collection of Cycladic and Ancient Greek Art which was accumulated by Nicholas P. Goulandris (1913-1983) and Dolly Goulandris (1921-2008). They started acquiring antiquities in the 1960's with the official permit granted by the Greek State. Gradually, they managed to create an impressive collection of exquisite artefacts of early Cycladic Art, some Minoan and Mycenaean pieces, an important assemblage of Geometric jewellery and other artefacts, as well as a series of excellent Archaic and Classical painted vases.

This highly valued collection specializes in the Cycladic civilization, an Early Bronze Age culture of the Cyclades in the Aegean Sea. However, the collection also includes pieces in a time line ranging as far back as the 10th millennium, from the Neolithic Age up to the Roman period. The collection's time line for the Aegean area begins with the **Neolithic Age** (6500-3200 BC), then it proceeds to the **Bronze Ages** (*Early* 3200-2000 BC; *Middle* 2000-1600 BC; *Late* 1600-1100 BC) and the **Iron Ages** (Geometric Period 1100-700 BC; Archaic Period 700-480 BC; Classical Period 480-323 BC; Hellenistic Period 323-31 BC; Roman Period 31 BC-AD 395).

Our guide is Philita, a mature slim woman, who drills us with her knowledge of the early history. Towards the end of the 4th millennium BC, profound cultural and social changes take place in the Aegean Region, signalling the end of the Neolithic way of life. The most important development is the introduction of metallurgy from the Near East. The use of metals substantially improves the quality of the tool kit in almost all sectors of activity: farming, tree-felling, architecture, shipbuilding etc. Bronze weapons alter the nature of warfare. New crops are introduced such as olives and grapes. There is an increase in maritime contacts and the widening of trading transactions.

Four distinct cultures develop in the Aegean: the Early Minoan culture on Crete, the Early Helladic on the Greek mainland, the early Cycladic in the islands of the Cyclades, and the Early Bronze Age culture of the Northeast Aegean islands. Among these cultures, the one that thrives on the small and arid Cycladic Islands holds a special place. Thanks to their strategic position and their mineral resources of marble and obsidian, these islands enjoy a privileged role in trade and become the crossroads and melting pot of diverse cultural influences.

The Cycladic islanders did not build large settlements containing monuments. One of their most notable achievements is the carving of marble. The sculpturing of figurines attain such a degree of accomplishment that these works are regarded as one the earliest forms of art in Europe. The marble figurines on display in the museum are simply exquisite and elegant creations.

Arriving back at The King George we need a relaxing soak in the bath after the busy excursions. For our evening dining we decide to visit a restaurant which we discovered during our walk down the busy central mall yesterday. By slipping down a side street we found this place. The owner gave us his business card which reads: IN THE CENTRE OF ATHENS, AT MITROPOLEOS SQUARE, IN VERY QUIET AND RELAXING PLACE WE ARE WAITING FOR YOU TO DISCOVER THE GREEK CUISINE THAT WE OFFER, OUR SPECIAL FRESH FISH OR MEAT DISHES, ALL MADE BY KAPETANAKIS FAMILY, AS MR. MANOLIS AND HIS WIFE PARASKEVI HAVE BEEN DOING FOR MANY YEARS WITH SUCCESS.

At 7.00 pm we call into the family restaurant called *Old Ithaki* where we enjoy a pleasant meal, alfresco by candle light in the balmy evening air outside. Sitting alone we seem to attract other customers to join with us. We order a BBQ groper and a Greek salad. The service is friendly but slow. We drink our Heineken beer, eat the salad and wait. He advertises fresh seafood, but we are thinking that he may be catching the groper. We are rewarded for our patience when the delicious barbeque fish arrives. Back at the King George hotel we catch up on the BBC World News and find that little has changed. They are still searching the Indian Ocean for the missing Malaysian passenger plane and Russia is hell-bent in the process of excising Crimea from Ukraine. It is time to retire before midnight.

Day 12
Monday March 24, 2014.

Piraeus, Athens

My alarm wakes us at 6.00 am as the dawn light of Athens filters in. Today we join our ship the *Aegean Odyssey* at the port of Piraeus, 12 km from the centre of Athens. Following a substantial breakfast we check the downstairs information board and find that our coach leaves for the port at 1.50 pm. There is much activity in the Constitution Square this morning. From our fourth floor balcony we observe hundreds of police and military who have taken over the square and blocked the entries. Tomorrow is Greek Independence Day and this activity is a dress rehearsal for the celebration. The Greek Guards in front of Parliament House are stepping out their slow elaborate high step march. This morning we want to take a photo of the guards in their fancy tunics and to visit the local Botanic Gardens situated behind Parliament House. It proves a difficult challenge.

We bravely set out on our mission but have to give up after circling the barriers around the police blockage. Except for one thoroughfare, the military have blocked entry to the streets around the square and closed the park. Around 11.00 am a grand march past takes place, led by the Police Band playing stirring music for the next thirty minutes. Suddenly they all pack up and go away. We may still have time to takes a wander into the Botanic gardens behind Parliament House.

Midday is checking out time, about 2 hours before our coach leaves for Piraeus. We allow ourselves an hour to visit the Greek marching guards on sentry duty in front of Parliament House and to visit the elaborate Botanic Gardens on the other side. The ceremonial march of the guards, striding out back and forth, is amusing to watch. We head to the gardens behind Parliament house. They are a haven away from the rush and din of the city. The old gardens contain a mix of well-established tree varieties and lots of ornamental orange trees in full fruit. Smaller flowers and shrubs are beginning to bloom. Further on we come to a small zoo stocked mainly with goats, peacocks, poultry and small parrots. A few young children rush about offering feed through the cages. The open yard area is a haven for pigeons which outnumber the permanent residents. We find a quiet shady spot to snack on a banana and then hurry back to the hotel.

Our coach leaves for the shipping terminal a few minutes late, but it takes little time to reach the port. We hand in our passports and are given our passenger cruise cards. At 2.30 pm a cheerful ship's director, Neil Horrock, greets us at the staircase as we embark. The tall fresh faced Englishman of solid build engages the boarding passengers easily with pleasantries. I ask him if he got over the Poms losing the Ashes. 'You can forget about joining us at the Captain's Table,' he quips.

We quickly orientate ourselves with the ship's features. Our cabin number 403 on the fourth deck, the Columbus Deck, is conveniently placed in the smartly designed ship, the *Aegean Odyssey*. We have time for a scrumptious mid-afternoon lunch in the Terrace Café and to organise our gear before the compulsory passenger safety drill at 5.00 pm. No sooner than this is completed than the ship weighs anchor and cruises out Piraeus Harbour, chased by a couple of fast moving Hellenic ferries.

At 7.00 pm we choose to dine informally in the Terrace Café rather than in the formal Marco Polo Restaurant. The meals are much the same and the friendly Filipino staff members provide you with VIP treatment. No sooner than we load our trays with soup, salads and chicken at the circular buffet than a waiter is on hand to take you to a table. They also offer trout with vegetables, pizza and wine. A selection of desserts, fruits and cheeses follow. I can feel my waistline expanding. For entertainment there is after-dinner music and song with *Blue Velvet* scheduled at 8.30 pm and an offering of light music with the *Odyssey Trio* at 9.15 pm. But Avril and I are weary from a wonderful 10 days of travel in Greece and we prefer to sojourn in our cabin to watch a bit of TV before retiring at 11.00 pm.

Attractive Greek village of
Lechovo, out from Kastoria.

Ancient Pella, an important seaside
centre in the Macedonian kingdom.

Shared memories: Avril with Alexandria and Rachel.

Rachel, George and Rafael.

At lunch with the Antoniadou family: Rachel, Marie, Sophia, George, Maria, Avril and I.

Maria and George at the old farmhouse that concealed Arthur after his escape.

The White Tower, Thessaloniki

Thessaloniki waterfront.

Springtime, northern Greece.

Destroyed by bombing in WW II, the Monastery of St Olympos near Dion, northern Greece is undergoing restoration.

Springtime, northern Greece.

Clifftop monasteries, Meteora.

Stairway to Clifftop Monastery, Meteora.

Ioannina, northern Greece.

Ancient arch bridge, out from Ioannina.

Avril views the replica display of a Neolithic Lake Settlement at Dispilio, Lake Kastoria, Greece.

Model interior of a Neolithic hut displaying domestic items of the era.

Avril and I at Lake Kastoria, township beyond.

Small Byzantine church built into a rock face at Kastoria.

Old Church of St Paul, Athens.

Athens, Parliament House.

The Parthenon.

View of Athens from the Acropolis.

The Acropolis, Athens.

A figurine from the early Bronze Age at the Museum of Cycladic Art, Athens.

Greek marching guards on parade at Parliament House, Athens.

CHAPTER 2

THE MEDITERRANEAN

Day 13
Tuesday March 25, 2014.

At Sea

The Aegean Odyssey is heading westwards across the Ionian Sea towards our first port of call, Syracuse, on the eastern coast of Sicily. The ship is sailing in a moderate swell and is expected to arrive at Syracuse at 7.00 am tomorrow. We will be passing near the 'Calypso Deep', the deepest part of the Mediterranean Sea where the African Plate meets the Aegean Sea Plate, creating the Hellenic Trench. I wake at sunrise, 6.19 am and the weather is a mix of blue and puffy white clouds. The forecast is for sunny conditions, ranging from low 10 C to high 15 C.

Breakfast is available at 7.00 am and we find only a few tables occupied when we arrive at 7.20 am. A sudden shower of rain forces our friends, Annette and Graham, from the Carrara area of the Gold Coast, to join us from their outside table on the Terrace Café. I have noticed Graham in Athens making quick sketches of museum artefacts. I find that he is into computer graphics and prints his art diaries in books, making two or three copies. We talk of the tremendous growth of the Gold Coast since the eighties. Graham says that the suburbs spring up around you. He once got lost in a newly built one. One Sydney lawyer nearing retirement wanted to subdivide his land at Mudgeeraba into pleasant rural acreage lots. But the council said he would have to divide it into smaller lots like another development next to his, in order to link in with a newly built freeway. So, as a result, he and the council made more money.

At 10.00 am we attend a lecture in the Ambassador Lounge. The lecture with Chris Adamson is entitled, *'An Introduction to Classical Archaeology'*. His lecture is an introductory guide to the ancient and modern history of Classical Archaeology. Chris speaks of the involvement and contribution made by Victorian explorers and modern technicians to Classical Archaeology.

He begins with the Scottish nobleman, Thomas Bruce, 7th Earl of Elgin who from 1803 to 1812 steals some classic Greek treasures from the Parthenon for his private collection. Lord Elgin bribes local Ottoman authorities into permitting their removal, including what is now known as the 'Elgin Marbles'. Fortunately, Thomas Bruce goes bankrupt and his collection is now on display for the public in the British Museum… unfortunately, not in a Greek museum.

The German, Heinrich Schliemann is one of the first to popularize archaeology. He is born in 1822, the son of a poor pastor. He observes a picture of 'Troy in Flames' in a history book given to him at the age of seven by his father. It remains embedded in his memory throughout his life. Heinrich begins his working life as an apprentice to a grocer and later works as a cabin boy on a ship. He has passion and a flair for languages and becomes fluent in eight or more, in particular, Dutch, English, French, Spanish, Italian, Portuguese, Russian and both ancient and modern Greek.

In 1846 he is working for a merchant trading firm which sends him to St Petersburg as an agent. In 1851 he decides to join one of his brothers in the Californian gold rush. He makes a fortune in a banking enterprise that buys and sells the gold dust won by miners. Returning to Russia he marries Ekaterina Lyschin, a niece of one of his wealthy friends. He founds his own trading business and furthers his fortune at the time of the Crimean War (1854-1856), as a military contractor.

The wealthy Schliemann is able to retire and pursue his interest in archaeology. With a copy of Homer's poem, *The Iliad*, in one hand and money in the other, he explores the ancient civilizations of Greece and Troy and claims to have found Troy. His method of using explosives to discover hidden archaeological treasures is considered quite destructive.

Augustus Pitt Rivers is another early archaeologist. In 1880 he inherits an estate of more than 32,000 acres in Cranborne from his cousin, Horace Pitt-Rivers, 6th Baron Rivers Chase. Born April 14, 1827 in Yorkshire, August Henry Lane-Fox is required to adopt the surname Pitt Rivers as part of the bequest. From 1883 to 1900 he uses his inheritance to finance his ambition of the excavation of ancient sites. He is influenced by the evolutionary writings of Charles Darwin and he views archaeology as an extension of anthropology. He amasses ethnographic collections from all over the world and methodically records his digs. He insists that all artefacts should be collected and catalogued as the key to understanding the past. Therefore, he breaks with the previous archaeological practice which verges on treasure hunting.

Sir William Matthew Flinders Petrie is another pioneering archaeologist and Egyptologist. He is born June 3, 1853 at Charlton, near Greenwich, London and dies July 28, 1942 in Jerusalem. His grandfather, Matthew Flinders, is the famous British navigator and explorer of Australia and Tasmania. Petrie invents a sequence dating method that makes possible the reconstruction of history from the remains of ancient cultures. His method of recording, by calculating and cataloguing, is the standard used today. He is knighted in 1923 for his contribution to archaeology.

Chris's lecture includes a brief outline of the significant events of Ancient Greek History. His handout, *'Ancient Greek History Crib Sheet',* lists the early periods of history of the **Bronze Age** (3000-1200 BC). The *Cycladic Period* is known as the Early Bronze Age, the *Minoan Period* is the Middle to Late Bronze Age and the *Mycenaean Period* is the Late Bronze Age. This Age collapses in c. 1200 BC. There is widespread destruction of cities and palaces across the Eastern Mediterranean.

The early **Iron Age** follows (1200-800 BC). From 1200-1000 BC is known as the **Dark Age**. The art of writing is lost; trade and exchange slows and population drops. From 1000 -800 BC is the *Geometric Period*, named after pottery decorations. Trading with the wider world increases. From 800-490 BC is the *Archaic Period*. Population grows and gathers in larger cities and in the associated emergence of 'Polis' city states. Greek colonies are founded around the Mediterranean. Tyrants rule many Greek cities. Democracy is established in Athens in 508 BC. Art and architecture develop.

The *Classical Period* follows from 490-323 BC. In 490 and 480/479 BC the Persian invasions are repelled. In 431-404 BC is the Peloponnesian War in which Sparta defeats Athens. In 336-323 BC Alexander the Great unites Greece and expands his empire across the Middle East, but he dies in early June 323 BC while suffering high fever lasting ten days. The Classical Period is considered the height of Greek cultural achievement in literature, philosophy, and art.

From 323-146 BC is the *Hellenistic Period*. Alexander's generals divide his empire into individual kingdoms for each to rule. Greek culture spreads widely throughout these kingdoms. The Hellenistic Period ends in 146 BC when Greece is conquered by the Romans.

At 11.30 am, Jenny Worwood outlines the shore excursion program for tomorrow at Syracuse which is located near the south-eastern corner of Sicily on the Ionian coast. Syracuse is built on an ancient Greek settlement founded by the Corinthians in 734 BC.

Around midday the sea swell strengthens and our ship sways from side to side and up and down. Avril needs to rest. I wake her at 1.00 pm and suggest lunch. With some reservation she still goes with me to enjoy a 'light lunch' of fish and chips with salad. A tempting dessert of fruit and ice cream follows. During lunch the Chief Officer, Claudiu Dunose, announces that the Captain's Welcome Cocktail Party set down for 6.15 pm has been postponed because of the rough swell.

At 3.00 pm Chris Adamson presents another lecture on Greek history. Greek cities begin establishing colonies in Sicily in c. 8th-7th BC. The Greek colonisation of Sicily is known as Magna Graecia or Greater Greece. The Greeks bring language and culture with them and leave behind a legacy of some of the finest remaining temple ruins anywhere in the Greek world. A main reason for the Greek expansion to Sicily is the shortage of land to inherit. Cities are desperate to get rid of people and many are forced to leave their homeland.

At 8.00 pm we dine in the Terrace Café. We ignore the smorgasbord of foods at the servery and order a rack of lamb from the chef's kitchen service. The delicious lamb is served with tasty roast vegetables. We choose a glass of red to go with the meal.

At the table next to ours is an elderly woman sitting alone. She is Barbara Currie from the Gold Coast where she lives in an eleventh floor apartment overlooking a wonderful view of the Broadwater at Southport. For a number of years she and her now deceased husband lived on a 40 acre avocado farm in Northern NSW. It was tough work, so they eventually sold up and moved to St Lucia in Brisbane. Following a cyclone, flood waters entered their unit during the devastating Brisbane floods in January 1974. Her daughter assisted Barbara to move to a Gold Coast unit when her husband died.

I ask if her family are in touch. 'Oh yes! I have had five children and I have to text them each day.'

'What will you do tomorrow?' I ask.

'Well I won't be visiting the historic ruins because I have seen enough on previous trips. I'll find some shops and have a coffee.' And of course, she'll text her family.

In our cabin we watch on TV Rick Steve's *Greek Peloponnese* and part of the film *Mamma Mia*. Tonight we adjust our clocks back an hour to allow for the time difference. Instead of being midnight it is actually 11.00 pm when we turn out the lights.

Day 14
Wednesday March 26, 2014.

Syracuse, Sicily

We wake at first light and go to early breakfast at 6.30 am. The weather forecast is for mostly cloudy skies with a possible shower, temperature range 11-17 C. At breakfast the port of Syracuse comes into view and soon after the *MV Aegean Odyssey* anchors a short distance from the docks.

Many a conqueror has set his sights on Syracuse, one of the largest and wealthiest cities of ancient Europe. It is the most important city of Magna Graecia. At the height of its economic, political and military powers, the city has a population of 300,000 and rivals Athens, Carthage and Rome. It defeats the mighty Athens in 413 BC and is home to many a great Greek, including Archimedes, the famous Greek mathematician and inventor.

Today's excursion will bring to life the rich history of this beautiful city. We are lucky with the weather as the morning skies turn blue and sunny. At 8.35 am a ship's tender takes to us ashore where we board a coach. Our guide is Liliana, a trim five foot nothing Italian.

The centre of town is the island of Ortygia which is 1 sq km in size and is connected to the mainland by three bridges. The island is the site of the original Greek settlers from Corinth who founded Syracuse in 734 BC. Today many visitors come here to walk and relax at the Foro Italica which is a beautiful promenade on the island.

Our coach leaves from Ortygia and weaves through narrow streets to Syracuse Archaeological Park situated in the northwest of the town. The ancient town is known as Neapolis and is home to a staggering number of well-preserved Greek and Roman remains. The main attraction is the Greek theatre, dating from the 5th century BC. Its cavea, the tiered semicircular seating space, is one of the largest ever built and it is still in good shape, despite the centuries. The 59 rows of seating could accommodate up to 15,000 spectators. This morning a team of workmen are at the site covering the tiered cavea with protective wooden seating in preparation for the centenary of the first ancient Greek play performed here in June 1914. The annual Greek theatre festival runs from the middle of May to the end of June. Fortunately they have not covered too much to interrupt our view of the ancient theatre. Higher up above the theatre at the ridgetop are a number of caverns. Liliana says they are catacombs of Christians, dating from the 1st century AD.

Situated nearby is an impressive Roman amphitheatre built in the 3rd century BC. It is 140 m long and one of the largest found anywhere. Of course, its function served a different purpose than the Greek theatre. Traditional circus fare was offered, with gladiators and wild animals providing spectacles of blood sport and violence. The rectangular hole in the centre is thought to be a drain for the blood and gore.

Another huge monument in the park is the 200 m long sacrificial altar built in the 2nd century BC by the Greek Sicilian king of Syracuse, Hieron II (c. 308 BC – 215 BC). The huge altar made it possible to sacrifice up to 450 bulls in a single day. This was one way to propitiate the gods and to remind friends and enemies that Syracuse had plenty of resources. Unfortunately, only the base of the huge structure remains. The walls of square blocks, columns, access ramps and statues were demolished by the Spanish in the 16th century in order to obtain stone to build the fortifications at Ortygia. 'Can you imagine 400 oxen being slaughtered here?' Liliana questions us.

What makes these monuments impressive is the fact that they have been carved straight out of the local bedrock. Just over the ridge from the theatre is the *Latomia Del Paradiso*, the ancient stone quarry that provided the building material. The limestone quarry is now beautiful parkland of green shrubbery dominated by citrus and olive trees. Water for the gardens comes from the mountains via an ancient aqueduct construction.

Liliana explains that the quarry once served a more sinister purpose. 7,000 Athenian prisoners were kept here after the Sicilian Expedition of 413 BC. Of most interest at this site is the *Orecchio di Dionisio*, a massive cave carved into the cliff face of the quarry that formed following years of mining. The famous 'Ear of Dionysius' is a 20 metre high slender pointed arch cut into the rock face that continues inwards for about 65 metres. The name was given by the famous Italian artist Caravaggio during his visit here in 1608. Legend tells us that Dionysius the Tyrant used it to imprison his bitterest enemies. The cavern provides particularly good Cathedral-like acoustics which meant that he could hear their conversations from outside.

Liliana is keen for us to try out the cave's excellent acoustics. She sings 'Santa Lucia' in excellent voice.

Our morning here is over and we return to Ortygia. Suddenly a small car darts out from a side street in front of our coach, bringing gasps from everyone. Our quick-witted driver blasts his horn in annoyance. Liliana announces, 'In France they drive on the right. In Britain they drive on the left. But in Sicily they drive in the shade.'

From the bridges at Ortygia, Liliana guides us on a short walk through narrow lanes containing the modern homes and shops of the local Sicilians. It leads to the real centre of Ortygia, the Piazza del Duomo. An imposing sight of towering Doric columns greets you upon entering the open pedestrian square which is home to the Duomo, the wonderful Syracuse Cathedral. More than any other structure in town, the cathedral illustrates the changing colonisations and architectural styles that have dominated the city over the centuries. Containing the additions made by various conquerors, the cathedral is a majestic hotchpotch of Greek, Roman, Byzantine and Norman features. Built on the original site of the 5th century Temple of Athena, the structure incorporates twenty-six of the original Doric columns.

The former Greek temple is now a fusion of pagan and Christian worship. In its heyday the temple was revered by the people of the Mediterranean. From miles away, sailors could see the golden statue of Athena shining like a beacon. An earthquake in 1693 caused the cathedral's façade to collapse. Rebuilt in Baroque style in the 18th century, the elegant façade steals the attention from the rest of the piazza.

The morning slips by and the last tender to our ship leaves at 12.30 pm. We have just enough time to visit another interesting historic church, Santa Lucia alla Badia, at the bottom end of the Piazza Duomo. Saint Lucia is the patron saint of Syracuse. According to legend, Lucia gives all her dowry money, left by her father, to the poor after her sick mother is healed at the St Agatha's shrine. Lucia's mother wants her to marry a rich pagan man. Instead Lucia breaks her engagement and offers her chastity to God. Her mother becomes very ill from a bleeding problem. So Lucia asks her mother to accompany her to St Agatha's shrine where they both pray all night. St Agatha appears to Lucia in a dream and gives her the good news that her mother is healed of her bleeding problem. Her mother finally agrees to comply with Lucia's request following her miracle cure.

This does not sit well with her pagan groom. He denounces Lucia as a Christian, so the governor of Syracuse sentences her to be deflowered in a brothel. This is in 304 AD, during the time of Roman Emperor Diocletian's severe persecution of Christians in the Roman Empire. The soldiers come to forcibly take Lucia to a brothel house, but no one can move her. They try oxen, witchcraft, and a thousand men, but she stands immobile. They claim she is heavier than a mountain. Finally, they torture Lucia to death by taking out her eyes with a fork and killing her with a knife in the throat. She dies as a martyr.

Behind the altar in the church is a magnificent painting depicting *The Burial of St Lucia* by Caravaggio. In 1608 the famous Italian painter escapes from prison on Malta and flees to Syracuse. His Roman companion, Mario Minniti, helps him get a commission to paint the altarpiece of the church. The most common theme in paintings of St Lucia is the depiction her martyrdom. Instead, Caravaggio decides to paint her burial. He is driven by the fact that the patron saint has been interred below the church. The scene shows hulking gravediggers and an armoured soldier taking up most of the lower portion of his canvas, seemingly twice the size of the huddled group of mourners. Caravaggio's paintings are renowned for his realistic observation of the human state, both physical and emotional and also with a dramatic use of lighting.

The weather has become inclement as we return to the ship. A few of us are splashed by the choppy waters that enter the sides of our tender. At 1.00 pm we enjoy a light lunch of fish, chips and salad. In mid-afternoon at 3.30 pm we attend a port lecture for our excursions over the next two days in Sicily.

At 5.50 pm Neil Horrocks calls from the bridge to alert us that we are approaching the Strait of Messina, the narrow channel which separates Sicily from the Italian mainland. He informs us that the Strait is 3.1 kilometres wide and 250 metres deep. Since 1957 there have been talks of building a bridge to link the two. It is estimated that this would cost over 6 billion Euros. In this earthquake zone it would require the construction of two pillars taller than the Empire State Building. We rush to the top deck to take a look, thinking that we are about to go through the strait. However, the strait is still a long way off and it takes nearly an hour to pass through. In gloomy skies and coldness we stand there shivering.

The Captain's Welcome's Party is next at 6.45 pm. We have 15 minutes to dress up. However, as it happens, we did not need to hurry as Captain Roland Andersson of Sweden is 30 minutes late. By the time of his arrival most of us have had two or more champagnes. He makes a short speech and then says, 'Skol'. We indulge in more drink as he departs.

We meet again with Barbara Currie and her friend Robin who resides in New Farm, Brisbane. Dressed in our evening wear we decide to dine formally in the Marco Polo Restaurant down in Deck 3. For starters we all have mushroom tart with truffle sauce. For mains Avril tries a pork dish and I have a Sicilian steak and beans. Barbara did not manage to make contact with her family today. She accepts my offer to send an Email to inform them of her well-being. Back in our unit Avril chooses to watch the film, *'Tea with Mussolini'*, which ends after 11.00 pm. But within a few minutes she is sound asleep. I retire a little before midnight.

Day 15
Thursday March 27, 2014.

Palermo, Sicily

We arise at 6.00 am and soon the *Aegean Odyssey* will dock at Palermo, Sicily's cultural, economic and tourist capital. There is a moderate sea swell and the weather forecast is for breezy conditions with showers, temperature range 11-15 C.

Palermo is a city rich in history, culture, art, music and food. Numerous tourists are attracted here for its pleasant Mediterranean weather, its renowned gastronomy and restaurants, and the Romanesque, Gothic and Baroque churches, palaces and other buildings.

Palermo, situated on the north coast of Sicily, is a bustling metropolis and has been capital of the island since Arab times (831-1042). It is filled with monuments and reminders of the many different phases of Sicilian history, from the archaeological remains of the earliest Phoenician settlement in 734 BC to the magnificent 19th Century neo-classical Teatro Politeama Garibaldi which overlooks the main square. There is something for everyone in Palermo.

This morning we will visit the Palermo Cathedral and the Palatine Chapel. Our Italian guide is Marilou, a pleasant woman in her forties, very chatty and knowledgeable. She is rugged up to avoid the cold and she cringes at the thought that so many in our coach are in short sleeves. She gets the driver to take us on a short trip through the beautiful city to showcase the highlights. Palermo opens like a fan from a circular backdrop of fertile green mountains. The long main avenue, Via Maqueda, is compared with the Champs Elysees.

The city contains splendid monuments, manicured parks, fountains and constructions. We drive by the magnificent Teatro Massimo, one of the most prestigious theatres in Europe, renowned for its opera performances. Designed by Giovan Battista Basile, work began in 1875 and was completed by his son Ernesto in 1897. The theatre is a majestic structure with a surface area of almost 8,000 square metres and a splendid neoclassical façade. A wide stairway is flanked by two bronze lions bearing the figures of Tragedy and Opera. Behind them are six huge columns which support a decorated roof façade in a large triangular pediment.

Marilou reminds us that Sicily is the biggest island in the Mediterranean and a stepping stone between Africa and Europe. It is bounded by the Tirreno Sea on the northern coast, the Ionian Sea on the eastern coast and the Sicilian Sea on the south-western coast. The fertile island is 60 percent hilly and contains the active volcano Mt Etna, the largest volcano in Europe, towering 3,330 metres.

Marilou briefly outlines the rich history of settlers and invaders who have been attracted to Palermo. They have left their mark on the island with a rich blend of architectural styles. The Sicanians arrive from the Iberian Peninsula about 10,000 years ago to establish their colonies beside the bay. In 734 BC the Phoenicians, a sea trading people from north of ancient Canaan, establish a small permanent settlement called 'Zis' on the natural harbour of Palermo.

The settlement passes to the Carthaginians who are the descendants and successors of the Phoenicians. In the 8th century the first Greek settlers establish cities in Sicily. The Greeks call the Carthaginian settlement *Panormus*, meaning *all-port* because of its fine natural harbour. Palermo becomes the centre of commerce and a power struggle develops between the Greeks and the Carthaginians. In 258 BC the Syracusans try to overpower Palermo, but are unsuccessful. However, the stronghold of the Carthaginians yields to the Romans in 254 BC during the First Punic War (264 to 241 BC). The long period under Roman rule is a peaceful time for Palermo, which grows into an important Roman trading centre.

Palermo falls into the hands of the Vandals when Roman power declines. The Vandals are an East Germanic group of tribes, originally from Scandinavia. They moved about Europe establishing kingdoms in Spain, and later North Africa in the 5th century. In 493 AD the Italian peninsula and all of Sicily falls to the Ostrogoths, another German tribe ruled by King Theodoric the Great. The Byzantines (Eastern Roman Empire) take over in the first half of the sixth century, to be turned out themselves by the Arabs in 831 AD.

At the beginning of the 11th Century the combined military invasion by Normans and Pisans (maritime power) undermines the Arab occupation, giving way to Robert Guiscard de Hauteville and his brother Roger by 1072.

The Norman influence declines near the end of the twelfth century. The Swabians (German people) then appear; Frederick II is their great ruler who attracts talented and innovative men of the time. The city declines when he dies in 1250 AD.

The Angevins (French rulers since 1266 AD) and the Aragonese (Spanish rulers) then take turns as rulers in Palermo. On the Easter Monday, March 30 of 1282, the Sicilian Vespers rebel against the rule of the French. A French soldier decides to search a Sicilian woman for weapons, offending her modesty and enraging the crowd that is on its way to evening prayer at the church of Palermo. A spontaneous uprising follows and quickly spreads across the island. Within six weeks 3000 French men and women are slain, accounting for nearly all the French in Sicily. The uprising and subsequent war destroys the strategic Mediterranean ambitions of Charles 1.

Known as the War of the Sicilian Vespers (1282 – 1302), the Sicilians turn to Peter III of Aragon for military assistance against Charles I, the Angevin ruler of Naples and Sicily. Peter III accepts the offer of the Sicilian throne and defeats Charles I who withdraws to Italy and establishes the kingdom of Naples. The struggle between the Angevin kings of Naples and the Aragonese kings of Sicily over the Sicilian throne continues for two decades until 1302 when the 'Peace of Caltabellotta' divides the old Kingdom of Sicily into an island kingdom and a peninsula kingdom. The Aragon dynasty keeps Sicily whereas the Angevin dynasty retains Southern Italy as the Kingdom of Naples. The Vespers' consolidation with the Spanish Aragonese is a prelude to the long-lasting domination of the Spanish in Palermo and on the island.

The War of the Vespers no doubt diverts the attention of Charles I away from the troubled Crusader states and Palestine in the Middle East. The fall of Acre to the Arabs in 1291 AD signals the end of the Christian presence there. Charles and his contemporaries would have bolstered the Christian position had they not become entangled in the domestic war.

The long debilitating War of Spanish Succession from 1700 AD ends with the Peace of Utrecht in 1713. The Treaty provides for a variety of territorial realignments; Sicily is handed to Duke Victor Amadeus II of the House of Savoy, one of the oldest Royal Houses in Europe. He has to return the island to King Philip V of Spain just five years later. In 1720 Spain passes Sicily over to Austria, but takes it back again in 1733 when Spain declares war on Austria.

King Philip V sends his son Charles to recapture Naples and Sicily. Young Charles rules Spain as King Charles III following the death of his father in 1746, then in 1738 he is crowned King of the Two Sicilies.

Charles III's descendants remain on the throne of the Two Sicilies in a continuous line, interrupted by Napoleon's period of occupation and the republican uprisings of Europe in 1848. The unrest prepares the way for the victorious campaign of Italian revolutionary leader, Garibaldi in 1860.

Our coach stops outside the majestic Palermo Cathedral which is a grand showpiece of the diverse mix of architectural styles of the preceding centuries. This splendid jewel is, without doubt, the world's most eclectic ecclesiastical structure which tells its story in stone -- Arab, Norman, Byzantine, Swabian, Romanesque, Gothic, Renaissance and Baroque. Today, Palermo's Cathedral is known as Saint Mary of the Assumption. Its history dates back to the early Christians who built a Christian basilica on the site. Arab records mention the existence of a large 'infidel' temple here when they conquer Palermo in 831. The Arabs turn it into the Great Mosque.

In 1072 the Normans wrest control of Palermo from the Saracens. Count Roger (Roger I) reconsecrates the Great Mosque as a Christian church. Roger 1 dies in 1101 and his young son, Simon of Hauteville, becomes Count of Sicily, with his mother Adelaide del Vasto acting as regent. Simon dies in 1105 at the age of 12 and his younger brother Roger II is successor. Roger II begins his rule as Count of Sicily and his mother Adelaide continues as regent to her younger son who was just 9 years old. At 32, Roger II is one of the most influential princes of Europe.

The death of Pope Honorius in February 1130 allows Roger II to gain a royal crown. For the election of a new Pope, Roger throws his support behind the candidature of antipope Anacletus II, rather than the favourite, Innocent II. In return for the support, Roger II is promised a coronation. Following the death of Antipope Anacletus II in 1138, Roger II needs to capture Pope Innocent II. Roger routs the papal army at Galluccio and forces Pope Innocent II to confirm him as king in the Norman Kingdom of Sicily. By the time of Roger II's death on February 26, 1154, at the age of 58, he has succeeded in uniting all the Norman conquests in Italy into one kingdom, with a strong centralized government.

The Norman-Arab style cathedrals at Palermo and nearby Monreale and Cefalu are born in the eleventh century and flourish into the twelfth.

In 1184, during the reign of William II (Roger II's grandson), the Anglo-Norman Archbishop, Walter Offamilio, a cousin of the Hauteville kings, commissions the construction of the Palermo Cathedral on the historic site. The Archbishop's aim is to surpass the glory of the magnificent Cathedral of Monreale.

Many renovations and additions have been made to the Cathedral of Palermo over the centuries. Our guide Marilou explains that these modifications have radically altered much of its unique Norman-Arab style.

The outside looks medieval and shows the development of Gothic style made in the 13th and 14th centuries. Four earlier Norman towers stand at each corner of the Cathedral. Its dramatic outline is surrounded by a marble balustrade containing sculptures in Baroque style. High above the main portal is a series of blind arches, columns, mullioned windows and intersecting arches.

Inside the huge edifice, the appearance changes to neoclassical. Marilou points out its many features such as a royal pantheon which shelters many tombs of Sicily's kings, including the first king, Roger II – born Mileto (Italy) on December 22, 1095, crowned in Palermo on December 25, 1130 and died there on February 26, 1154 (aged 58). The last royal burial here was Peter II in 1342.

Meanwhile, as we follow Marilou, a religious service is in progress and she is approached by a priest who reminds her that we are in a temple of prayer. She smiles and says, 'Please pray for all of us, father.' Marilou moves aside a little and continues her spiel as more tourists stream in.

On the right hand side of the presbytery is the Chapel of Santa Rosa, where a bronze railing protects a silver urn containing the mortal remains of the patron saint of the city. Marilou explains, 'Rosalie was the daughter of a nobleman who came to Sicily in the retinue of Roger II. She was born here in 1130. In her youth, her heart turned from earthly vanities to God. She left her home and took up her abode in a cave where she remained hidden from the world. She practiced great penances and lived in communion with God. She died a hermit in a grotto on Monte Pellegrino in 1160, unknown to the world. In 1625 during the outbreak of the Black Plague, a hermit had a vision of a woman who instructed him to search for her remains. The plague-ridden city was miraculously freed of the pestilence after relics of Rosalie were carried in a solemn procession through the city.'

Marilou suggests, 'If anyone is physiologically challenged, there is a toilet behind the second chapel to the right.' The weather has turned wet as we assemble in the outside portal in readiness for our visit to the Palatine Chapel, a short drive away. Our coach driver inches though crazy tight morning traffic. Marilou says, 'Here in Palermo the rule is 'No Rule at all'. You just take your chances'. Size counts and we arrive safely.

No visit to Palermo is complete without a visit to the site where the Norman Palace now stands. The Phoenicians establish the city as a trading colony around 750 BC, about the same time as the Greeks begin colonizing eastern Sicily. Three centuries later the Carthaginians (Phoenician descendants) arrive to develop and fortify the port city which was known as Zis, then successively as Panormos, Panormus, Balharm and finally Palermo.

Palermo becomes one of the main battlegrounds in the Punic Wars. Rome finally crushes Carthage and becomes the major power in the Mediterranean. The Romans rule Sicily for over six centuries from 211 BC to 440 AD. Following the fall of Rome, Palermo (Panormus) is visited by the Vandals and Goths, but they do not stay for long. Byzantium frees Sicily in 535 AD and integrates it into the Byzantine Empire.

The shoreline of Palermo recedes and the population dwindles. The Arabs restore the city in the 9th century and build a large citadel, al Kasr, over the walls of the old Carthaginian fortress. They erect administrative buildings on land claimed from the sea. The palace is abandoned by the Arabs and then restored by the conquering Normans. In 1071 Robert Guiscard and his younger brother, Roger, capture Palermo and the city is set to assume its place as an important European capital. Rival emirs cooperate with the invading Normans. Al Kasr becomes the fortress of Palermo and home of Sicily's rulers.

Almost everybody who visits Palermo comes to see the Palatine Chapel which is located within the Norman Palace. The palace has its start in the 9th century AD when the Emir of Palermo builds it on the site occupied by Roman and Punic (Phoenician- Carthaginian) fortresses. Then Roger II turns the sumptuous palace into the city's main fortress and, above all, he crowns the site by installing the magnificent Palatine Chapel. He commissions the

Chapel to be built in 1132 and it takes eight years to construct -- with the exquisite Norman-Byzantine mosaics taking a little longer. The sanctuary is dedicated to St Peter and has three apses with six pointed arches, three on each side of the central nave. Roger II does not include any Christian images in the nave. These are added later by his successors, his son William I (William the Bad) and grandson William II (William the Good).

Our coach stops outside the palace, beside the medieval walls of this ancient fortress. Marilou takes us up several flights of wide marble steps to a sweeping covered balcony that overlooks the quadrangle of an impressive courtyard. We continue along the balcony to the chapel which is set inside the fortified building.

Stepping into the king's chapel we witness a miraculous fusion of Latin, Byzantine and Arab architectural design. Byzantine mosaics blanket entire walls in a pattern of creamy marble inlaid with gold leaf. They depict a variety of saints and biblical scenes, some in unusual ways – Adam and Eve are shown with the forbidden fruit in their mouths. Some mosaics have a secular pattern, depicting oriental flora and fauna designs. The central image of Christ Pantocrator appears in the apse and the cupola. A huge royal throne is covered in mosaics near the entrance to the nave. The nave's ceiling consists of carved wooden coffers in a meld of the finest Arabic motif.

During Roger II's reign as King of Sicily (1130 AD to 1154 AD), the island becomes a great maritime power and also the channel through which Greek and Arab thought passes into Europe. The spirit of Roger's reign is gloriously expressed on the island, but nowhere more perfectly than the Palatine Chapel built during the 1130s and 1140s.

The palace falls into serious decay after the Normans leave. In 1555 the Spanish Viceroys begin to restore the palace into a royal residence once again. Today the palace is the seat of Sicily's semi-autonomous regional government.

We return to our ship for a quick bite before heading out at 1.30 pm to visit Cefalu, an hour's scenic drive along the coast. We are lucky to have Marilou again as our guide. Speaking four languages fluently, she is a font of wisdom. Cefalu is a charming hill town located on a headland jutting into the Tyrrhenian Sea. The beautiful drive passes through rich farming orchards of citrus trees and olive groves. Marilou says that Sicily is famous for its extra virgin olive oil. Our coach stops at a high point for a scenic view of this ancient fishing village, now a resort. The scene is dominated by a huge fortress rock with ancient fortifications used long ago. On either side of the dominant peak are harbours and sandy beaches. Cefalu takes its name from the Greek word *Kephaloidion*, meaning chief or head.

The main feature to see in the small township is its extraordinary Cathedral which overlooks a small central square containing a few cafes. Its superb façade is framed between two powerful towers. A flight of steps leads to the pavis, a courtyard which is fenced and adorned with statues. The upper and lower porticos are adorned with a mix of arches -- the small blind Moorish arches are at the top and larger Gothic arches are at the bottom. Begun by Roger II in 1131 the cathedral took a very long time to build and it remained partially unfinished.

Marilou explains the story behind the imposing Norman structure. Legend has it that King Roger II, seemingly faced with certain shipwreck, vows to build a splendid cathedral should he survive. Fortunately he escapes the storm and lands on the city's beach. Roger II commissions the Cathedral of Cefalu in 1131 soon after taking the throne in 1130. The structure is completed in little more than a year, but the decorations and furnishings take much longer, not until 1148.

Under his rule Sicily grows to become a major power. This Norman-Arab structure expresses the all-embracing spirit of Roger's reign. The main feature above the altar is the 12th century gold mosaic of Christ Pantocrator, one of the greatest representations of Christ in Christian art. But, apart from that, the Cathedral's plain interior is left barren and unfurnished. It seems that Roger II fulfils his vow and leaves. The Cathedral is far from finished at the time of his death in 1154. Not until 1257 does final consecration take place.

Marilou is anxious to show us an ancient Turkish washroom. A few of our group follow her down through narrow cobblestone laneways that lead to the site. The gurgling sound of flowing water is heard as we descend some steps that lead to a cavernous room containing a series of tubs. The water comes from an aqueduct feeding into a system of wash basins. It is here that the women of the village would gather to communicate and scrub their clothes, before the advent of washing machines.

We return to the square using another route. In a wall we come across a pretty shrine. Marilou says that you find these religious symbols all over Italy. Avril and I saw plenty during our self-drive in northern Greece. These shrines pop up randomly, particularly along country roads.

On our return from Cefalu, Marilou points out a huge factory complex as we near Palermo. 'That is the abandoned Fiat Factory. The parent company chose to close this branch because of economic problems. It is tough on those people to lose their jobs.' The Aussies on board tell her that Australia is experiencing the same thing with the closure of Holden, Ford and Toyota. She jokes, 'FIAT stands for Fix It Again Tony'; and for the Italian immigrants coming into Ellis Island, New York, TONY means 'To New York'.

Arriving at 6.00 pm we say farewell to our friendly and chatty host. Avril and I dine at 7.30 pm -- delicious roast pork, roast potato, vegetables and a small plate of Caesar salad. Avril reads her book from the ship's library, *'Family Baggage'*, by Monica McInerney and I catch up on notes till well past midnight.

Day 16
Friday March 28, 2014.

Palermo, Italy

The alarm wakes me at 6.00 am. I pull the curtain to ascertain the weather from the porthole. The sky is a mix of puffy white and grey clouds, suggesting rain at times. The ship's Journal says breezy with possible showers, and a temperature range of 9-17 C.

This morning our excursion takes us inland from Palermo to the picturesque town of Monreale located on the slope of Monte Caputo, part of a ring of mountains overlooking and surrounding the very fertile valley called 'La Conca d'Oro' – the Golden Shell, famed for its orange, olive and almond trees. At Monreale we will visit the Cathedral, considered by many to be the most beautiful Norman Church in Italy. Our coach follows the long main avenue leading from the port to Monreale, perched at 310 m and about 15 kilometres south of Palermo. Monreale comes from the Latin *'Mons Regalis'* meaning 'Royal Mountain'.

Our guide is Maggie or Marie-Jo, a stylish middle-aged Italian woman. On the way she points out an ancient Arab/Norman hunting lodge where once the Norman, King Roger II, his son William the Bad and grandson William the Good would retreat to after a day's hunting. The area becomes a favourite hunting ground for the Hauteville monarchs. In those days there were far more forests than today. Wild cats, boar and deer once roamed Sicily. The woodlands have long since given way to the city streets.

We are afforded a great view of the city as our coach ascends the winding mountain roadway leading to the cathedral. From the parking bay below the cathedral a steady walk is required to reach the picturesque square in front of the cathedral. Some of our group choose a 5 Euro taxi ride to avoid the steep climb. Maggie guides the rest of us up several flights of steps to the busy square. In sprinkling rain we assemble to enter the cathedral through a side door. On either side of the entrance are two bronze statues. On the right is the statue of King William the Good, his arms outstretched and offering the cathedral to the Virgin Mary on the left. William II became known as William the Good because his policy of clemency and justice toward the towns and barons, in contrast with his father, William 1 the Bad. William the Good (b. 1154, d. Nov 18, 1189, Palermo) was the last Norman king of Sicily.

Designed by William the Good in 1174, the cathedral offers visions of beauty, grace and the divinity. The exterior's thick walls and powerful towers have the look of an austere fortress. But just a step inside and one is struck by the cathedral's true glory. The large nave with its side aisles and grey granite columns draw your eyes upwards to 12th century gold mosaics that cover over one and a half acres of wall space. Above the columns (nine on both sides) are wonderful paintings of biblical scenes. Maggie says that 2000 kilograms of 24 carat gold was used in the mosaics. The bodies of William the Good and his father lie in two sarcophagi near the altar.

Maggie takes us into the Benedictine cloister courtyard of the former monastery that is attached to the cathedral. The monastery was built here at the same time as the Cathedral and the cloister is the only part now standing. The cloister contains 228 sets of twin columns which are linked by pointed Arabic arches. The columns support ornately carved capitals, depicting scenes in Sicily's Norman history and all manner of Biblical figures and mythological scenes. The carvings here in stone evoke a comparison with that of the Norman knights depicted in the Bayeux Tapestry which chronicles William the Conqueror's Battle of Hastings in 1066.

We are given some free time to view the Benedictine cloister court which forms a perfect square, measuring forty-seven metres on each side. The elegant rows of twin columns support ogival arches of exquisite Arab workmanship. The capitals were carved by Byzantine and Islamic artists. At the southwest corner is an Arab fountain of Moorish and Hispanic characteristics. It is like a mini cloister surrounded by its own four-sided colonnade. Jets of water provide a cooling atmosphere. Tradition says that William often washed his face in this fountain.

At 11.15 am we leave this delightful setting and return to the busy streets of Palermo for a special visit to Palazzo Gangi. Our young masterful coach driver, Antonio, weaves through chaotic city traffic to reach the site. Maggie says, 'You have to understand how to be fluid, otherwise you will be there all day.' Antonio deposits us and we take a short walk down a side street leading a small square where we see a couple of huge battered-looking doors, badly needing a coat of paint. Maggie knocks and a few minutes later a butler, dressed in a light gold jacket, opens the doors.

The atmosphere changes to opulence as we climb a marble staircase where we are greeted by a friend of its owner, Princess Carine Vanni Mantegna. The princess no longer lives here, and nowadays the non-residential palace serves as a museum of antiques. It was once the 15th century ancestral palace of the Princes of Valguarnera. In the 18th century the Princes of Gangi (Gangi is a province of Palermo) decided to remodel the aristocratic home, a vast undertaking which continues today under the auspices of Princess Mantegna.

The Palazzo Gangi is noted for its Sicilian Baroque ballroom decorated with Murano chandeliers, gold fittings and glittering mirrors. One of the several huge candelabras contains 102 lights. Imagine dusting all that! Here in 1882 Wagner composed the opening bars of *Pursifal* and in 1963 Luchino Visconti filmed the magnificent ballroom dance scene of Burt Lancaster and Claudia Cardinale in *The Leopard*.

We are served scrumptious deep fried finger food and a drink of juice or champagne poured by the butler. Upon returning to the *Aegean Odyssey* at 1.15 pm, we feel there is no need for lunch on board.

At evening dinner, Barbara Currie, our friend from Queensland, dines with us. The elderly lady wants to take up my offer to forward an email to her family. She has been unable to get a connection on her phone to send them a text message. She hands me a short note and email address of a family contact. On the menu is smoked cod, but we choose a delicious pork roast and vegetables.

At 9.15 pm the *Odyssey Trio*, a music group of talented artists from Romania, perform a wonderful concert. Of the three musicians, I note that one of the artists is the pianist, Bogdan Mandasescu, who performed splendidly during our cruise of South America last year. On that occasion he joined with the violinist, Teodor Radu, as a duo team. Tonight Bogdan teams up with Virgil-Florin Prisacariu on double bass and Catalin Sasu on violin to complete the trio. We are in for a treat as they play: *WIENER BLUT* (Viennese Blood) by Johann Strauss II (1825-1899); *AUF DER JAGD* (On the Hunt) by Johann Strauss II; *THE MERRY WIDOW* (Selections from) by Franz Lehar (1870-1948); *SALUT D'AMOUR* by Sir Edward Elgar (1857-1934); *CSARDAS* by Vittorio Monti (1868-1922); *FIDDLER ON THE ROOF* (Selections from) by Jerry Block (1928-2010); *ANNEN POLKA* by Johann Strauss II; *LOVE IS A MANY SPLENDORED THING* by Sammy Fain (1902-1989); and *SKYLARK* by Grigoras Dinicu (1899-1949).

I retire early at 10.30 pm as Avril watches the second episode of the First Series of 'Downton Abbey' on TV. The butler's droning voice soon sends me asleep.

Day 17
Saturday March 29, 2014
Trapani, Sicily

Overnight the *Aegean Odyssey* travels in calm waters from Palermo to Trapani, the capital city of the province with the same name on the westernmost tip of Sicily. Trapani is one of the nine provinces of Sicily which is an autonomous island region of Italy. Trapani province contains 24 municipalities with a total population of around 450,000, including 70,000 people who live in the city area. This compares with over 5 million for all of Sicily and over 60 million for Italy.

Sicily, with an area of 25,711 sq km, is the largest and most densely populated of the islands in the Mediterranean Sea. The island is separated from the Italian mainland by the Strait of Messina just 3km to the north. A map reveals Italy's long shoe-like peninsula seemingly booting the triangular shaped island into the middle of the Mediterranean Sea, almost to Tunisia in northern Africa, 160 km to the southeast. Sicily's strategic location has made it the world's most conquered island. This autonomous region of present day Italy has seen the rise and fall of various conquerors – Greek, Carthaginian, Roman, Vandal, Byzantine, Moslem, Norman, French and Spanish.

Sicily is mostly mountainous and enjoys a pleasant subtropical and Mediterranean climate. Average rainfall range is 400-600 mm on the plains and up to 1400 mm in the mountains. There is a plentiful supply of underground and spring water. The island is often subject to intense seismic and volcanic activity. Mount Etna towers above the city of Catania on the east coast. At 3,330 metres above sea level it is Europe's highest and most active volcano.

Sicily became inhabited about 10,000 years ago. The Elymians, the Sicanians and the Sicels were the three ancient indigenous peoples on Sicily before the Phoenicians and Greeks arrived on the island. The Sicels occupied Sicily in the east and gave their name to the island. The Elymians probably migrated from Asian Minor via Africa, maybe as far back as 6,000 BC. They established cities in northwestern Sicily, displacing or amalgamating with the Sicanians in these areas. Their two major cities were Erice and Segesta whose temples and amphitheatres are carefully being restored. According to Thucydides in his 'History of the Peloponnesian War', Egesta (Segesta) and nearby Eryx (Erice) were founded by colonists from Troy in the 2nd millennium BC. They call themselves Elymi and speak their own Elymian language. Later they adopt the Greek language and culture.

Trapani is founded by Elymians to serve as a port for its nearby city of Erice which overlooks it from Monte San Giuliano. By the 8th century the fishing village has developed into a prosperous Phoenician trading centre. A thriving business of trade develops between both the Phoenicians and then the Greeks upon their arrival to the island. Formerly, Trapani was called Drepanon, a Greek word for 'sickle', possibly because of the curve shape of its low promontory that juts out into the Mediterranean Sea.

The ancient Greeks sought to believe that the Elymians originated from the inhabitants of Troy. By identifying the Elymians to be a kindred race, the Greeks justify their occupation of western Sicily in order to oust the Phoenicians (Carthaginians) from that region. By 500 BC the native Elymian culture is Hellenised to the extent that little of the old society remains. They adopt many aspects of the culture of the Greek colonists, even erecting the remarkable temple at Segesta using the Greek alphabet to write their own language.

The Elymians find themselves torn by loyalties to the Carthaginians or to the Greeks. Boundary disputes arise as the Greeks seek to expand their colonies into western Sicily, especially the Greek colony of Selinus (modern day Selinunte), just sixty kilometres south of the Elymian city of Segesta. Selinus dramatically grows and prospers since its founding in 650 BC. This alarms the Elymians of Segesta and conflict with Selinus breaks out after 580 BC.

The Elymians ally firstly with Athens against Selinus. Athens responds by sending a fleet of 60 ships, but help never arrives. Instead, the fleet is redirected into the disastrous war against Syracuse. The Sicilian expedition of 415 BC-413 BC fails. Syracuse becomes the most powerful city in Sicily and is an ally of Selinus. For self-preservation the Elymians appeal to the Carthaginians to attack Selinus. They respond and Selinus is ultimately sacked in 409 BC. In the attack led by Hannibal, Carthage destroys Segesta's rival, slaughtering about 16,000 of the inhabitants in the process. But in doing so Carthage maintains its grip on the Mediterranean trade. As masters of western Sicily, they establish a garrison at Segesta. In 405 BC they sign a power sharing treaty with Syracuse to divide up the island.

However, just over a century later, Segesta turns on Carthage during the First Punic War (264 BC-146BC) and allies with Rome instead. The Romans conquer Sicily and are so impressed with the Elymians and their claim of Trojan ancestry that they do not require them to pay taxes to Rome. They are seen as cousins of the Roman people who also claim to have descended from the Trojans. Eventually, medieval Segestans abandon their city, favouring nearby towns such as Erice and Trapani.

Today the city of Trapani is still an important fishing port and the main gateway to the nearby Egadi Islands. It became the provincial capital in 1817. Trapani was badly damaged during WW II, when it was subjected to intense Allied bombardments. It has grown greatly since the end of the war, sprawling out virtually to the foot of Mont San Giuliano. Tourism has grown in recent years due to the city's proximity to popular destinations such as Erice, Segesta and the Egadi Islands.

This morning we plan to visit the ancient Greek colony of Selinus which was abandoned by 250 BC when Carthage forced the residents to relocate to Lilybaeum at the time of first Punic War with Rome. Lilybaeum is the scene of the first clash between the navies of Carthage and Rome during the Second Punic War in 218 BC. The present day city of Marsala in Trapani Province now occupies the site.

We wake to the alarm at 6.00 am and note that beautiful clear skies have returned after two days of unsettled weather. Sunny skies and an 18 C high temperature are forecast. Our ship docks as we breakfast at 6.45 am. At 8.00 am we are heading along the highway to Selinunte Archaeological Park, about an hour's drive away.

We travel along an excellent two lane highway passing olive groves, vineyards, wheat fields and plantings of melons, cherry tomatoes and eggplants. Our guide, Elena, says that olive trees 1000 years old have been found here and one estimated to be 1600 years old. She adds, 'I know prickly pears are a pest in Australia, but they are cultivated here for making marmalade jam. The soil is very fertile and this part of Sicily is free of snow and the summer is pleasant. The hot winds flowing from North Africa are tempered by the Mediterranean.'

Elena points out the flats for preparing salt, an old important industry. We see eucalyptus trees, a native of Australia, growing in low lying damp areas. 'They are growing there because of the malaria. The trees soak up the moisture and prevent mosquitos from breeding. We get a 4 months dry period over the summer, but we are still getting some rain at the moment.'

At 10.15 am we arrive at Selinunte Archaeological Park, considered the biggest and most imposing of Europe. It superbly illustrates the synthesis of Greek and Phoenician cultures. Selinunte is founded between 650 and 628 BC by the Greek colonisers from Megara Hyblaea near Syracuse. [Elena suggests that the city takes its name from the wild parsley growing at the nearby river Selinos (now Modione River).] The city is in constant conflict with its non-Hellenic neighbour, the Elymians, who have one of their important settlements at Segesta.

The Elymians are for a long time hostile to Carthage. But In 409 BC, the Carthaginians come to the aid of Segesta following its bitter rivalry with Selinunte. The Carthaginians lay siege to Selinunte and slaughter 16,000 of its residents. The ancient city never recovers. To prevent it from being conquered by Rome in 241 BC, the city is completely destroyed by what is left of its population. Devastating earthquakes in the early Middle Age cause further serious harm to its marvellous temple buildings.

During the Medieval period, even the memory of the ancient Greek city is lost. Later, Arabs and Byzantines establish residence here and Fasello rediscovers the lost city in the second half of the 16th century. The first excavations begin here in the first half of the 19th century and more recently the archaeological park is founded.

Excavations at the site have unearthed eight temples, altars and sanctuaries, as well as massive fortifications – all spread out over an area of approximately a square kilometre. On the Eastern Hill are three of the most important temples, all of Doric order. The temples of Selinunte are identified by letters, since it is not as yet possible to decipher what divinities they were consecrated to. They are simply Temple A, B C and so on.

We follow a long line of visitors to Temples E, F and G, located on the East Hill and dating to the sixth century BC. Temple E was rebuilt in 1958 and is possibly consecrated to Hera (goddess of marriage and childbirth). Temple F, the oldest temple on Eastern Hill, is probably consecrated to Athena (wisdom) or Dionysus (wine). Temple G, dedicated to Zeus or to Apollo, was once one of Greece's greatest temples, measuring 113 x 54 metres. The façade had eight columns with 17 along the long sides, each 16.27 metres high. Now wild parsley grows amid its fallen Doric columns, an evocative and unforgettable sight.

At 11.30 am we leave the park and return to the ship for a quick lunch before a 2.00 pm afternoon excursion to Erice. From its position 750 m above sea level, this medieval hilltop town has fabulous views over the entire western end of Sicily. Our coach takes us on an enjoyable scenic drive up the winding road to the classic little town at the top of the mountain of the same name.

Elymian settlements are known to exist here from the fifth century BC. From ancient times Erice becomes the subject of recurrent conflicts in the wars between the Greeks and the Carthaginians, because of its strategic importance. It is destroyed by the Carthaginians in the first half of the third century BC. Then the Romans control it after 241 BC. In Roman times visitors regularly come to visit the celebrated Sanctuary of Venus Ericina. In Medieval times Erice falls to the Arabs and then to the Normans.

Our guide for the afternoon is Gratcia (Grace) who takes us on a guided walk along the narrow winding cobblestone streets of this exquisite town of just 200 permanent residents. Norman architecture leads one to believe that it is a town out of the Middle Ages. However, Grace reminds us of the town's origins dating back to prehistoric times. Inside the Castle of Venus, a Norman construction of the twelfth to thirteenth century, Grace shows us the remaining vestiges to the Roman goddess of fertility, Venus Ericina, along with a sacred well and a Roman bath. The nearby Pepoli Castle soars 2,500 feet above the sea level. The Norman walls encircling the town incorporate original Phoenician fortifications – you can still see letters from the Phoenician alphabet carved in their surface.

From the Norman ramparts, on a clear sunny afternoon, Avril and I check out the panoramic views of Trapani countryside and beyond to the Mediterranean Sea and the Egadi Islands. We then seek out a cosy café for a cappuccino and one of the tempting little sweet delicacies.

At 6.00 pm we are on board the *Aegean Odyssey* for a briefing on tomorrow's visit to Valetta and Medina, Malta.

Following the briefing there is a lecture by Professor Jonathan Phillips, entitled *Malta and the Knights' Hospitaller*. The Hospitallers were (along with the Knights Templar) one of the great Military Orders of the Crusading Age (1095-1291). His lecture covers their origins as an institution offering medical help to pilgrims in the Holy Land, their emergence as an elite fighting force and as custodians of some of the great castles of the Levant (Eastern Mediterranean), such as Krak des Chevaliers near Lebanon. He describes the relocation of the Order to Cyprus, then Rhodes and finally Malta where they are the ruling power on the island for over 200 years before their expulsion at the hands of Napoleon in 1798.

At 7.30 pm we dine with Barbara Currie again. We have good news for her of an email from her daughter Kate who is grateful for our assistance. She thinks that her mother would at least try to reboot her mobile phone!

Avril watches the next episode of 'Downton Abbey' on our TV network and then reads till after midnight while I catch up with my notes.

Day 18
Sunday March 30, 2014.

Valletta, Malta

We are recommended to be up early to watch the entry into Valletta Harbour, one of the impressive sights in the Mediterranean. It is scheduled for 7.00 am so Avril and I decide to have the healthy breakfast on the Lido Deck 8, available from 6.30 am. I am relying on my alarm to wake us at 6.00 am, but I forget to set it. We wake at 6.17 am and need to rush. 15 minutes later we join a few stalwarts for breakfast. We munch our muesli and sip a hot cuppa tea. At that hour the sun is hidden by thick cloud and Avril had wished she had brought a scarf. The weather forecast is partly sunny, temperature range 13-17 C.

Malta is situated in the middle of the Mediterranean Sea, halfway between Sicily and North Africa. During the last Ice Age, Malta was a high mountain joined to Italy by land. Malta became a group of islands when the sea level rose as the Ice Age ended about 10,000 years ago. The Maltese archipelago, of which Malta is the main island, occupies a strategic position, about 90 km south of Sicily and about 350 km north of the Libyan coast. The surface area of the islands is 320 sq km. Malta and Gozo are the largest in the group of 5 islands, two of which are uninhabited. Almost the entire population of 400,000 lives on Malta. The islands have a dry Mediterranean climate with average annual rainfall of 500 points, about 20 inches. A desalination plant is necessary to convert seawater to fresh water.

Valletta is the capital of Malta, colloquially known as Il-Belt (English: 'The City') in Maltese. The city is located on Sciberras Peninsula on the south-eastern portion of the island. There is a harbour on either side: Marsamxett to the north and The Grand Harbour to the south. With an average depth of 36 m, the natural harbour is largest in the Mediterranean.

Valletta contains buildings from the 16th century onwards, built during the rule of the Order of St John of Jerusalem, also known as Knights Hospitaller. The Sciberras Peninsula, on which Valetta and the township of Floriana are built, was practically uninhabited when the Knights of St John arrive in Malta in 1530. The islands were a donation to the homeless knights from Charles V of Spain, the Holy Roman Emperor.

The Order is made up of knights from eight regions, each representing a language of Europe. The first Grand Master to rule in Malta is Frenchman, Philippe Villiers de L'Isle Adam. The Order finds around 15,000 inhabitants living frugally and always in danger of raids by corsairs. This situation changes dramatically with the arrival of the Order. The knights offer security, an efficient hospital system and many jobs to the local inhabitants, ushering in a Golden Age during their 268 years of rule (1530-1798). By the time the Order leaves Malta the population has reached 100,000.

At 7.00 am we see a pilot boat heading towards us as we approach The Grand Harbour. The harbour itself with its fortifications and impressive buildings is an inspiring sight. At 8.45 am we meet our guide, Marthese, a young Maltese woman, solid but shapely with flowing hair to her waist. She speaks monotonic English, sounding out every word, slowly in a precise manner. She tells us that she speaks Maltese which is a mixture of Arabic (65 per cent), English and Italian. The Latin alphabet is used and English is the official second language which is taught in schools to students from the age of five.

Marthese takes us on a walk through Malta's capital, Valetta, a city packed with historical interest. We immediately see evidence of English culture such as a red double decker tourist bus driving in the left lane, a red post box and phone booth. The World Heritage site is dominated by two magnificent buildings, the Baroque St John's Co-Cathedral and The Grand Masters Palace. We begin our walk at a beautiful park that overlooks the massive fortifications. Below are several canons which are fired at noon.

Marthese explains that the Knights of Order of St John came to Malta after the Turks drove them out of Rhodes in 1523, where they had been since 1309.

The Knights of St John's story begins in the 11th century. Many European pilgrims travel a risky journey to the Holy land. They often arrive sick and in need of assistance. Several Italian merchants from Amalfi appeal to the Caliph of Egypt to open a hospital in the Christian quarter of Jerusalem near the Holy Sepulchre.

Some Benedictines establish the Hospital of St John to cater for an influx of pilgrims between 1060 and 1070. During the First Crusade (1096-1099) Christians are fighting against the Muslims. Fortunately, the brave and Blessed Gerard Thom and other lay Benedictine brothers are able to remain to tend the sick in hospital. In 1099 Gerard and several knights break away from the Benedictines and found a new religious order, the Order of St John, dedicated to fight the Muslims as well as care for the welfare of Christian pilgrims. European noblemen are inspired by Gerard's compassion so they donate money and land to the Order which quickly rises to prominence and wealth. Soon it holds properties close to the major pilgrimage routes of Europe and points of embarkation in Spain, Italy and France. In 1113 the Order is formally recognized by the Pope.

However, in 1291 the Muslims capture the Holy Land, driving out the Christians. The Knights of St John shift their base to Cyprus and then to Rhodes in 1310. But in 1523 the Turks capture Rhodes and the Knights are without a home until the Spanish king gives them Malta in 1530. This gesture is not much of a prize as Malta is arid and infertile. Fresh water is scarce and the people are poor.

However, the Knights recognize the area is an excellent strategic site for a fortified city. The first structure to be built is the small star-shaped stronghold, Fort St Elmo on the Sciberras Peninsula.

In a square we see the bronze statue of Jean Parisot de la Vallette (1494- 1568). We learn from Marthese about the importance of Vallette's place in Malta's history. In 1522 at the age of 28 he is captured at the Siege of Rhodes and becomes a slave on a Turkish galley. Free again, the French nobleman becomes the 49th Grandmaster of the Order of Malta, from August 21, 1557. As a Knight Hospitaller he is the Order's hero and leader in commanding the resistance against the Ottomans at the Great Siege of Malta in 1565. At the age of 70 he fights with distinction during the 4 month siege. He dies from stroke in 1568.

Malta is strategically important for the control of the Mediterranean against the alarming growth of Muslim power. The Order prepares to defend the island against the inevitable invasion. The Maltese can only muster a force of about 9,000 who take up shelter in the walled cities of Birgu, Senglea and Mdina. Suleiman the Magnificent, the Ottoman sultan, intends to exterminate the knights once and for all. Suleiman had been magnanimous after defeating the Knights at Rhodes in 1522, but this time he is not planning the same generosity.

On May 18, 1565 the Turks send an armada of 81 ships with 40,000 troops. The siege lasts from May 18, 1565 till September 8, 1565. Firstly the Turks decide to bombard the Fort of St Elmo which stands alone on the Sciberras Peninsula on the site of Valetta. It bravely resists for a month until the Ottoman Turks capture it on June 23, 1565. But the victory comes at a cost. The Turks suffer heavy losses of 8,000 men, about a quarter of their whole army, in the siege. Their commander, Dragut Raise, is among the dead.

Afterwards the Turks behead 4 knights they have captured, nailing them to crosses and floating them across the harbour. In response, Grand Master la Vallette beheads Turkish prisoners and fires their heads from cannons.

The Turks then suffer heavy losses in an attempt to capture the cities of Birgu and Senglea. They abandon the siege shortly after on September 7, 1565 when a relief force of 8,000 Sicilians arrives in Northeast Malta. The Maltese attribute their deliverance to Divine help. Ever since then, that day has become a national feast day.

Immediately after the long hot summer siege, la Vallette writes to his European counterparts. He thanks them for their praise, but reminds them that the Order needs material help.

The encounter with the Turks reveals weaknesses in the Knights' original base at Vittoriosa, their fortified city on the south side of the Grand Harbour. So they move across the harbour and establish Valletta, an impregnable stronghold that has survived the centuries.

La Vallette erects the first building on the peninsula, the Church of Our Lady of Victories, in commemoration of his successful defence of the island against the Turks. Upon his death he is buried there, although his remains are later transferred to St John's Co-Cathedral.

The rest of the city is planned by the Pope's military architect, Francesco Laparelli. It is based on a grid-design with straight streets, centred on the Palace of the Grand Master of the Knights Hospitaller. Recovering from the trauma of the Great Siege, the city is remodelled by successive Grand Masters of the Order. The knights rebuild all their main buildings and churches. Valletta is essentially Baroque in character, with elements of Mannerist, Neo-Classical and Modern architecture in places. This display of confidence encourages the Maltese in the small villages to rebuild their churches in the Baroque style.

In 1675 a plague epidemic kills over 11,000 inhabitants out of an estimated 60,000 population. In 1693 a severe earthquake in south-eastern Sicily also hits Malta, causing immense structural damage but no deaths. During the French Revolution the Order loses most of its independence when much of its European territory is confiscated. These territories had provided financial support for the Order's stay and its building expenses on Malta.

In 1798 Napoleon Bonaparte takes control of Malta which provides a vital naval link between France and the Middle East for his planned Egyptian campaign. On September 2, 1798 the Maltese rise up in revolt. They blockade the French troops inside Valletta and the harbour fortifications. British and Portuguese ships send help. The siege takes two years until the French capitulate and the British take over Malta.

The Grand Harbour becomes the home port of the British Fleet of the Mediterranean. During the Crimean War, Malta proves a good staging depot for the advance to the east. During the First World War Malta is nicknamed the 'Nurse of the Mediterranean' for the hospital services it provides. World War II leaves major scars on the city, especially in the vicinity of the Grand Harbour. Families live and survive by using rock-cut shelters.

In 1942 Malta and its people are awarded the King George Cross by George VI in recognition of the island's courage. The George Cross now forms part of the national flag. Malta chooses to become a Republic with a President elected by Cabinet. Malta has a parliament of 69 elected members. Marthese tells us that Labour is in power by 9 seats over the Nationalist Party. The City of Valletta is officially recognised as a World Heritage Site by UNESCO in 1980.

Marthese claims that there are over 300 churches on Malta and one mosque. 98 per cent are Roman Catholic. We walk to St John's Co-Cathedral which has a plain exterior. It is Sunday and a service is taking place. Marthese allows us to take a peek inside but we must observe reverence. The magnificent Baroque interior transforms the church which glitters of gold and is an amazing experience to behold. The Cathedral contains Caravaggio's masterpiece, *The Beheading of St John*.

Continuing by foot we visit the Grand Master's Palace, designed by Gerolamo Cassar. It contains luxuriously furnished State Rooms and portraits of past Grand Masters. There are many pieces of knight's armour in the corridors, making you feel like you are part of former times.

Our coach takes us to Mdina, Malta's former capital, where much of the architecture dates to the Middle Age and beyond. Around 700 BC the site is fortified by the Phoenicians because of its strategic location on one of the highest points inland away from the sea. Around 60 AD the Apostle, St Paul, is shipwrecked off the coast and lives in a cave near Mdina. During his stay, he converts the Roman governor, Publius, to Christianity. We stroll through Mdina's narrow streets, devoid of cars, to visit St Paul's Cathedral which, according to tradition, is built on the site where Publius once lived. Our walk through 'the silent city' as it is known takes us to the city ramparts. This strategic position allows us a final panoramic overview of the island before returning to the ship.

Marthese, our guide suggests two souvenirs for us to consider. One is the eight pointed Maltese Cross, which represents the eight nationalities of the former knights of the Order. The other is a light liqueur distilled from prickly pears, which are cultivated on the island.

On board at 5.00 pm Jonathan Philips delivers another interesting lecture entitled, *The Origins and Impact of the First Crusade*. He delves into the thought processes of the medieval mind, the motives of the First Crusaders and the conquest of Jerusalem in 1099.

We head to the Charlestown Lounge after his interesting talk. It's time to relax over a Scotch and Dry. It comes served with a couple of tasty canapés. We sip slowly as the *Aegean Odyssey* departs The Grand Harbour of Valletta. Tomorrow we'll be at sea heading towards Crete. Different time zones mean we lose another hour in the process. So instead of bedtime at 11.15 pm, it is after midnight when the lights go out.

Day 19
Monday March 31, 2014.

At Sea heading towards Crete

We stir at 6.00am as the alarm rings. We are at sea and there is no need to be up too early, so I snooze until 7.15 am. Avril awakens me and wants to know if there is anything wrong, as I am usually an early riser. The morning is partly sunny with a forecast of 17C. Today we are heading eastwards across the Ionian Sea towards the Greek island of Crete. We will be passing over the Ionian Abyssal Plain before once again clearing the Hellenic Trench and making our approach to the western coast of Crete. The region of the Hellenic Trench is an eco-system for sperm whales and other aquatic life.

We take a light breakfast at 8.15 am and the Terrace Café is almost deserted. It seems that many passengers are also catching up on some rest. One couple, Carol and Rex, from Auckland, New Zealand join us. They enjoy travel and have travelled by Euro rail and car in France and Italy. But this is their first cruise and they are enjoying the experience.

At 10.00 am Ernie Rea presents a lecture, *'An Arab Spring in the Mediterranean: Where Muslims Disagree'*. This sounds a charming title for the grim reality of problems in the Muslim world. Ernie specializes in history of religions and regularly appears on the program *'Beyond Relief'* on BBC radio. He says something we all know: that all religions appear to have within them a division gene. He provides an explanation of what is happening in the Muslim parts of the Mediterranean and why the divisions within the body of Islam are impacting on the Western world in such a striking way.

Today countries in North Africa and the Middle East are witnessing violent events which, at least partially, have their roots in a religious division going back 1400 years. The world of Islam divides in two. **Sunny Muslims** are in the majority, consisting of approximately 85% of Muslims. **Shi'a Muslims** are a sizeable minority, consisting of approximately 15% of Muslims.

The quarrel between them is political rather than theological. It centres on the person who was chosen to succeed the Prophet Mohammed on his death in 632 AD. The Sunny claim that the community chose the person who possessed the qualities needed to provide political leadership to their young community. They did not expect this person, the *Caliph*, to have outstanding spiritual qualities.

The Shi'a felt that the choice should have fallen on the Prophet's closest relative, his son-in-law Ali. They claim that this was the Prophet's wish. But Ali was passed over three times. When he did eventually succeed to the office, he was an old man who died shortly afterwards. Ali's son, Hussein, led a rising against the new Caliph and was brutally murdered at the Battle of Karbala in Iraq. Shi'a Muslims commemorate his death at the annual Feast of Ashura. It seems that their struggles are ongoing and the West is being caught up.

At 1.45 pm we have a late lunch on the outside deck area of the Terrace Café where a warm plate of creamy mushroom pasta is available and a crisp slice of toasted garlic bread. It is warm and sunny with thin cloud so we order a pot of English breakfast and sit alfresco for a while, sipping freshly brewed black tea.

At 3.00 pm in the Ambassador Lounge Chris Adamson continues his absorbing series of lectures. This one is entitled, *'A Clash of Civilizations?'* The end of the Bronze Age (c. 1200 BC) was a period of war, piracy, migration and famine. As Cretans and Greeks were thrown together, they formed a new society, and a new identity. Apparently little was known about the disappearance of the Minoan civilization on Crete. Were they wiped out by the tsunami after Santorini? This does not explain evidence of fire. Were they victims of piracy? New research suggests that they were absorbed and replaced by an elite group from the Mycenaean culture from the Greek mainland.

Chris mentions the valuable work made by the eccentric British archaeologist John Pendlebury who dressed like the locals. The Nazi capture him behind enemy lines in WW II during the Battle of Crete, June 1941. They think he is a spy because he is not in uniform. So they shoot him. He is honoured and buried at Souda Bay Cemetery on Crete. Fortunately my Uncle Arthur Dawson does not suffer the same fate. He is captured on Crete and becomes a POW. He ends up in a German Work Camp in the present day Czech Republic, until escaping in the final stage of the war.

At 6.15 pm we attend an excursion briefing with Jenny Worwood to prepare us for tomorrow's visit to Knossos, Crete. Knossos is a Bronze Age site near Heraklion, on the northern coast of Crete. The site has been excavated and a palace complex found there. The palace is the largest Bronze Age archaeological site on Crete. It was the ceremonial and political centre of the Minoan civilisation and culture. The palace is partially restored under the direction of Sir Arthur Evans in the early 20th century.

Evans had a mansion built on the site, Villa Ariadne, for the use of archaeologists. For a short time it becomes the home of the Greek government in exile during the Battle of Crete in World War II. Subsequently, for three years it becomes the headquarters of the Third Reich's military governorship of Crete.

We plan a busy day there tomorrow. The drive to Knossos takes an hour and twenty minutes from Rethimnon and hopefully we will return by 1.00 pm. I have made enquiries about visiting Sfakia on the southern coast where there is a World War II memorial to the POWs captured by the Nazis on May 31, 1941. My Uncle Arthur was one of these. In the Battle for Crete the Allies successfully repel an ocean offensive and then inflict large casualties on German paratroopers. But finally, Crete is overwhelmed by German reinforcements and forced to surrender.

My uncle writes, *'Not enough significance has been made of Crete and the importance of the battle. Most of us were 'dead' sure that we won the battle. But it was so costly to supply the island. Getting supplies from Egypt was made more difficult because of the problems in the North African theatre of war, and it was decided that keeping Crete was too expensive.'*

German sources after the war say that the Battle for Crete was equally expensive for Germany. For two days it was debated in Berlin whether to continue the battle.

Arthur said, *'They were on the brink of calling it off when they decided to give it another go, and that was the turning point.'*

Arthur's mate George Blanche reported, *'They never used their paratroopers as a regiment again after Crete. One of the most important things about Crete was that it broke the myth of the unassailability of the Germans going through Europe unopposed. The Germans expected Crete to fall quickly and when it didn't, it delayed the invasion of Russia, which ultimately broke the Germans.'*

At 11.00 pm it is time to rest up for tomorrow's events.

Day 20
Tuesday April 1, 2014.

Rethimnon, Crete

Overnight the *Aegean Odyssey* sails in calm seas to our destination at the lovely port city of Rethimnon, Crete. Rethimnon is Crete's third largest town and one of the most picturesque, with a charming harbour and a massive Venetian fortress. Its delightful Venetian Ottoman quarter is a maze of narrow streets, containing houses of graceful wood balconies and ornate Venetian monuments. Minarets add a touch of the Orient.

The day promises superb weather, sunshine with a few clouds and a high of 19 C. It is Greek summer time and the sun has not yet risen when I arise at 6.00 am. The city street lights are still on as our ship docks while we are at breakfast. At 7.30 am I go to an outside deck as the first welcoming rays of sunlight herald a delightful spring day. The only sign of activity is a small white fishing boat plying the still waters of the harbour. However, on dockside our coaches have already arrived waiting to take us to Knossos.

Knossos was the ancient capital of the mythical king Minos. The original palace of Knossos was constructed around 1,900 BC. Our guide for the one hour 20 minute trip to the site is Ioanna, a worldly travelled Greek, informally dressed and sporting a short crop of fading blonde-rinsed hair. She came from the mainland 20 years ago to live on Crete. Her chatty tutoring commands attention. She tells us that Crete has a population of about 600,000 people, part of the 9 million in the whole of Greece. In 1913 Crete unified with Greece when it was liberated from the Ottoman Empire.

There are 30,000 inhabitants in the busy seaside township of Rethimnon. This is where the main body of German paratroopers landed in WW II. Hundreds were picked off as they made their drop and the Aussies captured 50 of them. But in the end the Allies were forced to retreat.

Ioanna points out the snow-capped Mt Ida, Crete's highest peak at 2456 m above sea level and located in the Central Range. Crete has rugged terrain, hilly and mountainous. It is literally goat country, mostly limestone, about 130 kilometres from east to west, and an average of 35 km from north to south. The island of Crete lies within a mild Mediterranean winter rainfall pattern and hot dry summers. The western end, which has a high mountain chain, receives a higher average rainfall than the east.

We follow the northern coast highway eastwards to Heraklion. On hilltops are numerous olive groves that thrive in the arid conditions. At the base of the hills are the citrus, especially oranges. Ioanna says that old settlements were built on top of hills to prevent attacks from pirates.

At 10.15 am we arrive in the modern city of Heraklion and drive through its bustling streets that lead us to the nearby archaeological site of Knossos, an important city in antiquity. Knossos was inhabited continuously from the Neolithic Period until the 5th c. AD. The Minoan palace is the main site of interest. It was built on the Kephala Hill which provided easy access to the sea and the Cretan interior. According to tradition, it is the seat of the wise King Minos. The Palace of Knossos is connected with thrilling legends, such as the myth of the Labyrinth with the Minotaur, and the story of Daedalus and Icarus.

The myth explains that Minos is the son of Zeus and the Phoenician princess Europa. He and his two brothers, Rhadamanthys and Sarpedon, are raised in the royal palace of Knossos. Minos marries Pasiphae, daughter of the sun-god Helios.

A dispute occurs over the true kingship of Crete. Minos asks the god of the sea, Poseidon, to send an offering as a sign of his sovereignty. Miraculously, a gleaming white bull emerges from the waves, confirming to all concerned that Minos is their true king. However, King Minos is so overawed by this magnificent beast that he refuses to sacrifice it to Poseidon. He decides to replace it with another.

In retaliation Poseidon sends Pasiphae into a sexual lust to mate with the huge beast. In order to do this she requests the help of Daedalus, master craftsman and inventor, to build her a hollow wooden cow. Pasiphae hides inside and the amorous bull mounts the wooden cow and has his way with her. As a result she conceives its child, a creature that is half man and half bull, known as the Minotaur. King Minos orders Daedalus to build the Labyrinth to hide the hideous Minotaur.

Meanwhile, the son of King Minos, Androgeos, attends the games in Athens. He wins every event, so he is murdered through envy by the other contestants. King Minos attacks Athens to avenge his son's death. In gaining control Minos grants peace to the citizens of Athens on the condition that every nine years they send seven of their finest young men and maidens to Crete as a sacrifice to the Minotaur.

Hearing this, the hero of Athens, Theseus, volunteers to go to Crete and to slay the Minotaur. Ariadne, daughter of King Minos and Pasiphae, falls in love with Theseus and asks Daedalus to help him. Daedalus gives her a flaxen thread to tie to the door of the Labyrinth. This helps Theseus to find his way out after slaying the monster. He succeeds and flees from Crete with Ariadne. In revenge the enraged King Minos locks Daedalus and his son Icarus into the Labyrinth. Eventually they escape by making wings from wax and feathers. Unfortunately Icarus' wings melt when he flies too close to the sun, and he drowns in the sea.

In 1900 AD the English archaeologist, Sir Arthur Evans, gives the name 'Minoan' to the Cretan civilization, taken from King Minos' name. The name may not have been the king's real name. Instead it may have been the hereditary title of Minoan rulers.

The earliest traces of habitation in the area of the palace go back to the Neolithic Period (7000-3000 BC). The site continues to be occupied in the Pre-palatial Period (3000-1900 BC), at the end of which the area is levelled for the erection of a large palace. This first palace is destroyed, probably by an earthquake in approximately 1700 BC. A second, larger palace is built on the ruins of the old one. This palace is partially destroyed about 1375 BC by a major conflagration (fire). The site it covers is occupied again from the late Mycenaean period until Roman times.

In Europe the Bronze Age starts about 2300 BC with the making of a few bronze tools and weapons. By 1200 BC bronze has replaced all stone tools. The Minoan period on Crete begins in the early Bronze Age and lasts from c. 2000 BC to 1400 BC. The Minoan civilization ends following the invasion and occupation of Crete by the Mycenaeans around 1400 BC. The Mycenaean period on Crete begins in the last phase of the Bronze Age, about 1400 BC and lasts until about 1100 BC.

In 1150 BC the Dorian Greeks destroy the Mycenaean civilisation in the Peloponnese, the peninsula and region of southern Greece, and by 1100 BC they reach Crete. The old Minoan and Mycenaean traditions of Crete are assimilated into the new Hellenic culture. This new culture eventually merges into the Classical Greek civilisation which has its centre in Athens.

Knossos today allows the visitor to visualize the palace as it once was and to understand its intricacies. Our tour takes us through this legend-rich, complex that sprawls across two hectares.

The first excavation of the historic site of Knossos is conducted in 1878 by Minos Kalokerinos of Heraklion. This is followed by long-term excavations (1900-1913 and 1922-1930) by Sir Arthur Evans who uncovers virtually the entire area. He pours his fortune into the effort and does a remarkable job for that time period.

A bronze statue of Sir Arthur Evans appears as we enter the grounds of the Palace of Knossos. The Palace reconstruction is a multi-storey complex which showcases the advanced level of technology attained by the Minoans and Mycenaean Greeks during the Bronze Age.

The Bronze Age artisans use a variety of building materials and lots of painted plaster; marble revetment (ornamental facing) and wall paintings adorn the rooms and passages. Some of the original structural features on show are: rooms with light-wells and *polythyra* (pier-and-door partitions); the use of beams to reinforce the masonry; and the complex drainage and water supply systems.

The earlier Old Palace was constructed around a large Central Court that overlooked an outside terrace known as the West Court. The terrace may have been used as a public meeting place as the roads lead here, from the town to the palace. Little remains of the West Façade of the Old Palace. It is thought that the upper floor of the West Façade had windows that opened onto the West Court. Ceremonies conducted here may have been conducted in conjunction with ceremonies taking place in front of a more elite audience in the Central Court. The Old Palace was severely damaged by earthquake or fire and rebuilt by the Minoans in c. 1375 BC. What we see today are the more prominent features of the New Palace, unearthed and reconstructed by Evans.

The entrance to the New Palace is from the southwest corner. Visitors follow along the West façade and arrive at the West Porch which contains a square portico with a central column. It leads to the Guardroom and continues to the Corridor of Processions. Fragments of wall paintings found here show a procession taking place.

On the West Wing of the Palace is the outstanding Throne Room, one of the most famous of rooms unearthed by Evans. A dog-leg stairway leads to its sunken room known as a *'lustral basin'*. The room contains an alabaster throne and the walls are flanked by benches and jars, evidence of anointing rituals. Such distinctive sunken rooms are found throughout the Aegean Minoan civilisation. Sir Arthur Evans names them lustral basins for the oil or perfume jars he finds in such rooms at Knossos.

Facing the Central Court, south of the Throne Room, are the remains of a Tripartite Shrine, the main sanctuary in Knossos. Nearby are storage rooms with vaults in the floor which are named the Temple Repositories by Evans. In the Treasury of the shrine he finds several Minoan snake goddesses buried there. Two of these restored treasures are must-see items in the Museum at Heraklion.

In a lower West Wing corridor, Ioanna leads us to the Great Sanctuary, a 16 metre wide chamber which displays a replica of the famous bull-leaping fresco. At ground level we are shown shrines and store rooms, many with enormous storage jars still *in situ*. They are used to store grain, wine, oil and other commodities.

The East Wing contains the residential quarters and large reception rooms, the most important being the Hall of the Double Axes and the Queen's Apartment. These rooms are approached by the impressive Grand Staircase. We descend four flights in the staircase of 54 stairs to reach the Hall of Double Axes which is a double chamber with an inner and outer space. The inner space could be closed off by eleven sets of double doors. Near the Hall of Double Axes is the Dolphin's Sanctuary which Evans assigns as the Queen's Apartment. The Dolphin's Sanctuary takes its name from a Dolphin Fresco which was found in pieces here by Evans. They probably fell from the floor above during the destruction of the palace. A replica of the fresco now adorns the north wall.

We continue to the North Entrance which Evans considers to be the main public entrance into the Palace. But the narrow doorway offers limited access and seems too small to be considered the main entry point. From here a road leads directly to the harbour of Knossos. This North Entrance is flanked by elevated stoas (covered walkways) -- one of these is decorated with the Bull Hunt fresco.

Ioanna shows us the Royal Road, one of the oldest and best preserved ancient roads in Europe. The stone-paved processional way divides in two as it approaches the palace. We follow the approach to the northwest corner of the palace where the road leads to an open-air theatre area. Our guide explains that it is the oldest example of a theatre construction in the world. The paved theatre area measures 13 by 10 metres. Its L-shaped area of steps offers limited standing room for about 500 people.

Ioanna explains that the numerous architectural finds from the palace are now housed in Herakleleon Archaeological Museum. We do not have time to see these exceptionally high quality works of art, pottery, vessels, figurines, and the original wall paintings. However, in our guided tour of the palace restoration this morning, we have seen grand replicas of the important pieces of art used at the site, including my favourite piece in the East Wing-- the Bull Leaping Fresco, depicting the three stages of this Minoan ceremonial sport of the 15th century BC.

Ioanna has detailed vividly the way of life of these ancient Minoans, so much so that we are the last of our 6 coaches to leave the site. We arrive back in Rethimnon at 1.30 pm.

I have another mission in mind which means Avril and I will have to skip lunch. I plan to hop in a taxi to visit the wartime evacuation scene of May 1941 at Sfakia during the Battle of Crete. Sfakia is on the other side of the island, requiring a long trip by taxi. Upon returning to the ship we quickly eat a banana we have stowed in our cabin and then we hurry into town to find a taxi at a waterfront square. Niko is willing to take us to Sfakia for a negotiated return fare of 140 Euros, a journey of at least an hour over the mountain range.

Niko is an elderly Greek of solid build who likes a cigarette or two. We begin our drive across the rooftop chain of mountains. The taxi twists its way to a high point just below the snowline of the Western Range. We see several goats roaming wild on the mountain slopes. At the top of the range is a pretty undulating valley, containing a farming community and some village stores at Amoudari and Imbros. Somewhere through these mountain passes the allies made their escape routes from the German onslaught. Allied ships waited to evacuate them from small ports such as Sfakia to the safety of Egypt.

Niko's taxi begins the winding descent into Sfakia. The view of the coastline is breathtaking. Niko stops at one of the few spots available to allow us to take a photo. A herd of goats crosses the road as we view the village farmlands on the coast near Sfakia. We eventually arrive at a sleepy picturesque waterfront village containing a cluster of restaurants saturated in white paint. The pretty village is bathed in bright sunlight and cocooned by the surrounding ridges.

Niko drives a few metres past a simple memorial and stops at the dock of a narrow deep water harbour, containing a few fishing boats. The water is so clear that we could see the bottom. I have my doubts that a warship would fit into the tiny harbour. But Niko has asked a couple of locals for the exact spot of evacuation. Apparently, barges were used to ferry the soldiers to warships waiting offshore. I begin to visualize stranded soldiers huddled against the narrow limestone ridgeline, awaiting their evacuation.

It is time for a coffee break and a quiet moment of reflection. Niko drives over to the sheltered beachside harbour with its complex of restaurants on the shoreline. A breakwater in front of shops provides shelter for a few small fishing vessels. The far side offers a picturesque view across the water towards the cafes and further on to the evacuation point beyond the memorial. Niko has to negotiate a narrow laneway at the back of the cafes in order to get to the breakwater. The scenery is so idyllic that it is difficult to imagine it ever being the wartime rendezvous for the fleeing allies. We take photos and Niko now returns to the cafes by taking a short-cut along the harbour front. He weaves his cab carefully through the main laneway full of chairs and tables belonging to the restaurants. Fortunately it is siesta time and the seats are empty of clients. At the end of the stretch we find a restaurant that is open and situated close to the memorial site around the corner.

A handsome young man who speaks English with a Scandinavian accent welcomes us to relax in the mid-afternoon sunshine at a front table next to the water's edge. His restaurant is called *Taverna Obrosgialos* meaning *In Front of the Shoreline.* He suggests we try his speciality, Sfakian pie (You have to be careful how you pronounce it) which is actually a local cheese spread between a thick folded crepe with a topping of local honey. It is a tasty treat to go with our cappuccino coffee. Niko is content to have an expresso, roll a cigarette and chat with a fellow middle-aged Greek until it is time to go.

I hurry around to the memorial for one last look and to reflect on another time when Arthur stood here waiting anxiously to be evacuated. **The memorial tells the story of the Battle of Crete:**

GERMANY ATTACKED NORTHERN MAINLAND GREECE ON 6 APRIL 1941 AND ALLIED TROOPS FOUGHT HARD OVER THE FOLLOWING 25 DAYS BUT WERE OVERWHELMED BY A SUPERIOR FORCE. THE ALLIES EVACUATED 50000 MEN, SHIPPING 25000 OF THEM TO CRETE TO DEFEND THE ISLAND WHICH WAS PIVOTAL IN CONTROLLING MUCH OF THE MEDITERRANEAN.

ON 20 MAY 1941, GERMAN PARATROOPERS AND GLIDERBORNE TROOPS INVADED CRETE. THEIR INITIAL OBJECTIVE WAS TO CAPTURE THE ISLAND'S THREE MAIN AIRFIELDS TO FACILITATE FURTHER AIRBORNE REINFORCEMENT. THESE AIRFIELDS WERE DEFENDED PRINCIPALLY BY NEW ZEALANDERS AT MALEME, AUSTRALIANS AT RETHIMNO AND BRITISH AT TRAKLIO WITH GREEK MILITARY AND VOLUNTEER CIVILIANS SUPPORTING ALL THESE AREAS.

THE INITIAL AIRBORNE LANDINGS RESULTED IN EXTREMELY HEAVY GERMAN CASUALITIES. BY THE END OF THE FIRST DAY MALEME AIRFIELD WAS CAPTURED WHILST AT RETHIMNO AND TRAKLIO THE GERMANS WERE FIRMLY CONTAINED. OVER THE NEXT TWO DAYS THE BATTLE HUNG IN THE BALANCE. AT MALEME AIRFIELD, AFTER FIERCE FIGHTING AND SUBSTANTIAL GERMAN REINFORCEMENTS, THE ALLIES WITHDREW EAST TO A LINE NEAR HANIA. HOWEVER BY 27 MAY THIS AREA BECAME UNTENABLE AND MOVEMENT BETWEEN THE THREE PRINCIPAL REGIONAL ALLIED ZONES BECAME IMPOSSIBLE. A FULL EVACUATION OF CRETE WAS ORDERED.

THE FORCE DEFENDING IRAKLIO WAS SUCCESSFULLY EVACUATED (28 MAY) BUT THOSE AT RETHIMNO, WHO HELD OUT LONGER THAN ANY OTHERS, WERE SURROUNDED AND SURRENDED (30 MAY). THOSE FROM HANIA COULD ONLY TURN SOUTH TO HORA SPHAKIA.

The memorial then tells the story of the evacuation of soldiers from Hora Sphakia:

IN MAY 1941 HORA SPHAKIA WAS A SMALL FISHING VILLAGE, THE LAST LIFELINE IN THE SURVIVAL OF A VALIANT BUT DEFEATED ALLIED ARMY IN THE BATTLE OF CRETE.

GERMAN AIRBORNE FORCES LANDED AROUND MALEME AND HANIA ON THE 20 MAY. FACED WITH INCREASING GERMAN REINFORCEMENTS AND LACKING AIR PROTECTION, ALLIED SOLDIERS SLOWLY WITHDREW CONCEDING MALEME (23 MAY) AND HANIA (27 MAY). EAST AT RETHIMNO AUSTRALIANS AND GREEKS WERE HOLDING BUT ESCAPE WAS BLOCKED AND IRAKLIO WAS NEVER AN OPTION. HORA SPHAKIA, LOCATED TO THE SOUTH ALONG A NARROW, TORTUOUS, ROUGH DIRT ROAD THAT STRADDLED THE MOUNTAINOUS SPINE OF CRETE, OFFERED THE LAST HOPE OF ESCAPE.

SO, EXHAUSTED AND HUNGRY 16000 BRITISH, NEW ZEALAND, AUSTRALIAN AND GREEK TROOPS WERE ORDERED TO WALK TO HORA SPHAKIA ON 27 MAY. ALONG

THIS DESPERATE ROUTE ALLIED TROOPS REPEATEDLY AMBUSHED AND DELAYED THE PURSUING GERMANS.

THE ROAD ENDED 3 KILOMETRES SHORT OF AND 500 METRES ABOVE THE TINY SHINGLE BEACH OF HORA SPHAKIA. OVER 4 SUCCESSIVE NIGHTS FROM 28 MAY, 11000 MEN MADE THEIR ESCAPE. BRITISH AND ALLIED WARSHIPS ARRIVED QUIETLY FROM ALEXANDRIA EACH NIGHT, RECEIVED THEIR HUMAN CARGO UNTIL 3.00 AM AND THEN SWIFTLY RETURNED TO AVOID GERMAN ATTACK.

HOWEVER THE EVACUATION ENDED ABRUPTLY WHEN LATE ON 1 JUNE THE GERMANS OUTFLANKED THE AUSTRALIAN REAR-GUARD HOLDING THE RIDGE ABOVE HORA SPHAKIA AND CAPTURED 5000 HUNGRY AND ABANDONED ALLIED TROOPS. FOUR YEARS OF HARSH CAPTIVITY IN EUROPE LAY BEFORE THEM, AND, FOR THE CRETANS, YEARS OF GERMAN SUBJUGATION AND BRUTALITY.

AFTER THE END OF THE EVACUATION, 600 MORE ALLIED SOLDIERS ESCAPED FROM CRETE BETWEEN JUNE AND SEPTEMBER 1941. THE LOCAL CRETANS OFTEN SHELTERED THEM, NOTABLY A GROUP HIDDEN AT PREVELI MONASTERY, NEAR HORA SPHAKIA. DURING THE OCCUPATION, CRETAN GUERILLA FORCES HARRASSED THE GERMANS BUT SUCH ACTION OFTEN INCURRED VIOLENT RETRIBUTION BY THE GERMANS ON THE CIVILIAN POPULATION.

The memorial lists the casualties on both sides:

	KILLED	WOUNDED	PRISONERS
BRITISH	797	263	6576
GREEK	546	800	5255
NEW ZEALAND	671	1455	1692
AUSTRALIAN	274	507	3109
BRITISH, AUSTRALIAN NAVY	1828	183	3 CRUISERS 5 DESTROYERS LOST
TOTAL ALLIED	4116	3208	16632
GERMAN	3986	2594	220 AIRCRAFT LOST

My Uncle Arthur tells the story of his capture at Sfakia. He is with his mate Bill awaiting evacuation to the safety of Egypt:

The night seemed to stretch into eternity. Finally we reach a position where we could actually see the beach. There were two ships side by side, and men were quickly climbing in. Bill and I were as good as away and talking about the first things we were going to do when we landed. The left hand boat was just about full when an Officer came hurrying down. He called out, 'Is there a doctor here?'

A figure stood up in that boat and said, 'Yes, I'm a doctor.'

I could see and recognise that he was Dr Gunther, regarded as our Unit doctor. The Officer called back, 'We need somebody to stay back with the wounded. Will you please come with me?'

Without a word Dr Gunther stood up, threaded his way through the men in the boat, and stepped back onto the beach. I was thinking, you poor bastard! What a hard thing to have to do! Bill then stepped over the gunwale and into the boat. I cocked one leg over the gunwale to follow when the sailor in charge of the boat dropped his arm between us and said, 'Sorry that's all for tonight. But don't worry; we'll be back again tomorrow night.'

Bill turned and shook hands with me. He said, "Don't worry, I'll have one set up for you in the Long Bar,' a favourite haunt of ours, and we parted…

With no food and nothing to do but wait, we didn't bother to stir from our spots until late in the morning. It was another fine and sunny day and about 9.00 am. A couple of officers could be seen approaching. They were still some way off and saying something to the knots of men as they passed.

The men for their part just stood there, talking seriously together. Obviously what had been said was pretty important. We waited expectantly to hear what it was, and when they arrived it was simple and to the point. 'Well chaps, we are sorry, but we are now all Prisoners of War.' To our howls of disbelief they replied, 'We surrendered two hours ago. All acts of war have now ceased. If there is anything you don't want to fall into the hands of the Germans, get rid of it now. They will be here shortly.'

We were all stunned… Somebody called out, 'Does anybody know the date?'

Somebody else called back, 'The first of June.' Good God, I thought, I've got a birthday at the end of the month, and I'll be a Prisoner of War.

For Arthur it seemed like a fanciful dream. Arthur notes:

It was almost impossible to accept the actuality of being prisoners. As yet no Germans had appeared… Most of us had not eaten for several days now, and for several months had been getting by the best way we could. We were in fact starving and could only hope to get something from the Germans.

There had not been the slightest sign of any local inhabitants since we had been here. But a little donkey tethered under the trees nearby indicated they couldn't be too far away.

In our hungry state that donkey meant food. In minutes it had been killed and carved up, with only the head and the hooves remaining. Fires were lit, with groups here and there, trying to cook their pieces as best they could. In most cases the ravenous men could not wait. Just grabbing the meat off their fires and tearing into it practically raw. Most could only watch, as one small donkey doesn't go very far.

Niko's taxi is waiting for my return from the memorial. Suddenly a group of university students from Manchester University, dressed in hiking gear, emerge from the hills to break the quiet ambience of Sfakia. I am told the university has annual visits here for study purposes. It's time to leave.

Niko's taxi arrives at the ship at 5.30 pm. We leave him a generous tip and return to our cabin. A note has been slipped under the door. Barbara Currie has been trying to catch up with us. Her note reads: 'Come and have a glass of champagne with me in cabin 810, Lido Deck – any time after 5.'

We make haste and report to Barbara's balcony suite on level 8. Robin and Margaret are also there. We apologise for being a little late after explaining the circumstances. Barbara's balcony cabin affords a grand view of the harbour. I take a photo of the city resting in the setting sun, the delightful panorama of harbour, and the snow-capped peak of Mt Ida in the background.

At 9.15 pm a local dance group from Crete is scheduled to perform in the Ambassador Lounge. We dine at 7.00 pm in time to be ready. Greece is one of the few countries in the world where folk dances are as alive today as they were in ancient times. This is a great opportunity to see a troupe of dancers performing local dances in traditional Cretan and Syrtaki dance costumes. Almost every dance has a story to tell and they continue to be passed on from one generation to another, keeping the traditional identity well and truly alive.

We are about to attend the performance when an announcement comes to advise that the dance troupe went to the wrong harbour and are hurrying to our ship, hopefully arriving in an hour. Our Director Neil hastily organises free drinks and for the *Aegean Odyssey Trio* to play lively music until the dancers arrive. It turns out an even better evening of entertainment. The dancers arrive dressed in traditional costumes and are wonderful. There is movement, hand clapping and foot stomping to rhythmic Greek music. In the end everyone joins in a large circle or two to participate in the dance finale.

Our bedtime is well after midnight.

Day 21
Wednesday April 2, 2014.

Rethimnon, Crete

My trusty alarm wakes me at 6.00 am. I am tricked into thinking it is sunrise, but I realise it is the yellow glow of lights from dockside. These lights are switched off at sunrise at 7.05 am, while we are at breakfast. The spring weather forecast is fresh and sunny, ranging from a low 11 C to a high 22 C. That is tempting enough for me to dress in shorts and collared T shirt for today's outing to Chania, for shopping and sightseeing. Several guys at breakfast are like-minded. The transfer to the centre from our ship takes about an hour. One of the ship's young shore excursion guides, William, is accompanying us. He hands out maps showing the city's streets and points of interest.

Chania is the second largest city of Crete and lies along the north coast of the island, about 70 km west of Rethimnon. We follow beautiful coastal scenery. To the right the jewel waters of the blue Cretan Sea gently lap upon soft white sand; to the left are small farms with olive groves and orchards and the encroaching towering snow peaks of the Western Range. We arrive 9.20 am in the heart of the old city outside the Municipal Market. The options for exploring the busy city are many, but we have a time limit of two hours.

The city of Chania can be divided in two parts: the old town and the modern city. The old town is situated next to the old harbour and is the matrix around which the whole urban area was developed. Venetian fortifications were built in 1538, of which the eastern and western parts have survived.

The Venetian Harbour and the accompanying lighthouse are landmarks of the city. The best preserved section is the western wall, running from Firkas Fortress to the Siavo Bastion. The waterfront is a perfect setting where locals and tourists may relax and reflect on the splendour of the harbour setting. Many Venetian townhouses have been restored and converted into chic restaurants. A visit to Roka Carpets in Zambeliou Street enables you to see a 400 year old loom in use, using methods that have remained essentially unchanged since Minoan times. The Archaeological Museum is housed in the former Venetian Church of San Francesco and contains objects from Neolithic and Minoan civilizations to the late Roman periods. The Maritime museum, located at the north-east end of the Venetian Harbour contains everything nautical with beautiful seashell collections.

Clearly one could spend a week or more here to enjoy the vibrancy and attractions. Nearby at Souda Bay is the War Memorial and War Cemetery in honour of the fallen during the Battle of Crete fought in May 1941. A few on our coach are hoping to visit the site. In the end most of our group decide to relax and explore the abundant shops and cafes. Avril and I head to one of the flashing green crosses that indicate a chemist. I need a pair of reading glasses. The rim of my only set broke four days ago, making it difficult to read. I usually bring a spare set of glasses with me while travelling, but not this time. I select a strength 1 set for 25 Euro to make do. The 1.5 strength are better and cheaper, but the only ones available are pink, somewhat like the ones John Lennon may have worn at a rock concert.

Avril and I then see an internet café and for one Euro we have access to high speed internet. I am able to catch up with important emails. In the past two days I have wasted at least an hour on the ship's satellite connection which fails to connect.

Avril is keen to window shop. Outside the internet café there is a shop full of bags, heaps of them. Avril has a weakness for such items and the store owner recognises this. He tempts her with a lovely black 'genuine' leather back pack similar to mine, especially reduced for her at 20 Euro. She convinces herself she needs it and then 'unconvinces' herself because of the assortment of bags she brought with her. We walk away and I see a hint of doubt and a little anguish as she mutters a little. 'I could throw away my *old* handbag,' she suggests. 'This *new* one would be better for travelling on aeroplanes.'

We stop a little way around the corner. 'It's your birthday soon,' I say. 'Let's go and take another look.' Avril comes away smiling, especially after the salesman shows her several storage spaces and hidden passages of her new purchase.

Half of our allotted time has gone so we decide to walk past numerous variety shops and cafes selling fish, vegetables, flowers, meat, bread and pastries, souvlaki, books, shoes and souvenirs. We step inside one of the small coffee stores and are greeted by a friendly middle-aged Greek man who asks, 'Where are you from?' How did he know we were not local? He smiles, 'What would you like?'

I order two cappuccinos. 'Ah! You have come to the right place. The best coffee is served right here.' And I am sure he is right. A quick look around and we see local Greek men enjoying their morning chat in his café.

His lively young assistant appears with two plates of delicious complimentary cake to try. 'I cooked this today and it is the first time I try it. You may think it not good.'

It is yummy and we praise her. 'That was so delicious.'

She is reluctant to accept our gratitude. She smiles and says, 'No, swear.'

We have just enough time to assemble at the market place to find our guide, William, who is holding the pink group sign to assemble for the coach. He is still waiting for stragglers, so we quickly slip into the market where Avril purchases some fancy honey olive oil soap. At 12.30 pm we arrive in Rethimnon for a delicious lunch on board the ship in the Terrace Cafe. We try the gnocchi, pasta with a spicy tomato sauce, and crisp toasted garlic bread. A glass of refreshing cold Heineken beer goes well with that. The dessert is a selection of fruits, cakes and ice-cream. I choose a tasty piece of rich cake and ice cream to go with our pot of English breakfast tea.

At 5.00 pm in the Ambassador Lounge is another interesting lecture with Jonathan Phillips entitled, *The Kings and Queens of Crusader Jerusalem*. He explores the challenges faced by the rulers of the Crusader States. He looks at the reigns of Queen Melisende (1131-52 AD) and King Baldwin IV, the Leper (1174-85 AD). He describes the response of the Muslim world to the Crusader presence in the Near East. He considers that the First Crusade is successful in 1099 AD because of the fractious disunity and fragmentation of the Muslim world.

Jonathan is making a TV series on the ancient world. He begins his lecture with an amusing clip from one of the bloopers. He is walking towards the camera and concentrating on the 220 words of his spiel when he suddenly vanishes from the screen. He has fallen into a hole at the digging site. Luckily his fall is cushioned by a layer of dust at the bottom. A big Texan pulls him out saying, 'Don't die on me dude.' This anguished sound was cut from the scene. Jonathan is dusted down, just a minor scratch and shock. He rings his wife to report his ordeal by saying, 'I am talking to you to let you know that I'm okay.' Upon hearing the news she bursts into tears. His university professor is stony-faced when told of the calamity.

Pina colada is the cocktail of the day at the special price of $5 US. We enjoy the treat in the Charleston Lounge after the lecture.

We dine at 8.00 pm in the Terrace Café. Tender roast veal is on the menu and a good variety of vegetables, salads and desserts. Avril and I see Barbara sitting alone so we join her. She has almost finished and is ready to retire to read *Ulysses* available from the library. I try to convince her to attend the special concert of classical music by the talented *Odyssey Trio* later at 9.15 pm. But she says she was up too early for today's excursion. She joins us for an extra glass of wine available with the nightly meal.

Many of the passengers are dining in the formal Marco Polo Restaurant on Deck 3, so our table waiters give us good service and like the opportunity to chat. Sherdon is a young man from Manila who has two girls, eight and two. He is on an eight month's contract and won't get home till November. Like most of the crew he is friendly and courteous. He keeps in regular touch with his family by Skype and email.

Another young, tall attendant, Stef, looks after the desserts. Tonight he recommends crème brulee. He serves me a slice and I move along to study the generous cheese selections. All the accompanying grapes have gone except two single ones. I joke that he is stingy with such a meagre supply. He offers to get me some and disappears to the supply room. Five minutes later he appears with a huge plate full of juicy fat red grapes. Barbara extends her stay to enjoy our tasty treat. Stef says he is doing business studies as well as a chef course. He hopes to start a small restaurant business one day, but he needs to save. His mother owns and works a rice field back home. He was two when he lost his father. He has two siblings. His elder brother does similar work to him and his younger sister is engaged to a business man, of which Stef smiles approvingly. Stef tells us that there are 100 crew members on board. Many are from the Philippines and some are from Indonesia and Eastern Europe.

We have dined and chatted for over an hour and then we head straight to the *Odyssey Trio's Concert* due to start in five minutes time in the Ambassador Lounge. It is pleasing to see a larger audience tonight since their last show on March 28. We manage to get front row seats as the concert begins.

The Romanian Trio are made up of Catalin Sasu on Violin, Virgil-Florin Prisacariu on Double Bass and Bogdan Mandasescu on Piano. The program features some wonderful numbers which display their extraordinary talent: *ROSEN AUS DEM SUDEN* (Roses from the South) Johann Strauss II (1825-1899); *SPRING* (from 'The Four seasons') Antonio Vivaldi (1678-1741); *TIK-TAK POLKA*, Johann Strauss II; *MEDITATION* (from Thais) Jules Massenet (1842-1912); *CARMEN* (Selection from) Georges Bizet (1838-1875); *PIROSKA* (Hungarian Fantasy) Traditional (arr. Harry Theis); *INTERMEZZO* (from Cavalleria Rusticana) Pietro Mascagni (1863-1945); *GRANADA*, Agustin Lara (1897-1970); *OBREO-ROMANIAN* (Medley of Folk Music) Traditional (arr. Odyssey Trio).

The appreciative audience are invited by Catalin to clap hands, stomp feet and shout 'Ole' at appropriate moments. It is an outstanding concert and a pleasure to congratulate the trio, especially for Avril and I to meet again with our friend Bogdan who was on the *Voyager* when we circumnavigated South America last year.

By midnight, it's time for that bedtime chocolate left on our pillows by our pleasant Filipino cabin steward, Alex. Our long day, beginning with the early morning excursion to Chania and ending with the evening concert at sea, has been exhilarating.

Fifth century BC Greek Theatre, still in use, Syracuse, Sicily.

Christian catacombs, fifth century BC, Syracuse.

'Ear of Dionysius', a pointed arch cut into the rock face, Syracuse.

Third century Roman amphitheater, Syracuse.

Palermo Cathedral, Sicily.

Twelfth century Cefalu Cathedral, a Norman structure in the reign of Roger II.

Monreale Cathedral near Palermo.

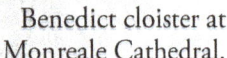

Benedict cloister at Monreale Cathedral.

Water fountain at Benedictine cloister, Monreale.

Ancient Greek Temple in Selinunte Archaeological Park near Trapani, Sicily.

Selinunte City, destroyed by Carthaginians in 409 BC, abandoned 250 BC.

Norman construction at Erice, a medieval hilltop town overlooking western Sicily.

Valletta Harbour, Malta.

Valletta Square, Malta.

Grand Master's Palace, Malta.

Mdina, a former capital of Malta.

St John's Co-Cathedral, Malta.

Relief markings on pillars at Monreale.

Syracuse Cathedral, Piazza Del Duomo, Ortygia, Sicily.

Storage Pots, Knossos.

Small harbour used to evacuate Allied soldiers in WW II, Sfakia.

Sfakia village, Crete, now dominated by waterfront cafes.

A knight in arms, Grand Master's Palace, Malta.

A tasty treat, Sfakian honey crepe.

Memorial honouring the Battle of Crete and the evacuation attempt at Sfakia in WW II.

Mdina, Malta.

Knossos, Crete.

Dolphin fresco, Knossos.

CHAPTER 3

THE HOLY LAND

Day 22
Thursday April 3, 2014.

At Sea sailing towards Haifa, Israel

At 7.30 am shafts of sunlight glimmer between the open curtains of our cabin. The forecast is for continuing sunny conditions, low 12 C to a high 20C. The *Aegean Odyssey* is sailing smoothly and heading in an east-south-easterly course towards Israel. We will be passing over the Herodotus Abyssal Plain and later in the day the Eratosthenes Tablemount. The latter is a large, submerged massif which rises 2000 m from the sea floor to a peak that is 690 m below sea level. It is one of the largest features of the Mediterranean seafloor. The *Aegean Odyssey* is scheduled to arrive in Haifa, Israel at 10.00 am tomorrow.

Two lectures are scheduled for today. At 10.00 am Ernie Rae's lecture is entitled *'Palestine in the Time of Jesus'*. He speaks on the political and religious background to the Jesus story and provides information on the main Biblical sites and their significance, including some hints on which ones are authentic. Ernie has visited Israel ten times and never fails to be impressed. He concludes his talk by saying that whether you are a Christian believer or not in the life of Jesus, we live in a world that has been dominated and influenced greatly by the Christian message… great architecture, literature, art and historic events.

At 11.00 am we attend the morning quiz on Israel trivia presented by our effervescent and amusing quiz master, the director Neil Horrock. At the same time we relax over a morning cappuccino from the Charleston Bar. Avril slips into the nearby library to get the daily Sudoku, crossword and news sheet, *Australia Today*, which tells us that the cigarette manufacturer Philip Morris is to quit Australia – too many have quit smoking!

At 3.00 pm Professor Jonathan Phillips has another lecture on the Crusades entitled *Crusader Acre*. His lecture offers some insight into the city we will be seeing, as well as some comments on the two major sieges of the city: in 1191 (Richard and Saladin) and a century later in 1291 (the end of the Crusader States). Jonathan has a book available, *HOLY WARRIORS – A Modern history of the Crusades*. The Financial Times says his book is 'Compelling, flamboyant and refreshing'.

At 4.45 pm we attend an excursion briefing on Haifa with Jenny Worwood. The *MV Aegean Odyssey* is due to arrive in Haifa, Israel at 10.00 am tomorrow and remain berthed until April 6. Over 30 passengers will disembark and about 100 new passengers will join the ship. Avril and I retire to the Charleston Lounge for a Scotch and Dry after the briefing.

At 7.40 pm we dine again at the Terrace Restaurant for a delicious roast lamb from the carvery and garlic prawns served with rice, cream sauce and broccoli. We finish with some tasty quality cheeses including gorgonzola and a few large red table grapes.

Day 23
Friday April 4, 2014.

Haifa, Israel

My alarm wakes me at 6.00 am as the *MV Aegean Odyssey* continues in calm sea conditions towards Haifa, Israel. The forecast is for sunny weather ranging from 12 C to a high of 22 C. I remember that it's my mother's birthday today. She was born 95 years ago in Newcastle NSW. But I can only pray for her, as she died 70 years young. The ship's satellite has poor internet reception so I would not be able to send her an email message if she was still here.

At 10.00 am immigration officials board the ship to process everyone for the purpose of stamping an entry card into Israel. Our face-to-face immigration process is very efficient and takes little time. A young smiling woman says, 'Hi William. Is this the first time you have been to Israel?' My answer is 'Yes'. She stamps my passport and says, 'Enjoy your stay and please come again.'

We relax in the Charleston Lounge with a morning cappuccino at 10.45 am. Lorraine from Boston sits and chats with us. She and husband Fred will be disembarking tomorrow and returning home on Tuesday. She has seen the Greek Islands before and is on this voyage to see the Holy Land. She says 27 passengers will be leaving the ship and over a hundred embarking. She thinks Avril and I are married and she asks how we met. We tell her we met through dancing and that we live separately. She has been married to Fred for 45 years. At that point a friend of hers joins us and wants to know the appropriate tip to give to her cabin steward. 'Tips are included in the trip,' says Lorraine emphatically. 'So I'm not tipping.' Her friend seems troubled. I too am taken aback as tipping is part of American culture. 'And if you think I'm tight my husband is worse. Frugal Fred I call him.'

At 11.30 am we take the early lunch available on the Terrace Café. We decide on spinach based pasta with crunchy garlic bread. The full afternoon excursion to Acre and Mount Carmel begins at 12.50 pm. Our guide, a very confident local man joins our coach and says, 'Shalom.' He continues, 'My name is Yair, which means *to shed light*. I am 41 years old, married with three children, a girl who is 8 and twin boys aged 6. My Holy task is to see us safely to our destination.' Given his holy sanction, I certainly hope our coach is not sabotaged!

We head towards Acre, a city on the northern coastal plain of Israel at the northern extremity of Haifa Bay. The city occupies an important location, as it sits on the coast of the Mediterranean, linking the waterways and commercial activity with the Levant (historic term for Southwest Asia). Acre is one of the oldest continuously inhabited sites in the northern region of Israel. Settlement began in the Early Bronze Age about 3000 BC. The Bible mentions *'Akko'* as a place from which the Israelites fail to drive out the Canaanites (Judges 1:31).

Greek historians refer to the city as *'Ake'*, meaning 'cure'. In Greek mythology, Heracles finds herbs here to cure his wounds. The name is changed to *'Antiochia Ptolemais'* and shortly after to *'Ptolemais'* following Alexander the Great's conquest of nearly the entire known world. Born in Macedonia in 356 BC and dying only 32 years later, he only reigns for 13 years. However his legacy lasts to this day. He overthrows the entire Persian Empire: from Asia Minor to Egypt and everything in between, including Israel.

Alexander's empire is divided among his four generals following his death in 323 BC. Although his empire is split, the Hellenism culture continues its spread to all parts of the divided empire. Greek becomes the universal language and Greek culture is required or encouraged.

Israel (Judea) changes hands between the Ptolemaic Dynasty (305 BC to 30 BC) and Seleucid Dynasty (312 to 64 BC). Ptolemy is one of Alexander the Great's generals who is appointed satrap of Egypt. The Seleucids are successors of Alexander the Great in the eastern part of his empire.

The land of Judea becomes a Jewish theocracy under the Syrian-based Seleucid rulers. The Jews are prohibited from practicing Judaism and their Temple is desecrated in an effort to impose Greek culture and customs on the entire population. In 166 BC the Jews rise in revolt. The Jews, led by Judah the Maccabee of the Hasmonean family, enter Jerusalem and purify the Temple in 164 BC. Further Hasmonean victories over the Seleucids in 147 BC restore semi-autonomy to Judea, as the land of Israel was called. Jewish independence is again achieved after the Seleucid kingdom collapses in 129 BC. This is known as the Hasmonean Period as recorded in Maccabees 1 and 2 of the Apocrypha.

Independent Hasmonean rule lasts for about 80 years (142-63 BC). In 63 BC the Roman general Pompey subdues Judea, ends the Hasmonean state and brings Judea into the Roman Empire. Antigonus II Mattathias is the last Hasmonean king of Judea. Antigonus leads a fierce unsuccessful struggle by the Jews for independence from the Romans. In 37 BC Herod orders his execution thus bringing an end to the Hasmonean dynasty. Herod the Great becomes king of Israel. He is designated 'King of the Jews' by the Roman Senate, effectively transforming the Hasmonean Kingdom into the Herodian Kingdom – a client of Rome.

In the Bible we learn that St Paul spends a day in Ptolemais (Acts 21:7). The first century Romano-Jewish historian, Flavius Josephus, calls the port city *'Akre'*. It is known as Akko following the division of the Roman Empire in 395 AD. Then Akko is administered by the Eastern ('Byzantine') Empire.

In the Battle of Yarmouk in 636 AD, Muslim Arab forces defeat the Byzantine army to capture the Christian City of Jerusalem. Acre comes under Moslem rule beginning in 638 AD. The Arab conquest brings a revival to the town of Acre, which serves as the main port of Palestine throughout the ruling Umayyad and Abbasid Caliphates and the following Crusader rule into the 13th century.

The Crusaders capture Acre in 1104 AD following a four year siege by King Baldwin I of Jerusalem. In Crusader times Acre is known as *St John d'Acre* after the Knights' Hospitaller of St John Order which has its headquarters there. Acre becomes an important link for the Crusader's advance into the Levant – the eastern Mediterranean. It gives them a foothold into the region and access to the prosperous Asiatic spice trade.

By 1170 AD Acre becomes the main port of the Levant. As a result, the kingdom of Jerusalem is regarded in the west as enormously wealthy. (The term *Levant* appeared in English in 1497, referring to Mediterranean lands east of Italy. It is borrowed from the French *levant* meaning 'rising', in reference to the rising sun in the east. Today historians and archaeologists use the term when referring to the prehistory and the ancient and medieval history of the region, notably when discussing the Crusades.)

Acre is the final stronghold of the Crusader States when much of the coastline is conquered by Mamluk forces. The Mamlukes are slave warriors of medieval Islam who overthrow their masters, defeat the Mongols and Crusaders, and establish a dynasty that lasts three hundred years. Acre capitulates to the Mamluk forces led by Sultan al-Ashraf Khalil in the bloody siege of 1291 AD. The Crusaders make a last stand, but their defence finally gives way and Mamluk warriors pour into the doomed city.

The survivors of the Order fight their way through to the port and board the Grand Master's waiting galley which sails to Cyprus. Eighteen years later the Order shifts to Rhodes and then, in 1522, to Malta where it remains until 1798 when Napoleon conquers the island on his way to Egypt.

In order to prevent any future return by Crusader forces, the Mamlukes leave the city in ruins, except for religious shrines considered sacred by the Muslims. For centuries the ruined city is little more than a fishing village.

The Mamluk era lasts from 1250 to 1517 when the Ottomans under Sultan Selim I capture what remains of the city. Towards the end of the 18th century the Ottoman rulers, Daher el-Omar and his successor Jezzar Pasha rebuild Acre's fortifications, using materials from the city's medieval ruins. The remnants of the Crusader walls are used as a foundation for new walls which are able to withstand Napoleon's siege of 1799. Impressive projects are undertaken such as the Jezzar Pasha Mosque. The older city begins to disappear beneath the new one. Excavations have proven that some of the finest Crusader structures have been preserved.

Visiting Acre is like being in a 5000 year time warp of history. Of particular interest to our group are the newly excavated Crusader's Halls, the Templar's Tunnel, the port and the Sea Walls.

Yair, a strongly built man, says he was born in Haifa and like all citizens of Israel he did his national service and trained as a paratrooper.

He provides us with a lively dissertation -- 'Haifa is only 280 years old and has a population of 30,000, whereas Acre, where we are going, is 4000 years old and has a mixed population of 80,000, about 75% Jewish and 25% Arab. Haifa has heavy industry, recycling and technology. It is the third largest city in Israel. Jerusalem is the largest followed by Tel Aviv. Haifa lies at the foot of Mt Carmel which is the centre of the Baha'i faith. But Acre is the holiest city of the Baha'i faith. It is the youngest monotheistic religion in the world with 7 million followers worldwide, including a big following in India.'

The Baha'i faith arose in Persia in 1844 at Shirazes. Siyyid Al Muhammad proclaims the imminent arrival of the Promised One, a messianic figure expected by Shia Muslims in Persia. He becomes known as the Bab (the 'Gate' in Arabic).The Bab proclaims the spiritual unity of all humankind and the differences of race are annulled. His proclamations provoke the Shiites who persecute his followers and put the Bab in prison for three years for claiming he is a prophet. They execute him by firing squad in 1850 and he achieves the status of a martyr. His remains are later brought secretly to Israel where they are interred in the Mount Carmel shrine.

The Bab's replacement and chief follower is Mizra Hussein Ali. In 1863 he claims to be the Promised One and he becomes known as Baha'u'llah (Glory of God). This troubles the Persians. They do not want another martyr so they expel him from Tehran in 1868 to the Ottoman penal colony of Akko (now Acre) where he dies in exile in 1892. From his prison he could gaze to Mt Carmel which he regards as sacred. This is where his followers have built an immense gold-domed shrine and the largest hanging gardens in the world.

Our coach advances along the modern highway to Acre. The highway is built on land reclaimed from the sea by the British who controlled Israel from 1917 to 1938, following the breakup of the Ottoman Empire.

Yair continues, 'Acre got its name by a miscalculation made by the knights of the Crusade, thinking they had reached the Biblical place of the same name.'

'There are 8 million Israeli citizens. Six million are Jews of all types. Some are serious, especially in Jerusalem. Some are party going, especially in Tel Aviv. And some are addicted to Facebook and texting. There are about 1.6 million Arab citizens in Israel who share the same rights.'

'Here we have freedom of speech, freedom of religion and freedom of the press,' he spruiks.

I ask Yair, 'Are the Arab citizens living here expected to do national service?'

He answers, 'That is an important question. They do not have to, only if they wish. But they must do other compulsory non-military work.'

Yair is a likeable man who loves his Jewish homeland which was granted to the Jews after the UN General Assembly adopted a resolution to partition Palestine on November 29, 1947. The aim was to partition Palestine into two states, one Jewish and the other Arab. The Jewish part was to be slightly larger than the Arab state: 56 percent and 43 percent of Palestine, respectively, excluding Jerusalem. The area of Jerusalem and Bethlehem were to become an international zone.

The Zionist leadership, pushing for a permanent homeland, accepts the UN plan, but the Palestinian Arabs and the surrounding Arab states reject it. The State of Israel is proclaimed when the British announces the termination of its Mandate over Palestine to take effect on May 14, 1948. The newly-created Israel immediately becomes a battleground as the armies of Egypt, Lebanon, Syria and Iraq attack. The Arab nations attack as separate units and prove no match against Israel's single unit command structure which is well-equipped with arms shipments from Czechoslovakia and three B-17 bombers that are purchased in America on the black market.

The war, which the Israelis regard as the 'War of Independence', ends in 1949 with the Arab states signing armistice agreements. Israel captures more territory than has been provided by the UN resolution and, in the process, they drive out over 700,000 Arabs, who become displaced persons known as Palestinians. As a result, the country once known as Palestine is divided into three parts, each under a different political regime. The State of Israel controls

77 percent of former Palestine; Jordan occupies East Jerusalem and the West Bank; Egypt takes control of the Gaza Strip (the coastal plain around the city of Gaza).

Yair is full of praise for the ANZACS and their legendary victory at Beersheba in 1917. He falsely believes the victory gives Israel its freedom. But this claim is historically incorrect. During the Great War, the Palestine Campaign sees the celebrated charge of the 4th Light Horse Brigade on the unsuspecting Turks. The ANZACS and Palestinian soldiers fight the Turks to free Palestine from Ottoman rule. The victory turns the tide that leads to the end of Ottoman rule in Palestine. However, Beersheba is never intended to become part of Israel under the 1947 UN Partition Plan. Instead Beersheba becomes one of the captured cities by the newly-created Israel. Its Palestinian inhabitants are sent fleeing and never allowed to return to their homes. The Palestinians now feel they are prisoners of Israel.

The Beersheba Commonwealth War Cemetery contains the graves of 175 Australian soldiers and lies at the edge of the sprawling city that Israel has renamed Be'er Sheva. An ANZAC-Israeli connection has set up a memorial statue in the park as a tribute to those who died in battle for the Jewish state. But any ANZAC-Israeli connection is fudging history. The ANZACS were fighting for King and Country some 31 years before the state of Israel was created.

Yair loves Australia which he visited after his compulsory military training as a paratrooper in 1994. He is 22 when he arrives at Bondi Beach, Sydney. He runs out of money by the time he reaches Tumbarumba in the Snowy Mountains. At this point a farmer, Mr Duffy, gives Yair a guided tour of his huge apple orchard and Yair works there for three months. To Yair's surprise, Duffy has installed irrigation technology imported from Israel. Yair laughs, 'I didn't eat apples for the next 12 months.'

Our coach deposits us at the bus station near the ancient city walls of Acre. We follow Yair on a tour of the magnificent underground rooms of the Knights Hospitaller compound. Yair has a unique way of making sure we do not get lost in the mix of tourists. He signals us with his trumpet which he blows expertly, providing entertainment at the same time. We enter the subterranean complex and encounter a row of high-ceiling chambers dubbed the **Knights Halls**. It is only in 1954 following excavations that the halls are cleared of debris that has filled them for centuries.

The most magnificent of the underground rooms is the **Crypt**, a refectory or dining hall of the knights. Three massive pillars support a vaulted ceiling 12 metres high. It is likely that Marco Polo dined here when he stopped in Acre on his way to China in 1148. One of the halls contains a captivating presentation of modern sculpture on the Crusader theme.

Yair leads us through a 45 m long underground passage which connects us with another building, **The Post**. It once served as part of the Order's infirmary. We continue along a thematic passageway known as **Templar's Tunnel** where we pause near a drink stand. A woman is using a hand press to squeeze pomegranate juice. It makes a refreshing drink and on a hot afternoon she is doing a rip-roaring trade. Avril and I enjoy the freshly squeezed juice while waiting for our group to catch up.

We emerge from the tunnel at the Sea Walls where our coach awaits to take us to our ship. We travel via Mount Carmel for a panoramic view of Haifa from the observation point next to Stella Maris Monastery. In very early times the top of Mt Carmel is a landmark for sailors approaching the Bay of Haifa. Mt Carmel is actually a coastal limestone mountain range stretching from Samaria to the Mediterranean, and ending in a promontory above Haifa. The 25 km long range varies from 10 to 15 km wide, with an average height of 500 m.

The mountain range contains over 1000 limestone caves and is a source of a plentiful supply of spring water. Lush Mediterranean vegetation covers its flanks and gorges: laurels, myrtles, cedars, pines, tamarinds, holm-oaks, carob and mastic trees. Mount Carmel's name is derived from the Hebrew word *kerem*, meaning beautiful orchard, vineyard or garden. Several books in the Old Testament refer to the region as a symbol of Israel's prosperity and fruitfulness (Amos 1:2; Jeremiah 50:19; Nahum 1:4).

From our observation point there is a magnificent view of Haifa Bay, our ship in the harbour. We see the clear blue Mediterranean Sea hugging the coastline northwards towards Acre. Nearby is the spectacular religious memorial of the Baha'i Shrine with its golden dome, marble walls and manicured gardens which cascade down the slope of Mount Carmel.

The Shrine is the world headquarters of Baha'i faith and was built in 1953 to contain the remains of the prophet-herald Siyyid Al Muhammad (1819-50) known as the Bab. The Shrine has nine sides representing the nine major religions of the world. The dome is covered with 14,000 gold-coated bricks. The beautiful terraced gardens surrounding the Shrine are often called the 'Hanging Gardens of Haifa'. There are 19 terraces, one representing the Shine of the Bab and the remainder for his first 18 disciples.

The history of Mount Carmel is closely linked with the Prophet Elijah who lived there in the ninth century B.C. Elijah's fire-lighting challenge is one of the Old Testament's most spectacular contests between Yahweh, the God of the Israelites, and the pagan deity, Baal. Elijah's challenge comes after successive kings 'did evil in the sight of the Lord' (1 Kings 16:30).

King Ahab marries the Phoenician princess Jezebel who turns his allegiance from Yahweh to her god Baal. She has Yahweh's prophets slaughtered. Elijah calls on Ahab to assemble 450 priests of Baal on Mount Carmel where he challenges them to call on fire to light a sacrifice. Baal fails to respond to the priest's cries. Then Elijah rebuilds the ruined altar and offers his sacrifice. Immediately fire comes from Heaven and consumes the offering, even though it has been soaked in water.

In the 12th century, during the Crusader occupation, groups of religious hermits begin to inhabit the caves of Mount Carmel in imitation of Elijah the Prophet. Within a century these monastic hermits become organized into the Carmelite Order under the guidance of St Berthold, originally a Crusader from France, and his successor St Brocard. Religious life under the Carmelite Rule involves solitude, asceticism and contemplation. Also known as the Rule of our Saviour, it continues to this day.

Papal approval for the Order is not received until 1226, a time of uncertainty for Christians in the Middle East. Some Carmelite friars return to their countries of origin and the Order spreads throughout Europe and flourishes throughout the Middle Age. However, its founders on Mount Carmel are exiled at the time of the Mamluk conquest of 1291.

The Carmelites return to Mount Carmel in 1631 and build the Stellar Maris Monastery in the 18th century. The monastery complex serves as hospital for Napoleon's soldiers during his unsuccessful siege of Acre (Akko) in 1799. The abandoned French soldiers are slaughtered by the Turks after Napoleon retreats.

In 1821 Abdullah Pasha, the ruler of Acre from 1820 to 1821 decides to build a summer palace in Stella Maris over the ruins of the Crusader fortress. He reuses the stones from the fortress as well as the stones from the ruined Carmelite Monastery. A lighthouse is added at the edge of Mount Carmel to help guide ships entering the Bay of Haifa, thus giving its name to the area-- *Stella Maris*, Latin for 'Star of the Sea'.

In 1831 Ibrahim Pasha captures Acre and exiles Abdulla Pasha to Egypt. He hands the palace building over to the Carmelites to be used as a Christian hostel. The Carmelites rebuilt their monastery in 1836. It is situated across the street from the old lighthouse. They accord their monastery's name of Stella Maris to Mary, the mother of Jesus, rather than to the magnificent lighthouse's view of the sea.

We only have about 30 minutes to admire the view of the beautiful surroundings and to take a quick walk in the garden park next to the Stella Maris Monastery and the church. Time does not permit viewing the beautiful church which contains vividly coloured Italian marble and dramatic paintings in the dome, one depicting Elijah being swept up to heaven in a fiery chariot. A cedar and porcelain statue of Mary, Our Lady of Mount Carmel, is above the altar. Below the altar, one can take steps leading into a cave where the Old Testament prophet Elijah is believed to have lived.

Opposite the monastery is a steep pathway leading down towards the Mediterranean to a large grotto, Elijah's Cave, where the prophet is believed to have meditated before his victory over the prophets of Baal, as described in 1 Kings 18: 1-40.

Yair's promise to deliver us safely to our ship has been fulfilled and he hopes we have seen Israel as a peaceful place of co-existence. 'Don't believe everything you read in the press. Tell your friends we are a safe and friendly place to visit, where Jews and Arabs are living harmoniously together.' Within three months of returning to Australia, three Jewish students are kidnapped and murdered, sparking an escalation in hostilities and retaliatory action by Israel against Palestinians in the Gaza.

Day 24
Saturday April 5, 2014.

Haifa, Israel

Avril and I arise before daybreak at 5.20 am and we take early breakfast at 6.00 am. At 7.50 am our coach is ready to take us to Jerusalem where we will stay overnight at the Grand Court Hotel. Today's full day tour takes in Nazareth and the Sea of Galilee, lasting 11 hours before we reach our destination in Jerusalem. Hotel check-in is not available there until after 8.00 pm due to the Jewish Sabbath. For the next two days we have been allocated an excellent guide, Isaac, a middle-aged Jew from Haifa. He has a strong voice and keeps us well informed with careful attention to detail and comfort.

Having been raised as a Christian, it seems surreal that I am visiting the birthplace of Christianity. We will be walking in the footsteps of Jesus during our visit to Nazareth and the Sea of Galilee. Our drive to Nazareth, the childhood home of Jesus, takes us through the fertile Jezreel Valley, south of the Lower Galilee region. The name Jezreel comes from two Hebrew root words meaning *'to sow'* and *'mighty'* or *'God will sow'* when put together. The valley is a beautiful broad plain only 32 km long by 12 km wide that stretches from the Mount Carmel Range in the west to the Jordan Valley in the east. The area has been the scene of more than 30 battles over the past 4000 years. Thousands have fought and died here: Egyptians, Canaanites, Israelites, Midianites, Amalekites, Philistines, Hasmonaeans, Greeks, Romans, Muslims, Crusaders, Mamlukes, Mongols, French, Ottomans, British, Australians, New Zealanders, Germans, Arabs and Israelis.

Biblical students know the area as Armageddon, the future scene of the Apocalypse, as explained in the Book of Revelations. This is prophesised as the final cataclysmic battle between the forces of good and the forces of evil, leading to the end of the world. Armageddon is a corruption of the Hebrew word *'Har Megiddo'* meaning *'the Mount of Megiddo'* and is an actual place in the Jezreel Valley.

The Bible contains a long history of prominent and mostly violent events at Jezreel. King Jehu ordered that the heads of King Ahab's 70 sons be placed in heaps at the gate of Jezreel (2 Kings 10:1-11). Ahab's queen, Jezebel, met her death by being thrown from a window of the palace of Jezreel and it was there that her body was eaten by dogs (2 Kings 9:30-35). Other events here include a victory by the Israelites, led by Gideon, against the Midianites and Amalekites (Judges 6:3); the victory of the Philistines over Saul and his sons (1 Samuel 31) and the victory of the Egyptians over King Josiah (2 Kings 20:29).

The morning is bright and sunny for our arrival at Nazareth. Here we visit the **Church of Annunciation** also referred to as the Basilica of the Annunciation which is one of the Holiest Christian sites. The Roman Catholic Church stands upon the site that is believed to be the house of Mary, where the angel Gabriel appeared and announced to Mary that she will give birth to Jesus (Luke 1). Greek Orthodox belief is that the Annunciation took place while Mary was drawing water from a local spring in Nazareth. Mary's well is located just below the Greek Orthodox Church of Annunciation, in the centre of Nazareth.

Our coach parks in downtown Nazareth and Isaac walks us up Casa Nova Street to the gate of the Basilica of the Annunciation. We mingle with tourists admiring the magnificent two-storey structure built in 1969 over the site of an earlier Byzantine-era Church commissioned by Emperor Constantine in 340 AD and completed in 470 AD. An Arab invasion in 638 AD destroys that Church. In 1109 AD the Crusaders arrive to the Holy Land and build a new magnificent Church. It is destroyed by the Mamluks in 1263 AD. In 1620 AD Franciscans purchase the ruins and the Church is rebuilt in 1730, and then enlarged in 1877. It is demolished and rebuilt (1955-1969) in its present form as designed by Giovanni Muzio.

Inside, we are struck by the simplicity of the large airy interior. Isaac explains, 'Churches here in the Holy Land are very humble and not bothered by elaborate art.' The walls have triangular sections to represent the Trinity; the towering cupola above is in the shape of an inverted white lily to denote Mary's purity. The cupola stands directly above a sunken grotto that contains the traditional cave-home of the Virgin Mary. We join a slow line of visitors descending a stairway leading to the Grotto of Annunciation. Inside the cave is an altar with the Latin inscription 'Here the Word was made flesh'.

Isaac is keen to show us the nearby church, the **Church of St Joseph**, a solid unpretentious building. It stands in the shadow of the soaring cupola of the Basilica of the Annunciation. A fond tradition holds that the Church of St Joseph is built over the carpentry workshop of the husband of the Virgin Mary. But there is no evidence to support that the cave over which the church is built is Joseph's workshop. A plaque on the wall reads:

'The church was built on the site of an earlier 12th – Century church.
The caves, granaries and wells in the lower level were used by the early dwellers of Nazareth. Later Christians turned the site into a worship place.
Travellers who visited the place in the 7th Century pointed out that this had been the location of the "Carpentry Shop of Joseph".
Later traditions identify the place as being "The House of Joseph'.

Isaac, allows us time to explore and find our way back to the coach. Inside the church are three noteworthy paintings: *The Holy Family, The Dream of Joseph,* and *The Death of Joseph in the Arms of Jesus and Mary.* A stairway in the church descends to a grill-covered crypt where caverns can be seen. Further on are openings to grain silos and water cisterns cut into the soft limestone by early dwellers.

Avril and I have time for a coffee before our coach heads north-east to the Sea of Galilee where we will have lunch at Ginosar kibbutz, situated north of Tiberias on Highway 90. On the way Isaac speaks on the geography of Israel…

'The Holy Land is an important location for three of the world's major religions. Israel is a small, narrow and semi-arid country lying at the junction of three continents: Europe, Asia and Africa. It is only 470 km in length and 135 km across at its widest point, with an area of 20,770 sq km. It is sandwiched in Southwest Asia between the Mediterranean and the deserts of Syria and Arabia. We are living on the edge of the Arabian Desert,' exclaims Isaac.

'The Mediterranean is to the West and the Jordan valley Rift is to the East. The mountains of Lebanon are to the North and Eilat Bay marks the country's southern tip.'

Israel has three main geographical areas: the coastal plain, the mountain region and the Jordan Valley Rift:

The **Coastal plain** is fertile and densely populated with most of Israel's major cities. The plain is only 4 to 7 km wide in the north, expanding as it moves southward to about 50 km. From north to south the plain is divided into the Galilee Plain, the Acre Plain, the Carmel Plain, the Sharon Plain, the Mediterranean Coastal plain, and the Southern Coastal Plain.

The **mountain region** separates the coastal plain from the Jordan Valley Rift in the east of the country. It stretches from Lebanon in the north to Eilat Bay in the south. Two major valleys interrupt the contiguous mountain region – the Jezreel Valley separates the Galilee Mountains from the hills of Samaria; and the Be'er Sheva-Arad Rift separates the Judean hills from the Negev highlands. Israel's highest mountain, Mt Hermon at 2224 m above sea level, is north of the hilly Golan Heights which are east of the Jordan River.

The **Jordan Valley Rift region** contains the Jordan Valley and the Arava. The Jordan Valley forms part of the larger Jordan Valley Rift. It extends from an outlet of the Jordan River at the Sea of Galilee to its inlet into the Dead Sea, a little over 100 km to the south. The Arava is a long savannah valley that stretches south from the Dead Sea to the Gulf of Eilat, between the desert hills of the Negev and the border with Jordan.

The Jordan Valley Rift forms part of the Syrian-African Rift which split the earth's crust millions of years ago. The 6,000 km long fissure extends from the Taurus Mountains in Turkey to the Zambesi Valley in Southern Africa. It marks the division between the continents of Asia and Africa and is subject to earthquakes and volcanic eruptions.

The Jordan River flows 320 km southward from its sources in the mountains, where Israel, Syria and Lebanon meet, and descends over 950 m on its journey to the Dead Sea. A large part of its length forms the border between Israel and Jordan in the north and the West Bank and Jordan in the south. For most of its course it flows well below sea level through the fertile Hula valley into Lake Kinneret (Sea of Galilee) which is 212 m below sea level.

It continues winding through the Jordan Valley before emptying into the Dead Sea; at 423 m below sea level it is the lowest point on earth.

The Dead Sea (known in Hebrew as the Salt Sea - Genesis 14:3) measures 67 km by 18 km and contains 30 percent salt, about 8.6 times greater than average ocean salinity. Its waters are rich in potash, magnesium and bromine, table and industrial salts. A high evaporation rate of 1.6 m annually, combined with large scale diversion projects undertaken by Israel and Jordan for their water needs, has accelerated the natural pace of recession in recent years. The 75 percent reduction of the incoming flow of water has caused the surface level to drop over 10 m since 1960.

Our journey in the northern district of Israel takes us by Kafr Kanna an Arab town in the Tur'an Valley in Galilee which was captured by Israel in the 1948 Arab-Israel War. Christians speculate that the town is Cana where Jesus performed his first public miracle at the Marriage at Cana, the turning of water into wine (John 2:1-12).

We arrive at Tabgha on the north-west shore of the Sea of Galilee, about 3 km south-west of Capernaum. Tabgha is at the foot of the Mount of Beatitudes where Jesus delivered his Sermon on the Mount. The name Tabgha is derived from an Arab mispronunciation of the Greek name *Heptapegon* meaning 'seven springs'. Nearby are seven warm sulphurous springs that enter the lake, attracting fish, especially in the winter months.

Tabgha is traditionally accepted as the place where Jesus performed the miracle of loaves and fishes to feed a multitude – 5000 men, plus women and children. According to Matthew Chapter 14, the miraculous feeding comes after Jesus learns that Herod Antipas has beheaded his cousin, John the Baptist. Jesus withdraws by boat to a private place, but the crowds follow on foot from the towns. He lands and sees a large crowd. Feeling compassion He heals their sick. It is getting late and His disciples urge Him to send them away, 'so they can go to the villages and buy themselves some food'.

There is not enough food to feed the crowd, except for five loaves of bread and two fish. But Jesus directs the people to sit on the grass. 'Taking the 5 loaves and the two fish and looking up to heaven, He gave thanks and broke the loaves... and the disciples gave them to the people. They all ate and were satisfied, and the disciples picked up twelve basketfuls of broken pieces that were left over. The number of those who ate was about five thousand men, besides women and children'.

Tabgha is also remembered for the third appearance of Jesus to His disciples after His Resurrection, when He tests Peter as leader of His Church. Pilgrims to Tabgha find the place a serene location for meditation, prayer and study.

The earliest building at Tabgha is a small chapel built around 350 AD by the Jewish convert to Christianity, Joseph of Tiberias. Emperor Constantine gives him permission to build churches in Galilee, specifically, in Jewish towns which do not yet have a Christian community.

A large monastery and a church are built in the fifth century, but these are destroyed in 614 AD by the Persian invasion. The Byzantine site is forgotten until the area's lands are bought in the 18th century by a Catholic-German association for the purpose of constructing a hotel for pilgrims. During the diggings for the construction, they discover evidence of the earlier church; but they cannot make excavations due to the Ottoman Law. Then in 1932, during the British Mandate of Palestine, two German archaeologists, Mader and Schneider, uncover a number of the Byzantine church's walls and mosaics. In 1981, the modern **Church of the Multiplication of Loaves and Fishes** is finally restored to its Byzantine form, incorporating portions of the original mosaics.

Tabgha is bathed in bright sunlight for our visit. Appropriately, large goldfish swim lazily among water lilies, seeking the shaded areas of a large pond in the courtyard of the church. Isaac gives us half an hour to observe the vibrantly coloured mosaic decorations inside. They are among the best in the Holy Land, featuring a whole floor of flora and fauna of the area – peacocks, doves, geese, herons, ducks, a flamingo and a swan, snakes, lotus flowers and oleanders. On the floor near the altar is the best-known mosaic featuring the miracle that the church commemorates. It depicts a basket of loaves flanked by two Galilee mullet. Beneath the altar is the rock on which many believe is the Table of Christ – where Jesus placed the loaves and fishes when he blessed them.

We proceed to Ginosar kibbutz for a relaxing lunch beside the Sea of Galilee. The food court is packed with hordes of tourists who help themselves at the buffet stations containing delicious hot and cold dishes. The Bible describes Israel as 'a land flowing with milk and honey' (Exodus 33:3; Deut. 31:20), one that conjures up a picture of a rich, fertile and productive land. The selection of local produce, pastries, desserts and wine on offer affirms that point.

On a hot sunny afternoon after lunch we arrive at Capernaum, the ancient fishing village and frontier post beside the Sea of Galilee which became the home town of Jesus during the years of his ministry. Among the Holy Land sites, the Sea of Galilee has changed comparatively little since the time of Jesus. Isaac takes our group to seats shaded by trees and talks to us about the history of the area.

Jews of the Hasmonean family establish Capernaum at the beginning of the 2nd century BC. It is built along the edge of the Sea of Galilee and it once had up to 1500 residents. The area is used for agriculture and fishing and extends 3 kilometres to Tabgha. Capernaum later falls into ruin.

By the third century, the town is described as *'despicable; it numbers only seven houses of poor fishermen'*. It is abandoned in the 11th century and its ruins lay undiscovered until 1838 when the American scholar, Edward Robinson, comes across a scene described as *'desolate and mournful'*. In 1866, the remains of the synagogue are identified by the English army officer and surveyor, Major General Sir Charles William Wilson. Franciscan Friar, Giuseppe Baldi of Naples, the Custodian of the Holy land, recovers the main part of the ruins from the Bedouins. The Franciscans built a protective fence to protect the ruins from vandals. They built a small harbour and plant palms and Australian eucalyptus to create seclusion for pilgrims.

Today the ruins are owned by two churches. The Franciscans control the western portion with the synagogue and a house claimed to be St Peter's house; The Greek Orthodox section is a short distance away and is marked by a white church with red domes. Built in 1931, it is dedicated to the Twelve Apostles.

Jesus leaves Nazareth and makes the ancient fishing town of Capernaum, on the northern shores of the Sea of Galilee, the centre of his ministry in Galilee. The heart-shaped freshwater lake is 21 km long and 13 km across at its widest point, with a maximum depth of 43 m. The lake serves as Israel's chief water supply. Jesus uses the lake, its boats and its shores to spread His Good News. It becomes his home town and the scene of many of His miracles.

Capernaum, is also St Peter's village where Jesus recruits His disciples, all fishermen, with miraculous catches and tells them that He will make them 'fishers of men' (Mathew 4:19; Mark 1:17). Four fishermen - Peter, Andrew, James and John – became His first disciples. Matthew the tax collector also dwells there and becomes a disciple. Fishing is the main industry in Jesus' time, with over 200 boats working the lake. Their catches are dried and exported all over the Roman world.

Isaac allows us time to visit the impressive, partly restored synagogue of the 4th or 5th century. The ornately decorated synagogue is the largest discovered in Israel and is believed to have been built on the foundations of the one in which Jesus taught. His teachings made a deep impression on the local people because, unlike the scribes, He taught with authority. (Mark 1:21-22). It was here that Jesus promised the Eucharist in His sermon on the bread of life: 'Very truly I tell you, unless you eat the flesh of the Son of Man and drink his blood, you have no life in you.' (John 6:22-59).

The original synagogue was built by a Roman centurion whose servant is healed following a declaration of faith that amazes Jesus (Luke 7:1-10). Jesus heals many people of illness or possession by the devil while teaching here, including Peter's mother-in-law and the daughter of Jarius, the leader of the synagogue. However, Jesus curses Capernaum, along with Bethsaida and Chorazin, because many of the inhabitants refuse to believe in Him.

Located between the synagogue and the lakeshore stands an ultra-modern Catholic church built in the shape of an octagon and is perched on eight sturdy pillars. Dedicated in 1990, the church hovers protectively over an excavation site believed to be the house of Peter where Jesus would have lodged. Franciscan excavators believe the house is in a small complex grouped around two irregular courtyards. The drystone basalt walls would have supported a roof of tree branches covered with earth. This flimsy roof arrangement is breached to lower a paralysed man on a mat for Jesus to cure (Mark 2:1-12).

Isaac now takes us to the panoramic hilltop site above Tabgha where Jesus delivers His Sermon on the Mount at the Mount of Beatitudes. The mountain is 175 m higher than the Sea of Galilee, yet 35 m under the sea level of the Mediterranean Sea. The site overlooks the northwestern shore of the Sea of Galilee and is one of the most serene places in the Holy Land. The vista extends across the water to the cliffs of the Golan Heights on the other side.

The Sermon on the Mount (Matthew 5:1-7:28) is a powerful summary of the fundamental teachings of Jesus. His proclamation of the eight Beatitudes begins with 'Blessed are the poor in spirit, for theirs is the kingdom of heaven…' (Matthew 5:3) The name Beatitudes originates from the Latin words *'Beti'*, meaning 'blessed', which is the prefix of each verse. The Mount of Beatitudes also is regarded to be the place where Jesus meets His apostles after His Resurrection, where He commissions them to 'go and make disciples of all nations, baptizing them in the name of the Father and of the Son and of the Holy Spirit' (Matthew 28:16-20).

The exact site of the Sermon on the Mount is unknown. Pilgrims commemorate the event at the modern eight-sided Church of Beatitudes built on the slope of the mount near the site of the fourth century Byzantine ruins. The modern church is built in 1938 for a Franciscan Order of nuns to a design by Italian architect Antonio Barluzzi. Interestingly, the church, monastery, hostel, gardens, farm and visitors centre were partly financed by Italian fascist dictator Benito Mussolini.

The octagonal-shaped church has colonnaded cloisters that blend elegantly with meandering pathways through the verdant landscaped gardens. The octagonal floor plan represents the eight Beatitudes and these are depicted in Latin in the upper windows. An altar in the centre is surmounted by a slender arch of alabaster and onyx. Around it, the floor has mosaic symbols representing the seven virtues (Justice, Prudence, Fortitude, Temperance, Faith, Hope and Charity).

Continuing our journey, we now drive through the city of Tiberias to Yardenit (Little Jordan) which is a popular Baptism site at the southern exit of the Sea of Galilee. Here the water flows into the Jordan River, eventually flowing into the Dead Sea located 100 km to the south. The Jordan River at Yardenit has a baptismal complex where Jesus is said to have been baptised by John the Baptist (Matthew 3:13). Every year over half a million tourists visit the site. Many Christian pilgrims from all over the world come here to perform baptism ceremonies, normally in small groups accompanied by a pastor.

We arrive to the large parking area on a sunny mid-afternoon and tourists are streaming into the centre. Inside are convenient dressing rooms and stairways to walk down into the waters. Groups of visitors are dressed in white robes ready for baptism following a prayer by the pastor. Isaac allows us half an hour to observe the scene or visit the restaurant and souvenir shop. The baptismal site on the banks of the Jordan is a scene of tranquillity and serenity, shaded by magnificent eucalyptus trees and the sweep of natural river flora.

On this warm and sunny afternoon I feel like plunging in and swimming the fifty or more metres to the opposite bank. I suggest to Avril that we paddle our feet at the water's edge below one of the narrow stairwells. Avril finds it refreshing and then it is my turn. She is bemused as I take off my shoes and socks ready to dip my feet into the cool calm waters of Jordan. Small golden fish surround my toes and start sucking at them. What a surprise! 'Pleased to meet you,' they seem to say.

We have time to share a refreshing drink before we continue the long drive, north to south through the fertile Jordan Valley and eventually to our hotel in Jerusalem. Israel enjoys a Mediterranean climate characterized by a hot summer and a cold rainy winter period. Isaac points out that the northern part of the Jordan Valley is several degrees warmer than adjacent areas. Temperatures of 40 C or more occur during the summers. Its year-round warm climate, fertile soils and water supply have made the region a key agricultural area.

Agricultural activity in the region dates back about 10,000 years. The export of produce from the valley to neighbouring regions begins about 5,000 years ago. The region's fertility is extolled in Old Testament (Deut. 31:20; Exodus 3:8). Modern methods of farming using portable greenhouses have brought about a sevenfold increase in the output of fruit and vegetables. Jordan, which borders Israel on the east side of the valley, has brought new areas under irrigation courtesy of the King Abdullah Canal.

Continuing south along Highway 90 towards the Dead Sea, the landscape gradually changes, becoming increasingly arid as it eventually dips to around 400 m below sea level. Flourishing in the area, thanks to modern irrigation methods, are date groves, vineyards and orchards. Flowers and vegetables grow in glasshouses. Occasionally we see shepherds attending their flocks of sheep.

This highway route travels through the disputed landlocked territory of the West Bank, a 5,628 sq km chunk of land east of Israel. It is home to 2.6 million Palestinians. Israel took control of it in the 1967 Six Day War and has allowed Jewish settlers to move in. About 500,000 Jewish Israelis are living in the West Bank in Israeli settlements (including 192,000 in East Jerusalem).The Palestinians consider it illegally occupied Palestinian land.

In 1967 Israel fought a war with Egypt, Syria and Jordan. Israel struck first, claiming that it was pre-empting an imminent Egyptian attack. Arabs disagree, casting Israel as the aggressor. In 6 days Israel routed the Arab powers, taking the West Bank and east Jerusalem from Jordan.

Israel has maintained control of the West Bank since the 6 Day War. For many Jews this is wonderful news because the West bank is the heartland of the Jewish State. Many Jewish Holy Sites here, such as the Cave of the Patriarchs in Hebron, were previously denied access to the Jews. Israel's control of the West Bank is by means of a military administration. This causes conflict in a territory full of Palestinians who are not happy about living under Israeli authority. Any future border resolution between Israel and the West Bank may have to involve a peace deal, probably through land swaps. So far, no set of leaders on either side has agreed on precisely where to draw the border.

Our road journey continues south bypassing the rich oasis city of Jericho, located near the Jordan River in the West Bank. At 250 m below sea level the city now supports a population of about 20,000. Israel handed over administrative control to the Palestine Authority in 1994. Many springs and date palms, in and around the city, have attracted human habitation for centuries. Jericho is perhaps the oldest inhabited city in the world, dating back to c. 10,000 BC to the Natufian Hunter-Gatherers. Archaeological digs have found the remains of more than 20 successive settlements in Jericho. The first permanent settlement developed near the Ein as-Sultan Spring in the Pre-Pottery Neolithic Age, c.9600 BC. Archaeologist, Kathleen Kenyon, discovered and excavated the Neolithic Tower that was built and destroyed in the Neolithic Age. She dates the 8 m tall by 8 m diameter tower to 8000-7000 BC.

In Hebrew the name Jericho means 'fragrant'. This area is the first destination of the Israelites into the 'Promised Land' when they cross the nearby Jordan River during the latter half of the Middle Bronze Age, c. 1200 BC.

The story of the Israelites begins with Abraham, about a thousand years earlier. God tells him to leave his homeland, promising to Abraham and his descendants a new home in the land of Canaan. Canaanites are identified in Genesis as descendants of Canaan, a son of Ham and grandson of Noah.

God commands Abraham, 'Take your son, your only son, whom you love, Isaac, and go to the land of Moriah, and offer him there as a burnt offering on one of the mountains which I will tell you' (Genesis 22:2).

Abraham trusts God, but he does not fully understand the mission that God is asking him to do. God leads Abraham to Mount Moriah where, in an act of faith, he obeys God and offers his son Isaac as a sacrifice. Of course, God intervenes and spares Isaac's life by providing a ram instead. Because of Abraham's obedience on Mount Moriah, God tells Abraham that his 'descendants will take possession of the cities of their enemies, and through your offspring all nations on earth will be blessed because you have obeyed me' (Genesis 22:17 -18). The Promised Land that God declares to Abraham is described in Genesis 15:18: 'To your descendants I give this land, from the river of Egypt to the great river, the Euphrates.'

God later confirms this promise to Abraham's son, Isaac, and Isaac's son Jacob, as recorded in Joshua 1:4. Later, Jacob's name is changed to 'Israel'. Jews believe that Jacob is given this name after wrestling all night with an angel. The name 'Israel' means 'one who wrestles with God'. 'Israelites' is one of the most common names for Jewish people in the Bible.

Jacob's descendants include 12 sons who become the heads of the 12 tribes of Israel; Judah is the leading tribe. Literally, a Jew means 'one from the land of Judah'. The word 'Jew' later is applied to any Israelite, regardless of his tribe. Jewish people are also referred to as 'Hebrews' (Genesis 14:13); 'children of Abraham' (Romans 9:7); 'daughter of Zion' (Zephaniah 3:14; Lam. 4:22; Micah 4:8; Zechariah 9:9; Isaiah 52:2) and 'God's chosen people' (1 Kings 3:8; Isaiah 46:6; 65:9).

God wants the Jews to wait before giving them the Promised Land because 'the iniquity of the Amorites was not yet complete' (Genesis 15:16). God promises to remove the iniquitous Amorites from the land where one day the Jews will live. Eventually the Amorites are destroyed as the Lord predicted (Numbers 21:31-32; Joshua 10:10, 11:8). God's Plan includes sending the Jews to Egypt for 400 years. The Promised Land is not given to their descendants until Moses leads them in the Exodus out of Egypt (Deuteronomy 1:8).

The Biblical history now moves to Jericho with Moses looking westwards across the Jordan from Mount Nebo in Moab to 'the plain of the valley of Jericho, the city of palm trees' (Deuteronomy 34.3). It is Joshua who the leads the Israelites into the 'Promised Land', probably about 1200 BC. The story describes how the city is taken and destroyed in an unusual way. The Israelites are told to march right round the city once each day for six days carrying the Ark of the Lord. On the seventh day they circle the city seven times, whereupon the priests blow their trumpets and the people shout with a 'great shout', causing the wall to collapse and allowing the Israelites led by Joshua to enter the city.

At first the Israelites settle in the hill country and in the south. In the following century, the Canaanites suffer an invasion from the Philistines who may have come from Crete. The Philistines agree to establish a coalition of five city-states on the southern coast of Canaan. In the 10th century BC, under the leadership of King David, the Israelites are able to break the Philistine power and vanquish the native Canaanites.

The Israelites now turn their attention to Mount Mariah. At the summit of Mount Moriah is the 'Foundation Stone', or simply Rock, which is a holy stone inside the Dome of the Rock, a Moslem shrine on Temple Mount in Jerusalem. Modern Jews identify the rock with references in the Bible relating to Mount Moriah. The Temple Mount is thought to have been built over this natural hill, the tallest in the Old City of Jerusalem.

According to Jewish oral tradition, the Talmudic sages, the creation of the world began 5766 years ago at the Foundation Stone on Mount Moriah. Jews consider the Rock to be the place from which the rest of the world is created. They claim it to be 'the navel of the world' -- the first bit of the world to come into being. It is the location from where God gathers dust that is made into Adam, Cain and Abel. It is where Noah offers sacrifices to God. The Jews believe the rock to be the place where Abraham almost sacrifices his son Isaac. This is where an important royal Canaanite city was built about 4000 years ago by the Jebusites.

In 1004 BC King David captures the ancient Jebusite fortress of Zion in the city of Jerusalem. Thereafter, 'the stronghold of Zion' is called the 'City of David' (1 Kings 8:1; 1 Chron. 11:5; 2 Chron. 5:2). Jerusalem has been known as the City of David for more than 3,000 years. 'Zion' is eventually used as a name for the city of Jerusalem as well as for the land of Judah and for the people of Israel as a whole (Isaiah 40:9; Jeremiah 31:12; Zechariah 9:13).

The area on Mount Moriah is thought to have been a threshing floor owned by Araunah the former Jebusite king. King David buys the site for 600 shekels of gold, rather than confiscate it. There around the Foundation Stone, David builds an altar to the Lord, so that a 'plague may be held back from the people' (2 Samuel 24:18, 21).

David's son, King Solomon, builds a glorious temple on the same site, referred to as the First Temple. It lasts for over 400 years until it is destroyed by the armies of King Nebuchadnezzar of Babylon in 586 BC (2 Kings 25:9). Seventy years later the temple is rebuilt on the same site by the Jews who return to Jerusalem following their Babylonian captivity. Over the next 400 years, under a series of Gentile rulers, the temple is often repaired and defiled.

In 20 BC King Herod enlarges the temple which becomes known as King Herod's Temple. It is this temple that Jesus cleanses (John 2:15). There is a close association between King David and Jesus Christ (Matthew 1:1). Both are born in Bethlehem and die in Jerusalem; both rise from obscurity to be kings; and both are devoted to God. Jesus is a descendant of David from the tribe of Judah (Revelation 22:16).

The finishing touches of King Herod's Temple continue until AD 63. However, in AD 70, during the siege of Jerusalem, the Roman armies led by Titus, destroy the temple as predicted by Jesus (Mark 13:1-2). The Jews become a scattered race. Only a portion of a retaining wall remains from that era, known as the 'Western wall' or the 'Wailing Wall'.

About 500 years later, Mohammed and his teaching of Islam begins in the Middle East, as the Roman Empire is fading. According to the Quran (same as Koran), in 621 AD Mohammed makes a miraculous night journey on a heavenly steed, Buraq, from Mecca to Jerusalem to lead in worship at 'the farthest mosque' (Surah 17:1). He is lifted into heaven and returns to earth to carry on his teachings.

Fifteen years later, Caliph Umar builds a small mosque to commemorate the prophet's night visit. The Al Aqsa Mosque ('the farthest mosque') is built on Temple Mount in 715 AD, and then rebuilt in 754, 780, and 1035. In AD 691 the construction of The Dome of the Rock is built over the rock where Mohammad allegedly ascends into heaven.

Our guide Isaac is highly sceptical of Islam's mythical and military claim on Jerusalem because it lacks historical support. Islam comes way too late to lay claim to 'The Holy City'. Isaac explains, 'Jerusalem is mentioned 823 times in the Bible, but it is never mentioned by name in the Quran.'

Islam claims that Muhammad's night journey in 621 AD begins with Muhammad praying in Mecca, whereupon the archangel 'Gabriel' brings him Buraq, the heavenly steed of the prophets. Buraq carries Muhammad to the 'farthest mosque' which Muslims believe is the 'Al Aqsa Mosque' in Jerusalem. But this mosque does not exist before Mohammad's death in 632 AD. At the time Palestine has not yet been conquered by the Muslim armies and not a single mosque exists there.

It was not until Caliph Umar conquers Jerusalem in 637 AD, after Muhammad's death, that a prayer house is built on the site of Temple Mount. It is fanciful to believe that a flying horse can transport a man from Mecca to a non-existent mosque in Jerusalem, a return journey of more than 2000 km in a single night. It is fanciful to believe that Muhammad alights and tethers Buraq to the Western Wall and then leads other prophets including Adam, Moses, and Jesus in prayer.

On the same night is the *Miraj*, the second part of Muhammad's journey. On this journey, Buraq takes Muhammad via a ladder to the heavens where he tours the circles of heaven to speak with the earlier prophets such as Adam, Abraham, Moses and Jesus who died hundreds or thousands of years earlier (Adam and Abraham were never prophets in the Bible). On his tour through the seven heavens, Muhammad is taken by the angel Jibril to meet God.

Moslems used to pray towards Jerusalem, but, on the basis of divine intervention, Muhammad changes this direction and directs Moslems to face the Kaaba in Mecca. The Kaaba is a cuboid building at the centre of Islam's most sacred mosque, Al-Masjid al-Haram, in Mecca, Saudi Arabia. Thus, in 621AD, when Surah 17:001 (one of the 114 chapters in the Quran) is revealed, the Sacred Mosque already exists in Mecca. The 'farthest mosque' is apparently identified with places inside Arabia, either Medina, or a town called Ji'ranah, about 10 miles from Mecca, which Muhammad visits in 630 AD.

The Umayyad Dynasty conquers and rules Palestine from 661 to 750 AD. The first Umayyad ruler, Muawiya, chooses Jerusalem as the place where he ascends to the caliphate. He and his successors engage in a construction program in the city, building religious structures, a palace and roads. They treat Jerusalem as their administrative capital. In 688-691 Caliph Amir Abd-ul-Malik builds the Dome on the Rock, right on the spot of the Jewish Temple. In 715 AD the Umayyad caliphate builds a second mosque on the Temple Mount and calls this one 'the farthest mosque', the al Masjid al Aqsa. In doing so, the Umayyad falsify history by giving Jerusalem a role in Mohammed's life and inserting Jerusalem into the Quran.

Jerusalem is never mentioned in the Quran and Muhammad never visits it. Islam's mythical and militant claim on Jerusalem is entirely without historical support. Rewards offering a million dollars have been offered for anyone finding 'Jerusalem' in the Koran (Quran).

This rock on Mount Moriah is the same one identified by Christians and Jews as the place where Abraham offered Isaac as a sacrifice; The Dome of the Rock edifice is believed to stand directly over the site where the Holy of Holies of both Solomon's Temple and Herod's Temple once stood. During the Crusades, Christians take temporary control of the Temple Mount, and the Al Aqsa Mosque is used as a palace and a church in 1099.

According to the Bible, the God, that first called Abraham to Mount Moriah, still has plans for that place. The City of David is the place where Jesus is to reign in the future. The Bible indicates that a third temple will be built on the site of Solomon's Temple (Daniel 9:27). The final chapters of the Bible describe a New Jerusalem where God's people will reign forever, bestowing eternal honour upon the earthly City of David.

No doubt this presents a difficult problem, given the political obstacles standing in the way. The religious activities on the Temple Mount are currently controlled by the Supreme Muslim Council (the Waqf). The Jerusalem Islamic Waqf is a trust, established in 1187 to manage Islamic structures in Jerusalem. The ownership of Temple Mount has been hotly contested by the three major religions for two thousand years. It is the holiest site in Judaism, the third holiest site in Islam (Mecca and Medina the other two) and a revered holy site to Christians.

The land of Israel is central to Judaism. The Jews have lived in the Holy Land since its conquest by Joshua 3,200 years ago. But they have not always been in political control and have not always been the majority of the land's population. The Romans destroy their temple and exile them in 135 AD. But they have never given up hope of returning to their homeland. For a Jew, living outside of Israel is like living in exile.

For many years the desire to return to their homeland remains a vague hope for the scattered Jews. Then, in the late 1800's, Theodor Herzl and Chaim Weizmann founded Zionism, a political movement dedicated to the creation of a Jewish State.

Herzl is born in Budapest in 1860 and is credited with being the founder of modern Zionism. His parents, though Jewish, have no religious sentiment. In 1878 his family moves to Vienna where he studies law at the University of Vienna. He joins the Germans' Student Society but leaves after two years in protest over anti-Semitism. In 1884 he is awarded a Doctorate of Law from the University of Vienna. He leaves law and becomes the Paris correspondent for the Vienna Free Press. He feels little attachment to his Jewish heritage, but he is brought face-to-face with the problem of anti-Semitism while covering the trial of Alfred Dreyfus, a Jewish Captain in the French Military.

Dreyfus is unjustly accused and convicted of passing secrets to Germany. In 1895, following a court martial, Dreyfus is publicly stripped of his army rank, clapped in irons and shipped to Devil's Island in French Guiana. The Dreyfus Affair blows up into a virulent political battle that shakes successive governments. A heated debate ensues about anti-Semitism and France's identity as a Catholic nation and as a Republic founded on equal rights for all citizens. President Emile Louber pardons Dreyfus on September 19, 1899, but it is not until July 12, 1906 that he is officially exonerated by a military commission.

The charges against Dreyfus bring out a wave of anti-Jewish sentiment that shocks Herzl into realizing the need for a Jewish state. His ideas are met with enthusiasm by the Jewish masses in Eastern Europe. In 1897, Herzl convenes the first Zionist Congress, backed by Jewish financial support of the Zionist groups and the masses. Herzl works hard to find a territory for the Jews. Sinai, Cyprus, Uganda, Alaska and Siberia are considered. But the only land that truly inspires Jewish people worldwide is their ancient homeland, at that time a part of the Ottoman (Turkish) Empire known as Palestine.

Herzl does not see his dreams fulfilled. He dies in Vienna in 1904 of pneumonia and a weak heart, overworked by his incessant efforts on behalf of Zionism. Nevertheless, during World War 1, the Zionist cause gains support from Great Britain. In 1917, Lord Balfour, the British foreign secretary, writes to Jewish financier Lord Rothschild, expressing British Government commitment to creating a Jewish homeland in Palestine. The letter is known as the Balfour Declaration.

Unfortunately, at the same time, the British promise the Arabs their freedom if they help to defeat the Ottoman Empire which, at that time, controls most of the Middle East and portions of Saudi Arabia and northern Africa. Thus, The Balfour Declaration supporting the establishment of a Jewish homeland in Palestine runs counter to the promise made to the Arabs - that Britain would limit Jewish settlement there.

After World War 1, the newly formed League of Nations assigns Palestine to the United Kingdom as a mandated territory. Initially, many Arab leaders are willing to give Palestine to the Jews if the rest of the Arab lands in the Middle East are under Arab control. However, the Arabs living in Palestine vigorously oppose the idea of a Jewish homeland and of Jewish immigration into the territory. Many riots break out and the British come to believe that the conflicting claims are irreconcilable.

During World War II the Jews who try to flee Nazi Germany are often turned back due to immigration limitations at the borders of every country, including the USA, Britain and Palestine. Many of the Jews sent back to Germany end up in the death camps of the Holocaust.

At the outbreak of World War II my Uncle Arthur is among the first contingent of Australian soldiers on their way to help Britain. They encounter firsthand the problem of a Jewish homeland soon after they embark in Palestine:

'Early one morning we disembarked at El Kantara (Suez Canal) bound for Palestine. The ship's captain was on hand and shook hands with every last one of us. He wished each man well and hoped he would be back in the next few months to take us all home again… The fact that it was mainly flat, open country, sparsely populated, with not a lot to see, didn't matter much. It was a welcome change from the open sea. Then again this was Palestine, the Holy Land, and surely that meant something.

We were vaguely aware that there had been some Arab Jewish skirmishes going on before we left home. Now that we were in Palestine we found that the troubles were quite serious, and that there was a strong British military presence to keep both sides apart. British Army Units were stationed permanently in the Country, and it was subject to military rule. And we were required to abide by that rule.

A strong guard system had to be mounted and care had to be taken of one's rifle and ammunition, against theft. Being hundreds of miles away from any actual War zone, made these precautions fretful and irksome, and quite foreign to our former easy-going approach.

For a week or two now the Arabs and Jews seemed to have lost interest in each other. The men took this as a sign that a bit too much had been made of the situation in order to keep us under control. They began to get restless… One or two hardheads decided to do something about it and slipped away from camp. We were many miles from Tel Aviv, the Capital and nearest city. Somehow they managed to con a lift and to come back with glowing accounts of the delights and amenities to be had there. Contrary to our belief, there were little evidence of British Army controls and the British soldiers were able to visit there. This was downright discriminatory in our eyes and made us fret even more…

There was a small Jewish village called Rehovat just a few miles along the road to Tel Aviv. We would be permitted to go there on leave. It was a small village serving a small community and in no way geared with a sudden influx of troops. We found that in half an hour we had covered just about everything. It was just a poor substitute for the real thing and we quickly lost interest in going there.

Then there came an intriguing request that spread through the Unit like wildfire. One of our men had made an official application for permission to marry. The man concerned had organised a job for himself as Cook's helper, but he spent the greater part of his time running a fairly big two-up game… He mostly was untidy and smeared a bit from his chores. He was a tall, dark and lean bloke, that when dressed up could look quite presentable. But this happened so seldom that we could not figure out how he could be seen as instant desirable and marriage material.

The lady concerned had to present herself at our orderly room in connection with the application and she was a beauty. Officers and staff fell over themselves in a bid to make her welcome… She was a Jewess from Rehovat… smartly dressed and totally feminine. She returned a few times in connection with her application… Her man would be summoned, and on occasions during a two-up game, he was known to say, 'Bugger her. She can wait,' until summoned again…

There had to be an angle and for a while we couldn't figure it out. Then the penny dropped. Hitler had deported quite a lot of German Jews on a couple of ships to any country who would take them. Nobody would, citing mostly, that they had no papers. Germany wouldn't issue any, so they were forced to roam the world. Finally, in desperation, they ran their ships ashore on the beach at Tel Aviv and scattered into the countryside. Without proper papers, they were stranded here. Some were reputed to have quite large fortunes and investments in different countries, but only available to them if they could get there and establish their identities. This proposed union had to be a legal angle to overcome this problem… The marriage did go through…

At long last proper leave did come through and the monotony of isolated military life was lightened by touches of civilian living. We were able to go on one day leave to Tel Aviv and then Jerusalem. The modern everyday life of a large city like Tel Aviv made us feel civilised again. There were cafes to eat and drink in and the beach was a good one. In Jerusalem there was the fascination of the very ancient and of Biblical history. Those almost forgotten Sunday school stories now came to life at the scenes of some of those happenings. There was the Via Dolorosa, or Way of the Cross along which Jesus was driven before His crucifixion. There were the marked stopping places. There was the Dome of The Rock, an Islamic Temple (shrine) covering the stone Abraham is said to have prepared to sacrifice his son to God…

The British Military Establishment had a permanent School of Instruction set up at a place called Sarafand. Our Australian Establishment took advantage of this by sending along regular intakes for training… We asked the instructors what had happened during the troubles between the Jews and the Arabs. They told us of what had happened at Sarafand… Arabs had a penchant for creeping in and snatching a sentry. They would take him away and hand him over to their women. These playful ladies would disembowel him and fill his stomach with stones. They would then cut off his genitals, stuff them in his mouth and sew his lips together. They would hand his body back to their men who return and leave it in the centre of the Barrack Square, all this without being seen. The impact on morale could only be imagined.'

The British are unable to come up with a solution that will satisfy either Jews or Arabs, so after World War II, they hand the problem to the newly-founded United Nations. They develop a partition plan, dividing Palestine into Jewish and Arab portions. The plan is ratified in November 1947. The British troops pull out of Palestine when the mandate expires on May 14, 1948. The outraged Arabs fight a year-long war to drive the Jews out. The new state of Israel wins this war and every subsequent Arab-Israeli War since then. The Arabs keep losing territory every time they attack, but they have never given up hope.

Today, approximately 5 million Jews live in Israel, more than a third of the world's Jewish population. The Jews make up 80 percent of the inhabitants in Israel. Non-Jews who become citizens of Israel have the same legal rights as the Jewish citizens. About half of all Israelis are Mizrachim, descended from Jews who have been in the land since ancient times or were forced out of Arab countries after Israel was founded in 1948. Most of the rest are Ashkenazic, descended from Jews who fled persecution in Eastern Europe, or immigrants who came at various times. About one percent of the Israeli population are the black Ethiopian Jews who fled during the Ethiopian famine in the late 1980s and early 1990s.

Most Jews today support the existence of the state of Israel. But a small number of secular Jews are anti-Zionist. And a small group of Orthodox Jews object to the existence of the state of Israel by maintaining that it is a sin to create a Jewish state when the Messiah has not yet come. The Jews reject Jesus because He failed. Two thousand years after He came to the nation of Israel as their Messiah, Christ is still rejected by the Jews. In their eyes, they believed that the Messiah, the prophet which Moses spoke about, will come and deliver them from Roman bondage and they will become its rulers.

On the other hand, Christians believe in Jesus and accept Him as Lord and Saviour. They accept the Trinity – by claiming that God revealed Himself as one in three Persons: the father, Son, and Holy Spirit. However, Muslims reject the Trinity and claim Jesus was one of the most important prophets – not God's Son. Muslims do not believe Jesus died on the Cross. Allah would not allow his prophet to die a torturous death, so Allah took him up to heaven (Surah 4:157-158). They believe Jesus will be a follower of Muhammad when he returns to kill the Antichrist. Everyone who does not accept Islam will be slain. The Bible says Jesus was crucified then resurrected and ascended into heaven – in front of eyewitnesses. Christians believe that Jesus will judge the world in true righteousness when He returns.

Muslims believe that paradise can be earned through keeping the Five Pillars of Islam – 1. The **Testimony of Faith** (the *shahada*: There is no deity but Allah. Muhammad is the messenger of Allah); 2. **Prayer** (*salat*: Five ritual prayers must be performed every day); 3. **Giving** (*zakat*: Almsgiving is a certain percentage given once a year); 4. **Fasting** (*sawm*: Muslims fast during the Ramadan in the ninth month of the Islamic calendar); 5. **Pilgrimage** (*hajj*: Muslims must make the pilgrimage to Mecca in Saudi Arabia at least once).

Christians believe that sinful man can never measure up to the Holy God (Romans 3:23; 6:23). Sinful man may be saved only by God's grace through repentance and faith in Jesus (Acts 20:21; Ephesians 2:8-9)

Allah tells Muslims to kill anyone who rejects Islam, converts to Christianity, or becomes an atheist. Alternatively, Jesus tells Christians to love Muslims because He wants Muslims to join Christians in heaven. "You have heard that it was said, 'Love your neighbour and hate your enemy.' But I tell you: Love your enemies and pray for those who persecute you" (Matthew 5:43-44).

We are now close to our destination of Jerusalem. The road detours Jericho and passes the entrance to another Jordan River crossing, the Allenby Bridge. Continuing on, we arrive at the T-junction where you may continue southeast to the Dead Sea, less than 10 km away or head 27 km west to our destination in Jerusalem.

Arriving at sunset Avril and I take our first view of the Holy City from the Mount of Olives. Standing out in the fading sunlight on Temple Mount is the impressive Dome of the Rock. The golden dome of the famous Islamic shrine can be seen all over Jerusalem. This Islamic holy place on Temple Mount is built over a site that is sacred to Jews, Christians and Muslims. Commissioned by Caliph Abd al-Malik in 688 AD and completed in 691AD, the Dome covers the sacred rock where Muhammad prayed during his Night Journey from Mecca to Jerusalem and back to Mecca on a winged steed called Al-Buraq (Quran 17).

Some sources say that the Caliph's real purpose in building the Dome of the Rock was to erect a beautiful Muslim shrine to showcase the superiority of the new faith of Islam to both Jews and Christians. He wanted to emphasise the superior truth of Islam over both Judaism and Christianity. His building spoke to the Jews by its location over the sacred Foundation Stone

Measuring 20 metres across and 35 metres high, the roof of the Dome was originally made of gold, but was replaced with copper and then aluminium. The aluminium is now covered with gold leaf, a donation from the late King Hussein of Jordan in 1993. He sold one of his houses in London to fund the 80 kilograms of gold required.

The shrine is meant to outshine the splendour of Christian churches. Strangely, its rich ornamentation was the work of Syrian Christians. Its 'founding inscription', written in old Arabic Kufic script along the top of inner octagonal arcade, challenges the Christian belief in the Trinity and the Divinity of Jesus. It reads:

'O you people of the Book, overstep not bounds in your religion, and of God speak only the truth. The Messiah, Jesus, son of Mary, is only an apostle of God … Believe therefore in God and his apostles, and say not 'Three'. It will be better for you. God is only one God. Far be it from his glory that he should have a son.'

The Dome of the Rock symbolises the transformation of Jerusalem – once a Jewish city, then a Christian city, into a Muslim city.

Jerusalem today is a city both culturally and religiously diverse. It is located on a plateau in the Judean Mountains between the Mediterranean Sea and the Dead Sea. One of the oldest cities in the world, it is considered holy to the three major Abrahamic religions – Judaism, Christianity and Islam. Israelis and Palestinians both claim Jerusalem as their capital. Israel maintains its primary governmental institutions there; the State of Palestine untimely foresees it as its seat of power. However, neither claim is widely recognized internationally.

Our busy day ends when we reach the Grand Hotel. The Sabbath has ended and we must eat first before they allocate our hotel rooms. The checking-in time is after sunset and the rooms now must be prepared for our group. The harried staff members are unable to cope. Rooms do not get allocated till after 9.00 pm and some guests do not get into their rooms till after 10.00 pm. Then some find the rooms have been double booked. It is a shemozzle much like Faulty Towers. Avril and I do well to get our room key at 9.00 pm. I spend time catching up with emailing till then. We find our room comfortable and it contains an electric jug to make a welcome cuppa tea.

Day 25
Sunday April 6, 2014.

Jerusalem

I awake refreshed at 5.30 am following a good night's rest. The day is bright and sunny as we prepare for a day in Jerusalem and Bethlehem. It is springtime but we expect hot conditions nearing 30 C. The buffet breakfast is a bit of a scramble with at least 200 plus people jostling to find where to get what. There is plenty of variety, but it takes time to negotiate the crowded buffet. I do a good job of jostling to get back to my table only to find there are no spoons for my muesli!

At 8.20 am we start the day by visiting the Mount of Olives again. It is a long ridge to the east of Jerusalem, once covered with olive trees and the scene of many biblical events. At 820 metres it is Jerusalem's highest peak and offers a clear view of the Old City and its environs.

The Old Testament tells of King David fleeing over the Mount of Olives to escape when his son Absalom rebels (2 Samuel 25:30). The New Testament tells that Jesus visits here to pray or to rest. He often travels over the Mount of Olives on a 40 minute walk from the Temple to the little village of Bethany, about 3km from Jerusalem. It is a favourite place for Jesus to spend the night at the home of the siblings Mary, Martha and Lazarus. It is here in a cemetery just below the village that Jesus raises Lazarus from the dead. His sisters send for Jesus when Lazarus is dying (John 11:1-44). But Jesus delays His arrival until four days after the burial, 'so that the Son of God may be glorified'. Arriving at the tomb, Jesus calls, 'Lazarus, come out!' To the amazement of mourners, the dead man walks out. The miracle confirms the determination of the religious leaders in Jerusalem to have Jesus put to death.

Jesus goes down from the Mount of Olives on his triumphal entry to Jerusalem on Palm Sunday. On the way He weeps over the city's final destruction (Luke 19:29-44). It is here on the Mount of Olives that Jesus addresses His disciples, foretelling His Second Coming (Matthew 24:27-31). And He prays here with His disciples the night before He is arrested (Matthew 26:30-56). From here He ascends into heaven (Acts 1:1-12).

Many Jewish pilgrims used to sleep under the olive trees until the destruction of the Temple on Temple Mount in the Old City of Jerusalem. Roman soldiers camped on the Mount of Olives during the siege of Jerusalem which led to the destruction of the city in 70 AD.

From our viewpoint on the Mount of Olives, across the Kidron Valley, the morning sun illuminates the eastern wall of the Old City. The Old City, originally built by King David in 1004 BC, has always been considered the centre of the world. Ancient maps show Europe, Asia and Africa situated in a circle with Jerusalem at the centre. Over the centuries, Jerusalem has been cherished and glorified by kings, rulers and conquerors. Multitudes of pilgrims, students, beggars, merchants, warriors and slaves and tourists like Avril and me have come here to walk its streets. Jesus was crucified here; Jews built their Temple here and Mohammed rose into heaven.

The walled area of the Old City is now a 0.9 sq km centre within the modern city of Jerusalem. The Old City constituted the entire city of Jerusalem until 1860 when the Jewish neighbourhood of Mishkenot Sha'ananim is established.

In the centre of the Eastern wall facing us is the blocked-up double gateway known as the Golden Gate. The gate was built in the 6th or 7th century over the ruins of the second temple gate and sealed in the 16th century. It is also known as Beautiful Gate and the Gate of Eternal Life. It is a Holy site for the three faiths – many Muslim, most Jews and Christians see it as the place of the Last Judgement. Christians believe it is the gateway where Jesus entered on Palm Sunday.

The Golden Gate is the oldest of the eight gates in Jerusalem's Old City walls, and the only one not rebuilt by Suleiman the Magnificent in 1537-42 AD. The Golden Gate was walled up by the Arabs in 810 AD and has remained closed for 12 centuries.

Muslims expect Jesus to return to our world at the 'end of the age' to participate in the Final Judgement. Christians believe it will be Jesus who will conduct that Final Judgement. The Jews believe that the Messiah will descend the Mount of Olives on Judgement Day from the East and enter Jerusalem again through the Golden Gate (Zechariah 14:4-5). Hence the Golden Gate is also known as the Gate of Mercy. For this reason, the adherents to all three faiths have always sought to be buried as close as possible to the Golden Gate. The assumption is that the dead in the immediate vicinity will be the first to be raised.

In the Middle Ages the Jews are forbidden to bury on Mount Moriah. Instead they bury their dead opposite the gate and to the south on the Mount of Olives. This Jewish cemetery is the oldest in continuous use anywhere in the world. A plot here may cost $50,000 or more. The Christian cemetery lies in the Kidron Valley, sadly in poor condition. The Muslim burial area is on the eastern Temple Mount hillside. Their burial chambers are crammed up to and surrounding the Golden Gate.

Following the Ottoman conquest of Israel (1517), Sultan Suleiman the Magnificent rebuilds the crumbling walls of the Holy City of Jerusalem, from 1537 to 1542 AD, to protect its people against marauding Bedouins and from the possibility of a new Crusade. He seals off the Golden Gate in 1541, some say to prevent the Messiah's entrance. Muslim thinking is that a holy man would not defile himself by walking through a Muslim cemetery.

There have been attempts to open the Golden Gate and shatter an Old Testament prophecy that 'This gate shall be shut, it shall not be opened, and no man shall enter in by it; because the LORD, the God of Israel, hath entered in by it, therefore it shall be shut' (Ezekiel 44:2). In the Six Day War of 1967 some members of the Jewish military suggest catching the Jordanian defenders off guard by blowing open the sealed Eastern Gate. But the leader of the group, an Orthodox Jew, vehemently protests the thought, stating that 'the Eastern Gate can only be opened when the Messiah comes.'

In 1917 Muslim leaders in control of Jerusalem try to break the prophecy. On the exact day some workmen are sent to demolish the ancient stone gate the hand of God intervenes – the city of Jerusalem passes out of Muslim control into the hands of the British.

Our tour continues down to the Garden of Gethsemane near the foot of the Mount of Olives. The garden is well known to the disciples as it is close to the natural route from the Temple to the summit of the Mount of Olives and the ridge leading to Bethany. This is where Jesus goes to pray with his disciples on the night before he is crucified.

The garden is only 1200 sq m in area and contains ancient and gnarled olive trees. Some olive trees in Israel are over 3000 years old. The trees here give that impression, but all the olive trees were cut down by the Romans for their siege equipment before they capture Jerusalem in 70 AD. It is possible that the Gethsemane olives are descendants of those in the garden at the time of Christ because shoots come back from the roots when an olive tree is cut down. The treasured fruit from the Gethsemane olive trees is harvested each year and the oil is pressed for Gethsemane sanctuary lamps; the pips are used to make rosary beads and given to notable pilgrims to the Holy Land.

At this point we enter the **Church of All Nations** which is built over the rock on which Jesus is believed to have prayed after the Last Supper. The Gospels of Matthew, Mark and Luke tell that Jesus leaves eight of the disciples together in one place and he withdraws with Peter, James and John. He asks them to stay awake with Him while He prays. There they witness a taste of heaven in His Transfiguration – this is the miracle of dazzling brightness emanating from His whole Body, produced by an interior shining of His Divinity. The disciples explain that Jesus 'threw Himself on the ground' (Matthew 26:39) and in His anguish 'His sweat became like drops of blood falling down on the ground' (Luke 22:44). But the three disciples, all fishermen, used to working through the night, could not stay awake 'because of the grief' (Luke 22:45).

Then a group from the chief priests and elders arrive to arrest Jesus. They are being led by Judas, who betrays his Master with a kiss.

An atmosphere of sorrow and reverence pervades the Church of All nations as you step inside. The architect, Antonio Barluzzi, has designed the interior in semi-darkness to evoke the night-time of the Agony of Christ. Subdued natural light filters through violet-blue alabaster windows. In front of the high altar is a flat outcrop of rock which Christian tradition identifies as the Rock of Agony where Jesus prayed. Inside the ceiling domes are the national symbols of many donor countries that have contributed to the cost of its construction. The wrought-iron wreath around the Rock of Agony is donated by Australia. The wreath is the form of a crown of thorns with olive branches.

We now head across the road to our coach which drives us up the steep eastern slope to visit the Old City, opposite the church and Gethsemane. Today the Old City is roughly divided into four uneven quarters, known since the 19th century as the Muslim Quarter, the Christian Quarter, the Jewish Quarter and the Armenian Quarter. The current population of about 40,000 resides mostly in the Islamic and Christian quarters.

The Old City is less than 50 acres in area and is the hottest piece of real estate on earth. According to Jewish tradition, all of creation began in Jerusalem. The city is enclosed by 4 kilometres of strong protective walls built by Suleiman in the 16th century. The walls contain 12 m high notched towers for firing arrows or guns. Visitors may enter by one of seven gates. An interesting stroll around the Old City walls, with stops at the seven gates would take up most of the morning.

We stop at Dung Gate close to the gold-topped Dome of the Rock on the Temple Mount. For hundreds of years residents of the city took their trash out through this gate which offered easy access to a refuse site in the valley below. Dung Gate leads to the Western Wall in the Jewish quarter. The Western Wall is a 187 foot (57 m) high section of the ancient wall of Herod's temple that is the sole remaining remnant of the Second Temple destroyed by the Romans in 70 AD. The wall is on the western side of the Temple Mount and extends almost 500 metres. For the Jews this remnant of what was the most sacred building in the Jewish world quickly became the holiest spot in Jewish life.

During their 1,900 years of exile, Jews would make the difficult pilgrimage to Palestine just to have the chance to pray at the Western Wall. The Jews refused to abandon Jerusalem despite great expense, the dangers of disease, and lack of water and marauding bandits. A final insult awaited the visiting Jews during the 1000 plus years that Jerusalem is under Muslim rule. Arabs would dump their rubbish at the Wall to humiliate the Jews.

The Wall becomes known as the 'Wailing Wall' because of the endless tears, shed by Jews yearning to rebuild Jerusalem. Following the 1948 Arab-Israeli War, the Western Wall is captured by Jordan. Jerusalem becomes a divided city when the ceasefire lines are drawn and once again the Jews are banished from visiting the Western Wall. They are permitted only to gaze across the barbed wire barrier. But Israel recaptures the Wall in the 1967 Six Day War when their paratroopers enter the Old City through the Lion's Gate. There comes a triumphant cry, 'The Temple Mount is in our hands.' Grown men weep and dance – finally, after 2000 year in exile, Jerusalem is united under Jewish control, with free access for all.

Israel immediately razes Arab housing and mosques near the wall to create today's open plaza. Isaac allows us time to visit the wall. I must wear a head covering. A kippah is provided free of charge. The prayer area in front of the wall is divided into separate sections for men and women. Ultra-Orthodox Jews oppose women's prayer services at the Wall. They maintain that prayer services may only be conducted by males. They have been known to throw chairs and other missiles at praying women. Avril and I wisely separate at this point.

I wander over to the men's section and observe bearded Jews, book in hand, beseeching the Wall in fervent prayer. I see prayer notes inserted in the cracks of the Wall, a Jewish custom that was revived by the Israeli Defence Minister Moshe Dayan who was one of the first to reach the wall in the 1967 Six-Day War. Some American-Jewish newspapers carry advertisements for services that insert such prayers on behalf of the sick. The Hebrew expression 'The walls have ears' is claimed to originate from these visits.

Time does not allow a look inside the Haram esh-Sharif, or Noble Sanctuary, as the Muslims call the Temple Mount. The Mughrabi Gate is the only gate that the Islamic Waqf allows non-Muslim visitors to use for visiting the Temple Mount complex. It is open only a few days per week for a few hours of viewing. It is difficult to see anything more than the main features of the Temple Mount area, such as the Dome of the Rock and Al-Aqsa Mosque and the Islamic Museum.

The Pinnacle of the Temple Mount is the high point in the south-east corner above Kidron Valley. In 62 AD James the Just, brother of Jesus and pastor of the early Christian church, is martyred by being thrown down from the pinnacle. He survives the fall, only to be stoned to death while praying for forgiveness for his persecutors.

Stephen, the first martyr of the Christian church, is also martyred near the Temple Mount (Acts 6:8-7:60). Stephen is dragged out of the city through the Damascus Gate and is stoned to death outside the city. The gate that bears his name commemorates the traditional area where he dies. St Stephen's Gate is the Christian name of the gate which is also known as Lions' Gate. It is located on the north-east side of the Old City, close to the Golden Gate.

Our guide, Isaac, has arranged an assembly point at the arched entry into Moslem Quarter. It is close to Lions' Gate, the starting point of the **Via Dolorosa**. The most important and meaningful thing for Christian pilgrims to do while in the Old City is to walk the Via Dolorosa, the route that Jesus took between his condemnation by Pilate and His crucifixion and burial. It is a noisy experience with vendors vying for your attention. Old stone buildings rise up on either side of narrow crowded streets in a never ending Oriental bazaar where you are tempted to buy almost anything.

The Via Dolorosa, meaning 'the sorrowful way' is the 500 metre route which Jesus travelled on the day of His crucifixion, beginning near Lions' Gate and ending at the **Church of the Holy Sepulchre**. Christians believe the Church of the Holy Sepulchre to be the holiest place on earth. It is the site of the most important event in human history – the place where Jesus Christ rose from the dead.

Christianity begins not as a religion. Instead it begins as a movement of people who follow a charismatic preacher, a holy man named Jesus, on his wanderings as he does His teachings and healings. He comes to Jerusalem where Jewish priests see him as a trouble maker and a threat to the social order. So they organise the Roman authorities to have him executed.

His followers, a Jewish sect, now interpret the life, death and resurrection of Jesus as the most miraculous event in all history – an event which will have profound significance affecting God's relationship with the Jews and ultimately all mankind. From this backwater of the Roman Empire, the Disciples of Christ, particularly St Paul, will risk their lives in spreading the Good News throughout the Empire – right to the very heart of Rome.

The Romans try to beat down Christianity but fail. By the end of the 4th century Christianity has taken over the Roman Empire as the official state religion. It becomes illegal to do any form of public worship other than Christianity in the entire Roman Empire.

The triumph of Christianity is an extraordinary victory in the background of Rome's pagan and idolatrous world. The reversal begins with Jesus being executed by the Romans as a public criminal and a threat to the social order. Then three centuries later, in the face of Rome's threatening social and political problems, the Emperor Constantine legalizes Christianity. Now Jesus is hailed as a God, part of the one, true God who is the God of the new Christian Roman Empire.

Constantine becomes the enlightened leader and defender of the Christian faith. His father Constantius becomes the Western Emperor in 305 AD and spends some time in Britain putting down a rebellion among the Picts and the Scots. He dies at York and after his death the young Constantine brings his mother Helena to live at court at Byzantium, the capital of the Eastern Empire. Byzantium was the ancient Greek city founded by Greek colonists from Megara in 657 BC.

The Roman Empire is rocked by civil war in the 4th century and Constantine has to defend his position against different Roman factions. In the year 312 AD Constantine has a dream visualizing a flaming cross in the sky. Beneath it are words written in Greek: 'By this sign you shall conquer.' Luckily for Christendom there is a bishop nearby to interpret the vision. Constantine becomes patron of this bishop's branch of the church that has Old Testament as well as the New Testament teachings as part of its canon. Constantine embraces Christianity and orders a Christian symbol to be painted on his soldier's shields. He proceeds south to the Tiber, where his victory over the Emperor Maxentius gives him control of the Western Empire.

Constantine now becomes the Western Roman Emperor and soon after he uses his power to address the status of Christians by issuing the *Edict of Milan* in 313 AD. The Proclamation legalizes Christianity and allows for freedom of worship throughout the Empire. For a time Constantine stands by as others rule the Eastern Roman Empire. Then in 324 AD Constantine defeats Licinius and wins control of a united Empire. Soon after his triumph, he establishes the city of Constantinople (modern Istanbul) on the site of Byzantium, making it the new capital of the Roman Empire in 330 AD.

Constantine continues to embrace Christianity and he wants to resolve religious conflicts in order to eliminate confusion, controversy and contention within the church. The emperor sees quarrels within the church not only as a threat to Christianity, but also a threat to society as well. So in 325 AD he orders the Council of Nicea to take place and calls upon the church leaders to settle their disagreements and become Christlike agents to help bring about unity, peace and love within the church. The aim is to unify the Christian church with one doctrine of Christian faith, especially on issues of the Trinity, the deity and humanity of Jesus Christ. He prods the 300 bishops in the Council to make a decision by majority vote defining who Jesus is. The doctrine they produce is one that all of Christianity will follow and obey, called the 'Nicene Creed'. The Council of Nicea overwhelmingly affirm the Apostles' teaching of Christ – that He is the one true God and the Second person of the Trinity with the Father and the Holy Spirit.

Constantine's aged mother Helena converts to Christianity and is so turned on by the faith that she travels to Judea to make a pilgrimage on behalf of her son. In 326 AD she visits the Holy sites where the stories of Jesus take place. Helena is an old woman of nearly eighty and her aim is to clear the holy places of three centuries of accumulated debris. Christians living in Jerusalem at that time help to point out the location of Calvary and Jesus's tomb to Helena and her travelling companion, the historian Eusebius of Caesarea.

They claim that the Holy site is buried beneath Jerusalem's Temple of Venus (or Jupiter) which has been built by Emperor Hadrian a century after Jesus' crucifixion. Hadrian built pagan temples in the city after the Jewish revolt of 135 AD. Helena orders the temple to be torn down, and, with the help of Judas Kyriakos, she clears the mound that covers the Holy Sepulchre. They find three crosses buried in a cistern not far from the hill of Calvary.

Helena has Bishop Macarius of Jerusalem carry out tests to discern the True Cross. A sick woman of rank, who is near death, touches each of the crosses in turn. Her condition does not change by touching the first and second crosses. But the instant the third cross is touched her sickness is expelled and she suddenly recovers. Helena declares this cross to be the True Cross.

In 326 AD Constantine immediately orders the building of the Church of the Holy Sepulchre, which is completed by 335 AD on the site of the discovery by his mother. Constantine abandons the sacred space of the Temple Mount that is so important for the Jews. Instead he religiously relocates the centre of gravity of the city to the places where Christ has suffered, where He has been buried and where He has risen from death.

Constantine has other churches built on sites detected by his mother Helena. According to Helena's travelling companion, Eusebius, she was responsible for the construction of the Church of Nativity in Bethlehem and the Church on the Mount of Olives – i.e., the sites of Christ's birth and ascension. It is also claimed by Theodoret of Cyrus that Helena finds the nails of the crucifixion and has one placed in Constantine's helmet and another in the bridle of his horse to keep him safe.

Helena leaves Jerusalem and the Eastern provinces in 327 AD to return to Rome, bringing with her large parts of the True Cross and other relics, which she stores in her palace's private chapel, where they can still be seen today.

The True Cross is installed in the Church of the Holy Sepulchre until 614 AD when the church is burned by invading Persians. The True Cross is carried off to Ctesiphon and fifteen years later Emperor Heraclius recaptures it, keeping it in Constantinople and then returning it to Jerusalem. The restored church is destroyed again by Moslems in 1009 and then partially rebuilt. The Crusaders complete the reconstruction in 1149 and this is essentially the church that stands today. The sprawling Church of the Holy Sepulchre displays a conglomerate of architectural styles, bearing the scars of fires and earthquakes, deliberate destruction and reconstruction down through the centuries.

Miraculously the True Cross is recovered and remains in Christian hands for another 88 years. Defeat of the Crusader armies at the *Battle of Hattin* on July 4, 1187 allows the relic to fall into Muslim hands. Saladin is said to have tied the relic to his horse's tail and ridden through the streets, dragging it in the dirt. It is claimed that Richard the Lionheart tries to get the True Cross back, but it is never again in possession of Christians. Strangely, fragments of the cross continue to be discovered, bought and sold. The Christian reformer John Calvin would point out later that if all the existing fragments of the True Cross are assembled they would fill a large ship.

The Via Dolorosa pilgrimage has been followed since early Christianity. The pilgrimage down 'the sorrowful way' becomes safe to do so after Constantine legalizes the religion. Originally, the Byzantine pilgrims would follow a similar path to the one taken today; but they do not stop along the way. They do not know exactly where each specific event (called stations) takes place. But Helena shows them the precise spots that commemorate fourteen incidents that took place along the Via Dolorosa. These fourteen stations become accepted by Christian tradition, though five of these are not recorded in the Bible.

Each of the 14 Stations of the Cross along the Via Dolorosa is marked with a plaque, but these small signs can be difficult to spot. Fortunately, we have our guide Isaac to point us in the right direction. *Stations 1 to 9* lead us to the Church of the Holy Sepulchre: *Station 1* is Jesus's condemnation by Pontius Pilate. The event is said to have occurred at the site of Madrasa al-Omariya, a school 300 metres west of the Lions' Gate; *Station 2* is where Jesus takes up His cross. It is located next to the Franciscan Monastery; *Station 3* is where Jesus falls for the first time under the weight of His Cross. It is located near a small Polish chapel at the junction with al-Wad Road; *Station 4* is where Mary watches her Son go by with the cross and is commemorated at the Armenian Church of Our lady of the Spasm; *Station 5* is where Simon of Cyrene is forced to help Jesus carry His cross (Mt 27:32, Mk 15:21, Lk 23:26). It is located on the corner where the Via Dolorosa turns west off al-Wad Road; *Station 6* is located at the top of a steep hill. It is where St Veronica wipes Jesus's face with her handkerchief, leaving an image of His face imprinted on the cloth. The relic is now kept at St Peter's Basilica in Rome; *Station 7* is where Jesus falls for a second time, near the Franciscan chapel at the Via Dolorosa's junction with Souq Khan al-Zeit; *Station 8* is where Jesus consoles the lamenting women of Jerusalem (Lk 23:27-31). The site is across the market street and up some stairs opposite a souvenir Bazaar. Here we see a cross with Greek inscription, 'NIKA', meaning *Victory*, written on the wall of the Greek Orthodox Monastery of St Charalambos; at *Station 9* a Roman pillar, next to the Church of the Holy Sepulchre, marks the site of Jesus' third fall.

Stations 10 to 14 are all inside the Church. The square in front of the Church is crowded with pilgrims and the scene is difficult to come to terms with. A favourite song sung by Christians at Easter goes, 'There is a green hill far away, outside a city wall, where the dear Lord was crucified and died to save us all.' But where is it?

The Bible does not reveal the precise location of *Golgotha*, the Aramaic word meaning 'the skull'. *Calvary* is the Latin form of the word. Scriptures state that the crucifixion takes place outside the city of Jerusalem, though near it (John 19:20, Hebrews 13:12). Jewish law does not allow executions and burials inside the city. The Romans would select conspicuous places by major highways for their public executions. Undoubtedly, Jesus is crucified on a hill near a well-travelled road, since passers-by mocked Him (Mt 27:31, Mk 15:21, 29-30).

The Church of the Holy Sepulchre is inside the walls of today's Christian quarter of the Old City. The Bible requires that Golgotha lie outside the city walls. But this does not disqualify the Church as the authentic site identified by St Helen in 326 AD. The walls that surround today's Old City are not the same walls of Jesus' day. They are the expanded ones built in the 16th century by Turkish Sultan Suleiman the Magnificent.

Isaac gets us to turn hard right and ascend a steep and curving flight of stairs of about 5 m, rather than follow the majority of tourists into the gloomy interior of the ground floor which houses Christ's tomb. The stairs leading to Calvary open onto a floor that is level with the hilly outcrop on which Christ is crucified. This is *Station 10* where Jesus is stripped. On the floor of Calvary are two chapels, side by side, Greek Orthodox on the left, Catholic on the right. The liturgical decorations illustrate the vast differences between the Eastern and Western churches.

The Catholic **Chapel of the Nailing to the Cross** is the site of *Station 11*. The ornate Greek **Chapel of the Crucifixion** is Station 12. Between the two chapels is the Catholic altar of **Our Lady of Sorrows,** which is *Station 13* (Jesus is taken down from the cross).

Isaac takes us down another flight of steep stairs leading back to the ground floor. Here we see the Stone of Anointing, a long table length of reddish stone flanked by candlesticks and overhung by a row of eight lamps. Some pilgrims kneel and kiss it with great reverence, but it is not the stone on which Christ's body is anointed. On the wall behind the stone is a beautiful Greek mosaic depicting, in three parts, Christ being taken down from the cross, His body being prepared for burial and His body being taken to the tomb.

Isaac takes us away from Calvary to the main floor of the church which is crowded with a long line of pilgrims waiting to enter the stone Edicule containing the Tomb of Christ. This is **Station 14**. The entrance to the monument is flanked by rows of huge candles and Greek Orthodox priests are controlling admission. Inside are two chambers. The outer one is known as the **Chapel of the Angel** which has a pedestal containing a piece of the rolling stone believed to have been used to close the tomb. A low doorway leads into the **tomb chamber** which contains the marble slab where it is believed Jesus Christ lay buried for three days. In 1555 it was deliberately split by order of the Franciscan guardians of the Holy land, lest Ottoman Turks should steal such a fine piece of marble.

There is insufficient time for us to join the slow moving queue for a view inside the tomb chamber. Isaac advises us to continue the route through the Christian Quarter of the city to the Jaffa Gate where our coach awaits to take us to Bethlehem, the birthplace of Jesus. The highlight there will be a visit to the **Church of the Nativity** which will be our final stop before returning to our ship.

Isaac says that he has enjoyed our company so much that he wants to reward us with a gift which turns out to be a packet of Dead Sea mud. Avril and I look askance at each other as Isaac hands us our wonderful elixir. We are thinking, 'How will this flush down the ship's plumbing?' And it is as heavy as lead. 'Will it get through customs and how much will the excess baggage cost by the time we get to our final destination in Prague?'

Scientists still do not know why this mud, from the lowest place on earth, is so beneficial for the skin and body. Yet I am told that hundreds of clinical trials conducted in hospitals worldwide have shown that the high concentration of Dead Sea minerals is almost instantly effective in improving the skin's natural processes, easing rheumatic pains and providing inner calmness and tranquillity. The black mud, harvested from the banks of the Dead Sea, is in fact the alluvial silt washed down from the surrounding mountains and deposited on this inland salt sea. The mineral-rich mud contains high levels of magnesium, calcium, potassium, strontium, boron and iron.

We stop to enjoy a delicious buffet lunch at another kibbutz before continuing to the West Bank city of Bethlehem. In Hebrew, Bethlehem means *'house of bread'*. The city is perched on a hill at the edge of the Judean desert, about 9 km south of Jerusalem. Bedouin people from the desert, pilgrims and tourists are among the daily mix of cultures to be found in its town market and its narrow ancient streets. Along the main streets and ancient markets are shops selling jewellery and handicrafts of carved olive wood, a tradition that dates back to the beginnings of the town. In 1995 Bethlehem came under the administration of the Palestinian Authority, though Israel retains control of entrances and exits. Israel has built a separation wall which severely affects Bethlehem's economy and the movements of its residents. The barrier runs along the city's northern side.

Bethlehem is celebrated by Christians as the birthplace of Jesus Christ. **The Church of Nativity** is built over the grotto believed to be the location of Jesus's birth in a stable. The gospels of Matthew and Luke agree that Jesus was born in Bethlehem and raised in Nazareth. According to Luke 2:7, Mary 'laid Him in a manger because there was no room for them in the inn.' The Gospels do not mention a cave. However, less than a century later, around 160 AD, the writings of Saint Justin Martyr (100-165 AD) and others mention that Jesus is born in a cave. Today there are houses still existing close to the cave location. In those times the cave would have been used for stabling and storage – thus the use of the manger for His birth was practical.

In 326 AD, Constantine and his mother St Helena commission a church to be built over the cave. This first church is dedicated on May 31, 339. The octagonal floor plan is placed directly above the cave. In the centre is a 4 metre wide hole surrounded by a railing to provide a view of the cave. Portions of the floor mosaic survive from this period. Up to this point, the Romans have tried to wipe out the memory of the cave by planting a grove dedicated to the pagan god Adonis, lover of Venus. They establish his cult in the cave.

The place of Christ's birth is a dimly lit rock cave, far from the Christmas-card images honouring the birth. The Grotto of the Nativity is enlarged when the original church is built in order to make room for pilgrims, and the replacement of a silver manger is installed. Also beneath the church is St Jerome's cave. The scholarly Dalmatian priest does not approve of the changes: 'If I could only see that manger in which the Lord lay!' he pleads earnestly. 'Now, as if to honour the Christ, we have removed the poor one and placed there a silver one; for me the one which was removed is more precious…'

St Jerome (342-420 AD) lives an ascetic lifestyle and works in Bethlehem for 36 years from 384 AD. He spends 30 years in his underground study translating the scriptures from Hebrew and Greek into Latin. Known as the 'Vulgate', it remains the authoritative version for Catholics until the 20th century. St Jerome is the great patron saint of libraries and of translators. He dies in 420 AD and his body is later transferred to Constantinople and then to Rome, where his bones now rest in the Basilica of St Mary Major.

St Helena's church is burnt down and destroyed in a revolt between the Jews and Samaritans around 530 AD. It is rebuilt in its present form in 565 AD by Byzantine Emperor Justinian 1. The Persians spare the church during their invasion in 614 AD because, according to legend, their commander Shahrbaraz is moved by the depiction inside the church of the Three Magi wearing Persian clothing.

The Crusaders take Jerusalem on June 1099 and the church is used primarily as a coronation church for Crusader kings. Baldwin I and II are crowned there. In 1165-69 the Franks and Byzantines cooperate to make repairs and additions to the interior of the basilica and the grounds.

The church is neglected in the Mamluk (1250-1517) and Ottoman periods, but not destroyed. In the 1482 King Edward IV of England sends English oak and tons of lead to renew the roof. Two centuries later the Turks loot the lead to melt into bullets to use in the war against Venice. The roof rots and most of the rich mosaics on the walls of the nave are ruined. Much of the church's marble is looted by the Ottomans for use in other buildings of the region, and some now adorn the Temple Mount in Jerusalem. Earthquakes in 1834 and 1837 and a fire in 1869 inflict significant damage to the belltower, the church's structure, and the furnishings of the cave on which the church is built.

In 1847 the theft of the religiously significant Silver Star displayed above the Grotto of the Nativity helps fuel an international crisis between the Russian Empire and the Ottoman Empire over the occupation of the Holy Places. The theft is seen as one of the catalysts of the Crimean War (1854-56).

In 1852, shared custody of the Church of Nativity is granted to the Roman Catholics and the Armenian and Greek Orthodox churches. The Greeks care for the Grotto of the Nativity. In 2012 UNESCO places the basilica on its list of World Heritage Sites. It is also placed on the List of World Heritage in Danger because damage, due to water leaks, deems it to be endangered.

We follow Isaac and approach a small low rectangular doorway in a fortress-like wall of limestone blocks. A sign above on the wall reminds us of ongoing repairs to the church. It reads: 'RESTORATION OF THE CHURCH OF NATIVITY -- PHASE 1: ROOF AND WINDOWS RESTORATON...' The doorway is just 1.2 m high and is known as **The Door of Humility**. It was created around 1500 AD to prevent looters from driving their carts in, and also to force even the most important visitor to dismount from their horse upon entering the holy place. Isaac jokes, 'This doorway has been here for thousands of years. Do not break it now. And there is a stair up here so watch your step as well.' For Christians it seems appropriate to bow low in the place where God humbled Himself to become man.

Inside, we find today's Church of Nativity cool and dark, and the bare interior has no pews. The nave contains 44 red limestone columns, thirty of which carry Crusader paintings of Saints and of the Virgin and Child. But age and lighting conditions make them hard to see. There are trapdoors in the floor of the nave which allow us glimpses of the 4th century mosaic floor, surviving from Constantine's original basilica. Isaac lifts one of the trapdoors protecting the ancient mosaics to reveal a complex pattern of geometric designs depicting birds, flowers and vines.

The basilica is now almost wholly a Greek Orthodox place of worship. The Armenian Orthodox owns the northern transept. The main altar of the Greek Orthodox section is adorned with icons and lamps and a service is taking place when we arrive. Steps to the right of the altar lead down to the Grotto of the Nativity where the Catholics have the site of the Manger and the adjoining **Chapel of the Manger** next to the Nativity Grotto. The Grotto is a rectangular cavern and a silver star in the floor marks the very spot where Christ is believed to have been born.

In the upper church, Isaac leads us through a door in the north apse to the adjoining **Church of St Catherine of Alexandria** which is the parish church for Bethlehem's Roman Catholics. The 19th century church shares a wall with the 6th century Church of Nativity. This is the church from where the Midnight Mass on Christmas Eve is celebrated and beamed from Bethlehem to a worldwide television audience. Christians in the Western world celebrate Christ's birthday on December 25, whereas the church at his birthplace still has 13 days to wait for the Greek Orthodox observance on January 7 and a further 12 days for the Armenian Christmas.

St Catherine of Alexandria is widely venerated as a 4th century Christian martyr from Egypt, though there are few reliable facts about her life. Tradition states that she is of noble birth and well educated. At the age of 18 she challenges the emperor Maxentius for persecuting Christians and worshipping false gods. The enraged emperor orders her to be tortured on a wheel, hence the term 'Catherine wheel'. She touches the wheel and it breaks so she is then beheaded. She is ranked with St Barbara and St Margaret as one of the most helpful Saints in heaven.

The present church is simple and modern. It was built in 1882 on the ruins of a 12th century Crusader church and the foundations of St Jerome's monastery of the 4th-5th century. In 1948, Antonio Barluzzi (architect of the Holy land) restored the church and created the beautiful cloister near the main entrance of the church. From atop the main entrance is a statue of the Virgin Mary and below her is the statue of St Jerome, guarding the courtyard. Inside the sanctuary is a window display showing St Francis and St Augustine in the Nativity scene. On the surrounding walls there is a painting of the Nativity scene depicting angels and St Joseph adoring the newly born baby.

A narrow stairway on the right hand side of the nave leads down into a complex of caves and rock-cut chambers containing a number of **chapels**. They include the **Cave of St Jerome**, who translated the Vulgate version of the Bible; the **Chapel of the Holy Innocents** commemorating the children killed by King Herod; **St Joseph's Chapel**, recalling the dream in which an angel warns Joseph to take the Holy Family to Egypt; **Chapels of St Paula** and her daughter **Eustochium**, who travelled with St Jerome and helped him with the monastery; and the **Chapel of St Eusebius**, who led the monastery after St Jerome's death in 420 AD.

It has been a warm sunny day as our excursion comes to an end. From Bethlehem our coach takes about two and a half hours to reach Haifa. The ship is preparing to sail to Cyprus after a safety drill. Another group of about 100 passengers, mainly British, have joined the ship.

The Knights Halls, underground rooms, Acre.

Templar's Tunnel, Acre: juicing pomegranates.

Haifa Bay, view from Mount Carmel looking towards Acre, Israel.

Grotto of Annunciation in the Church of Annunciation, Nazareth.

Old Synagogue in Capernaum, a fishing village and centre of Jesus' ministry in Galilee.

Mount of Beatitudes overlooking the Sea of Galilee.

Church of Beatitudes at Mount of Beatitudes.

Christian Pilgrims at Yardenit on the Jordan River, a popular baptismal site.

Old City of Jerusalem, view from the Mount of Olives.

Gnarled olive trees in the Garden of Gethsemane.

The sealed Golden Gate in the Old City walls, Jerusalem.

Jews in prayer at the Western Wall.

Arched entry to the Moslem Quarter, Old City, Jerusalem.

A crowded street in the Via Dolorosa.

Entry point into the Church of the Holy Sepulchre.

Mosaic depicting the
birth of Christ.

Pilgrims entering The Door of
Humility at the Church of Nativity.

The Church of Annunciation, Nazareth, Israel.

Church of Beatitudes at Mount of Beatitudes.

Calvary.

The Church of Annunciation, Nazareth, Israel.

CHAPTER 4

THE AEGEAN

Monday April 7, 2014,

Limassol, Cyprus

In dim light I stir to check the alarm which I forgot to set for 6.30 am. I still have 25 minutes of valuable snooze time. It's daybreak as the *Aegean Odyssey* sails towards Limassol, Cyprus, where we are scheduled to arrive at 8.00 am. At 7.15 am Avril and I are at breakfast in the Terrace Café as we enter the harbour. There is nothing exceptional to see like entering Valletta in Malta or Rio or Sydney, but the day is bright and sunny. The temperature is comfortable about 16 C, expecting a high of 24 C.

The Republic of Cyprus is an island country in the Eastern Mediterranean located northwest of Israel, south of Turkey, north of Egypt and east of Greece. It is the third largest island in the Mediterranean with an area of 9,251 sq km and third most populous with about 1.2 million people.

Limassol is a city of about 100,000 inhabitants on the southern coast of Cyprus located between two ancient cities, Amathus and Kourion. Our morning excursion will be to the spectacular archaeological site of Kurion, an important city kingdom containing many monuments which date from the Roman period.

The history of Limassol is largely known by events associated with the Third Crusade when in 1191 the English King Richard I, the Lionheart, captures the city from the renegade Byzantine ruler, Isaac Comnenus. On July 20, 1189, the future king of England is invested as Duke of Normandy and on September 3, 1189 he is crowned King Richard I in Westminster Abbey. On hearing the news of the fall of Jerusalem to Saladin, he and King Philip II of France agree to go on the Third Crusade. In September 1190 they arrive in Sicily where they learn that King William II of Sicily has died and his cousin Tancred has seized power. He has been crowned as King Tancred I of Sicily although the rightful heir is William's aunt, Constance, wife of Emperor Henry VI. He has imprisoned William's widow, Queen Joan, who is Richard's sister, and kept the money she inherits in William's will. Richard demands his sister's release and she is freed on 28 September, but without the inheritance.

The presence of foreign troops on the island causes unrest and in October the people of Messina revolt and demand that the foreigners leave. Richard attacks Messina and captures it on October 4, 1190. He burns and loots the city and establishes his base there. This creates tension between the two kings, Richard and Phillip. But Richard stays in Messina until Tancred agrees to sign a treaty on March 4, 1191. The Treaty is signed by Richard, Phillip and Tancred. Under the terms, Joan is to have 20,000 ounces of gold as compensation for her inheritance. Also,

Richard proclaims his nephew, Arthur of Brittany, as heir to Sicily to whom Tancred promises to marry off one of his daughters when Arthur comes of age.

Tensions mount between Richard and Phillip and the two kings meet to clear the air, including the end of Richard's betrothal to Phillip's sister, Alys, who is thought to have been the mistress of Richard's father, Henry II. Following the tempestuous winter on Sicily, Phillip II and his contingent of crusaders proceed to the Holy Land without the English/Angevin forces. On April 1, 1191, Richard's fleet leaves Messina for Acre but a storm disperses his large fleet. Richard's galley finds safe harbour on the island of Rhodes on April 22, but the ship carrying his sister Joan, the widowed Queen of Sicily, and his new fiancée, Princess Berengaria of Navarre, is missing. On May 5, after some searching, Richard's fleet sails into Limassol harbour on the south coast of Cyprus to find the ship carrying the royal ladies. They have avoided shipwreck but are in a precarious position aboard an unseaworthy vessel; they are in danger of being held for ransom if they go ashore. The survivors of wrecks have been taken prisoner by the island's Byzantine ruler, Isaac Comnenus.

Richard orders Isaac to release the prisoners and to return the treasure from his wrecked treasure ship. Isaac refuses, so Richard lands his troops and captures Limassol. Isaac avoids capture, but they face each other off in a battle at Kolossi, the later site of the Hospitaller Commandery. Richard puts the forces of Isaac to flight with no casualties of his own. The Byzantine ruler enjoys little support among the population because of his despotic rule, so they abandon him. Isaac surrenders and agrees to make peace with Richard by joining him on the Crusade. Richard returns to Limassol and on May 12 he marries Berengaria and has her crowned Queen of England.

Isaac changes his mind and tries to escape by fleeing into the mountains in an attempt to re-establish rule over the island. Various princes of the Holy Land have arrived in Limassol, particularly Guy of Lusignan. All declare their support for Richard and they capture the whole island by June 1. Isaac Comnenus surrenders to Richard a second time despite having three unassailable castles where he might seek refuge. He cannot trust his garrisons for their loyal support. He sets only one condition for his surrender – that he not be placed in irons. Instead Richard confines him in shackles made of silver. He dies three years later in Syria, trying to incite the Sultan of Konya to attack the Byzantine Empire.

Richard sees the strategic importance of Cyprus to the Crusader kingdoms, barely 270 kilometres east of Sicily. It is a fertile island, capable of producing grain, sugar, olives, wine and citrus fruits. But he is in a hurry to get to the Holy Land to join the siege of Acre before his rival King Phillip II of France can claim credit. He leaves Cyprus on June 4, 1191, exactly a month after his arrival. He cannot possibly rule Cyprus himself so, a year later in 1192, he sells the island to the Knights Templar for 100,000 pieces of gold.

Richard has made an agreement with the island's Greek nobility to let them retain their laws and customs. But the Templars seek to impose Latin rituals and excessive taxes on the population. Subsequently, within six months, following a bloody revolt against them, the Templars realize they lack the manpower to quell the rebellion. They are forced to return the island to Richard who promptly sells it a second time to his vassal and former King of Jerusalem, Guy of Lusignan of the French dynastic family. Following Guy's death, two years later, Cyprus passes to his elder brother and successor Aimery de Lusignan. He is recognized as King of Cyprus by Henry VI, Holy Roman Emperor. This begins the medieval kingdom of Cyprus, a stable Latin dynasty lasting about 300 years (1192-1489).

In 1473 the Republic of Venice assumes control of the island following the death of James II, the last Lusignan king. His widow Queen Catherine Cornaro reigns as figurehead. In 1489 Venice formally annexes Cyprus following Catherine's abdication. The Ottoman Empire frequently raids the island and in 1539 they destroy Limassol. In 1570 the Ottomans conquer the island following a full scale assault with 60,000 troops.

The history of Cyprus dates back to the Stone Age. A Neolithic village, Khirokitia, existed here around the 10th millennium BC. Cyprus is home to the oldest water wells in the world. Mycenaean Greeks settle here in the Bronze Age around 2,000 BC. Subsequently the island is occupied by the Assyrians, Egyptians and Persians. Alexander the Great seizes the island in 333 BC. Following his death it is ruled by Ptolemaic Egypt, the Classical and Eastern (Byzantine) Roman Empire, Arab caliphates, the French Lusignan dynasty, the Venetians, followed by the Ottomans between 1571 and 1878. It is placed under British administration on June 4, 1878 and formally annexed by Britain on November 5, 1914 in response to the Ottoman government's decision to join World War I on the side of the Central Powers.

Independence is granted in 1960. Violence between Greek Cypriots and Turkish Cypriots commences in 1963 and is still unresolved. Greek Cypriot nationalists stage a coup on July 15, 1974, attempting a union with Greece. This sparks the Turkish invasion of Cyprus. The Turks capture the present day territory of Northern Cyprus, resulting in the establishment in 1983 of a separate Turkish Cypriot political entity in the northern third of the island. The process leads to the displacement of over 150,000 Greek Cypriots and 50,000 Turkish Cypriots. The occupation is considered illegal under international law. The Republic of Cyprus, according to international law, has *de jure* sovereignty over the island of Cyprus and its surrounding waters, except for the British Overseas Territory of Akrotiri and Dhekelia administered as Sovereign Base Areas.

At 8.20 am our coach arrives at Limassol to take us to the Roman ruins at Kourion. Our guide is Julia, a tall slim middle aged Cypriot woman of olive complexion, smartly dressed in a neat black suit. She adds a thick Greek accent to her English, many words ending with the vowel 'a'.

Kourion settlement dates back to the 16th century BC and was recorded by numerous ancient authors including Ptolemy and Hierocles. It was also called *Curias* (Pliny v. 13) or *Curium* in Latin. The city endured from antiquity until the early Middle Ages.

Kourion Archaeological site is situated on the southern shores of the island to the west of the river Lycus (now called Kouris), Today the site lies within the Akrotiri Sovereign Base Area which is a British Overseas Territory. The site is maintained and administrated by the Republic of Cyprus according to the Treaty of Establishments. In 2012 the Cyprus EU Presidency ceremony was held in the ancient theatre of Kourion.

On route to the ancient Greco-Roman cultural site we pass lots of orange groves which formerly grew sugarcane. Julia says that Kourion's location once held great strategic importance in the Middle Ages and once contained large facilities for the production of sugar from the local sugarcane, one of Cyprus's main exports of the period.

Our first stop is at the House of Eustolios, a palatial private house of the late Roman period, with its stunning mosaic floors and unique complex of baths. It has a commanding view of the coastline. In the distance is Mt Olympus, the tallest peak on the island at 1951 metres. Some of us are distracted by the Red Arrows flying squad out on a morning training session from the nearby British Air Base.

A short walk away is the magnificently restored Roman theatre, built in the second century BC and enlarged in the second century AD. Up to 2000 spectators once watched gladiators perform in this arena. Today the site's wonderful acoustics and stunning sea views make it ideal for summer musical and theatrical performances. George, from our group, tests the acoustics by singing the French National anthem. He receives well-earned applause from those perched high in the arena. Three Aussie women criticize him for not singing Waltzing Matilda, so they make a brave but feeble attempt to outdo the fellow Aussie.

At 11.00 am we drive a short distance to the Sanctuary of Apollo which contains a sacrificial altar and a well-constructed bath house for the athletes. We move to a stadium where once Roman chariot races were held. Most of the stone work has been removed but you can still see the course outline. The circuit is probably a kilometre long, having two 300 metre straights and sharp corner turns of about 100 metres each.

On our return to the seaside town of Limassol we stop for a photo of the medieval Kolossi Castle. Today it consists of a single story keep within an attached rectangular enclosure, or bailey, about 30 by 40 metres. The former Crusader stronghold held great strategic importance during the Middle Ages. It is situated on a coastal plain on the southwest edge of Kolossi village, 14 km west of Limassol. The area was named Kolossi after its feudal lord, Garinus de Colos. In 1210 the fief was transferred to the Knights of the Order of St John of Jerusalem (Knights Hospitallers) by the Lusignan King, Hugh I.

The original castle was built in 1210 by the Order of St John. Having lost Acre in 1291, the Hospitallers transfer the base of their activities to Kolossi in 1301/02. Rival factions in the Crusader Kingdom on Cyprus lead to the castle being taken briefly by the Knights Templar in 1306. In those days the Templars are a very strong political power. But it is returned to the Hospitallers in 1313 when Pope Clement V issued an edict abolishing the Knights Templar.

The present castle was built in 1454 by the Hospitallers under the Commander of Kolossi, Louis de Magnac, whose coat of arms can be seen carved into the castle's walls. An opening above the entrance gate allowed the castle's occupants to pour boiling water or tar over unwanted entrants.

The area around the castle contains sugar cane plantations dating back to the 14th century. The area is also known for its sweet wine, *'Commandaria'*, possibly the oldest continually- produced and named wine in the world. It has been known for centuries as Commandaria after the Templars' *Grand Commanderie*, the seat of the Supreme military commandment there. The wine flowed at the wedding banquet of King Richard the Lionheart's marriage to Berengaria of Navarre at nearby Limassol. He declared it to be 'the wine of kings and the king of wines'.

We continue into the old town of Limassol to walk about the shops and to relax at one of the busy cafes in the main street. In front of us is the medieval castle which now serves as a museum. Limassol castle was built on the Byzantine Fort in the 14th century. Inside the old fort was the Chapel of St George where the marriage between Richard the Lionheart and Queen Berengaria of Navarre took place. He crowned her Queen of England in 1191 before going on to conquer Cyprus.

Avril has a latte and I enjoy a cool beer before returning to the ship. At 4.45 pm we attend the briefing for our next port of call tomorrow when we visit Tasucu, Turkey. Following this there is a wonderful lecture by Ernie Rea entitled, *'Saint Paul: Hero of Western Civilization?'* Ernie tries to reconcile the conflicting accounts of Paul's letters and what the author of the Acts of the Apostles has to say. Ernie considers why the main message of Paul's letters becomes so important for the subsequent history of Western Civilization.

At 6.30 pm we attend the Captain's Welcome Cocktail Party. We chat with Gaynor Rea, wife of Ernie the lecturer. She loves the story I tell of my Uncle Arthur, three times on the run as a POW in WW II. She is also interested in our four months of travel around South America last year. She was pleased to accept a voucher to download a copy of my book, *Cruising the Latin Tapestry,* which I wrote with Avril's help.

We are sipping our champagne with our new friends, Barbara and Robin. It is now 7.00 pm so Avril, Barbara and I retire down to the main restaurant for formal dining, seeing that we are all dressed up for the occasion. Another lady, Clare, from Toronto joins us to make a table of four. At 10.30 pm we decide on an early night as we have to be up early for a full day excursion tomorrow. I set the alarm for 5.30 am before retiring. We are scheduled to arrive in Tasucu Harbour, Turkey at 7.15 am.

Tuesday April 8,2014,

Tasucu, Turkey

My alarm wakes me as the *Aegean Odyssey* is approaching Tasucu Harbour. It is still dark as we take breakfast at 6.00 am. Sunrise is at 6.21 am and sunset at 7.12 pm. The ship docks at 7.15 am and our coach is ready for departure to Mamure Castle and the ancient city of Anemurium. We are issued with a Turkish landing card as we proceed ashore. The grey skies turn sunny and the expected temperature range is a low of 10 C to a high 20 C. Avril bravely wears shorts for today's outing.

Our guide for the full day excursion is Hande, a short nuggetty Turkish woman, delightfully cheery with a warm persona. We see a couple of long curved wings on the wharf and wonder what they are. 'They are wind turbines for power generation,' says Hande. 'The coastline is windy and they will be used to produce electricity,' she says.

We set off for the three hour journey that will take us westwards on a coastal drive to the ancient hillside city of Anemurium. It is located on a peninsula jutting into the Mediterranean which the Greeks termed 'windy cape'. The city was inhabited from the 4th century BC to the 7th century AD and reached its height as a trading centre under Roman rule. Many of the ruins date from that time.

The journey provides for spectacular coastal scenery of the blue Mediterranean. The mountainous road twists awkwardly before descending to Anamur, a lovely coastal village of summer houses and small farms. On a clear day it is possible to see the silhouette of the island of Cyprus, about 64 kilometres away. Hande points out a group of nomads camped on a hillside and their accompanying herd of goats. 'There are still nomads here in Anatolia, probably about 1700,' she says. 'The government is trying to get education to the children.'

Hande continues, 'Turkey is the only country that is in Europe and Asia. When you get to Istanbul you will be on the European side. Here we are in the Asian side, called Anatolia.'

At Anamur we observe many glass houses which grow bananas and strawberries. Hande announces, 'The bananas here are not the big ones that come from South America. They are smaller, but very sweet and tasty. We grow figs, apricots and olives. From the olives a fragrant perfume is made using crushed grape leaves and flowers mixed with olive oil.'

Hande now provides a brief outline on historical events. 'The Ottoman Turks led by Osman in 1300 established an empire that extended from Vienna down to Egypt and across North Africa to Morocco and into Spain. It lasted for over 700 years until WW I. Then the Turkish Republic commenced following an Independence War led by Mustafa Kemal Ataturk. The last Sultan of the Ottomans and his entourage were forced to leave for Europe and other places. Some didn't even know how to live because they were used to having everything done for them.'

'April 23 is our National Day. In 1924 a New Constitution was drawn up and the country was modernised. Turkey at the time was worn out from the war. It was a tired country with not many young left and they were poorly educated. We changed the education system and the alphabet to Latin. We adopted the Swedish system of Law. For example, in a divorce there was an equal split of property. The dress style changed -- no longer Fez caps or pantaloons. The transport was improved to provide for a railway network. Ankara was selected as the capital and political head. But Istanbul remains the economic powerhouse with a population of more than 15 million people. The minimum wage here is about $600 US per month. Teachers get about double that. Family ties are important. There are no homeless people because the families support one another. You'll find beggars in Istanbul, but they are refugees from Syria and other places.'

At 10.40 am we arrive at the ruins of Anemurium. The ancient port city is located about 6 km southwest of Anamur and built on the facing slopes of Cape Anamur at the southernmost tip of Anatolia. There is no information on when the city was founded, except that it flourished as a small Roman town between c. 100 BC and 600 AD. No ruins earlier than the Roman Empire have been found in the area. The fact that the city's name appears on a list of ports dated 4th century AD indicates that the city was in existence during that period. Ancient sources state that the name of Anemurium means 'windy place.' The first city walls were built in the first century AD, and the city was governed by Antiochus of Commagene for a period (38-72 AD).

Due to its proximity to Cyprus, Anemurium was a stopover, especially in the Roman Era. The city was connected via land to Germanicopolis, one of the most prominent Roman cities. Therefore, it became a major commercial city from where the natural resources of the region were being exported.

Anemurium was captured by the Sassanians (a Persian dynasty) in 260 AD. In the 4th and 5th centuries AD, pirates from Taurus Mountains ravaged the city frequently. In 650 AD, frequent Arab attacks caused the city to be abandoned.

Hande takes us through the complex as rain threatens. Anemurium city consists of two parts, namely upper and lower cities. The most monumental structures are located in the lower city where the stone walls are still partly intact and contain many mosaics. There are three public baths, a small theatre or Odeon, a large concert and meeting hall, the palaestra or wrestling and physical exercise area. Around the city walls are many single and double layered vaulted tombs which have wall paintings and mosaics. The mosaics testify to the wealth of a community that minted its own coins.

Rain starts falling as I observe this impressive site. I dash for shelter in the former ancient bath house until the rain eases. In its heyday it contained changing rooms, a hot section, a warm section and a hall with a pool. At the entrance a sign written in Latin says 'Welcome to the baths, have a good bath'. I don't need a bath. I catch up with Avril who is sheltering in our coach. We leave in pouring rain accompanied by a loud clap of thunder. This glimpse into Roman life poses some tantalizing questions about why this city was abandoned.

On our return we call into the town of Anamur to dine on Greek cuisine at a local restaurant. We start with Turkish bread and a selection of hummus, sea weed and salads, followed by lentil and bean soup. The main dish is savoury meat balls, chicken kebab and rice. The dessert is a very sweet chocolate profiterole. Water, tea and coffee are free, but some of our group prefer to take advantage of the wine and beer bar.

Our next stop is Mamure Castle which we passed on the way to Anemurium. The sight of its stark façade soaring out of the sea may once have struck awe in the heart of would be conquerors. Today its 39 towers and surrounding moat inspire photos, even though it is still raining. I forget to bring an umbrella so I am soaked by the time I dash down to the moat and the sea wall facing the Mediterranean Sea to get my Kodak moment of its impressive walls. Avril is more sensible and quickly returns to the coach. She graciously parts with her bright neck scarf which I use to towel myself down.

Mamure Castle was built by the rulers of the Armenian kingdom of Cilicia on the foundations of a fourth century Roman castle. Designed to protect against pirates, it is repaired during the Byzantine Era and during the Crusades. The Seljuk Turkish Sultan, Alaeddin Kaykubad I, captures the castle in 1221 and he builds a larger scale castle using elements of the earlier fortifications. The castle changes hands a few times before it is annexed by the Ottoman Empire in 1469. It is subsequently repaired in the 15th, 16th and 18th centuries and in that time a part of the castle is used as a caravanserai (roadside inn).

Continuing our return journey, Hande takes us to the Cave of St Thecla and the ruins of a church called Ayatekla. In early Christianity St Thecla is a young noble virgin who overhears St Paul preaching in her neighbour's house. Learning to fear nobody but God, she chooses to live in chastity. She converts to Christianity and is persecuted for her beliefs, but she survives life threatening situations. Authorities sentence her to be eaten by wild beasts, but she is saved when the female beasts protect her against the male aggressors. She travels, preaching the word of God, and becomes an icon by encouraging women to also live a life of chastity. St Thecla is revered by the Byzantines who build a splendid church in her honour above the cave where she shelters from her persecutors. The church, called Ayatekla, is now in ruins, but the cave beneath is a place of pilgrimage for Christians.

At 5.10 pm we are back on board the ship. Avril and I head for the bar for a Scotch and Dry. We sit with a couple who preferred to stay on board with about 100 others, rather than face the 3 hour road trip which was a highlight for us. We describe the scenic journey and I think they are having second thoughts about their missed opportunity. At 5.45 pm we attend the shore excursion briefing with Jenny Worwood for tomorrow's visit to Antalya, Turkey.

We again dine with Barbara Currie in the Terrace Café. Our friend Graham, who dined with the Captain in the Marco Polo restaurant last night, walks by and stops to chat. Tonight the captain is sitting with a couple of officers across from us. I say to Graham, 'I notice you are not dining with the captain tonight.' He smiles uncomfortably and whispers, 'I think I must have done my dash.' Graham then repeats a story that the captain painfully revealed to him. As a young officer his ship calls into New Zealand where he meets a wonderful Kiwi woman. He tells her that he will return to her. It is another two years before his ship arrives. He rings and her mother answers,' Oh Roland, you're too late. She married yesterday.'

Wednesday April 9, 2014,

Antalya, Turkey

During the night the *Aegean Odyssey* sails smoothly westwards, hugging the southern Turkish coastline of Anatolia facing the Mediterranean Sea. I am up at 6.20 am just before sunrise at 6.32 am. The weather looks promising despite the forecast of partly sunny skies with possible showers and thunderstorms, a low of 11 C and an expected high of 21 C. Avril and I will take our rain gear for the full day of shore excursions.

Our ship docks in Akdeniz Port, Antalya, slightly ahead of the scheduled time of 8.00 am. The cruise port is 15 kilometres from the small charming historic centre of Antalya which is now a sprawling modern city with a population of about two million. Antalya is the most popular resort destination in Turkey, attracting international visitors to its long sunny beaches, east and west of the city. The modern city of Antalya did not appear until after World War II.

The historic centre of Old Antalya, called Kaleici, surrounds the Roman harbour, once the city's port, now the yacht harbour. Many buildings here date from Ottoman times and a few from Roman times. Some have been restored as houses, boutique hotels and restaurants.

King Attalus II of Pergamon is looked upon as the founder of the city around 150 BC, during the Hellenistic period. It was named Attalea in his honour and served as a naval base for his powerful fleet. Attalea became part of the Roman Republic in 133 BC upon the death of Attalus III, nephew of Attalus II, who bequeathed his kingdom to Rome. The city prospered during Roman rule and was part of the Roman province of Pamphylia Secunda, whose capital was Perge.

Pamphylia is the narrow strip of land in southern Anatolia that curves along the Mediterranean Sea between Cilicia and Lycia. The region had seen centuries of Anatolian conquerors before the Romans: Hittites, Phrygians, Lydians, Persians, Alexander the Great and his successors. The Pamphylians, meaning *'of mingled tribes or races'*, were a mixture of aboriginal inhabitants, immigrant Cicilians and Greeks who became Hellenised in Roman times.

Along the Turquoise Coast, as it is known, we will be visiting the important Greek and Roman ruins at Perge, Aspendos and Side. Our first stop will be at Side, about 90 km from Port Akdeniz, one of the most ancient towns around Antalya dating back to the 5th century BC. Located on a peninsula and sandwiched between two stretches of golden beach, Side has the best of both worlds; the spectacular ruins of the ancient city and the modern shops and restaurants.

At 8.45 am we board the coach and meet our guide Yauze, a knowledgeable middle-aged Turk whose presentation is clear and concise. We are impressed with the drive through the sprawling modern city of Antalya. It sits along the southern coast of Anatolia on a narrow coastal plain protected from cool northerly winds by the impressive Tarsus Mountain Range. Yauze explains that the city's population has increased from 200,000 to over a million in 15 years. 'But it is not as big as Istanbul which has over 15 million and is the second biggest city after Shanghai (debateable). Turkey has 76 million people and the country is 300,000 sq miles in area (783,562 sq km), bigger than France, Germany and Texas.'

Antalya has a long pebble beach front and we see some people swimming in the smooth Mediterranean waters. A little further along a few rod fishermen have their lines out while they sit and chat in the refreshing spring weather.

'This beach will become very crowded in the holiday season from May to October,' says Yauze. 'Today will be a pleasant temperature in the 20s. In July and August is becomes very hot, about 30 to 35 C.'

He points to the high range of mountains surrounding Antalya. 'Those are the Tarsus Mountains and they average 3000 metres. You have heard of Noah's Ark and Mt Ararat. It is the biggest mountain in the range at 5165 metres. Look! You can still see some snow on those peaks. But down here the winter is pleasant.'

I am thinking, 'What an ideal place for a holiday. It's one of those few places in the world where you could spend the morning skiing and the afternoon swimming, all in one day.'

Our drive takes us past many modern apartments of six or more storeys in height, ideally located near the long stretch of beach. There are several well-maintained parklands, some with playgrounds and fountains. I overhear someone in the coach say, 'This is Turkey's Parramatta Road.'

The urban setting eventually gives way to lush farms, spreading over the fertile plain. 'We can grow anything here except coffee,' say Yauze. 'Farmers can get three crops a year and the hothouses can get four or five crops. We have orchards of citrus, olives, pomegranates and more.'

Yauze continues, 'We do not have any oil and our gas prices are the most expensive in the world… $2.50 US per litre and taxed at 17.5 %. Our speed limit is 70 km/h in the city and 90 in the country.' I am thinking, 'Wow! Gas is half the price in Australia and we complain.'

On the way we pass through the township of Serik, famous for its traditional oil wrestling. 'The men smother themselves with olive oil and the bouts often last until exhaustion sets in,' says Yauze.

At 11.00 am our coach arrives at Side – the name means pomegranate. Yauze takes us for a stroll through the busy bazaar area of the narrow peninsula to the end square in front of the small picturesque ancient port which traditionally served the Romans. A few leisure craft are berthed inside. One is full of tourists and it is about to take them on a cruise through the narrow entrance. In the square is a bronze statue of Ataturk the founder of modern day Turkey.

Yauze leads us to the edge of the harbour to the site of the Temple of Apollo which has several columns offering dramatic photo opportunities. We mix with several people armed with cameras, but no one is allowed to enter its reconstruction site. Ten minutes later we walk back through the bazaar to visit the ancient Roman amphitheatre, a huge complex which once served the ancient city of Side.

A few miles outside Antalya lay the isolated sites of Aspendos and Perge, (about 60 km and 30 km respectively from Port Akdeniz), once part of the ancient kingdom of Pergamon. Our coach drives to the site of Aspendos located on the Eurymedon River and splendidly backed by the Taurus Mountains. This was a major port in Roman times. In the fifth century Aspendos had become the most important city of Pamphylia. At that time the Eurymedon River was navigable as far as Aspendos and the city prospered from trade in salt, olive oil and wool.

To date only parts of Aspendos have been excavated, but the well preserved Roman theatre was one of the most spectacular buildings of its time. The theatre was built by two wealthy brothers during the reign of Marcus Aurelius in the 2nd century AD. The architect Xenon gave it a public entrance, dressing rooms, a colonnaded gallery, rows of marble seats and suites for the dignitaries, as well as a canopy to protect patrons from the weather. The founder of the Turkish Republic, Ataturk, asked that the theatre be used. The acoustics are so perfect that during performances, microphones are not even needed.

We continue our drive to the site of a marvellous aqueduct at Aspendos, an example of Romans engineering that brought water from the mountains to the city. At the site Avril is attracted to a stall selling pottery. She purchases four small decorative bowls and then gets conned into buying a lacy neck piece for 3 Euro. An old woman approaches and offers her a piece of cotton. The next instant a neck piece is thrown over Avril's shoulders and she is lassoed into buying it.

At 1.00 pm it is time for lunch at a huge restaurant in an orchard setting beside the Eurymedon River. Today it has to cater for our entire mob from the *Aegean Odyssey*, about 200 people. They do well with a buffet style meal as we hog into a selection of salads, hot food and the popular chicken kebabs straight from the BBQ oven.

After lunch at 2.15 pm we visit the Perge Archaeological site, whose impressive ruins date back to around 1,000 BC. Legend has it that the city was founded by two Greek seers returning from the Trojan War. Perge may have played an important role in the spread of early Christianity. It is mentioned in the Acts of the Apostles as a place where St Paul visited to preach. The inhabitants once worshipped the goddess Artemis, but the Virgin Mary took her place. We visit the basilica where St Paul preached his first sermon in 46 AD before heading out to spread the Word across the Eastern Mediterranean.

The stadium here is one of the best preserved in Anatolia, consisting of a large area where over 12,000 could watch athletic competitions. The vaulted areas under the seating once were shops and the owner's names were inscribed in the marble. Our guide Yauze takes us through the Roman Gate, the entrance to the city. We follow a fine colonnaded avenue that once took the ancients to their Nymphaeum, the Baths complex and the Agora. We see the results of ongoing work which is still uncovering this ancient city – the round towers, the Hellenistic walls and the grooves of chariot wheels in city streets.

Yauze points to scrubland that still contains much of the abandoned city following the fall of the Roman Empire. I am left wondering, 'Who was the last street vendor to make a sale before this magnificent city of over 30,000 people was finally abandoned?' The city eventually silted from flooding and remained covered until present and ongoing attempts uncovered its former glory. Yauze thinks the destruction of the nearby forests for fuelling the Roman baths may have caused erosion and silting up of the abandoned city.

At 5.30 pm we return to the ship in time for tomorrow's shore excursion briefing on Fethiye. At 6.15 pm following the briefing we attend Ernie Rae's lecture entitled *'The Orthodox Church'*. Ernie outlines the history, beliefs and practices of the second largest Christian Church and the dominant one in most of the areas through which we are cruising. He offers an analysis of the principal political and social issues confronting the Orthodox Church today.

The lecture ends at 7.00 pm and we head for a dining table in the Terrace Café. Once again we sit with Barbara Currie. She is happy to again text her daughter in Australia. Barbara has stayed on board since Israel rather than face the energetic shore excursions. We are tired too, but there is the Classical Concert with the *Odyssey Trio* tonight at 9.15 pm. We hurry back to our cabin to scrub up in time. It features works by Strauss, Rogers, Williams, Kalman and others: WEIN,WEIB UND GESANG (Wine, Women and Song) Op.333, Johann Strauss II (1825-1899); (Selections from) THE SOUND OF MUSIC, Richard Rodgers (1902-1979); UNTER DONNER UND BLITZ (Thunder and Lightning) Op.324, Johann Strauss II (1825-1899); GROBES POTPOURRI (from Die Csardastfurstin / The Gipsy Princess) Emmerich Kalman (1882-1953); (Theme from) SCHINDLER'S LIST, John Williams (b. 1932); ZIGEUNERTANZ (Hungarian Fantasie) Hans Zander (1905-1985); ROMANIAN RHAPSODY (arr. Odyssey Trio) George Enescu (1881-1955).

Thursday April 10, 2014,

Fethiye, Turkey

My alarm wakes me at 6.30 am, thirty minutes before the *Aegean Odyssey* is scheduled to arrive in Fethiye. A weather check from our porthole suggests more sunny weather with a forecast high expected of 18 C. We attend breakfast at 7.10 am and get ready for our excursion set to leave at 8.35 am. We will be visiting the ancient cities of Patara, Xanthos and Letoon.

Fethiye has a fine natural harbour which contains a flotilla of sailing vessels in its marina. A modern complex of shops and restaurants are a short walk from where we dock.

Contemporary Fethiye is located on the site of the ancient city of Telmessos, whose history dates back to 5th century BC. Telmessos was once the most important city of Lycia, a former geopolitical region in Anatolia on the westernmost section of Mediterranean Turkey, now in the provinces of Antalya and Mugla. Its ruins can be found all over Fethiye which is one of the few cities in the world where sarcophagi can be found on the streets. The city was renamed 'Fethiye' in 1934 in honour of Fethi Bey, one of the first pilots of the Ottoman Air Force, killed on an early mission. Fethiye is now a tourist town and an excellent base for exploring inland Turkey.

Our guide for the morning is Attilla, a chatty middle aged Turk of average height. His family settled in Turkey from Greece when he was a boy. He says he is Moslem but he smokes and enjoys a beer. 'It is my short cut to heaven,' he announces. This morning we will visit three archaeological sites of Lycian antiquity: the city of Patara with its impressive agora, Xanthos whose people won fame for valour in battle, and Letoon, once the area's most important sanctuary.

Some of Turkey's most intriguing ruins are to be found in the region known as Lycia, a mountainous place mentioned in Hittite records of the 14th century BC. 'Lycia means '*land of light*,' says Attilla, 'And Anatolia means '*land of the east*'. The Anatolia region formed about 640 million years ago, rising from a limestone sea base to form these mountains. They contain rich marble deposits for building. So geologically we are a relatively young country and the main problem is that the Anatolia region is still a bit shaky. In 1957 a big earthquake hit Fethiye.'

The views of the mountains, covered with a green carpet of pine, offer a perfect contrast against the turquoise of the Mediterranean coastline. This is a tourist's mecca and known as the Turquoise Coast. 'We have a dry season of almost no rain for 5 months. But the area stays green from the underground water,' says Attilla.

Our drive includes a rest stop before continuing to Patara about 80 kilometres from Fethiye. Attilla runs through the complex history of the area. 'We are the crossroads of civilization. Our history probably begins 13,000 years ago. People buried their dead so that their heads faced east towards the sun. 9,000 years ago urbanisation began. About 6,000 years ago there was a mixture of cultures arriving. Pirates of Lycia settled and peoples from the East arrived, the Cretans. The Hittites arrived in the 1250 BC from the north. From the east came the Mesopotamians. The Greeks came to settle following the Trojan War (c. 1194-1184 BC). The Persians came from the Far East in 546 BC, followed by the Athenians and the Spartans. Alexander the Great came next and we became part of his Empire. Then it was split among his generals when he died in 323 BC. Lycia saw an independent era from 168 BC to 43 AD, the first democracy in history. Then the Romans conquered and in 43 AD we became part of the Roman Empire.' George, a Sydney GP, congratulates Attilla for the brief history.

At around 10.00 am our coach arrives in the ancient city Patara. The story of Santa Clause begins here. Patara is the birthplace of St Nicolas, born on March 15, 270 AD. His wealthy parents, who are devout Christians, die in an epidemic while Nicholas is still young. Nicholas uses his whole inheritance to assist the needy, the sick and the suffering – obeying Jesus' words to 'sell what you own and give the money to the poor'. He dedicates his life to serving God and is made Bishop of Myra while still a young man. He becomes known throughout the land for his generosity to the needy, his love of children and his concern for sailors and ships. He is one of the Bishops who attend the council of Nicaea in 325 AD. He dies December 6, 343 AD in Myra and is buried in his cathedral church.

Once a thriving port, Patara counted Hannibal, St Paul and Emperor Hadrian as important visitors. Pilgrims came here to worship the shrine of Apollo and to consult the oracle. The Greek historian, Herodotus (c. 484-425 BC), tells us the oracle worked only part time because Apollo went on vacation in the summer. Patara's ruins include the impressive agora (market place), the newly evacuated theatre (until recently half buried in sand), and a fine Propylon that whispers of the past as it overlooks all the remains of the silted-up harbour.

We drive to Xanthos, the capital city of ancient Lycia, set above a bend in the river with commanding views of the entire valley. Here, Lycian ruins mingle with Byzantine basilicas decorated with fascinating mosaics. Lycians gained their reputation as fierce warriors here, twice burning their own city and fighting to the death rather than submit to invading Persians and Romans.

Our final stop is Letoon, the sacred cult centre of Lycia. The sanctuary site near Xanthos was one of the most important religious centres in the region. A well preserved theatre rises above the little village that surrounds the site. Attilla says, 'There are more than a thousand ancient theatres in Turkey and I've visited most of them.' He leads our group to the bottom of the theatre while I take a track leading to an archway above which was formerly the grand entrance to the theatre. Attilla directs the group below to look above to the grand entrance. At that moment I emerge through the archway and triumphantly raise my arms. Attilla announces, 'The king emerged through that archway and look there he is.' The crowd hails me as their king. From this vantage point I see a peaceful scene of a grassy paddock with a few grazing sheep.

We now walk along a pathway of very old olive trees towards the sacred temples. Attilla says that there are at least eighty varieties of olives in the region. Some grown near the sea have a nice salty flavour.

We come to a triad of temples dedicated to the three national deities of Lycia – Leto and her twin children Apollo and Artemis. The three temples reminded the Lycians of their archaic religious system, where female deities prevailed. Leto is the mother of Apollo, her womanish son, and Artemis, her mannish daughter. They form the heart of the sanctuary and are identifiable by their foundations. Parts of the ongoing excavations are half-submerged below a rising local water table. A population of frogs and terrapins add to the charm.

At 1.40 pm our coach is the last to return to our ship. It is lunchtime and the restaurant is crowded. We bypass the queue at the main servery and go to the outside balcony where delicious pasta is cooked and served straight to your plate. The queue at the servery has swelled by the time we have eaten our tomato and vegetable pasta as well as the selection of desserts and ice cream.

Later we enjoy a Scotch & Dry and at 6.00 pm we join the Happy Hour on the Observation Deck for a Pina Colada at the special rate of US $5 each. For dinner we select roast chicken, jacket potato and vegetables. We have the usual red wine and select a couple of cheeses from the cheese board, including Pont Leveque. The joys of shipboard travel are the choices of food and drink, until you get home!

Friday April 11, 2014,

Rhodes, Greece

I arise a few minutes before 6.00 am. Sunrise is at 6.39 am, about the same time as we take breakfast of cereal, fruit and toast. The weather forecast is mainly sunny with a possible shower and a high of 18 C. Rain fell overnight and there are heavy puffs of cloud about suggesting more rain. The *Aegean Odyssey* docks in Rhodes at 7.30 am, about half an hour ahead of schedule.

Rhodes is the principal city on the island of the same name in the Dodecanese, Greece. The Dodecanese are the furthest Aegean island group from the Greek mainland. The name Dodecanese means 'twelve islands'. Rhodes and Kos are the two largest and most fertile of the main group which includes about 150 smaller islands. Hugging the south eastern edge of the Aegean Sea and facing the shores of Anatolia, the Dodecanese are about 15 km from mainland Turkey. Their total land area is 2,670 sq km and about 200,000 people live on 26 of the inhabited islands.

The island of Rhodes covers an area of 1404 square kilometres and is one of the largest and most beautiful of the Greek islands. The population exceeds 100,000 and has 44 picturesque villages. The landscape mainly comprises of hills and low mountains, the majority of which are covered with forest. The island's climate is subtropical and healthy. The summer heat is moderated by fresh winds while the winter is nearly always mild, with long periods of sunshine. Water is abundant on the island and is exported to Greece.

Rhodes has been famous since antiquity as the site of the Colossus of Rhodes, one of the Seven Wonders of the Ancient World. The Colossus features in literature, in many poems, and famously in Shakespeare's Julius Caesar. The citadel of Rhodes, built by the Hospitallers, is one of the best preserved medieval towns in Europe, which in 1988 was designated as a UNESCO World Heritage Site. Unsurprisingly, the city has become a popular international tourist destination.

The city of Rhodes today contains the old walled city and the new one. Our ship is berthed within walking distance of the old walled city. The most important places within it are the Palace of Knights, the Archaeological Museum, the Byzantium, the medieval ramparts of the city, the temple of Venus, the Byzantine churches, the Hebrew synagogue and more.

The Dodecanese have had a turbulent history due to their strategic position en route to the Middle East. Rhodes in prehistoric times is inhabited by Telchines, Heliades, Phoenicians, Cares and Minoans from Crete. The islands are ruled by the Mycenaean Greeks from the 15th century BC until the arrival of the Dorian Greeks around 1100 BC. The islands develop a thriving economy and culture in the centuries of the Dorian period which sees Rhodes and Kos emerge as the major islands in the group. By the early Archaic Period, in the 6th century BC, the Dorians establish three major cities on Rhodes: Lindos, Kamiros and Lalyssos. These cities, Kos and the cities of Knidos and Halicarnassos on Asia Minor form a federation called the Dorian Hexapolis.

This development is interrupted by the Persian Wars around 499 BC and the islands are captured for a brief period. In 478 BC Athens defeats the Persians and the cities join the Delian League dominated by Athens. The Peloponnesian War breaks out in 431 BC and by the time it ends in 404 BC the Dodecanese are largely removed from the conflict, enjoying a period of relative peace and prosperity.

In the year 408 BC, the three cities of Rhodes unite to build a new capital on the northern end of the island, keeping the same name. The united Rhodes dominates the region for the coming millennia. Other islands in the Dodecanese also prosper. Kos is the site of the school of medicine founded by Hippocrates.

However, the Peloponnesian War has weakened the entire Greek civilization's military strength and it lay open to invasion. Between 336 BC and 323 BC Alexander the Great, King of Macedonia, sweeps through Persia and Asia, conquering an empire that stretches from the Balkans to modern-day Pakistan.

Following Alexander's death, the islands are split up among his many generals. The islands form strong commercial ties with the Ptolemais in Egypt. Trade flourishes throughout the Aegean in the 3rd century BC. Rhodes develops into a maritime, commercial and cultural centre. Its coins circulate throughout the Mediterranean.

The famous Colossus of Rhodes statue, erected by Greek sculptor Chares of Lindos in 280 BC, symbolizes their wealth and power. The enormous bronze statue is built to commemorate Rhodes' victory over invading Macedonians in 305 BC, led by Demetrius 1, son of Antigonus, a general under Alexander the Great. The large statue honours the Greek Titan God of the Sun (Helios), the patron god of Rhodes, and is one of the Seven Wonders of the Ancient World. It stands 31 metres tall at the entrance of the harbour and takes almost 12 years to complete.

The story of its construction begins after the death of Alexander the Great. His empire is split and a new scene for political struggles begins, in which the successors of Alexander fight for supremacy. The most important kingdoms are Syria, Egypt and Macedonia, of which Greece is still a part. These kingdoms are called Hellenistic, and the term is also applied to the whole period following Alexander's death until the final conquest of the Greek areas by Rome (c. 330-30 BC).

During the struggles among the different dynasties, Rhodes has to pay a price also. In 305 BC the city is besieged by Demetrius Poliorketes, a Macedonian king who is fighting against Ptolemy, king of Egypt. It is a typical dynastic struggle prompted by greed for more power. Demetrius wants Rhodes to take his side, and, when the Rhodians refuse, he besieges the fortified city. His attempt fails and the Rhodians sell the siege machines he leaves behind. In 280 BC they use the money to build the enormous bronze statue to commemorate the victory. In the same century, the mighty statue is destroyed in the earthquake of 226 BC.

In 164 BC Rhodes signs a treaty with Rome and the islands become important allies, enjoying privileges and friendly relations. Rhodes is an important schooling centre for Roman noble families. But these privileges are lost in 42 BC in the upheaval following the assassination of Julius Caesar in 44 BC. Cassius invades and sacks the islands. They are absorbed into the Roman Empire proper, becoming the 18th Province of the Roman Empire, which includes Crete. Titus makes Rhodes the capital of the *Provincia Insularum*.

In 50 AD, the Apostle Paul makes Rhodes a significant Christian centre and later it becomes part of the Byzantine Empire. Saint John also visits the islands several times. The apostles succeed in converting the islands to Christianity and fostering them to be among the first dominantly Christian regions. In 95 AD St John is exiled to Patmos in the northern Dodecanese where he writes the *Book of Revelation*.

In 395 AD the Roman Empire splits into Eastern and Western halves. The Dodecanese are included in the Eastern part which evolves into the Byzantine Empire. Here the islands remain for nearly a thousand years, apart from a few invasions.(In 620 AD the Persians conquer Rhodes and in 623 AD the Saracens (Muslims) take control.)

In the late 7th century AD, Rhodes, directly threatened by the Arabs, is fortified. A small but strong fortress rises for the first time to the northwest of the ancient great harbour. With the passing of time the defences expand and Rhodes gradually becomes an impregnable fortified city.

In 1249 Rhodes is conquered by Genoans who essentially rule until 1309, when the Knights Hospitaller of the Order of St John capture the island. The Knights built massive fortifications which prove successful in repelling invasions from the Sultan of Egypt in 1444 and Mehmed II in 1480. However, in 1522, the citadel of Rhodes falls to the forces of Suleiman the Magnificent. He arrives with a force of 200,000 men and 400 ships to subdue 700 knights and 7,500 men. This is the second and ultimately successful attempt to expel the Knights of Rhodes from their island stronghold. Both sides fight to exhaustion and a truce is declared which allows the remaining knights to march out of the town. They board 50 ships and flee to Crete and subsequently to Malta in 1530, from where the Hospitallers can continue their actions against the Muslims.

Suleiman's victory comes at a high cost, losing 20,000 men, but it secures Ottoman control of the Eastern Empire. The Turks stay several hundred years until 1912, when the islands are taken by the Italians.

During World War II, Italy joins the Axis Powers which use the islands as a naval base for staging their invasion of Crete in 1941. The islands become the scene of ferocious battles between German and British forces in 1943-44, after the surrender of Italy in September 1943. The Germans prevail in the Dodecanese Campaign. The islands remain occupied until the end of the war in 1945… even though the Germans are driven out of mainland Greece in 1944.The Dodecanese only join the Modern Greek state in 1948, after centuries of rule by Crusaders, Ottomans and Italians.

Our busy day on the island begins with a visit to Lindos, a destination of both historic and scenic interest, about an hour's drive from Rhodes. This Doric town rose to power hundreds of years before Christ and continued to thrive into the Middle Age. Our guide is Iphigenia, a pleasant and shapely Rhodian woman in her thirties, who informs us that Rhodes receives about 2 million visitors in the peak tourist season between May and October.

The drive passes several almost modern hotels which are empty. In a month's time most of the 100,000 rooms will be filled with tourists. Rain is threatening as we arrive at a high parking spot above the picturesque city. Eventually, the threatening clouds clear into a bright sunny day. The site offers sweeping views over St Paul's Bay where the Apostle is said to have sought shelter during a storm.

The Acropolis of Lindos is the main physical attraction on Rhodes. It sweeps upwards from the blue waters of the Mediterranean and requires a demanding but scenic walk to climb the pathway that leads to the top. Alternatively, it is accessible by 'Lindian taxi' – a hired donkey. The Acropolis is surrounded by the contrasting 12th century Crusader fortifications that cling to the rocks above the village. We wind our way through narrow streets full of souvenir shops to the summit where the Doric Temple of the Lindian Athena was built in the 4th century BC. The archaeological jewels at the summit are the double-winged portico and elaborate Propylaca, a gate on the edge of the precipice. The panoramic view of the whitewashed houses contrasting with the blue of the Mediterranean is unforgettable. Below us is the azure cove of St Paul's Bay where the Apostle landed in 58 AD. A favourite resort since the time of Julius Caesar, Lindos is home to writers, artists and craftsmen. Avril and I purchase some souvenirs at the small shops as we descend the pathway to the village.

At noon our coach continues on a delightful journey around the island to the Aegean side where we visit Besion Pottery factory for a pottery demonstration. By now most of us are more interested in getting back to the ship for lunch. But this well established craft factory and wholesale outlet has us fascinated. A craftsman, Demetri, shows his skills and forms a beautiful vase in little time. It will dry for four days before a pattern is engraved for firing in a kiln. Then another artist will add colours to the pattern and it will go in the kiln again. The results depict unique Greek patterns and symbolic scenes of high quality craftsmanship. Avril and I cannot resist purchasing a few pieces.

We return for lunch at 1.45 pm, an enjoyable tomato based pasta with a couple of mussels in shell. At 2.30 pm we head out to the old walled city less than 500 metres from the ship. We spend a busy three hours strolling through the cobbled streets which are full of restaurants and souvenir shops. Our aim is to visit two of the museums recommended by our guide this morning: the Archaeological Museum and the Grand Master's Palace.

We stumble across the Archaeological Museum which is rich in artefacts dating back to Neolithic times. On display are two exhibitions, inaugurated in 1993, celebrating the 2400th anniversary of the foundation of the city of Rhodes in 408/7 BC: 'RHODES RROM THE 4th CENTURY TO ITS CAPTURE BY THE TURKS (1522)' and 'ANCIENT RHODES – 2.400 YEARS'. One could easily spend the day here but we are pressed for time. The museum has an impressive display of mosaics, once featured on floors and walls of ancient homes. The figurines and statues are wonderful, particularly the beautiful naked figure of the goddess of love, Aphrodite of Rhodes. I declare to Avril, 'Look, that's Aphrodite. I recognize her from her breasts.'

We walk to the hill top where the Grand Master's Palace was built to serve as a fortress in times of war. The roughly square building, 80x75 m, is constructed around a large courtyard measuring about 50x40 m. It was built at the end of the 4th century to act as the citadel of the early Byzantine fortress. It continued in this role in the period of the Knights of St John (1309-1522). In peacetime it was the residence for the Grand Master as well as a meeting place for senior knights. Inside is a fantastic exhibit of items depicting life and culture in the time of the knights.

During the period of Turkish rule (1522-1912) the palace served as a prison. It continued this function under the Italians, until the decision was taken to restore the building. We leave the palace to explore the cobblestone streets of the Avenue of Knights which still exude a noble and forbidden aura. Its lofty buildings stretch in a 600 metre long unbroken wall of honey coloured stone blocks and its flat façade is punctuated by huge doorways and arched windows.

Searching for a way to our ship, we have coffee in one of the restaurants. Suddenly we realize that our ship leaves in 30 minutes so we ask for the bill. The coffee is strong and not particularly tasty. He wants 9 Euro which is double what we expect. Avril hands him 10 Euros and he hesitates to keep the extra Euro as a tip. Avril insists on the change so it comes in loose coins. 'I did not like the coffee which was too dear, so he wasn't getting a tip,' says Avril. We walk briskly and I pause to take one last snap of the ship in the harbour. The gangway is about to be hauled in. 'Hurry!' calls Avril.

Saturday April 12, 2014,

Santorini, Greece

My alarm wakes me at 6.00 am as the *Aegean Odyssey* sails in smooth waters towards Santorini. An hour later we are at breakfast and surrounded by the steep crescent-shaped cliffs of the volcanic island. Formally known as Strongyle or Thera in antiquity, the island is the remnant of a volcanic caldera and is largest in a small, circular archipelago of the same name. It forms the southernmost member of the Cyclades group of islands.

Our ship settles inside the beautiful deep dark blue harbour of Santorini caldera. We cannot anchor as the sea around is 380 metres deep. A flourishing civilisation existed on the island in second millennium BC until a volcanic eruption about 3,600 years ago destroyed all life there and much of the island sank beneath the waves.

The story of Santorini begins millions of years ago when Europe and Africa were still joined. What is today the Aegean Sea was once a land mass known as Aegeis which linked mainland Greece with Asia Minor and Crete. Following geographical upheavals, Aegeis sank beneath the surface about six million years ago and waves rushed in to take its place. The mountain peaks of the old mainland protruding above the surface of the sea are now the islands of the Aegean Sea.

At that time Santorini was little more than two or three insignificant islets. Then about 80,000 years ago a volcano appeared there. Ash originating from this huge eruption can be found on the seabed stretching from Italy to North Africa and almost to Crete. The crater poured out viscous liquid from the bowels of the earth to form a cone which gradually grew to cover the surface of the sea. It eventually joined up with the islets to form a circular island with a diameter of about 15 kilometres.

Around 2000 BC the island is inhabited by people who call it Strongyle, meaning Round Island. At that time the Minoan civilisation is reaching a peak on Crete. Then around 1450 BC a huge catastrophic eruption obliterates all life on Strongyle. The eruption of Santorini is one of the largest volcanic eruptions in recorded history (sometimes called the Thera eruption). The volcanic dome collapses and the greater part of the island sinks beneath the sea. All that is left above the surface of the sea are parts of its perimeter, like huge arms encircling a sea-filled basin - the Santorini caldera. These arms of land are the islands that we see today—Santorini, Thirassia and Aspronisi. Eighty-four sq km disappears to the bottom of the sea, almost half of the former island.

The eruption comes at the height of the Minoan civilization. The explosion may have resounded across Europe as far away as Scandinavia. Its vast pall of black smoke and ash covers the Aegean Sea and a gigantic tsunami 250 metres high rises up and races off at a speed of 350 kilometres an hour. In less than half an hour the huge tidal wave reaches Crete, 110 kilometres to the south, and may have led indirectly to the collapse of the entire Minoan civilization. Another popular theory holds that the Thera eruption is the source of the legend of Atlantis.

We could not have hoped for a more perfect day to visit a place which has been on my wish list, ever since the 1980's. Year after year I drilled my Grade 5 students about the huge explosion on Santorini that led to the theory of the lost city of Atlantis. I am looking forward to our visit to the site of the archaeological dig at Akrotiri where a complete town has been discovered under the ash.

Our ship remains adrift offshore as we are transferred by a local tender to Athinios where we join a waiting bus to visit the northernmost tip of the island to experience the unique village of Oia. High on the steep pumice heights are white painted houses that appear like snow-topped mountains. Our local guide is Nicolette, a beautiful young woman with golden shoulder length hair. She has the looks of the goddess, Aphrodite, and her knowledge of Greek archaeology holds us in the palm of her hand.

Nicolette informs us that she is from Athens and now lives in a village on Santorini. The island's population of 15,000 swells to three times that during the peak tourist season, including about 6,000 itinerant workers from other parts of Greece and Europe. She explains, 'Athens empties in the tourist season from May to August. They come to the islands. It's almost impossible to rent accommodation.'

Nicolette pours out more statistics, 'The huge eruption 3600 years ago caused a caldera to be created. The eruption buried the island in pumice. The most recent volcanic activity was in 1950 and the last big earthquake was in 1956. Pumice is quarried and mixed with limestone to form cement which has been exported.'

'The soil here is very fertile,' she says, 'the pumice absorbs humidity and irrigates the plants and grapevines.' She points to the grapevines that are small and circular like bird nests. 'They are shaped like that to protect the grapes from strong wind. There is no need to water the vines as they absorb moisture from the soil. The vines have been cultivated since historic times. Wine is one of our main exports. The wines are expensive, but pure and not mixed. We also grow cherry tomatoes to make tomato paste. We grow a local cucumber, egg plants and produce yellow split peas.' I notice a few Australian eucalypts flourishing here. Nicolette explains, 'We grow the eucalypt for shade and their beauty.'

'There are 14 villages on the island and Santorini is the southernmost island in the Cycladic islands. Delos is the birthplace of Athena and Artemis. Eros is another island in the Cyclades and is the birthplace of Homer. The houses are painted white to reflect the light and to create air conditioning inside. Here there are 300 days of sunshine. Our water is collected in winter and we need extra supplies from a desalination plant. Bottled water for drinking comes from Crete. Some of our homes are built into the ground to make them earthquake proof and to provide an even temperature.'

At 11.00 am we arrive at the village of Oia and we are allowed more than an hour to explore its whitewashed houses, blue-domed churches and coffee shops carved into the cliffs. In the perfect spring sunshine we stroll along the narrow cobblestone streets where wealthy sea captains built their mansions, now converted to cafes, boutiques and art galleries. We are spellbound by the breathtaking views in all directions. Avril buys me a Santorini cap to replace a hat I lost – a bad habit of mine. We purchase postcards and I forward one to our dance group back home. I add a fridge magnet to my collection and then we slip into a rooftop café for a morning coffee. Avril says to the waiter,' What a wonderful view you have here!' He replies, 'And I work here every day—pretty boring, huh.'

At 12.15 pm our coach drives to the southern end of the island to visit Akrotiri, the Aegean's most important archaeological site. Akrotiri was abandoned after the severe earthquakes in 1625 BC. It was covered in pumice by the volcanic eruption and forgotten except for the legend of the lost city.

Nicolette informs us that Professor Spyros Marinatos led the excavation in 1967, continuing until his death in 1974. The former Minoan settlement site was closed to the public for over six years and recently reopened following works to protect the excavations. Inside the protective covering we walk around this amazing city and get an insight into the culture that laid the foundation for Greek civilization. We view the streets, paths, squares, wall paintings, murals and toilets with flushing systems. The people knew how to build two-storey houses and they decorated their homes with colourful pottery and wonderful paintings. They tilled the earth and produced wheat and olive oil. They owned sheep, made cheese and fished. The value of Akrotiri is that it is the only original archaeological site in Greece, not a reconstruction.

At 1.30 pm we continue to tiny Pyrgos, once the capital, where we sit down to lunch at Pyrgos Tavern Restaurant. From its privileged location it offers stunning views all over Santorini. The modern circular shape building and adjacent windows offer a spectacular view of the Santorini caldera. The restaurant was recently renovated to provide a spacious area for reception and social events. It even has its own helicopter pad. Our lunch starts with a Greek salad, hommos and yoghurt followed by a tomato ball and moussaka. Dessert is a sweet cake, honey and semolina.

Following a short drive after lunch, our excursion ends at the beautiful village of Fira. It has historical and contemporary churches, souvenir shops and many stores of dazzling Greek jewellery. Local souvenirs include sea sponges, pumice and black basalt rocks. I am not tempted to add rocks to my luggage as I already have a heavy packet of Dead Sea mud from Israel. At 3.30 pm we return to our ship via a cable car which takes 3 minutes to descend to the awaiting tender shuttle below the village.

In our cabin we find an official looking envelope stuck under the door. It is an invitation from Matthew Swire, the Hotel Manager, requesting the pleasure of our company for dinner at 7.15 pm tonight in the Marco Polo Restaurant. RSVP is 4.00 pm so I need to ring straight away to confirm. At 5.30 pm it is time for a sundowner of whiskey dry in the Charleston Lounge. We chat with friends Peter and Judy from Sydney and at 6.00 pm we move to the Ambassador Lounge for a briefing by Jenny Worwood on tomorrow's visit to Delos and Mykonos. It is then time to scrub up and join the Hotel Manager for dinner. Two other couples join us for a pleasant evening.

Sunday April 13, 2014,

Delos and Mykonos, Greece

We are awake at 6.00 am and on our way to breakfast at 6.50 am. The sun beams its strong golden rays, heralding a lovely spring day. At 7.30 am the *Aegean Odyssey* anchors off the uninhabited island of Delos where it will stay until midday to allow us time to visit the ancient religious centre of the Cyclades. The island of Delos is situated near the centre of the Cyclades archipelago. It is one of the most important mythological, historical and archaeological sites in Greece. In the early 19th century excavations uncovered the abandoned ruins of a whole dead city. The excavations are among the most extensive in the Mediterranean. Ongoing work is taking place under the direction of the French School at Athens. Many of the artefacts found here are now on display at the Archaeological Museum of Athens.

At 9.00 am we take a tender ashore where we meet our guide, Kostantis, a handsome well-built Greek man. The archaeological site of Delos is unique, being located on a small, narrow, barren island 5 kilometres long and 1,300 m wide. The island is devoid of vegetation except for a good quantity of spring flowers growing like weeds among the ruins. On our long walk through the ruins we see a profusion of red poppies, daisies, statice, the inevitable Scotch thistle and more.

It is hard to believe that this small island, rocky and barren, once supported a flourishing economy and thriving culture for centuries. But its historical importance as a religious centre distinguishes it as one of the best known and highly developed sites in the ancient world. The majority of ancients chose Delos as the religious place and mythical setting for the birth of Apollo. This is probably due to the fact that Delos is bathed with sunlight from daybreak till sunset, unhindered by high mountain masses.

The name Delos in ancient Greek means 'visible'. It got its name because they believe it appeared from amid the waves. In ancient Greek myths, Leto is the representation of motherhood. She suffers many misfortunes because of her relationship with Zeus. Hera, the wife of Zeus, becomes enraged by his newfound love escapade, so she gives an order that no place is to receive Leto. When Leto is ready to bring Apollo and Artemis into the world, she cannot find a place to give birth. Zeus implores Poseidon to help him. Poseidon then strikes the sea with his trident, somewhere among the Cyclades, and the small island of Delos appears. The persecuted Leto takes refuge there and delivers two new gods of Olympus into the world, the twins Apollo and Artemis.

The first settlements on the island date to the Third Millennium. Probably the first inhabitants are the Carians, Leleges or Phoenicians. An important settlement develops on the island during the Mycenaean period (1580-1200 BC). Around 1000 BC, the Ionian Greeks settle on the island, making it their religious capital and building a temple for the worship of Apollo. By 700 BC Delos has become an important religious centre of worship. The island becomes a focal point for many pilgrims and a commercial harbour is established.

Domination of the island by the Athenians begins in the middle of the 6th century. In 550 BC, Peisistratos, the tyrant of Athens, thinks that the dead would infect Apollo. Therefore, he quarantines that section of the island that can be seen from the temple by removing all the tombs from there.

During the Greco-Persian War of 492-479 BC, Persia subjugates the Ionians of Asia Minor and the nearby islands. The Persian fleet loots the islands in 490 BC, but Datis does not inflict any damage on Delos. Instead he pays due homage to the sanctuary. During this period, the sanctuary on Delos loses much of its radiance.

Delos resumes importance after the defeat of the Persians. In 478 BC the first Athenian Alliance is created and Delos becomes the centre of Ionian culture as well as the headquarters of the Alliance and where its coffers are located. Gradually however, the influence of the Athenians increases and in 454 BC the treasury of the Alliance is transferred to the Acropolis of Athens, an event which leads to a storm of protest and condemnation.

In the years 426-425 BC a new quarantine of Delos is carried out. The Athenians, ravaged by plague, attribute the pestilence to the rage of Apollo, so they decide to appease him. They order the purification of Delos by transferring all their dead and their grave offerings to nearby Rineia – a hilly island four times the size of Delos and separated by a small strait of 700 metres at the narrowest point. Births and deaths are forbidden on the sacred island. Henceforth, all women about to give birth and all people on the verge of death must transfer to Rineia. During the same period, the Athenians establish a brilliant festival, the *'Delia'*, which takes place every five years. Pilgrims from Athens would travel to the sacred island to conduct a procession to the Temple of Apollo.

Delos becomes independent for a brief time after the end of the Peloponnesian War (404 BC). It is short-lived and in 394 BC the Athenians re-establish their dominance on the island. However, in 314 BC Delos becomes independent again and also the religious centre of an island alliance under the protection of the Egyptian Ptolemies who become rulers of the Aegean Sea. In 250 BC Delos comes under the influence of the Macedonian kings. The period 314-166 BC is an important period for the island as it gradually becomes an important cosmopolitan Mediterranean port with an average population estimated to be 25,000.

In 166 BC the Roman Senate decides to take control of Delos, making it a free port in order to supplant the trade at Rhodes. The Romans expel all the Delians, ceding control to the Athenians and establishing Athenian colonists. Delos is transformed into the most important harbour in the Aegean. The island's commercial role exceeds its previous religious importance. As a consequence of its rapid economic development, the population increases and its composition changes. The city has a cosmopolitan character. Apart from Athenians and other Greeks, Delos is the home of Italian, Syrian, Egyptian, Phoenician, Jewish and Palestinian settlers.

But doom is approaching. In 88 BC Mithridates, the king of the Pontus (historically, a region on the southern coast of the Black Sea), raids the island as part of a revolt against Roman rule. He destroys everything that is Roman. The sanctuary treasures are looted and the city razed to the ground. The entire population is slaughtered or sold into slavery. The Romans regain it, but the great era of maritime trade ends in 69 AD when Athenodoros pillages it and destroys whatever is left of the sacred island.

During the Middle Age and more recent times, a host of dealers in antiquities have passed through Delos and looted it. Even the inhabitants of the neighbouring islands frequently organize visits in order to take pieces of marble which they use in their own buildings. In 1872 the French Archaeological School begins a formal excavation which uncovers the main monuments on the island. Excavation is continuing on the 95 ha site where more than two thirds is still to be uncovered.

Our walk over the site with Kostantis covers four main areas: the **Maritime Quarter** next to the harbour, the **Theatre District**, the **Sanctuary of Apollo** and the **Lion District**.

The **Maritime Quarter** was the main residential area when the city was at the peak of its prosperity. Here we see the ruins of beautiful villas, some with fine mosaics still *in situ*. The House of Masks has the renowned mosaic of Dionysus riding a panther.

We move on to the **Theatre Quarter** containing the great classical theatre of Delos which could seat 5,500 people. Delian builders began its construction shortly before 300 BC. Next to the theatre is a huge cistern for the collection of water. It contains nine sections of well-preserved vaulted partitions.

The **Sanctuary of Apollo** was the ancient heart of Delos. It once contained three great temples dedicated to Apollo – *The Great Temple of Apollo, the Temple of the Athenians and the Porinos Naos*. Sadly, little remains for us to see of the temples. The construction of the *Great Temple of Apollo* began around 477 BC, but it was neglected after the treasury was transferred to Athens in 454 BC. The Doric structure with six rows of 13 columns measuring 29.6 m by 13.4 m was finally completed around 200 BC.

The *Temple of the Athenians* (built 425-17 BC) was a Doric amphiprostyle building with six columns on the façade and a total area of 17.8 m by 11.4 m. The inner chamber contained seven statues on a semicircular pedestal and was probably home to the archaic statue of Apollo. The third great temple, *Porinos Naos* (built 550-25 BC) measuring 15.7 m by 10 m was the original home containing the treasure of the Delian League.

The **Lion District** is renowned for the famous *Terrace of the Lions*. From the 7th century about nine elegant lions made of Naxian marble, a coarse-grain white marble from the Greek Island of Naxos, guarded the sanctuary, looking out to the *Sacred Lake*. The oval Sacred Lake, drained in 1926, is where the sacred swans and geese of Apollo were kept. A palm tree has been planted in the centre to honour the one which Leto clutched while giving birth to her divine twins, Apollo and Artemis. The lions we see on site are replicas.

Our excursion to this fascinating island ends with a visit to the museum which protects these monuments, including 5 weathered original lions from the Terrace of Lions. The Delos Museum has one of the most important collections for the history of ancient sculpture, and a unique collection of objects relating to the private life of the Delians in the Hellenistic period. On show is an abundance of pottery, clay figurines, and miniature works of art, as well as fascinating mosaics and wall-paintings.

At 12.30 pm we return to the ship by tender in time for lunch. The *Aegean Odyssey* then sails a short distance to the island of Mykonos, a whitewashed resort that is the very image of a Greek isle. It is called the 'white island' because the township is awash in pure-white painted houses, windmills, walls, laneways and staircases, which captivate tourists by the droves every summer. The abundance of white and the contrasting crystal blue waters of the Aegean make Mykonos one of the leading summer holiday spots on earth. Colourful flower baskets of geraniums and pretty creeper vines adorn stairways and window sills. This dazzling island reflects, opal-like, the sparkles of red or blue from painted window frames, roofs, doorways and railings. One can expect the sun and the sea to be in harmony here for at least 300 days a year. Of course, Apollo, the god of the sun, was born on the neighbouring island of Delos from whence we have come. And the island takes its name from Mykonos, the son of Anios who was descended from the god Apollo and the nymph Roio.

For a number of years after the World War II, Mykonos was little more than a way-station on a trip to Delos. The few island inhabitants led a poor simple life restricted to fishing and farming within the confines of its 88 km long hilly and picturesque coastline. Visiting artists and socialites loved to spend peaceful and carefree summer days here. Gradually, more and more people discovered its dreamy idyllic setting. Given today's mass media, the secret of Mykonos' tranquil lifestyle has spread worldwide and now the island has become a scene of excess summer madness.

We have only a short afternoon to embrace this welcoming scene. At 2.45 pm we take the ship's tender ashore for some free time in the township. The street area is a labyrinth of complicated passages, designed to confuse attacking pirates. The island was once the headquarters of the Corsair fleet and a place where pirates recruited for their ships. The cooling breezes that fan the island on hot summer days have played an important role in the naval history of Mykonos. For many years the island relied on this source of energy for its windmills and for its shipping, which was the main driving force of the economy.

In ancient times Mykonos becomes a member of the Delian (Athenian) Alliance, following the defeat of the Persians. Mykonos and the rest of the Aegean Islands pay a yearly tribute to the Athenians. Dominance by Athens lasts from 478 BC until 393 BC. The Cyclades avoid taking part in the campaigns of Alexander and his successors. Mykonos mints its own coins in this period. The island enjoys a period of economic prosperity following the seizure of the Cyclades by the Romans who proclaim Delos as a free port in 166 BC. This ends in 88 BC when Delos is destroyed by Mithridates.

In the Byzantine period, Mykonos belongs to the Maritime Theme, a kind of administrative division of the Byzantine Empire. The Venetians become rulers of the Cyclades in 1207. Their rule lasts, with brief interruptions, until 1537 when Barbarossa captures Mykonos without resistance. He abducts many of the inhabitants and others take refuge on nearby Tinos which is still under Venetian control.

In 1615 the Community of Mykonians is founded with a degree of self-government under the Turks. During the Turkish occupation, Mykonos develops into a naval island on which piracy is conducted. Mykonos sailors are regarded as the most experienced in the country. Out of a population of 3000 there are at least 500 sailors on the island. The absence of men away at sea means that there were 4 women for each man left on the island. More than 100 ships ply trade with Turkey and the Peloponnese. France, England and Holland have consulates there.

Mykonos is able to offer a significant number of ships and trained crewmen during the Greek War of Independence (1821-1832). The Turks attempt a landing on the island In October 1822. But the Mykonians, under their heroic woman leader, Manto Mavrogenous (1796-1848), successfully repulse the attack. The brave Greek woman makes a significant contribution to the fight for independence, using all her large fortune for armaments, personally taking her place on the battlefield and enlightening foreigners to support the Greeks in their struggle against the Ottomans. Liberation and the recognition of Greece as an independent nation come in 1830.

Today we visit these narrow winding streets, designed to thwart pirates. They are now lined with tempting souvenir shops, galleries and boutiques. Along the waterfront, near the area called Little Venice, the seaside cafes are ideal for drinks and coffee. This is where we head after a visit to view the windmills which are the most recognizable landmarks of Mykonos. Dating from the 16th century they were used for grinding grain for shipment when Mykonos was a major seaport between Venice and Asia. With ample year round supply of wind, Mykonos was the perfect location needed to refine grain and compact it for export. We walk around the edge of the town's harbour and up a steep hill to view the wind mills that now function as a tourist attraction.

On the way back we decide to take a short cut through the centre and end up guessing which turn to take. At one stage a church bell rings and a crowd of Greeks, holding arms, files through a narrow alley towards the church which is decked with floral wreaths in readiness for a funeral service.

Eventually we arrive at the busy waterfront cafes where I make use of their free Wi-Fi by ordering our drinks. The ship's satellite service, slow and unreliable, is next to useless. I am able to achieve email contact with our family and do some banking in a few minutes while I relax with a Heineken beer and Avril enjoys her latte.

At 5.00 pm we return to the ship and at 6.30 pm we attend the briefing for tomorrow's shore excursions to ancient Ephesus and the city of Izmir. At 7.00 pm we dine again with Barbara Currie. We have become good friends and she hands us her personal card hoping that we will visit her on the Gold Coast in the future.

Monday April 14, 2014,

Izmir, Turkey

My alarm wakes me at 6.00 am as we approach Izmir, Turkey. The sea conditions are smooth and the morning sky is overcast. The forecast is for partly sunny conditions with the temperature ranging from 11 C to 21 C.

At breakfast Izmir comes into view and looks nothing special from the dockside. But it is the historically important seaport hub for today's visit to the ruins of ancient Ephesus and the Izmir Archaeological Museum. Izmir has an impressive history stretching back to 3000 BC when the Trojans founded the city on the Bairiki Ridges. This is the birthplace of Homer who is thought to have lived here in the 8th century BC. The ancient city, known for most of its history as *Smyrna*, grows to become one of the most advanced cultures in Anatolia, alongside Troy.

The 5,000 year old city is one of the oldest in the Mediterranean basin, located at a central and strategic point on the Aegean coast of Anatolia. The ancient city of Smyrna rose to prominence due to its excellent and defensible port and its good position for inland trade. Izmir is now the second biggest port in Turkey after Istanbul. The modern city is now an important port in Turkey for exporting its various agricultural and industrial products. It contains a modern and busy commercial centre, set around a huge bay and surrounded by mountains.

In the first millennium BC Izmir, then known as *Smyrna*, ranks as one of the most important cities of the Ionian federation. The ancient city is known as *Smyrna* until the Turkish Postal Service Law of March 28, 1930 makes 'Izmir' the internationally recognized name. The original name is thought to have been taken from the ancient Greek word for myrrh, *'smyrna'*, which was the chief export of the city in ancient times.

Historical records indicate that the Aeolians are the first Greek settlers here. They are eventually taken over by their Greek Ionian rivals who flee from the Doric invasion of Greece around 1000 BC. The Ionians settle in Izmir and its surroundings. Izmir becomes richer through trade with its neighbours, especially Lydia. This lasts until the Lydians decide to conquer the city around 600 BC. Soon afterwards the Persians conquer Lydia. Then in 334 BC Alexander the Great ends Persian sovereignty, with his arrival to Anatolia. His conquests usher in the Hellenistic period. After Alexander's death, his generals follow his wishes and re-establish Smyrna on Mount Pagos in Kadifekale, a hill located within the urban zone of Izmir. The city becomes tied to the Pergamon Empire in 197 BC and then it passes to Roman rule in 133 BC when Eumenes III, the last king of Pergamon, is about to die without an heir.

Izmir prospers under Roman control. The Romans transform Izmir into an important trade and harbour city. At that time it is regarded in the west as the centre of Asia. The Romans build roads linking Kadifekale to Sardis, the ruined capital of the ancient kingdom of Lydia, about 80 km west of Izmir, and Ephesus, 70 km to the south of Izmir. Izmir is destroyed by an earthquake in 178 AD, but is rebuilt. In 324 AD the Roman Empire is divided into two and Izmir becomes part of the Byzantine Empire. Ephesus becomes an important cultural and religious centre in the classic Hellenistic, Roman and Byzantine period.

In 1076 AD, Izmir is conquered by the Seljuk Turks. It returns to the Byzantines in 1098, but it is taken over by knights when Istanbul is invaded by the Crusaders in 1204 AD. In 1415 AD Mehmet incorporates Izmir into the Ottoman Empire. Under Suleiman the Magnificent, it becomes a thriving, sophisticated city and a huge trading centre. Despite frequent earthquakes, it develops into a cosmopolitan city with a Greek Orthodox majority, Armenians, Jews and Muslims. Numerous languages, spoken by locals and visiting traders, can be heard in the streets.

The Ottoman Empire comes to an end following their defeat in World War I. The majority Greek population in the area is granted a mandate over Izmir from the Allies. Athens takes control over the whole Aegean region. Then rising tensions leads to an outbreak of war as the Greeks push further into the heart of Anatolia in an attempt to unite the Greek communities of Asia Minor. But the Turkish army, led by Mustafa Kemal Ataturk, launches a counter-attack and seizes the city. In the struggle for liberation, Turkish forces torch 70 percent of Izmir to the ground. The 'Great Fire' ends the multinational authority of the city and the Greek and Armenians are expelled. Ataturk formally takes control of Izmir on September 9 1922, which is celebrated as the day of the city's liberation.

Izmir's metropolitan area extends along the outlying waters of the Gulf of Izmir and inland to the north across the Gediz River Delta, to the east along an alluvial plain created by several small streams and to a slightly more rugged terrain to the south.

Our guide today is Mdsut who is a graduate in political science and business administration. He says, 'My name means *'lucky or happy man'*.' His experience of the sites and the best photo spots proves useful during our morning and afternoon excursions. He is certainly energetic and keeps us on the move. As we leave Izmir he informs, 'Izmir is Turkey's second major port and third in population at 4 million after Istanbul at 15 million and Ankara the capital at 6 million. Our city is an industrial city that processes much of the country's produce such as beer, wine and meat and fruits.' He points out the quince orchards as we follow a dual lane highway to Ephesus. 'We make quince jam, a favourite here in Turkey.' says Mdsut.

The impressive archaeological site of Ephesus is less than an hour by coach from Izmir. The city played an important role in both Greek and Roman history. The cosmopolitan city was, in its heyday, on a par with Athens and Rome. Once it was the home to over 250,000 people. The site affords a snapshot into the daily lives of the Greeks and their conquerors, the Romans. The seaside port that once fuelled the city's prosperity in antiquity has now silted up leaving the grand sites frozen in a state of remarkable preservation, nine kilometres from the sea.

Over the centuries, Ephesus was a sacred centre to Artemis, a Roman stronghold and later, a centre for Christianity. There is evidence that St Paul and the Virgin Mary visited the city, along with a cast of characters including General Lysimachus, the bodyguard of Alexander the Great during the conquest of Asia. He was assigned to govern Thrace in the distribution of satrapies following Alexander's death in 323 BC. Famous lovers, Mark Anthony and Cleopatra, also may have visited Ephesus.

Ephesus must be the crown of the many archaeological sites in Turkey. Today we find it crowded with tourists from many parts of the world. 'Ephesus receives one million visitors a year and it is not peak season yet,' says Mdsut.

We are fortunate that the weather is sunny and not too hot. The ruins of ancient Ephesus are remarkably well preserved allowing a clear impression of ancient life. One of the highlights is an inside viewing of the excavated and partially restored Terrace Houses. These homes were originally inhabited by the city's wealthy citizens and are decorated with rich mosaics and frescoes.

The Library of Celsus completed in 135 AD is another impressive structure with its splendid columned façade, built to hold 12,000 scrolls. Celsus was a polemical writer against Christianity in the second century AD. He wrote his work *True Discourse* as a polemic against the Christians in approximately 178 AD. He ridiculed Christians because they advocated blind faith instead of reason. Oddly, the House of Love, the city's brothel, is situated at a not so discreet distance opposite the library. For the first time in my life I enter into a brothel. But where is my Roman Goddess? Oops, the second! I forgot about the one in Pompeii where I visited a decade ago.

Mdsut walks us down a long wide marbled avenue, featuring the Corinthian columns, still standing today, of the stoa encircling the Trade Agora. He stops and points to a lady's shoeprint cut into a block of marble. 'She is advertising for clients and the arrows show the location of her room. See that rectangular shape next to it. Now you know that they even accepted credit cards in those days!' he jokes.

We continue along the wide marbled avenue that once led to the ancient port. Few places bring antiquity so vividly to life. We come to the magnificent Grand Theatre, with a seating capacity of 24,000. This is where the apostle St Paul once preached his sermons. He arrived there in 50 AD. I climb the ancient stairs that once seated crowds of Romans. From a vantage point high up in the theatre I see a different crowd wandering the streets of Ephesus. Suddenly I see an anxious face in the crowd. It's Avril wondering where I am. The shore excursion manager spies me and waves his lollypop stick. It's time to go.

At 1.00 pm we return to the ship for lunch on board, before heading out into the city. Our lunchtime selection of food can be obtained from three serveries in the Terrace Café. To save time we always head to the outside deck of the Terrace for the pasta and pizza selections. The chef quickly cooks a hearty pasta dish in front of you. Today he has a tomato blend with fetta and eggplant. From nearby outlets we add a slice of crispy garlic bread, a wrap of mince, a kebab of lamb and a small bit of salad.

At 2.15 pm our coach drives us through the busy streets of Izmir to visit the Archaeological Museum which houses a marvellous collection of antiques. A large collection of early Greek and Roman coinage is a prime exhibit here. We are also attracted to the bronze statue of a naked Greek athlete in running pose. Bronze statues are rare because much of the metal in those days was recycled. This one however was recovered from the sea, the result of a shipwreck.

Mdsut allows us 30 minutes to walk through a crowded bazaar in the centre of the city to explore its busy shops. Our final visit is to see the ancient Agora, set on the slopes of Izmir's highest hill. Mdsut begins to explain its function when suddenly a cry to prayer echoes from the loud speaker of a nearby minaret. This is now Islamic prayer time which must take place before the sun sets, because Moslems are not worshipping the sun. For my unaccustomed ears it sounds like someone is in great pain and writhing in agony.

The ancient market of Smyrna was constructed during the rule of Alexander the Great. We need to descend into the arch covered ancient market place which still has a functioning water supply. The ingenuity of the ancient craftsman stretches the imagination. Their capability in building this wonderful stone-arched structure is amazing. A water supply to the market stalls, long since abandoned, still functions today.

At 5.30 pm our coach negotiates the busy peak hour traffic in order to return us to our ship. We mix with crowded banana buses, taxis, cars and motor scooters -- all scrambling home at the end of the working day. At 6.00 pm it is time to enjoy a whiskey dry in the Charleston Lounge while listening to our talented Director, Neil Horrocks, play light music on the piano, including 'I Still Call Australia Home.' At 7.20 pm we dine once more with Barbara Currie who then retires for a good night's sleep. She thought the afternoon city excursion involved too much walking. On the way back to our cabin we pass the duty free shop. I know that Avril has been eyeing off one of the lightweight *Aegean Odyssey* windproof jackets, so now is the time to fit her out for her birthday in four days' time.

At 9.15 pm in the Ambassador lounge is the final concert of the Odyssey Trio, not to be missed. We are so impressed by the talented musicians that I purchase their DVD after the show. I ask Bogdan if he knows what his mate Theo is up to these days. Bogdan and Theo, a violinist, were on the *MV Voyager* last year performing as the Voyager Duo. 'Oh... I think he is in Romania somewhere and wants to get married.' Tonight they perform *AN*

DER SCHONEN BLAUEN DONAU (By the Beautiful Blue Danube) Op. 314, Johann Strauss II (1825-1899); (Selection from) *MY FAIR LADY*, Frederick Loewe (1901-1988); *UNGARISCH* (Hungarian Fantasie) Jo Knumann (1895-1952); *AVE MARIA* Charles Gounod (1818-1893) and Johann Sebastian Bach (1685-1750); (Overture from) *DIE FLEDERMAUS* (The Bat) Johann Strauss II (1825-1899); *OCCHI NERI* (Impressione Russa) Adalgiso Ferraris (1895-1966); *OBREO* – Romanian Folk Medley, Traditional (arr. Odyssey Trio).

Tuesday April 15, 2014
The Dardanelles and Sea of Marmara, Turkey

The *Aegean Odyssey* sails smoothly through the night and we will spend the day at sea passing through The Dardanelles and Sea of Marmara on the way to Istanbul. I wake at 6.28 am after a comfortable sleep. Avril and I are at breakfast just after the sun rises on the east and a full moon appears on the west. A clear day beckons for viewing our scheduled entry into the Dardanelles at 11.00 am. The Dardanelles, formerly known as Hellespont, is a narrow strait in northwestern Turkey connecting the Aegean Sea to the Sea of Marmara. It is one of the Turkish straits, along with its counterpart, the Bosphorus. The strait is 61 km long but only 1.2 to 6 km wide with a maximum depth of 103 m. Water flows in both directions along the strait, from the Sea of Marmara to the Aegean via a surface current and in the opposite direction via an undercurrent.

At 9.30 am we attend a lecture with Professor Jonathan Phillips entitled, *'The Fourth Crusade and the Sack of Constantinople'*. In April 1204 the armies of the Fourth Crusade put Constantinople, the greatest city in the Christian world, to the sword. The lecture explores how and why the Crusaders turned against their fellow Christians in one of the most infamous episodes in the history of Holy War.

At 11.00 am an announcement comes from the bridge of our imminent arrival at the Dardanelles. It is a time of reflection as we contemplate the carnage of Gallipoli in WW I. The unsuccessful attempt by the allies to take Istanbul and put Turkey out of the war proves a costly mistake. Both sides suffer great losses as the Turks fought bravely to defend their homeland. This modern siege is remembered solemnly each year on ANZAC Day 25th April. Next year will be the centenary of the landing. We observe a one minute silence as we pass the British monument at the Gallipoli landing site.

At 12.45 pm we have our usual lunch of pasta and crunchy garlic bread. It is then time to sort out our luggage to prepare for disembarkation tomorrow. At 3.30 pm we attend a briefing and guideline session from Jenny Worwood. Our tagged luggage is to be placed outside our cabins before midnight and we must vacate our cabins by 8.00 am tomorrow. This allows the cabin stewards to prepare for the ongoing passengers who will travel to Athens. The large group of Aussies who embarked at Athens a month ago will be heading home. Avril and I will be staying over to visit Troy and Gallipoli.

At 5.00 pm we attend the final lecture for the cruise, again given by Professor Jonathan Phillips, entitled *'Saladin – Life and Legend: The Legacy of the Crusades'*. He examines the career of Saladin, the man who conquered Jerusalem from the Crusaders in 1187. He speaks on Saladin's personality, his motives and his leadership qualities to understand why, down the centuries, he has enjoyed such extraordinary popularity in both the West and the Muslim Near East.

Again we dine with Barbara Currie who passed on a rumour that seven of the delightful Filipinos have received their marching orders, four female and three males. I check this out with a female waiter who is one of those affected. She is one of those ever smiling and courteous workers who ensure that we are well served. 'Is it true that you are going home?' I ask.

She confirms that management forced her to rescind her contract. 'They told us that we do not have the right attitude which is untrue. I wrote that I am being forced to sign this. He then tore it up and made me sign another.' she said.

I remember the night we dined with the Hotel Manager. He revealed that cruise ships run on a very tight budget. But it is appalling to treat staff like this. I believe that fewer passengers will be on board for the ongoing voyage to Athens and perhaps this is the real reason for sacking their workers.

A Roman bathhouse for athletes at the Sanctuary of Apollo, Kourion, Cyprus.

Roman chariot course, Kourion, Cyprus.

Kolossi Castle, former Crusader stronghold, Cyprus.

Road development on the Mediterranean coastline of Anatolia near Anamur, Turkey.

Ruins of Anemurium, former Roman town at Cape Anamur on the southern tip of Anatolia.

Mamure Castle on the Mediterranean, Anatolia.

Ayatekla Church ruins near the Cave of St Thecla.

Roman built harbour at Kaleici in Old Antalya.

Roman aqueduct once brought water to Aspendos.

Market place at Aspendos.

Abandoned city of Perge in Anatolia, Turkey.

Natural harbour at Fethiye on Turquoise Coast, Anatolia.

Excavated theatre at ancient Patara.

Agora at Patara, a region once known as Lycia.

Xanthos, capital city in ancient Lycia.

Theatre entrance at Letoon, Lycia's cult centre.

Sacred temple area, Letoon.

St Paul's Bay from the Acropolis of Lindos, Rhodes.

Pottery demonstration, Rhodes.

Grand Master's Palace, Rhodes.

Avril at the Avenue of Knights, Rhodes

Clifftop café on Santorini.

Deep blue of Santorini caldera, Aegean islands.

Akrotiri Archeological Site on Santorini.

Ground-hugging grapevines in pumice soil, Santorini.

Delos mosaics, old religious centre of the Cyclades.

Ancient theatre district on uninhabited Delos Island in the Aegean.

Wine press, Delos Island in the Aegean.

Windmills on Mykonos Island in the Aegean.

Marbled avenue leading to the ancient port at Ephesus.

Library of Celsus in the ancient Roman city of Ephesus, Turkey.

Grand theatre where St Paul once preached, Ephesus, Turkey.

Shopping area, Izmir, Turkey.

Ancient agora of Smyrna, Izmir, Turkey.

Goddess Artemis on a Roman column at Perge.

Bronze statue, Izmir Museum, Turkey.

CHAPTER 5

TURKISH DELIGHT

Wednesday April 16, 2014,
Istanbul, Turkey

This morning our voyage on the *Aegean Odyssey* comes to an end. We wake at 5.00 am to the noise of the ship's docking manoeuvres at Istanbul. Our small vessel is sandwiched between two huge multi storey passenger liners that require more than 70 coaches to take their passengers on shore excursions. We take breakfast at 6.30 am, a few minutes after sunrise at 6.23 am. The clear skies promise a nice spring day. Our luggage has been cleared overnight to our hotels and we will find it in our rooms after the morning excursion to the Hagia Sophia and Topkapi Palace.

We board our coach at 9.45 am and Thelma our guide welcomes us to her city. She is a young intelligent woman, a Moslem like 97 per cent of the Turkish population. She does not push her faith. She dresses in Western street clothes, jeans, blouse and no head covering. Turkey is a secular society thanks to the founder of modern Turkey, Mustafa Kemal Ataturk who democratised the society and brought in sweeping reforms following the collapse of the Ottoman Empire after W W I. There is freedom of religion despite most of the 15 million inhabitants in Istanbul following the Muslim faith. Thelma says there are 3115 mosques in Istanbul alone. But she warns, 'There have been attempts to restrict some of the freedoms to Moslem values. But I believe, hopefully, that Church and State will remain separate.'

Thelma rattles off more stats about her religion as we drive to our destination, the Hagia Sophia. 'Our religion dates back to the 7th century when the Holy words of the Koran were written in 622-632 by Mohammed. It is based on 5 Pillars. The **First Pillar** is *the acceptance sentence* that Allah is the only God and Islam is the path according to the Koran. And that you will be a good person. The **Second Pillar** is *prayer*. It requires you to pray five times a day. The minarets you see are spaces to call the followers to prayer, much like the Christians who use a church bell. Our calendar is based on the lunar year so the times of prayer before and after sunset vary. We are meant to wash our hands, feet and face before entering a mosque. There is a tap outside for this purpose. The **Third Pillar** is *fasting* in the Ramadan, a full lunar month during which there is no eating or drinking during the day time. This can be very difficult if the Ramadan falls in the hot summer. The **Fourth Pillar** is *pilgrimage*. We are expected to visit Mecca and Medina at least once in a lifetime. You must be free of all debts before you can do this. The **Fifth Pillar** is *alms*. You give a fortieth of your income to the poor or for a worthy cause.'

Thelma also manages to squeeze in a history lesson on Istanbul and Turkey, listing all the significant events of the last two and a half millennium – The story of Istanbul begins in 657 BC when early Greek colonists from Megara, a city-state near Athens, found the ancient city of Byzantium on the site that later becomes Constantinople (modern Istanbul). The city is rebuilt and reinaugurated as the new capital of the Roman Empire by Emperor Constantine the Great on May 11, 330 AD, and subsequently renamed Constantinople. Under Constantine, Christianity spreads in the city and becomes the state religion in 391 AD. With the death of the Emperor Theodosius I in 395 AD, the Roman Empire is separated and Constantinople becomes the capital of East Roman or Byzantine Empire. Between the years 527 – 565 AD, in the reign of Justinian, many new buildings are constructed, the first of which is the Hagia Sophia, built in 537 AD. The Arabs attempt to conquer the city many times from 666 until 870 AD.

Disagreements between the Roman Catholics and Eastern Orthodox Church increase and the two churches separate in 1054 AD. Constantinople becomes the religious centre for the Eastern Orthodox Catholics as a result of the East-West Schism or Great Schism. The Byzantine split with Roman Catholicism arises when Pope Leo III crowns Charlemagne, King of the Franks, as Holy Roman Emperor in 800 AD.

In 1204, Latin Crusaders of the Fourth Crusade, capture and ruin the city. Historian Jonathan Phillips sees the Sack of Constantinople as one of the most notorious events in European history, resulting from a typical clash of cultures. The Fourth Crusade is a Western European armed expedition on a mission intending to conquer the Muslim-controlled Jerusalem by means of an invasion through Egypt. Instead, the army of perhaps 20,000 men and a fleet of about 200 ships crewed by Venetian sailors and warriors break in and begin to loot the greatest metropolis of the Christian World.

In the 14th Century the Ottomans besiege the city, first by Bayezid I in 1390 and then by Murad II in 1422. In 1453 the Ottoman armies, commanded by Mehmet II, conquer the city and adopt the name Istanbul. It becomes the third capital of the Ottomans after Bursa and Edirne. The city becomes the centre of the whole world of Islam after the Ottomans conquer Egypt and bring the Caliphate to Istanbul.

During WW I, on the night of March 15, 1919, the city is captured by the allied armies. The Sultanate and Caliphate are abolished and the former Ottoman Empire collapses as a result of choosing the wrong side. The Supreme Allied War Council authorizes the Greeks to occupy Izmir and Bursa.

Rising tensions and military action follow between Turks and Greeks in Anatolia. In The Turkish War of Independence (1919-1923) the Greeks push further into the heart of Anatolia in an attempt to unite the Greek communities. The Turks, led by Mustafa Kemal Ataturk, successfully counter-attack and their victory sees the expulsion of the Greek and Armenian communities from Anatolia. Ankara becomes the capital of the new Republic of Turkey on October 13, 1923. The old Ottoman Empire was once 25 times bigger than today's Turkey. Since the establishment of modern Turkey, the Turkish name of the city, Istanbul, has replaced the name Constantinople in the West.

Thelma also does remarkably well to squeeze in a geography lesson. She explains that the majority of Turkey, 97 percent, is on the Asian or Anatolia side and only 3 percent is on the European side. Istanbul is the only city in the world established on two continents. Istanbul is established on both sides of the Bosphorus - the strait that forms the boundary between Asia and Europe and connects the Black Sea and the Sea of Marmara. She says, 'The city is a bit like an apple pie. On the European side you will find the historic peninsula part to the south, and the Galatia District to the North. Also the European side is the trade and business centre, whereas the New City on the Asian side is more of a residential area.'

Her lectures end as we arrive at the Hagia Sophia whose name means 'holy wisdom'. This great architectural beauty was accepted as the greatest and most sacred piece of the city during the Byzantine Age. It was used as a church for 916 years from the date of its construction (537 AD) until the date Istanbul was conquered by the Ottomans (1453). It then served the Moslems for 481 years as a mosque.

The building was opened to visitors as a museum in February 1935. It is the third most visited museum in Turkey. Today is no exception as we join a long queue in order to gain access to admire the unrivalled architectural masterpiece. The best construction material and best masons were brought to the city from all over the country, and for 5 years, over 100 masters and 10,000 labourers worked on the construction. The marble used for the inner decoration of the church was transported from all the Mediterranean countries, especially from the quarries of Anatolia. The four green granite columns on both sides of the nave came from the Harbour Gymnasium in Ephesus. Special tiles and bricks were brought from the island of Rhodes in order to build the giant dome with lighter material.

We venture on to view the Topkapi palace, the seat of the Ottoman sultans from 1465 until 1856. The Palace is unlike any other. The main features are the magnificent gardens with the buildings around it, rather than a single feature building surrounded by gardens. The imperial residence could house 4000 people and features decorative courts, gardens and harem rooms. We enter two gateways to reach an impressive garden courtyard where we join another long queue to see Oriental treasures. On display are the 84 carat Spoonmaker Diamond, an Emerald Dagger and an array of golden treasures and valuable porcelain.

At 1.00 pm we conclude our morning excursion and are driven to the Intercontinental Hotel for checking-in. We find our room at a high vantage point on the 16th floor overlooking the Bosphorus. At 2.10 pm we order a quick snack of fish and chips and coffee. The coffee arrives, but at 2.40 pm we are still waiting for the meal. We need to leave for our afternoon excursion. But we are no longer hungry, having eaten a plate full of Turkish bread while we waited. The head waiter apologises and hands us his card. 'You may have a free meal tonight,' he says.

At 3.00 pm we visit the must-see Blue Mosque. It is the greatest and most splendid mosque in Istanbul. Finished in 1616, this monument is renowned for its cascading domed exterior. Of equal note is the Mosque's sumptuous interior that features 20,000 hand-made ceramic tiles and some of the finest examples of marble carving. Designed to hold 10,000 worshippers, the special acoustic design enables the Imam to be heard by all. To enter we must take off our shoes and put them in a thin plastic carry bag. Women must wear a hat or head cover. Avril uses her floral scarf. We walk on the soft red carpet to gaze in awe at the large central dome. Some Moslems are worshipping quietly in a roped off section. We speak in hushed tones, take pictures and leave. The outside premises feature a lovely garden of tulips and pansies in full bloom, a double flower cherry tree and a public fountain. Despite the crowd it looks serene.

At 4.00 pm we hasten to Matis carpet warehouse to view spectacular Turkish rugs made from wool, cotton and silk fibres. We are seated and offered a cup of hot green apple tea. Rugs are rolled out in front of us, each one looking a masterpiece. The silk ones change their design appearance depending on how you view them. It may take 6 months or more for a couple of village weavers to prepare the intricate designs. Of course they cost several thousand dollars for the more spectacular examples -- well outside my budget, even with the 40 percent cut for us, plus free delivery to anywhere in the world. I decline the temptation on the excuse that I am confused over which one to buy.

We head to the world renowned Grand Bazaar within walking distance from Matis carpets. We have little more than an hour to check it out before our coach pick-up arrives at 6.30 pm. One would need all day to investigate the maze of alley ways. It is one of the largest covered markets in the world, containing 60 streets and 5,000 shops. Into this maze of vaults and skylights come 250,000 to 400,000 visitors daily seeking jewellery, ceramics, carpets, embroideries, spices or perhaps just a cup of green apple tea. The market is a place to shop and haggle. We are looking for pretty bracelets for gifts. But nothing seems a bargain anymore since the market has had a facelift. One bracelet attracts my eye and I inquire. He says 69 Euro, then 55 and, as I walk away, it is down to 40 Euro. I keep walking and buy some Turkish delight sweets as we hurry for our coach, otherwise we would have to catch a tram or taxi.

We dine in the main restaurant of the hotel and our friends Graham and Annette from the ship join us. The head waiter who promised a 'freebie' was true to his word. For mains I have a delicious bass and Avril a tasty beef noodle dish. We are treated to a whiskey and dry, a desert and a variety of fruit. Graham and Annette are also delighted. By joining us their meal is also on the house.

Thursday April 17, 2014,
Istanbul, Turkey

The alarm wakes me at 6.00 am. The early morning sky promises a fine day ahead, with light cool breezes, a strong sun and a predicted maximum temperature of 18C. At 8.30 am we are on a visit to view the Basilica Cistern and the Archaeological Museum. Our excellent local guide is Attila, a handsome middle age man who imparts his knowledge clearly to us, 'Some call me Attila the Hun,' he jokes. We are about to discover what lies beneath Istanbul.

The entrance of the underground cistern is just across from the Hagia Sophia Museum which we visited yesterday. Near the entrance is a small obelisk and beside it a signpost denoting distances to all parts of the world. It served as the historic starting point of the ancient road network when the centre of the Roman Empire came to Constantinople. All roads lead to Constantinople.

We step inside the dimly lit cistern and see rows of marble columns. Mystical music from a flute provides a touch of eeriness. Below the pathway leading around the temple-like structure is the reservoir which once provided the city's water supply. The only ripple on the surface is from the fat carp swimming lazily below. Occasionally a droplet of water falls from the ceiling above the columns.

Over sixty cisterns are built during the Byzantine Period and the Basilica is the biggest. These huge tanks are needed because there is not enough water inside the Byzantine ramparts that surround the city. The water is supplied from rivers and sources in the Belgrade Forest which is 25 km north of Istanbul. During wars and sieges, enemy soldiers could destroy the ducts bringing water to the city or by poisoning the water. To prevent this, large cisterns are constructed for storing water.

In 532 AD the Byzantine emperor, Justinian I, has the Basilica Cistern built after the bloody Nika Revolt which is sparked by rioting factions of chariot racing fans. The Hagia Sophia is destroyed during the riots and 30,000 rioters are slaughtered in the attempted upheaval against Justinian. During the tumult the palace complex next to the Hippodrome is under siege and fires destroy much of the city. The week long riot in January ends when Imperial troops storm the Hippodrome, killing the remaining rebels. Justinian exiles the Senators who have supported the riot and he rebuilds Constantinople and the Hagia Sophia. The Basilica Cistern is completed in a very short time of two months. It is designed to service the Great Palace and surrounding buildings.

The cistern is closed and forgotten by the city authorities when the Byzantine emperors relocate from the Great Palace. But the cistern is still in use until the 16th century and for a short time following the Ottoman conquest of 1453. The Ottomans simply use it as a dumping ground for junk, including corpses. In the mid-19th century someone is fishing in the garden and discovers the old cistern which is then restored and used again to supply the city's water until the 1900's.

The cistern is opened for the public to visit after restoration work is completed in 1987. 'People can now hire the complex to hold weddings or other social functions,' says Attila.

We follow him down a path to the end where two Medusa heads are used as column bases. One is placed sideways and down and the other is placed upside down. Attila explains, 'These were probably used to ward off evil spirits. Scenes of the James Bond movie, *From Russia with Love,* were filmed here.'

Attila informs, 'The cistern has 336 marble columns. They were salvaged from different Roman structures.' He points to the capitals. Some are plain and others are Doric. 'The Romans were good at recycling from other sites. The cistern is 70 m wide and 140 m long. The columns are placed apart every 4 m and the total water capacity is 80,000 cubic metres. Its height is 8 m and its surface area is about 10,000 sq m (1 ha).'

From the cistern we follow Attila down the street to the entrance of Istanbul Archaeological Museums. The pathway leading to the museums is a riot of colourful tulips. There are three museums in the complex: the **Museum of the Ancient Orient**, the **Tile Museum** and the **Archaeological Museum** itself. The Museum of the Ancient Orient was constructed by the Academy of Fine Arts in 1883 and has the most distinguished examples of pre-Asian civilizations brought from Egypt, Anatolia and Mesopotamia. The most interesting works here are the lion sculptures from the 14th century BC.

The Tile Museum was the first building constructed upon the order of Mehmet II (the Ottoman conqueror in 1453) in 1466 and it is one of the oldest buildings of Topkapi Palace. It was used as an entertainment hall in the Ottoman times. It is now used as a department where Turkish-Islamic tile and ceramic works have been exhibited since 1967. These artistic works of art are magnificent.

We spend the bulk of our limited time in the main Archaeological Museum. Its façade was inspired by two of its prized sarcophagi which are on display as you step inside the main hall. One is of Alexander the Great displaying epic conquests and the other is of the Weeping Women mourning the loss of a nobleman. Attila describes the funeral scenes of the Weeping Women on the sarcophagus of the Roman noble man, 'It is likely that these crying women were paid to weep. In Roman times women were employed to add sorrow to the occasion. The tears may have been collected and handed to the family. The more collected, the more the honour for the deceased.'

In 1887 these tombs and others came from the necropolis of Sidon to Istanbul. The need for a new exhibition building arose. Today's building was constructed by Alexander Vallaury in 1891 through the efforts of Osman Hamdi Bey, master of Turkish museology. The majority of the collections were transferred to this building.

Attila explains, 'Osman Hamdi Bey inspired the Ottoman Empire to protect the ancient treasures from being stolen or vandalised. He had the museum established to house priceless treasures which trace civilization as far back as mythical Troy in 4,000 BC. Laws were passed in the 1880's to establish what could and what could not be taken out of the Empire. At first it involved a three way split, a third to the excavator, a third to the state and a third to the owner. Strangely some of the best bits ended up in London. Now, nothing can leave the country.'

Today 800,000 of the 2.5 million works of art in all of Turkish archaeological museums are housed here in the Istanbul Archaeological Museum. However, only one tenth of these works are able to be displayed.

Our interesting morning ends at midday. On our way to the hotel, Attila turns to politics. He speaks on the corruption taking place at the highest levels.

Our afternoon is spent sorting out our luggage ready for our move to another hotel tomorrow. I also spend time in the business room confirming and printing our boarding passes for the flight from Istanbul's airport to Budapest on Monday April 21, 2014. At 7.30 pm we decide to eat out and we stumble upon a restaurant desperately searching for a couple of strangers like us. The red wine of Turkey is rough and the meal of mixed grill of meats and salad is average. We are slotted into a corner near the doorway which is opened and shut frequently by the scouts looking for more clients. A blast of cold air shoots towards us each time. No wonder they have scouts looking for customers. We are happy to leave.

Friday April 18, 2014.

Istanbul, Turkey

I sleep to 6.20 am as there is no need to rush, especially as the day is full of cloud and a shower or two of rain is expected. Today is Good Friday which is of little significance here in a secular country with a largely Moslem population. It's business as usual. The most significant event today is Avril's birthday. She has been carrying a gift package from her treasured friends, 'Trish' and Barry, all the way from Australia. It is now time to open it. The contents reveal a pair of sparkling hoop ear rings.

We will be moving on to another hotel, the Best Western Senator, after breakfast. At 7.00 am we venture down to breakfast and take the opportunity to bid farewell to a few of our Aussie friends we met on the *Aegean Odyssey*.

At 11.30 am we catch a taxi to our new hotel which is located in the heart of the old city of Istanbul. According to my itinerary the Best Western Senator is one of best hotels in the city of Istanbul, offering fantastic views and perfect decoration. It aims at offering exceptional customer service and making guests feel at home. It is located within walking distance to popular attractions such as the Grand Bazaar, Topkapi palace, Blue Mosque and Underground Cistern. The problem is that we have already been to these main attractions. From our room on the first floor I peek over a grimy backyard with two or three cats. A young woman comes out to feed them and to water a couple of pot plants. The laneway below is a short cut to the busy main drag from where we were dropped by our taxi so that we could walk to the hotel.

In hindsight, we should have stayed where we were or booked a hotel on the Asian side where we have to catch a plane to Budapest in 3 days' time after our visit to Gallipoli and Troy. Still our room, without a view, is comfortable, despite it not having a kettle to make a cup of tea and despite the noisy loud speakers calling Moslems to prayer. The members of staff are courteous and the concierge makes a call to Hassle-Free Travel to confirm our 8.30 am booking for tomorrow's trip to Troy by private car. I am puzzled when he says to be ready at 6.30 am for the bus as they need to pick up other passengers. 'Your pick-up will be here first,' he says.

'But breakfast is at 7.00 am,' I complain. 'And why do I need to be picked up by a bus?'

He answers, 'No problem, I can make up a breakfast package to collect from reception. You will go later by car.' I am still not convinced.

It is time to have a coffee and to read the fine print of my arrangements. It reads… 'tour by car ex Istanbul… pick up, Best Western Hotel Istanbul at 8.30 am… please be waiting in the lobby.' I return to the desk and this time a young woman understands. She rings the company and hands me the phone. I confirm that we do have a private car as stated, leaving at 8.30 am.

We return to our room to sort out our gear for the overnight trip down the peninsula tomorrow. At 4.30 pm it is time to have a whiskey in the downstairs bar. At 7.45 pm we walk to one of the street restaurants for a meal of calamari and vegetable spring rolls for starters and grilled fish for mains. Avril says, 'Guess what? It's Good Friday and we are eating fish.' I have a beer to toast her birthday and Avril has a glass of white wine.

Saturday April 19, 2013,

Canakkale, Turkey

I am awake at 5.00 am but snooze until the alarm rings at 6.00 am. We are ready for breakfast at 7.00 am and check out of the Best Western Senator at 8.10 am. We wait for our private car to take us to see the ancient ruins of Troy. The weather has cleared and hopefully the day will be fine and mild. At 8.30 am our guide for the day arrives as scheduled. We are ushered into a white sedan and soon our driver is whisking us out of the city. Our guide is Ercan Yavuz, a 41 year man of slim athletic build. He has a good command of English, having graduated in languages and history at university. He has passed rigorous tests in order to become a guide and he is allowed to work up to 200 days per year. The Turkish government ensures a high standard for tourist guides and all must wear their ID cards or face a fine of two thousand Turkish liras, about $700 US,

Today we will be visiting Troy which was once the stronghold of changing civilizations which build on top of one another. From the Early Bronze Age of 3000 BC until 400 AD, a total of nine civilizations are identified on the site, beginning from Troy 1 to Troy 9. In addition, archaeologists have identified another dating to 3500 BC. Ercan hands us a package from Hassle-Free Travel Agency containing our itinerary for the next two days. Our trip involves a five hour drive down the Gallipoli Peninsula to Eceabat where we plan to have lunch at 1.30 pm at Maydos Restaurant. On the way we take a couple of short breaks for coffee and the rest rooms. Ercan keeps us informed on a variety of interests, including politics, which he claims is corrupt. 'The political players keep manoeuvring to hang onto power by keeping a tight rein on the press. Protests by young city people are exposing their corruption. Twitter was banned for a short time before the recent mayoral elections. Then it was relaxed after the elections. I have to watch the world news to receive a balanced view of my country.'

During our drive to Troy, Ercan points to the battle fields near Gallipoli where we will visit tomorrow. He declares, 'The Ottoman Empire lasted from 1299 to 1922 and had 38 Sultans. They lost their lands by siding with the Germans in WW I. Some of the ostracised ancestors have returned and are trying to claim some of their land back.' Ercan laughs and scoffs at the very impertinence. He adds, 'Tonight we will be staying in the city of Canakkale which commemorates the Freedom from Ottoman rule on March 18.

Ercan states other eventful days celebrated by Turkey, 'April 23 is a public holiday declared for National Independence and Youth Day. October 29 is a public holiday for the Foundation of the Turkish Republic. And May 19 is Remembrance Day for Ataturk. This great man inspired the Turks to their valiant victory over the ANZAC forces at Gallipoli in 1914. He then led the 3 year War of Independence Battle that settled the borders of Greece, Bulgaria and Turkey in 1924. An agreement was reached and there was an exchange of population between Greece and Turkey.' I explain that I know a Greek family in Northern Greece that was involved in the swap. (This is the family at Pefkodassos who rescued my uncle during WW II.)

Mustafa Kemal Ataturk, the father figure, who inspired his nation to victories in WW I and its Independence, was lucky to survive these great victories. Ercan says, 'Ataturk was brilliant at maths and read 17,000 books in his lifetime. He would read a book on the battlefield; he encouraged his men to do the same. There are many people called Mustafa because it is the first name of Mohammed. But Ataturk was given the nickname Kemal by his teacher because he was smart and wise. This distinguished him from the rest of the class. Ataturk is the Turkish name of his ancestors and now no one is allowed to use it.'

'He was leading his men to make a stand against the ANZACS when an Australian, Eric William Tulloch, saw him waving to his men. Eric took a shot at Ataturk which missed, fortunately, for the Turks who were about to run. Their leader stood firm and courageous. In another incident a bullet hit Ataturk's pocket watch he had in his chest pocket. The watch smashed but he survived. On another occasion, pounding shell fire was creeping up on his unit as he urged them to stay put. They were in the next target range, but the shelling suddenly stopped.'

At a service station we stop for petrol and I note the many varieties of Turkish delight sweets on sale. I mention this to Ercan. He informs us, 'These sweets were once the reserve of the Sultans. Nowadays they are traditionally presented to the mother by the groom when her daughter wants her permission to marry. In return the groom, seeking the mother's approval, is given a cup of Turkish coffee full of salt. He must drink it if he wants to get married.' Ercan shudders at the thought, 'I have never been keen to drink coffee after this experience.'

A shower or two accompanies our drive down the peninsula as we approach our luncheon stop at Maydos. Springtime fields of yellow canola flourish amid the pine and the olive trees. Ercan announces, 'We have had a very mild winter and the season should be good. However, we need more rain.'

At the waterfront of the Dardanelles we reach Maydos Restaurant, perfectly placed to watch the passing ships. 'These are international waters,' explains Ercan, 'about 400,000 ships pass through each year. The narrow strait is 61 km long and 1.2 to 6.5 km wide, connecting the Aegean Sea with the Sea of Marmara. On May 10, 1810, Lord Byron swam 3.1 km to the other side of the Hellespont (Dardanelles). Now a commemorative swim is held every year and about 100 international swimmers are given approval to hold a race after health checks. Shipping is held up to allow the race. The fastest swim was an incredible 45 minutes,' claims Ercan. I ask him to explain how the Dardanelles got its name. 'It was named after King Dardanos, one of the early Greek kings.'

Our lunch is a bowl of tasty tomato soup and a freshly cooked sea bream… quite yummy because the weather is breezy and cool outside the restaurant. At 2.30 pm we catch the ferry to Canakkale on the Asian side. The crossing is negotiated in 10 minutes, but we are stuck in traffic for a while as our driver negotiates a way out of the city of over 100,000 inhabitants. Ercan says that Canakkale was only a small fishing village before the Greeks left. It now has a university population of 25,000 students. He smiles, 'There is a university here called *The University of the 24 Th March*. Turkish families send their students here because it is considered a safe city.'

Forty minutes later we arrive at the famous site of Troy, home of the Trojan horse and Helen of Troy. The lands between the Dardanelles, Sea of Marmara and Edremit Bay were called 'TROAS' in ancient times. It may be that the ancient settlement mentioned in the *Iliad* as TROIA, ILION or ILIOS took these names from the two kings, TROS an ILOS.

Troy was accepted as a legendary city for ages. Not many people believed in the existence of Troy. But its location is clearly depicted in the *Iliad* with the word *'Hellespont'*, the ancient name for the Dardanelles, and *'Mount Ida'*, the highest mountain of the Troad. Zeus, father of the immortals, used to watch the Trojan War from the peak of Mount Ida.

Today the ruins of Troy are 30 kilometres from Canakkale. From the ancient hilltop of Troy one may observe the famous plain where the Trojan War took place. With a little imagination you may feel the excitement of the Trojan War as the cool north breeze blows in from the Dardanelles. It is fascinating to visit Troy because it is a mythical place in the history of the West, where Homer sings of its mythical heroes in the *Odyssey* and the *Iliad*, the beginnings of Western literature.

There is not a great deal left to see in Troy today, but its ruins speak to us in a way that time has been unable to destroy. There are traces of succeeding civilisations in Troy's many layers of earth. These are the remnants of the civilisations that replaced one another dating back to 4,000 BC. The various levels that can be seen are numbered from I to IX and each one can be followed by observing the instructions on indicator boards. Archaeological excavations began in Troy in 1871 on the Hill of Hisarlik by a German named Heinrich Schliemann who was stubborn, far-sighted and rich.

The various levels are explained to us as Ercan guides us around the site. But, firstly, we must clamber into the replica of Troy's legendary wooden horse placed near the entrance. It affords a marvellous view of the ancient city. The urge to climb its staircase is irresistible. You poke your head out of a window for a photo.

At Troy 1 are the remains of two towers that supported a gate. Troy II is reached by a stone-slabbed ramp. According to Schliemann, it enclosed the ancient treasury of Priam, King of the Trojans. In Troy III and IV (2,500-2,000 BC) are the remains of a few roads and houses that may have formed a village. Troy V preserves the ruins of buildings surrounded by a wall.

Troy VI displays an open space 200 m in diameter, containing the remains of thick walls, 90 m long and 6 m high. It protects a citadel that has trade links with Mycenae and Greece. This, according to Homer, is the birth place of Priam, king of Troy during the Trojan War. Troy VII dates from the time of the heroes as narrated by Homer. Archaeologists suggest that it is burned by the Greeks around 1,200 BC. Troy VII is rebuilt by a population, originating in the Balkans. Lasting for the next 400 years, Troy then falls into oblivion.

Troy VIII dates from 700 BC when the town is reconstructed by Greek colonists and the Temple of Athena dates from this period. Known as New Ilium, the town is sacked by the Persians. The ruins at the Gate of Dardanos are where, in the *Iliad*, the Trojan hero, Hector, is killed by Achilles.

By 85 BC, during the times of Julius Caesar, Ilium Novum, or Troy IX has become rich and prosperous. Here Augustus and Caracalla, the Roman Emperors, spend long periods of time. But after its conquest by the Turks, Troy once again falls into oblivion.

It takes the imagination of a German born businessman, Heinrich Schliemann to discover Troy. Born in 1822 in Mecklenburg, he believes every line of Homer's *Iliad*. He wants to prove to the world that the legendary Troy actually exists. He starts making plans to discover Troy. He needs limitless money to support the excavations. He makes immense fortunes at various times during his life. He is a banker in California during the gold-rush. He amasses a fortune through the black-market by supplying materials for the Russian army during the Crimean War (1854). During his life he visits half the countries of the world and learns a dozen languages. He has three children by his Russian wife. He divorces her and later in life he decides to go to Greece to seek his dream.

Frank Calvert, an Englishman, who acted as American vice-consul for the Dardanelles, had done some preliminary digging at Hisarlik. Believing that he had found Troy, he invited the British museum to begin excavations. He wanted the British to have the honour of discovering Troy, but his proposal came to nothing. When Schliemann arrives on the scene, Calvert decides to help him.

In his quest, Schliemann thinks a Greek wife would be ideal for him. He writes a letter to Vimpos, a Greek priest, to help him. He writes, 'She should be poor, beautiful, a Homer enthusiast, dark-haired, well-educated and possessed of a good and loving heart.' Vimpos collects photographs of suitable young Athenian girls and Schliemann selects the picture of a 17 year old girl named Sophia. In a short time he marries Sophia and then turns his attention to the subject of Troy.

Schliemann reaches his goal in May, 1873. He suddenly notices some metal objects as he is standing near a trench with Sophia. None of the workmen has noticed it. To avert their attention he turns to Sophia and says, 'You must go at once and shout PAIDOS.' This is the Greek and Turkish word meaning 'rest period'. 'Tell them it is my birthday, and I have only just remembered it. Tell them that they will get their wages today without working.' The treasure he finds is like nothing that has ever been seen before. It consists of a copper shield, a copper cauldron, a silver vase, a gold bottle, two gold cups, a silver goblet, three great silver vases, seven double-edged copper daggers, six silver knife blades, thirteen copper lance heads, two gold diadems, fifty-six gold earrings and 8750 gold rings and buttons. With the help of Calvert, the treasure is smuggled out of the country and Schliemann returns to Athens.

With great enthusiasm he pronounces that he has made the 'greatest discovery of the age'. He declares that the treasure he has found is the 'Treasure of Priam' and Hisarlik Hill is the legendary 'City of Priam'. The Greeks refuse to accept the treasure because they are afraid of trouble with Turkey.

Amin Efendi is put in prison for failing to keep a close watch on the excavations. The Turks take Schliemann to court for half of the treasure. The trial lasts a year in Athens and the Greek judges find in favour of the Turks and order him to pay 50,000 francs. Schliemann thinks the treasure to be worth one million. As a gesture of friendship he sends five times the amount to the Archaeological museum in Istanbul. He also sends seven large vases and four sacks filled with stone implements, part of the treasure found at Troy. That proves enough to melt the ice. Schliemann's collection ends up in a German museum. It is seized by the Russians during WW II and now the treasures are held in a Russian museum.

The weather closes in towards the end of our interesting visit to Troy. Being close to the Dardanelle Straits, the City of Troy is exposed to prevailing winds. It becomes cold as we trudge around the site. Ercan suggests a coffee stop on the return to Canakkale where we are booked into the Hotel Akol, Canakkale. We bid farewell to Ercan who has been hired for another tour tomorrow. Another specialist guide will receive us in the morning.

Sunday April 20, 2014,

Canakkale, Turkey

We are up at 6.00 am to prepare for our private Gallipoli ANZAC sector tour at 8.00 am. Our new guide is Izzet Yildirim, a professional tour guide who lives in Canakkale and specializes in the Gallipoli area. Once again we cross the Dardanelles by ferry from the Asian side at Canakkale to the European side at Eceabat. This is the narrowest point of the Dardanelles at 1.2 kilometres. Izzet tells us that the name Dardanelles, which was known as Hellespont in ancient times, is a combination from the ancient King Dardanos and the mythical Princess Helle. According to mythology, when the children of King Athamas, the twins Phryxus and Helle, were sent away by their grandmother, they were mounted on a flying ram with a golden fleece which was given to them by Nephele, the Goddess of the Cloud. Whilst flying over the straits, Princess Helle fell off the ram into the water, giving the basis for the name Hellespont.

Izzet says that Canakkale is also a combination word from *'Canak'* meaning pottery and *'Kale'* meaning castle. On either side of the strait are castles built by the sultans for the purpose of controlling the trading route and collecting taxes.

We begin our tour of the Gallipoli Campaign area at Brighton Beach, a lovely flat area of beach, a perfect spot for the ANZAC's plan to launch their attack on April 25, 1915. However, mistakes are made in the darkness and they are put ashore in high ground north of their objective at ANZAC Cove. Izzet points to a rugged area two miles further north where the ANZAC forces overshoot their planned landing beaches. The soldiers come ashore at Ari Burnu, a narrow beach which is swept by Turkish gunfire. They are confronted with sheer cliffs instead of the expectation of low foothills. Their advance to the heights of Sari Bair is halted by a division led by Turkish Colonel Mustafa Kemal Ataturk. The ANZAC's are driven back to beach and they dig in, earning their nickname *'diggers'*. Izzet jokes, 'From the Allied forces launching sites at Lemnos and Thasos, it was Chaos where they landed.'

More seriously, Izzet explains the reasons for the Gallipoli Campaign. By early 1915 there is deadlock on the Western Front and the Russian army is struggling in the East. The First Lord of the Admiralty, Winston Churchill becomes the driving force behind a grand scheme to strike at the Central Powers on a new front in south-eastern Europe. Churchill hopes to knock Turkey out of the war and open up a much needed relief route to Russia through the Dardanelles.

The campaign begins with an attempt by naval power alone to force through the Dardanelles. Early bombardments on the coastal ports fail and on March 18, 1915, three Allied battleships are lost to Turkish mines.

In light of this failure, British Secretary of State for War, Lord Kitchener, appoints Sir Ian Hamilton to command a 70,000 strong Mediterranean Expeditionary Force which consists of the British 29th Division, a Newfoundland battalion, Indian troops, two divisions of untried Australian and New Zealand Army Corps (ANZAC), a Royal Navy Division and a French colonial Division. Its mission is to clear the way for the Royal Navy to capture the Turkish capital of Constantinople (now Istanbul).

The British 29th Division plan is to land at Cape Helles and push inland to capture Achi Baba. The ANZAC's plan is to land in the area further north, at Gaba Tepe, and to strike the Sari Bair heights. Gaba Tepe, or Kabatepe, is a headland overlooking the Aegean Sea in what is now the Gallipoli Peninsula National Historic Park.

The attack is launched on April 25, 1915. It meets a combination of unexpectedly hostile terrain and ferocious Turkish defence which soon stops any potential advance. The campaign degenerates into the familiar deadlock of trench warfare. The Turks cling grimly to the high ground while the Allies below find it difficult to dig trenches. Disease caused by extreme heat and unsanitary conditions proves as deadly as the Turkish gunfire as the deadlock continues.

On May 19 the Allies successfully defend their position in the face of unsuccessful Turkish attempts to drive the invaders back into the sea. The Allies inflict so many casualties on the Turks that a truce has to be called to allow them to reclaim their dead from the battlefield. 'This is when the ANZACS see their enemy in a new spirit,' Izzet explains. 'They exchange tobacco and cigarettes. Then they return to their trenches, separated only by this narrow roadway. The Aussies throw some bully beef into the Turkish trenches. A reply comes back written in French -- No more bully beef; send cigarettes!' The area still bears the scars of Turkish and Allied trenches and tunnels. 'It is nicknamed *'Johnston's Jolly'* because he thought he could jolly-well *'stick it'* to the Turks,' says Izzet.

On August 6, Hamilton, with his force doubled to eleven divisions, tries to break the deadlock with an assault on Sulva Bay. Five divisions are to link the Sulva beachhead with those at Anzac and seize the heights at Teke Tepe at the heart of the peninsula.

A diversionary attack is launched at Helles and at Anzac two attacks take place. At Lone Pine the Anzacs are successful but unable to hold their position. At Sari Bair (The Nek) the Australians are cut down as they advance. Confusion leads to the advance on Sulva being stopped and, by the time it is resumed, the Turks have sent in reinforcements.

Further desperate actions in August see the Anzac, British and Indian forces attempt to take Chunuk Bair, but they are eventually forced back. The final actions take place on August 21 at Hill 60 and Scimitar Hill. The Anzac and Sulva forces attempt to join and take the heights, but are driven back with no gains.

In October, with the campaign stalled, Hamilton is relieved of command. He is replaced by Sir Charles Munro who immediately recommends that the Allies evacuate. This proves the most successful part of the entire operation. Anzac Cove and Sulva Bay are evacuated in December 1915 and the Helles area emptied of troops by January 9, 1916. This marks the ironic end to a campaign that costs the lives of almost 36,000 Commonwealth, 10,000 French and around 86,000 Turks.

During our visit to the sights there is frantic activity preparing for the 99th commemoration of the Gallipoli Campaign, just 5 days from now. Workmen are adjusting the portable seating and moving boxes of media equipment in readiness for the Dawn Service at Anzac Cove Commemoration Site and services at the Lone Pine Australian Memorial and the Chunuk Bair New Zealand Memorial.

Izzet shows us the gravesite of ANZAC legend, John Simpson Kirkpatrick, who bravely rescued many wounded soldiers with his donkey before he was killed on May 19, 1915, aged 22. A few metres away from this quiet beachside cemetery, bathed in sunshine, Avril notices the grave of another young soldier by her surname, Lees.

We drive up to the Lone Pine Memorial where another pine tree has been planted beside the graves to replace the one destroyed during the fighting. The seeds of the original tree were taken to Australia and propagated. One of the propagated plants is returned and is now flourishing at the entrance to the memorial. On the wall of the memorial are the names of those unidentified soldiers who were killed or died from disease and were buried at sea. The youngest is a 14 year old by the name of Wilson who dies of enteritis. Inside the Memorial Housing, Avril adds our signatures to the Visitors' Book. Outside the Memorial is a group of Kiwis, dressed in the all black rugby colours. They are holding a quiet vigil until I interrupt them. They yell, 'How you're goin' mate? Where you're from?' I answer, 'Melbourne,' to which one replies, 'Oh! One of my relations lives there.'

We visit the New Zealand Memorial at Chunuk Bair and nearby there is the huge bronze statue of the Turkish hero, Mustafa Kemal Ataturk, who defends the heights by showing leadership under fire. Many brave young men on both sides lose their lives here in the heat of August, 1915.

The Gallipoli Peninsula is now a National Park dedicated to preserving that time in history. In 1934, Ataturk, who became President of the Turkish Republic, said, *'Those heroes that shed their blood and lost their lives… you are now lying in the soil of a friendly country. Therefore rest in peace. There is no difference between the Johnnies and the Mehmets to us where they lie side by side here in this country of ours… You, the mothers, who sent their sons from far away countries, wipe away your tears, your sons are now lying in our bosom and are in peace after having lost their lives on this land they have become our sons as well.'*

Enriched by our experience and pilgrimage, we leave the Anzac site as a developing cloud cover wipes away the morning sunshine. We return to Maydos Restaurant, at Eceabat, where we enjoy a tasty lunch of soup, salad and whiting fish fillet. Here Izzet meets another group of six, including an Aussie family of four. They will visit the Anzac memorial sites this afternoon while our driver returns us to Budapest, a drive of four and a half hours in showery weather.

We are in need of a whiskey by the time we arrive at the Best Western Senator at 5.00 pm. We head out to find a restaurant and are greeted by a young jovial, rather shortish waiter who suggests we try a goulash fired in a clay pot. 'You won't be disappointed,' he assures us. 'If you don't like, then it will be free.' Out comes the clay pot on a salted pan with flames roaring around it. He seizes the pot with clamps and cuts the top. Inside is a delicious casserole which we tuck into. We return to the hotel well- satisfied with our few days in Istanbul and Turkey.

Monday April 21, 2014,

Istanbul to Budapest

Today we fly to Budapest from Istanbul's Sabiha Gokcen Airport which is located on the Asian side of the city, about an hour's drive from our hotel. Several months ago I booked two no frills tickets for 180 Euro with WIZZ Air. This was 4 times cheaper than any other offer on the internet. Yesterday afternoon the concierge of our hotel arranged a private car for 50 Euro to leave at 10.00 am. This will allow ample time to catch our flight WB 2398 due to depart at 2.35 pm and to arrive in Budapest an hour later.

I snooze till 6.20 am despite my alarm clock's attempt to wake me at 6.00 am. The day is a fine spring day, sunny and refreshing. Those April showers that persisted during yesterday's return to Budapest from the Gallipoli landings have gone.

At 10.00 am our private car arrives with enough room to carry 5 more passengers. We stretch out and enjoy the brisk ride across the huge city. A high six-lane bridge arches the Bosphorus in order to cross from Europe into Asia. Arriving at 11.15 am we find ourselves with more than 3 hours spare. Sabiha Gokcen is a modern award winning airport. Security takes place at the entrance. Check-in and immigration follow. WHIZZ Air doesn't open for check-in until 12.30 pm, two hours before the flight, so we are more or less twiddling our toes until then. We are first in line but the low budget airline catches up with me. I didn't read the fine print and we are charged 60 Euro for each suit case, almost as much as the booking charge. I would have paid far less if I had selected the luggage option payment on the internet site. WHIZZ then requests all passengers to stand in line for boarding, even though the plane had not yet arrived. So we stand there nonplussed for 30 minutes. Then there is a rapid last minute dash to obtain the best seats because seats are not allocated on a no-frills airline.

We arrive at Budapest at 4.15 pm and take 30 minutes to clear immigration. It is easy to find a taxi by following markers in the tiled floor. We are not through the terminal door when a taxi driver approaches us. We follow him outside and down a long footpath leading to his taxi. Avril is happy to be relieved of her luggage. He wastes no time in whisking us to the Sofitel Chain Bridge Hotel. His fare is 36 Euro and I settle for 40 Euro. We will be here for two nights before the APT River Tour starts. We will stay a further two nights with APT in the same hotel. We arrange to keep the same room.

The bell boy follows us with our luggage to our room on the fifth floor. It affords a magnificent view over the Danube to the other side. Below us, stretching the river is the beautiful and famous Chain Bridge. 'You are in Pest. The other side is Buda,' says the bell boy. 'You will find plenty of shops if you turn right; there are plenty of bars and restaurants.'

It is Easter Monday. The main business centre is closed but there are makeshift stores set up in and beyond the busy city square. Heavy rock music is echoing out from a stage and drowning out conversation. We walk past stall after stall selling various craft and souvenirs as well as mouth-watering Hungarian food such as Hungarian goulash, kebabs, sausages and pizzas. We haven't eaten since breakfast so we purchase two delicious kebabs and share a pint of beer. Earlier I found an ATM and withdrew about 100,000 Huszezer Forint in local money, worth $490 Aussie dollars. (About 2000 HF equal $1 Australian dollar). We decide to head to a stall where we saw the Hungarian goulash being served in a hollow loaf of bread. We are too late. Most of the store owners are packing up their portable stores. It is a balmy evening and we stumble upon a restaurant and bar called *Boom and Brass*. A stylish female singer sways to the beat of a keyboard player as they entertain diners with pleasant and popular old time melodies. Avril and I could easily dance to the rhythmic beat if there was enough floor space. We order some goulash and a glass of wine for the sum total of 5421 Forint, less than 25 Aussie dollars. It hardly makes a dint in my 100,000 HF.

Around 9.00 pm we trudge back to our hotel and put on a jug for a cuppa. Avril is tired and soon falls asleep. From our window I admire the serene night view of the lights on the Chain Bridge linking Pest with Buda.

A long queue waiting to enter the Hagia Sophia, Istanbul, Turkey.

Garden area outside the Blue Mosque, Istanbul.

Archaeological Museum, Istanbul.

Sarcophagus displaying a conquest by Alexander the Great

Replica Trojan Horse at Troy.

Markers indicate succeeding civilizations at Troy.

ANZAC Commemoration Site, Gallipoli Peninsula, Turkey.

Headstone of ANZAC legend, John Simpson Kirkpatrick.

Gravesite of ANZAC legend, John Simpson Kirkpatrick, 'the man with the donkey'.

Lone Pine Memorial Cemetery, Gallipoli.

WW I trench warfare site at Gallipoli.

Turkish casserole cooked in a clay pot, Istanbul.

Turkish casserole cooked in a clay pot, Istanbul.

Inside the Blue Mosque, Istanbul.

Turkish rugs at Matis carpet warehouse.

Entry point to the Grand Bazaar, Istanbul.

CHAPTER 6

THE DANUBE

Tuesday April 22, 2014,

Budapest, Hungary

At 7.20 am Avril wakes me with a cup of tea. It is unusual for me to sleep in, but our time in Turkey has kept us busy. We arrived late yesterday afternoon in Budapest where we are staying at the Sofitel Chain Bridge Hotel. Tomorrow we will catch up with an APT River Cruise group for a couple of days here in Budapest before heading down the scenic Danube River to Nuremberg in Germany and then travelling by coach to Prague. Today we are free to explore the city but it is raining. Everyone I know, who has been to Prague, proclaim how wonderful the city is. The rainy weather will test this proclamation after breakfast when we head out to do some shopping.

We don our wet weather gear and walk about the city. Avril needs some Euro. There are a number of banks, but she is unable to find one that dispenses Euro. She is advised to take the local currency and to swap it for Euro at one of the money exchanges. She extracts 75,000 Hungarian Forint (HUF), equivalent to $378 Aussie dollars.

I am on the lookout for another high definition SD card for my camcorder. I look into a couple of shops but I cannot find a photo outlet that stocks the quality I want. On our search we call into a souvenir shop that specializes in Hungarian handicrafts. Avril's eyes light up as she finds an exquisite piece of embroidery with colourful tulips. We are walking around in light rain and decide it is time for a coffee break. There are many choices but we decide to call into the 'Boom and Brass' where we dined the previous evening. For something light to go with the Americano we have chocolate pikelets, a tasty treat swimming in a yummy cream base.

At 1.00 pm it is still raining when we return to our hotel. A hint of late afternoon sunshine appears as we are sipping our Scotch and Dry down in the hotel bar. A waiter chats with us and we explain to him that we will be joining the APT river cruise group tomorrow. We are hoping for better weather. He checks his iPhone and finds that a finer day of 23 C is forecast.

For the evening meal we venture out at 8.30 pm to find a restaurant that has Hungarian cuisine. People dine late here so the night is young. We finish up at the Duna Csarda, a Hungarian restaurant specialising in grilling food on the stone. We share a tender loin of pork which comes sizzling on a hot stone. You cut it into pieces and turn it on the stone until it is cooked to your preferred taste. You dip it and the side pieces of roasted potato chips into the tasty yoghurt sauce provided. A musician dressed stylishly in a white coat pours out a mix of Hungarian and old time favourites on his keyboard. A group of young women are dining in the far corner. One rushes over to sing along side of the musician while her friend takes photos on her iPad, no doubt to be forwarded on Facebook!

Our tasty meal and red wine costs less than $25 Australian. It is a delightful way to spend the evening.

Wednesday April 23, 2014,

Budapest, Hungary

I snooze in until my alarm annoys me enough to arise at 6.20 am. The rays of bright morning sunlight reflect a picturesque image of the opposite bank onto the waters of the Danube River. I grab my camera to capture the magic. No wonder, Liszt, Strauss, Mozart and other artists were inspired to compose their classical waltzes as a tribute to its graceful beauty.

My guide book tells me that Budapest has a population of 2.55 million. There's no other Hungarian city like Budapest in size and importance. Its natural charm makes it stand apart. Straddling a gentle curve in the Danube, the city is flanked by the Buda Hills on the west bank and the beginnings of the Great Plain to the east. Architecturally, it has enough Baroque, Neoclassical, Eclectic and Art Nouveau elements to satisfy anyone. Budapest is the nation's administrative, business and cultural centre. Everything of importance starts and finishes here.

Hungary is at the very heart of Europe. This kidney-shaped country has a long history, a rich culture and strong folk traditions. The landlocked nation covers about 104,000 sq km (39,919 sq miles). Most of the east is flat, but the northwest has rolling hills and low mountains. Almost 55 percent of the land is suitable for agriculture, allowing Hungary to be almost self-sufficient in food.

Hungary's population of about 9.9 million is decreasing by 0.25% annually. Magyars (Hungarians) form the largest ethnic group and 90% of the population. The Roma (Gypsies) comprise 4% of the population. Hungary's impact on Europe's history and development has been greater than its present size and population would suggest. There are Roman ruins, ancient castles and Turkish minarets in Baroque cities.

Founded in 1000 AD, Hungary is powerful until 1526 when the Turks occupy lands that include Budapest. In 1686, the Austrian Habsburgs annex the lands that have been under Turkish rule. Unrest in 1867 eventually leads to Hungarian autonomy within the Austro-Hungarian Empire.

Hungary is stripped of more than two-thirds of its territory after WW 1. Ambition to recover its lost territory draws the nation into WW II on the Axis side (Germany, Italy and Japan). The Germans occupy Hungary when leftist partisans try to negotiate a separate peace in 1944. The Nazi begin deporting hundreds of Jews to death camps at Auschwitz. In April 1945, Hungary is liberated by the Soviet army. However, in 1947 the communists take complete control of the government.

Anti-Soviet student demonstrations prompt Soviet tanks to move into Budapest in 1956, and more than 25,000 people die. Hungary begins moving towards full democracy in 1989 and the last Soviet troops leave the country in June 1991. Hungary joins the EU in 2004.

The story of Budapest begins only in 1873 with the administrative union of three cities that have grown together: Buda, west of the Danube; Obuda to the north; and Pest on the eastern side of the river. Previously these city areas have been occupied for thousands of years. In the late 19th century, under the Austro-Hungarian monarchy, the population of Budapest soars. Many notable buildings date from that period. The city suffers damage in both World Wars, and the 1956 revolution leaves structures pockmarked, though many have now been restored.

At 10.30 am we check in at the APT desk in the lobby. There are no tours until tomorrow morning – a guided tour of Budapest. Avril and I head out again to foot-slog around Budapest. I am still searching for a high quality SD card. An information centre provides us with a map to help locate two Photo shops. I can't read its fine print, so Avril navigates. The first of the shops is still using celluloid film and old cameras. The second shop has a closed door with a small front window. At first we walk past the nondescript site. But I reel round and peer inside, hopefully. We squeeze into a tiny room where an attendant is serving two customers. You couldn't swing a cat. The other attendant leans over to serve me. I have hit the jackpot. He has two high speed definition SD cards with ample 16 GB capacity, so I purchase both. We have been walking briskly for almost two hours. It is time for lunch. At a bistro close to our hotel we have a light snack, aerated water and coffee Americano.

At 5.35 pm it is time for a Scotch and Dry in the hotel bar. We liked the hot stone meal at Duna Csarda last evening so we decide to try the seafood which has a dozen prawns for Avril and I to share, plus the baked potato chips. I have a tall glass of beer and Avril has a glass of white. For dessert I try the tasty Hungarian Strudel and Avril settles for the ice cream.

Thursday April 24, 2014,

Budapest, Hungary

I do not set the alarm but I arise at 6.15 am, a few minutes later than usual. From my grand view of the Danube from the fifth floor hotel room I see the city beginning to stir. There is hazy cloud about, but the weather should be fine for our excursion of Pest and of Buda on the other side of the river. At 9.30 am we join the Green Group, one of the three APT coaches. Our experienced guide is Katalin Decsenyi who speaks English, French and German. She has her own web site and may be found on www.budapestprivatetours.hu. Her dry wit keeps us amused. She is a Jew from a tough Jewish family who survive Auschwitz and The Holocaust. Her mother is 10 and her father 15 when Eichmann sends half a million from Budapest to face the gas chamber in April 1945. The Jews are safe here until 1944 when Hungary changes sides to support the Allies. The Nazi seize a fortune of Jewish property. Now, as a result, her parents and other Holocaust survivors receive ongoing lifetime compensation payments every year.

Katalin explains, 'The USSR saved many Jews, but they stayed too long. The Communists confiscated everything in 1948 and built a huge Statue of Stalin in the public square. This was pulled down during the revolution in 1956, but they replaced it with one of Lenin. You may be asking, did they get their property back when they left in 1991? Well no one pays rent anymore. I pay only 2 Euro per month for my apartment in lower Buda. Some former business owners did not get their businesses, but they receive compensation vouchers. If you wish, you can buy a good 80 sq metre apartment here for US $120,000, half that in the country or double for new apartments.'

We begin our drive from Pest by following the lower river road of the Danube. Katalin says, 'When the river floods, we can only use the higher level road. All river traffic stops during a flood. On rare occasions the river freezes and you can walk across to Buda.' As we pass the Chain Bridge she comments, 'This is where we built our first bridge to cross the Danube. It was first built by the British 160 years ago. All the bridges were destroyed by retreating Germans during the war.'

The Chain Bridge is considered to be one of the wonders of the world at the time of its construction in 1849. At that time a temporary pontoon crossing is available for use during summer and autumn until the bridge is built. During winter the pontoon is disconnected to protect it against drifting ice. The only way to cross during wintertime is by ferry. In 1820 Count Istvan Szechenyi misses his father's funeral when the ferry service is halted for a week due to bad weather. The aggrieved count resolves to build a permanent bridge across the Danube.

In 1836 Szechenyi asks English Civil Engineer, William Tierney to design the bridge. In 1842, Scottish engineer Adam Clark begins the construction of the Chain Bridge which measures 375 m long and 16 m wide. A legend has it that Clark is so proud of his masterpiece that he will challenge anyone to find any fault with his work. It is claimed that he commits suicide when someone discovers that the lions at either ends of the bridge do not have tongues. Yet another rumour claims it was the sculptor of the lions who threw himself off the bridge. This happens during the opening ceremony, on November 20, 1849, when a spectator proclaims the missing tongues. Both rumours are false and the lions do have small tongues.

The bridge ignites the economic revival of Hungary by linking the provincial towns of Pest and Buda into a fast growing metropolis. In 1945, near the end of World War II, the bridge is blown up by the retreating Germans in an attempt to halt the advancing Red Army. It is rebuilt as an exact copy of the original and reopens in 1949, a century after the inaugural opening.

On our way through Pest, Katalin points out the major public buildings and the city zoo. We drive around a huge public square called Hero's Square, a World Heritage Site. At its centre stands the Millennium Monument with its towering thirty-six metre Millennium Column topped with a statue of the archangel Gabriel. Legend has it that the archangel appears to St Stephen in a dream and offers him the crown of Hungary. Stephen is declared a saint for his efforts in bringing Christianity to Hungary. Around the base of the monument are equestrian statues of ferocious warriors. The statues depict the seven founding Magyar chieftains who in 896 AD conquer the Carpathian Basin, the area now known as Hungary. Katalin says, 'In 1896 there were big 1,000th celebrations to mark the occasion. Remember that date. All major public buildings here date from that year.'

'Stephen became Hungary's first king on Christmas Day AD 1000. Saint Stephen converted the people to Christianity,' she continues.

'Good Stephen,' says Katalin proudly, 'Our bus driver is Stephen -- Yah!'

Katalin explains the method of cooking the famous Hungarian goulash. 'You fry the onion in oil and then add the paprika to taste. Then you add the meat and brown it. You the add water or stock as you go, plus a few vegetables to taste. If you add more water it becomes soup. If you get more guests, just add more water.'

We pass by the busy Jewish Quarter containing the Great Synagogue. The twin-towered building built in 1859 is the second largest synagogue in the world. It has a museum containing a harrowing exhibit on the Holocaust. Behind the synagogue is the Memorial of the Hungarian Jewish Martyrs dedicated to those who perished in the death camps. Katalin explains, '100,000 Jews still live in Budapest. But not all are practicing Jews. Although I am from a Jewish family, I do not live as a Jew.'

Our coach now crosses one of the nine bridges that span the Danube, from the flat side of Pest to Buda Hills on the western side of the Danube. Katalin directs our attention to some stately mansions as we approach the top of Castle Hill. 'This is what I call the Beverley Hill section of Buda. Unfortunately I live in the lower Buda.' She points to a bike lane in a leafy parkland and says that she rode her bicycle from her apartment to Pest to be with us this morning. 'The bike lanes will take you all the way to Austria. On the way there are bicycle petrol stations where you can fill up with beer.' We all laugh. 'It was very easy for me this morning going down. But it will be more difficult when I return.'

In the thirteenth century the first citizens arrive at Castle Hill, seeking protection in the hills of Buda after Mongol tribes invade Hungary. In 1243 King Bela IV builds a keep surrounded by thick walls, but no trace of it remains. The foundations of today's royal castle are laid in the fourteenth century when King Lajos the Great completes a Romanesque style castle in 1356. Buda castle has been besieged thirty-one times since then. Around 1396 Sigismund of Luxemburg replaces this early castle by a Gothic style palace with an impressive Knight's Hall. Construction continues in the fifteenth century, following the marriage of King Matthias Corvinus and Beatrix of Naples in 1476. The great Hungarian king thinks that Sigismund's palace is too sober and small, so he orders the construction of a new palace in Renaissance style. Many Italian artists and craftsmen accompany the new queen, lured by the city's prosperity.

The Turks invade and rule the city between 1541 and 1686. Their occupation leaves the city in ruins. Budapest is recaptured and Hungary's new rulers, the Habsburgs, built a new smaller palace in Baroque style between 1714 and 1723. Empress Maria Theresa extends the palace, but the great fire of 1810 and the Hungarian revolt against the Habsburgs destroy much of the new palace. Following the Austro-Hungarian Compromise of 1867, the Habsburg palace is rebuilt to express Hungary's independence. The reconstruction is seen as symbolic since no monarch has lived there since 1541.

During World War II the Germans depose the last resident, Miklos Horthy, regent of Hungary, in 1944. The castle is ruined again in the battle between the German armed forces, the Wehrmacht, and the Red Army. Reconstruction of the castle commences in 1950 and the original Baroque dome is replaced with a classicist version. Ruins of the fifteenth century castle are discovered and incorporated in the new Buda Castle, known as the Royal Palace. Today the interior of the palace is austere compared to its predecessors. However, the magnificent Buda

Castle with its 300 m long façade is still an imposing complex that overlooks the city from its elevated position atop Castle Hill, some forty-eight metres above the Danube.

On Castle Hill we alight from the coach to spend an hour walking the cobbled streets in order to admire the impressive eighteenth century Baroque houses, the Gothic architecture and the panoramic scenes of the Danube. The main streets of the World Heritage Site still follow their medieval paths, since building began there in the 13th century. Some houses date back to the 14th and 15th centuries and a number of buildings are still in private hands. Castle Hill is still a residential area and cars are banned except for residents and workers.

The massive Royal Palace occupies the far end of Castle Hill. Inside are the Hungarian National Gallery and the Budapest History Museum. Our time is limited so we head towards Trinity Square which forms the heart of Buda's Castle District. This square at the highest point of the area was once the main marketplace.

The centrepiece of the square is Trinity Column, designed by Phillip Ungliech and built between 1710 and 1713 by the council as a memorial to celebrate the end of the plague that ravaged the city in 1691 and 1709. At the top of the Baroque column we see a sculpture of the golden Holy Trinity with angels and saints and at the base is King David praying to end the plague.

Facing the square is the majestic Matthias Church, the most important one in Buda. It features a colourful tiled roof and contains lovely murals inside. The historic church is over 700 years old and is the scene of several coronations. In 1476 it is the venue for the royal wedding of the great Hungarian King Matthias to Beatrix of Naples, hence its name. Following the Austro-Hungarian Compromise of 1867, Matthias Church is the scene of a massive coronation ceremony for the crowning of Franz Joseph and his wife Elizabeth, and thereby establishing the Austro-Hungarian Empire. Katalin reminds us that Franz List's *'Hungarian Coronation Mass'* is played here for the first time at the coronation.

Katalin leads us across the square to the well-known Fisherman's Bastion which offers wonderful panoramic views of Budapest. On the way we admire a statue of the first Christian king of Hungary, St Stephen. He is shown mounted on his horse atop an ornate pedestal featuring decorated reliefs.

We only have an hour to soak in this time capsule. Katalin carefully explains the directions for us to meet the coach at 12.15 pm. 'You must turn here. If you go straight on you will end up in Romania in two days' time.'

To the south of Castle Hill is Gellert Hill, a 235 m high hill overlooking the Danube. Unfortunately it is not on our schedule, but the views from the Citadella (Citadel) at the top Gellert Hill offer stunning views of the Parliament building and both directions of the Danube. The fortress was erected by the Habsburgs in 1854 following the suppression of the 1848-49 Hungarian revolution and War of Independence.

At the end of Citadella is the Liberty Statue, designed by Hungarian sculptor, Zsigmond Kisfaludi Strobl, and erected in 1947 by the Soviet's to commemorate the Nazis' defeat. Standing at 14 metres tall, the gigantic statue of a woman is proclaiming freedom. The Gellert Monument is visible from almost anywhere in town and is most impressive at night when it is floodlit.

Gellert Hill is named after the 11th century bishop St Gellert, who converts the Magyars to Christianity. Legend says that the Bishop is put to death by pagans who put him in a barrel, rolled it down the hill and threw it into the Danube. His statue holds a cross and faces Elizabeth Bridge. Designed by Gyula Jankovits and erected in 1904, it can be seen from many parts of Pest.

Fortunately, at the appropriate time, we are all accounted for. From Castle Hill Katalin takes us to a huge market place for some shopping. Guess when it was built?' asks Katalin. '1896,' we reply.

The lower section of the market contains shops full of produce, and the upper section provides mainly for cafes and handicrafts. In the hour available for shopping we buy a few lovely Hungarian souvenirs. Avril purchases a small Hungarian doll in traditional dress, a collector's spoon and a colourful bracelet. At 1.30 pm we return along a scenic route beside the riverside of Buda and cross the Chain Bridge to our hotel. We observe our river ship, the *MS AmaLyra,* ready for our cruise tomorrow.

We decide on a light lunch and a drink at the Boom and Brass. I have a fruit cocktail and Avril chooses an ice coffee. It is probably all we need. However, we order a burger thinking it will be a light meal. It comes with the works and heaps of chips, which we cannot finish. We return to the Sofitel and tidy up our gear in readiness for embarkation of the *MS AmaLyra* tomorrow. At 5.00 pm we are sipping a Scotch and Dry in the hotel bar. At 8.15 pm Avril suggests a light quick meal and drink at the English pub. It proves to be the worst meal on tour. I order a pork chop to go with my beer. It looks like a thick piece of cardboard covered with melted cheese on top of a pile of greasy chips. I simply push it aside. Avril does slightly better with jacket potatoes and a little salad which she generously offers to me. Back at the hotel we finish sorting out our main luggage which needs to be placed outside our rooms by 9.00 am in the morning.

Friday April 25, 2014,

Budapest

    Today is ANZAC Day and by the time I wake at 5.55 am the Dawn Service would be over in Australia and at Anzac Cove at Gallipoli. Sunrise here in Budapest is at 5.38 am but today the weather is cloudy and overcast.

    At 10.30 am we join an optional tour to Puszta, on the Great Hungarian Plain. This vast World Heritage region stretches to Hungary's east and showcases pristine natural grassland habitat, which is fundamental for the country's agricultural heritage and the region's native flora and fauna. The wet skies have set in and light rain is falling as we drive for nearly an hour. Our guide from Budapest is Gabriella, a light framed and neatly dressed woman. She is knowledgeable but her monotone weak voice does not command much attention beyond the front seats where Avril and I sit. She repeats much of what Katalin revealed to us yesterday.

    Puszta is a horse ranch that showcases the traditional horsemanship of the Magyar horsemen. In the blink of an eye, a rider on his horse at full gallop fires an arrow to hit a target. Another thrusts a spear into the wooden frame to demonstrate how deadly an attack on horseback could be. Cracking whips bring puffs of smoke but the horses are trained to ignore it, a requirement in the heat of battle. A champion horsewoman shows the dressage skills of her horse. Another man stands on the rump of two horses as they gallop around the track.

    We are shown the ultra-clean stables where the 86 champion horses reside. The ranch museum is stocked with many trophies gained over the years. A film of a trophy win is shown of a rider and wagon negotiating tricky obstacles. We visit the ranch's farmyard animals where a turkey expresses it annoyance. Baby lambs, white and black, hide close to their mothers. A woolly pig listens intently as our guide explains how tasty the flesh is of its breed. A small horse takes a nibble of my jacket as I brush past it on my way to a covered wagon attached to two white horses; another wagon is attached to two black horses. We are taken for a ride around the ranch. The horses have no trouble powering a load of about 16 passengers around the terrain. The wagons pull into to a huge ranch complex with restaurant facilities.

    Inside are rows of tables where about a hundred people are tucking into their soup and a tasty BBQ. Lively music from 5 musicians is rousing enough to dance to. We take our seats at the back of the hall as the musicians whip up the stirring *'William Tell Overture'*. The musicians move towards us and play a mix of old time favourites and some Hungarian gipsy tunes. Avril and I get up to dance it is so much fun. Katalin, our guide for yesterday's excursion, comes over to congratulate us.

    The skies are still weeping rain as we return to Budapest. At 3.30 pm we board our river ship the *MS AmaLyra*. The ship's newspaper, *The Daily Cruiser*, has a quote for the day: 'Every day is a new life to the wise one.' It announces, 'We are pleased to welcome you aboard your floating luxury hotel for this amazing cruise that lies ahead. Get settled in your new home away from home, get to know some of our crew members, and enjoy your first night aboard.'

    Avril and I quickly settle and enjoy a cup of tea in the Lounge at 5.00 pm. At 6.00 pm in the Lounge there is a Welcome Cocktail, an Information Briefing and Safety Drill. Attendance for the Safety Drill is compulsory. We are introduced to the main crew members including the Captain, Andreas Zarwel, from Germany. The Cruise Manager, Csaba Tamas, announces the various countries that have joined the ship. Avril and I are the only Aussies. There are many from the USA and Canada. The Americans seem keen to chat with us. One man, a Vietnam veteran, chatted with Avril. He told her that he loves our country and has visited Australia seven times to join reunions.

At 7.00 pm the Welcome Dinner is served in the onboard restaurant prior to sailing from Budapest. Gypsy violinists walk around to entertain us with Hungarian melodies. Sailing out of Budapest at night is unforgettable. At 9.00 pm we have our cameras ready to catch the illuminated city skyline, its golden lights mirrored in the Danube.

Saturday April 26, 2014,
Cruising day to Bratislava

At 6.20 am we arise after our relaxing first night of the river cruise. From our cabin we see mainly a forest of green on the banks of the Danube. The sky is overcast and the weather forecast is for scattered thunder storms, temperature ranging from 11C to 19 C. Breakfast is available at 7.30 am and we find ourselves one of the first customers. There are a good choice of cereals, hot food, meats, breads and pastries. On the special menu, a full English breakfast is available, pancakes and waffles. I start with my usual preference of muesli and mixed fruit. From the special menu I order eggs Benedict to go with my coffee. Avril has her corn flakes and the chef cooks her fried eggs to have with her toast. We chat with a Canadian couple and their mother, a sprightly granny worrying about where the cereals are and also the coffee, hopefully 'not too strong'. The gentleman and I enjoy a conversation on currency rates and the world economy. He is a former Brit who now lives in Ontario in a small town near Lake Superior. He loves the cold winters for skiing and the glorious hot summers.

This morning we enjoy a relaxing cruise on the Danube between Hungary and Slovakia. Slovakia's roots can be traced to the 9th century state of Great Moravia. Subsequently, the Slovaks become part of the Hungarian Kingdom, where they remain for the next 1,000 years. After the dissolution of the Austro-Hungarian Empire at the close of WW 1, the Slovaks join the closely related Czechs to form Czechoslovakia. Following WW II, Czechoslovakia comes under Communist rule within Soviet-dominated Eastern Europe.

The peaceful 'Velvet Revolution' sweeps the Communist Party from power at the end of 1989 and inaugurates a return to democratic rule and a market economy. On January 1, 1993, the country undergoes a nonviolent 'Velvet Divorce and splits into Slovakia and the Czech Republic. Slovakia joins both NATO and the EU in the spring of 2004 and adopts the Euro five years later.

Slovakia is primarily mountainous, with relatively warm summers and cold and humid winters. The warmest region is Bratislava and Southern Slovakia where the temperatures may rise to up to +30 C in summer, occasionally to 35-37 C. Its size is 49,035 sq km with a population 5.5 million. The capital, Bratislava, has population of 462,000.

At 11.00 am we are due to arrive at the biggest lock on our cruise, Gabcikovo. However, the *AmaLyra* is ahead of schedule and we arrive at 9.30 am. The lock is an important part of Slovakia's electric power grid, providing 20 per cent of its electricity. The lock takes only about 30 minutes to lift us 18 metres. The starboard side is almost touching the wall of the lock as we rise. Another river ship joins us on the passage through the lock to enter the large Gabcikovo-Nagymros Dam. It was built between Hungary and what is now known as the Czech Republic. The project's goal is to prevent catastrophic floods, improve river navigability and produce clean electricity. Only a part of the project has been finished in Slovakia, because Hungary first suspends then tries to terminate the project due to environmental concerns. This causes an international dispute and both parties have to turn to the International Court at The Hague for a ruling.

The Danube is Europe's second longest River. From its source in the Black Forest in Germany to its mouth in Romania it flows for a total of 2,848 kilometres. Ever since ancient times the Danube has exercised a magical attraction. Along its banks the remains of the earliest human settlements have been found: the 'Venus of Willendorf' was discovered in the Wachau Valley in Lower Austria and a statuette from Carasija near Belgium – two of the oldest representations of the human form in sculpture.

On its route from west to east, the Danube traverses ten countries and unites the most diverse peoples, religions and cultures. The banks of the Danube are densely lined by monuments which bear witness to an eventful history: mighty castles, lofty monasteries and sumptuous palaces. The varied scenery along the Danube's course is the source of legend and myth. It is navigable for 2415 km, almost its entire length. Now, via the Main Danube Canal, the Danube River links with the Rhine River, thus making it possible navigate from the Black Sea to the North Sea.

At 10.30 we join our Cruise Manager, Csaba for a briefing on the detailed sailing schedule and upcoming events. He is a tall athletic Hungarian with piercing blue eyes. His pleasant and amusing comments are delivered in a heavy accent. He is 40 years of age and was brought up under the strict rule of Communism which offered no personal freedom. He says, 'You were bound by its rigid rules. It was a difficult adjustment to make to a free society.'

He reads out *'The Seven Wonders of Communism'*:

>   Everybody has a job
>   Everybody has a job but nobody works
>   Even though nobody works, the five-year plan is fulfilled 110 percent
>   Even though the five-year plan is fulfilled 110 per cent there is nothing in the stores
>   Even though there is nothing in the stores, people have everything they need
>   Even though people have everything they need, they keep stealing
>   Even though people keep stealing, nothing is reported stolen.

At 1.00 pm we arrive in Bratislava which is often called 'Beauty on the Danube'. It has a long history that has been strongly influenced by people of different nations and religions. From 1536 to 1783 the city is the capital of the kingdom of Hungary (a part of the Habsburg Monarchy territories). In 1993 it becomes capital of the newly formed Slovak Republic. In the 1990s and early 21st century, its economy booms due to foreign investment.

The old town is located just steps away from the ship. It abounds in charming houses and buildings which mostly have been restored and repainted after the fall of Communism. Almost the entire city centre is a pedestrian zone and a delight to walk around.

At 2.30 pm Avril and I take part in the Bratislava Communist Tour to visit a selection of landmarks from the city's communist past, such as Liberty Square and the Soviet War Memorial. Our guide is Eve, a mature Slovakian patriot. She has lived under communist rule. Light rain is falling as we begin our tour. 'I have something important to tell you,' she says, 'The weather is crying tears because you are leaving us today.'

I am thinking how dingy the city looks. The grotty buildings at riverside are full of graffiti. But this quickly changes as Eve points out new structures that are replacing the stark facades of those built during the communist rule following WW II. A huge double pylon bridge, called *The Bridge of the Slovak Uprising*, spans the Danube. Nearby is the impressive upside down pyramid building. Our little red bus commences a climb up the hills overlooking the city. The hillside contains the homes of the wealthy and the embassies. 'There is the real White House' says Eve, 'The other one is in the USA.'

We stop at the Russian Memorial which contains the bodies of the 6845 Russians who freed Czechoslovakia from German domination in WW II. '6845 is interesting for two reasons,' says Eve, '45 is the year that the Russians freed us and 68 is the year of our uprising against Russian Communist Rule.'

'In 1948 the Communist nationalized all property. In 1968 Alexander Dubcek led the movement towards democracy. Some 60,000 people were killed or imprisoned. But it was the end for Communism. Liberation came in 1987 and Dubcek became leader of the new Democratic Party in 1992. He was killed 10 days later in a car crash which occurred on a straight piece of highway. So work that one out,' says Eve.

'All major public buildings and palaces, formerly nationalized and turned into apartment housing, could be claimed back. But the families living there could not be cast out. Instead they are rented less than 100 Euro per month. This causes friction because a normal rent would be about 1800 Euro.'

Eve says the former Czechoslovakia separated peacefully to become the Czech Republic in 1991 because it suited their leadership. 'Slovakia was the less advanced and a hindrance to the Czech Republic. We joined the EU and adopted the Euro, whereas the Czech Republic still retains their currency. They are not fully committed to the EU. Foreign investment flowed here and our unemployment level dropped from 22% to 7.5%. It's beginning to rise again, but that's because of the small towns away from Bratislava. Here in the city unemployment is only 2.5 %. The average wage here is about 850 Euro per month.'

From the austere Russian Memorial we drive to Bratislava Castle, once the home of a royal family until the Hungarians conquered the lands in 1000 AD. The castle has been destroyed and rebuilt over the years. It has high towers in each of its corners. The historic castle is painted white to enhance its recent restoration as a museum. Eve says, 'We were lucky to escape bombing during the war. This was because they concentrated on the industrial sections outside the city.'

Bratislava Castle stands on an isolated rocky hill, directly above the Danube River. From its vantage point in what is called the 'Little Carpathians Landscape Area', it offers excellent views of Bratislava, Austria and parts of Hungary. Straddling the Danube below us is the impressive 'Bridge of the Slovak Uprising', the first asymmetrical suspension bridge in the world. Built in the years 1967-72, the steel road bridge is hung on a pylon 84.6 metres in height and spans the Danube with a length of 431 m and a width of 21 m. A flying saucer shape restaurant is perched on top of the pylon.

Standing in the parkland and backdrop of the castle is a beautiful bronze statue honouring St Elizabeth of Hungary (1207-1231). The plaque below the statue states:

The daughter of King Alexander II and his wife Gertrude, Elizabeth spent her childhood at Bratislava Castle. After the death of her husband Ludwig of Thuringia (died of a heavy fever while fighting with the Crusaders) she took a vow of poverty and devoted her life to others, particularly the poor and the sick. Canonized in 1235 she is revered by Sisters of St Elizabeth as their patroness.

At 5.15 pm we are back on board the *AmaLyra* for our whiskey and dry. At 6.45 Csaba, our Cruise Manager, outlines tomorrow's visit to Vienna. At 7.00 pm we have an excellent dinner in the Restaurant and are joined by two couples from Los Angles – Leonard, a retired credit manager and his wife Jen, a teacher; Norman and his wife Nora were also on our tour with Eve this afternoon. After dinner we retire to the lounge to be entertained with a great performance by *The Aphrodites*, a Slovakian ladies group who play classical instruments. The five women dressed in flowing white sleeveless gowns and bolero jackets play a delightful combination of long time favourites from Andrew Lloyd Webber and ABBA as well as local Gypsy music. The quintet is made up of three string instruments (violin, viola and cello), a flute and piano.

Sunday April 27, 2014,

Vienna, Austria

The weather promises a magnificent day as the *AmaLyra* arrives in Vienna, the capital of Austria and by far its largest city. At 6.00 am sunrise the morning sky is deep blue and cloudless. The forecast is sunny all day with the temperature rising from 10 C to 22 C. I peer through the condensation on my cabin window as a woman wearing a backpack briskly walks by. The tree-lined walkway in front of pastel terrace houses displays sereneness in the morning sunshine.

After breakfast we look forward to exploring the grandeur of Vienna's monumental buildings lining the famous Ringstrasse, the prestigious boulevard that forms a 57 metre wide Ring Road around the old city of Vienna. On December 20 1857, Emperor Franz Joseph 1 issues an order to demolish the old defensive walls that protect the Hofburg palace complex. The city walls no longer offer protection against modern weaponry, as proven in 1809 when Napoleon's French army blows up the Hofburg bastion.

Vienna, with nearly 2 million inhabitants, is a truly elegant and romantic city situated in the historic and cultural heart of Europe. The city receives a year-round stream of tourists who come to view the historic face of this designated UNESCO World Heritage Site. The historic city centre contains many architectural delights, including grand imperial palaces with Baroque interiors, peaceful gardens and parks, museums flanking magnificent squares, notable monuments and the Hofburg, where the Hapsburg rulers lived, loved and married into empires.

For centuries Vienna has attracted a galaxy of artists, musicians and thinkers. Many musical prodigies once lived and worked here, including Wolfgang Amadeus Mozart, Joseph Haydn, Ludwig van Beethoven, Franz Schubert, Johannes Brahms, Gustav Mahler and Arnold Schoenberg. Their efforts can be seen and heard in the various museums throughout the city.

Music was initially reserved for the imperial court of the Habsburg family and the aristocracy, but with the rise of the middle class in the late 1800s, music also becomes an important part of bourgeois life. Classical music flourishes in Vienna with compositions for the waltz, including those created by Johann Strauss the Elder and then, even more famously, by his son. Popular music also flourishes as migration from all parts of the Hapsburg Empire introduces new styles of music and dance.

Vienna is also famous for its cuisine. Traditional Viennese food is quite hearty, with a strong emphasis on meat such as the famous *Wiener Schnitzel*. This speciality is a pork cutlet fried in a coating of egg and breadcrumbs. Everyone agrees that the Schnitzel should have the gold-brown colour of a Stradivarius violin.

Hearty soups often include *Knodel* (dumplings) or pasta. Apple strudels and Salzburger Nockeri (a fluffy soufflé) are popular Austrian desserts. The country has excellent lager beers, including Gosser, Schwechater, Stiegl and Zipfler. The famous Sacher Torte is a sinfully rich chocolate cake invented by Franz Sacher for a famous Austrian politician. Back in 1887, as many as 400 a day were baked at Hotel Sacher and shipped to Berlin, Paris and London. These days, 12 pastry chefs make about 550 a day and as many as 3000 daily around Christmas. The cake consists of two layers of dense semi-sweet chocolate dough, a thin layer of apricot jam in the middle, and dark chocolate icing on the sides and top. Traditionally it is eaten with whipped cream as most Viennese consider 'die torte' too dry to be eaten without.

The Austrian countryside is a mountainous and a popular year-round holiday destination. The landlocked German speaking Federal Republic is 83,871 sq km in size and contains of over 8 million people. It is bordered by eight countries: the Czech Republic and Germany to the north, Hungary and Slovakia to the east, Slovenia and Italy to the south, and Switzerland and Liechtenstein to the west.

Many Europeans come here to enjoy hiking and biking in the summer and winter sports in the winter. Meadows and forests cover much of Austria where more than half the country is mountainous. Three chains of mountains run west to east: the Northern Limestone Alps, the Central (or High) Alps and the Southern Limestone Alps. The tallest peaks are in the Central Alps, including the 3797 m Grossglockner.

My tour book says, 'Everyone's seen Julie Andrews spinning around in *The Sound of Music*, but there's more to Austria than forests and snowcapped peaks. In the country where Mozart composed and Strauss taught the world to twirl, you don't need to search hard for culture – it waltzes right up to you.'

Vienna is situated away from the main flow of the Danube River. The *AmaLyra* reaches Vienna by the *Donaukanal* (Danube Canal) which cuts across the Danube floodplain called *Lobau*. Ten per cent of the Danube River cuts its way through Austria, passing through Linz in Upper Austria to Krems and Tulln in Lower Austria. The Danube, an international waterway, rises in the Black Forest Mountains of western Germany and flows 2,872 km southeast through Central and Eastern Europe before emptying into the Black Sea via the Danube Delta in Romania, Ukraine and Moldova. In doing so the second longest river in Europe passes through or touches the borders of ten countries: Germany, Austria, Slovakia, Hungary, Croatia, Serbia, Bulgaria, Romania, Ukraine and Moldova.

The Danube has played a vital role in the settlement and political evolution of Europe. Its waters have long served as a vital commercial highway. Its banks are lined with castles and fortresses which formed the boundary of great empires. The Roman Empire used the Danube as their northern border. For centuries it formed the north western border of the Ottoman Empire. Between the late 14th and 19th centuries the Ottoman Empire competed firstly with the Kingdom of Hungary and later with the Austrian Habsburgs.

Our coach departs for the Vienna city tour at 9.00 am. Reyna is our local guide, of slim athletic build and slightly balding. He has a pleasant smile and speaks fluent English, a requirement in any tourist capital in Europe. Reyna quickly outlines some of the delights of the imperial city as we take the Ring Road to St Stephen's Square. There are so many features to point out: churches, mainly Roman Catholic, interesting statues, fine architecture, parks and cafes.

Our first stop is at St Stephens Square in the heart of Vienna. The magnificent centrepiece of the Square (Stephansplatz) is St Stephen's Cathedral with its towering Gothic spires, the very symbol of the city. There is a lively bustle as visitors check inside the huge Gothic structure, while others soak up the sunshine in the square outside. Some are enjoying a ride by horse and coach, available on one side of the Cathedral. They may not realise that they are sitting in coaches once owned by royalty.

St Stephen's Cathedral is first mentioned in a document dated 1220 as a simple Romanesque parish church belonging to the bishopric of Passau. For centuries, St Stephen's Square is located just outside the walls of the Roman fortress of Vindobona and is a burial ground. By 1732 the area has long been incorporated into the city and, for hygienic reasons, Emperor Charles VI bans any further burials there.

Reyna explains that in 1358 the Habsburg Duke Rudolf IV raises the status of St Stephen's to an Austrian national shrine. Construction of the 137 metre south tower commences the following year and is completed 75 years later in 1433. The 134 metre Gothic building is the tallest in Europe in its time. In 1467 Rudolf has plans for a second tower of equal height on the north side, but the task proves formidable. Emperor Friedrich III takes on the challenge, but the shortage of finance leads to its abandonment in 1511. The shorter north tower now houses the great bell of the cathedral, the Pumerin.

Reyna allows us half an hour free time to explore the ornate interior of the Cathedral and its surroundings. Outside St Stephen's Cathedral you find the *Faiker* stand. Tourists may enjoy a ride in a typical *Faiker*, a Viennese term for a two- horse-drawn carriage. The 'Faiker' also refers to the carriage driver who can be hired to take you on an easy pace ride through the quaint streets of Vienna's old centre. There is no end to the delights of the imperial city.

We emerge from the crowded interior of the cathedral and search for Reyna among the stream of visitors in this popular square. He is waving his 'lollypop' and beckons us to follow him. We walk from St Stephen's Plaza and follow the route of an old Roman moat, now covered by wide pavement. A large part of the street layout goes back to Roman times. We walk along the Graben, meaning '*ditch*'. It is a wide prestigious shopping street that follows the former ditch that defends the Roman citadel of the first century. Beneath the streets are underground cellars interconnected by a network of tunnels. These are constructed under Habsburg rule and are used for stores and workshops. They are used to save many lives during the bombing raids of World War II. But there is also tragedy when a direct bomb-strike blocks the single entry to one of the air raid shelters. Several hundred people are buried alive and perish.

We come to an impressive statue called *The Plague Monument*. Reyna informs us that in 1689 an epidemic of bubonic plague breaks out in Vienna. It spreads like wildfire, claiming thousands of lives. Emperor Leopold 1 vows to erect a monument to give thanks for the end of the epidemic and this is the result. Many artists and architects work on the project which is completed in 1694. The richly ornamented column stands 18 metres in height and is an outstanding example of the high Baroque Period in art.

At the pedestal of the column is the figure of an ugly woman falling into an abyss, an allegory to depict that the plague has been overcome. The allegory also metaphorically represents the Christian victory over Islam during the Turkish sieges by the Ottoman Empire, most recently in 1683. A female figure to the left is pointing her crucifix towards heaven, symbolizing the victory of the Catholic religion. Above this, is the kneeling figure of Emperor Leopold 1, gazing up at the nine choirs of angels in the clouds above him. The magnificent monument symbolizes that Habsburg rule was founded in faith.

Our walk leads to the Hofburg palace complex. It is the largest palace in Europe, covering an area of 240,000 sq m, with 18 wings and 19 courtyards. The old castle is mentioned in records dating back to 1275 when King Ottokar II of Bohemia seizes power from the Babenberg dynasty. He completes the building of the four-square Gothic citadel with its four towers. On August 12, 1278, Ottokar is defeated by Rudolf I von Habsburg in a battle on the Marchfield, to the north-east of Vienna. For the next seven centuries the Hofburg is the centre of the gigantic Habsburg Empire.

Over time the Habsburg emperors develop the Hofburg into a complex of individual wings and four-square citadels with an intricate network of secret passages and stairways. Since the 17th century the entire complex has been known as the Hofburg. Emperor Leopold 1 inaugurated the work to connect all its various wings to provide its present character as a single fortress. Today, the Hofburg is the official seat of the Austrian President and it serves as a congress centre for international organisations.

A visit to the Hofburg is like an imperial march through history, art and luxury. Here you will find more than two dozen museums and collections of international standing. There are the Imperial Apartments where one finds the Imperial Silver Collection of the former Habsburg monarchy. There is the Art and History Museum containing works by Bruegel, Raphael, Rembrandt, van Dyck, Durer, Holbein and other great masters. Other exhibits include the world's largest collection of historic musical instruments, the largest platypus collection, the Empress Elizabeth Museum and the Court Hunting and Armour Museum. The Hofburg contains cafes, restaurants, squares and parks to soak up the imperial ambience. It has a Spanish Riding School where the art of classical riding has been retained to the present day. At the Imperial Court Chapel you can celebrate High Mass with the Vienna Court Music, the Vienna Boys' Choir and members of the Vienna State Opera. At the Imperial Treasury in the oldest part of the Imperial Palace you will find the most important treasure chamber in the world, including the imperial crown.

Our visit to the Hofburg is limited to an explanation of its features by Reyna. In front of St Michael's Wing he shows us traces of the old first century Roman wall foundations that have been excavated and left exposed for public viewing. A portal from St Michael's Wing leads to the Imperial Chancellery Wing which is flanked by two statues of Hercules. The numerous statues of Hercules in the Hofburg date back to Emperor Charles VI who identifies himself with the major hero of Greek mythology.

Reyna leads us past the Spanish Court riding School where we see the famous Lipizzaner horses in their stables. For more than 400 years the Spanish Court Riding School has cultivated the classical art of horsemanship. The School is opened by Emperor Charles VI who moves from Spain to Vienna following the death of his brother Joseph 1 in 1711. It is the only institution in the world where the classic equestrian skills have been preserved and are still practised in their original form. It takes years of training to fuse horse and rider into an inseparable unit in order to perform the precision of movement in harmony with the music. The beautiful white Lipizzaner stallions are all bred in western Styria where they spend their formative years. The stallions enter the world black or brown in colour which turns white between the ages of 7 and 10 years. Their training, over a period of years, begins when they reach the age of four.

Our walk continues to the palace wings surrounding the Josefsplatz. In the middle of the square is the statue of Emperor Joseph II, erected during the reign of Franz II. It depicts Joseph as a Roman conqueror, complete with toga and laurel wreath. The Habsburg rulers believe that they are the descendants of the ancient Roman Emperors. In the ornate building behind his statue is the world famous Baroque hall of the National Library. Atop the façade of the library is the statue of Minerva, the Roman Goddess of Wisdom, who triumphs over jealousy and ignorance. Another one is of the titan Atlas who carries a golden celestial globe on his back.

Our morning visit in the city centre leaves us wanting more. One would need a long vacation to taste its cultural and historic heritage. Reyna walks us to a meeting point near the famous Vienna Court Opera House at Karlsplatz. We have an hour of free time to soak up the atmosphere. Avril and I spy Café Mozart, a busy coffee restaurant near Vienna State Opera. We plan to return here after a tour of the opera site.

Eleonora Gonzaga, wife of Emperor Ferdinand II, brought opera from Italy to Vienna. To her honour, in 1861, the architects August Sicard von Sicardsburg and Eduard van der Null won the commission to design the opera house. They decide to build it in Italian Renaissance style to commemorate Eleonora. With its grand entry facing the new Ringstrasse, this monumental building is intended to become the highlight of the Viennese Romantic Movement and to raise the profile of the city to new heights of prestige. However, history is not always sympathetic. The construction drags on for eight years and Viennese public tastes change strongly, viewing the Opera House as outdated. To make matters worse, the Ringstrasse (Ring Road) is raised by one metre so that only three steps remain of the grand stairway entrance. The jokes go around that it has 'sunk'. Even the Emperor expresses criticism which proves too much for Eduard van der Null. The architect commits suicide on April 4, 1868. Sicardsburg does not survive the completion either. In the same year, on June 11, he suffers a stroke and dies.

The Opera House is ceremonially opened on May 25, 1869 with a performance of Mozart's *Don Giovanni*. Nowadays, the Vienna State Opera contributes greatly to the Vienna's heritage. It is internationally recognised for its televised transmissions of the Opera Ball and its close association with the Vienna philharmonic Orchestra. Nowadays, the Opera House offers approximately 50 operas and 20 ballets every season between September 1 and June 30.

Avril and I stroll around the entire surrounds of the Opera House and we are suitably impressed. Street vendors are out offering pamphlets and advice for its concerts, but we already have a booking to see a concert performance by the Vienna Resident Orchestra tonight. Half of our free time is over so we to head back to our meeting place with Reyna for our return coach. We have just enough time to sit al fresco at Café Mozart for a delicious Viennese coffee, apple strudel and Sacher Torte.

For Lunch on board the *AmaLyra* at 12.30 pm we decide on simple pasta meal. We need to be ready for an afternoon visit of Schonbrunn Palace and its extensive gardens beginning at 1.30 pm. The palace is the former summer residence of the imperial family with a history dating back to the early Middle Age. The complex is one of the world's foremost treasures and is a major tourist attraction in modern Vienna, receiving 1.5 million visitors annually and up to 12,000 per day. Our coach is one of many to deposit their tourists outside the palace entry. The estate has been added to the UNESCO World Cultural Heritage List in 1996 and includes the palace and its ancillary buildings, a huge park with its numerous architectural features, fountains and statues, together with the zoological garden.

The estate is known from the 14th century as the *Katterburg* and belongs to the manor of the Abbey at Klosterneuburg. It lay far outside the walls of the city and contains a small dairy farm and a small mill on the River Vienna. In 1569 Emperor Maximillian II purchases the Katterburg and erects an imperial hunting lodge. Following the death of Maximillian in 1576, his son Rudolph II succeeds him. He provides funds to maintain the estate, but he never uses it. His brother Matthias succeeds to the throne in 1612 and uses the grounds for hunting. According to the legend, he discovers the 'fair spring' (German: '*Schoner Brunnen*') that later gives its name to the estate.

Matthias dies in 1619 and is succeeded by his cousin Ferdinand II. The Emperor and his wife Eleonora habitually choose Schonbrunn as a venue for hunting parties. After Ferdinand's death in 1637, the estate becomes his widow's residence. Eleonora has a summer residence built there. Finished in 1642, she leads an active life and is famed for her interest in the arts. The mansion and deer park are destroyed during the second Turkish Siege of Vienna in 1683. In 1686 the estate passes into the possession of Emperor Leopold 1, who decides to build a magnificent new residence for his son Joseph 1. Money was no object at first, but construction of the side wings falters owing to financial difficulties resulting from the War of Spanish Succession (1702-13) and the remaining building work is abandoned following the sudden death of Joseph 1 in 1711.

The unfinished palace is used as a dowager's residence again until 1728 when Emperor Charles VI, brother of the deceased Joseph 1, acquires Schonbrunn. He eventually gives it to his daughter Maria Theresa around 1736. Her accession to Archduchess and Empress heralds an epoch of splendour for Schonbrunn. Under her personal supervision and of her architect, Nikolaus Pacassi, the former hunting lodge is transformed into an imperial residence for the first time in 1743-1773, acquiring the Rococo appearance it still largely has today.

Rivalry between the Habsburgs in Austria and the Bourbons in France ensures that the stately jewel of Schonbrunn Palace compares favourably with the Palace of Versailles. Schonbrunn has 1441 rooms which house the imperial couple's 16 children and the numerous court officials and servants who have to be provided with accommodation. Maria Theresa's husband, Emperor Franz 1 Stephan of Lorraine, takes personal interest in the arts and sciences. Our guide mentions that he also had 5 mistresses and about 30 more children – no doubt a good Catholic! Children aside, he expands what is still the world's oldest zoo in the huge area of Schonbrunn Park. Maria Theresa takes the death of Franz Stephan in 1765 very hard. The widowed empress spares no expense to furnish his memorial rooms in the East Wing of the palace.

Maria Theresa's last project, undertaken in the 1770s, is the laying out of the gardens. Johann Ferdinand von Hetzendorf is engaged to give the palace park their architectural features, including the Gloriette, the Neptune Fountain, the Roman Ruin and the Obelisk. The avenues, fountains and open spaces are enhanced with numerous statues and sculptures. The remodelling of the palace and gardens is finally completed shortly before Maria Theresa's death in 1780. The palace remains unoccupied for two decades until Emperor Franz II (I) uses it as his summer residence. In 1805 and 1809 the French army occupies Austria. Napoleon uses Franz 1 Stephan's memorial rooms as his living quarters.

This afternoon a special guide escorts our group through the main rooms of the palace – no photos and no stopping. We are agog as we move through an opulence of Rococo and Baroque furnishings, chandeliers, ceiling frescos and galleries of art works depicting the life of the Habsburg rulers. Of particular splendour is the Great Gallery room, forty-three metres long and 10 metres wide. Its three ceiling frescos depict the allegories of the Austrian Crown lands, Peace and War. Ironically, during WW II an unexploded bomb destroys the *Allegory of War*. Our guide mentions a sum of 100 million (Euro) spent on its renovation.

The Great Gallery provides the perfect setting for grand receptions, balls and festive banquets. Maria Theresa enjoyed celebrating the 'name-days' of family members. On such occasions there was usually a ball as well as theatre and ballet entertainment provided by her children. Since the foundation of the Republic in 1918, the Great Gallery has continued to be used for concerts and receptions. On June 3, 1961 it was the meeting place for the historic encounter between the American president John F Kennedy and the Soviet premier Nikita Khrushchev.

The Hall of Ceremonies showcases a remarkable cycle of paintings commissioned by Maria Theresa, depicting a socio-political event that took place in 1760. The paintings show the marriage of Joseph, the heir to the throne, to Isabella of Parma, granddaughter of Louis XV of France. Like most marriage arrangements by Empress Maria Theresa, this was a political move to ensure France's support for Austria. The largest of these monumental paintings shows the entry of the Bourbon princess on October 5, 1760 against the backdrop of the Vienna Hofburg. Other paintings depict the marriage ceremony in the Hofburg parish church, the noonday wedding banquet and the evening banquet held in the Redoute Ballroom. Another painting shows the *serenata* which took place a few days later at which the imperial family is seated in the front row. The paintings depict in fine detail the buildings, the people, their clothing and even the food and tableware. These paintings took years of work in the studio of Martin van Meytens. Photography had not been invented in those days so the artwork displayed in the Hall of Ceremonies and throughout the palace rooms form a spectacular photo album of their life and times.

Our guide points to a small figure in a sea of faces attending the serenata. It is portrait of the young Wolfgang Amadeus Mozart who was added to the rows of onlookers. Mozart was six years old when he played for Empress Maria Theresa in Schonbrunn Palace. He is reported to have climbed onto her lap and kissed her at the end of his performance.

The palace gardens are one of the seven most important Habsburg parks and gardens. The Great Parterre extends from the palace complex to the foot of Schonbrunn Hill. The Baroque style layout of the parterre has been preserved largely unchanged since it was laid out in the 1770s, during the last decade of Maria Theresa's life. This dominating feature of the parkland is divided into eight sections of different sizes, separated by clipped hedges. At the foot of Schonbrunn Hill is the splendid Neptune Fountain erected in 1776 and at the summit is the Gloriette, a colonnaded neo-Classical structure built the year before. Atop the triumphal central arch of the Gloriette is a massive imperial eagle perching on a globe. There is a viewing platform on the flat roof of the balustrade.

The grounds are extensive and nowadays they are administered by the Federal Parks Service in Vienna and Innsbruck. It would take all day to take in all the features of the palace garden. We have barely an hour left, following our tour through the palace. We decide to follow a leafy axial path to the east leading towards the Obelisk Fountain. The lofty obelisk is inscribed with hieroglyphs and rises above a rocky mound in a pool. The impressive fountain contains river gods and lively water cascades. We return via a pathway that takes us to the Neptune Fountain below the Gloriette. The huge pool contains a rocky landscape populated by the sea-god Neptune and his entourage. Thetis, the goddess of the sea, is kneeling at his feet and is accompanied by Tritons, half man and half fish, with their conch-shell trumpets.

At 4.00 pm we need to find our coach. Hopefully, it is somewhere among the long queue of coaches waiting outside the palace grounds. We take the central path through the Great Parterre, ignoring the Maze and the Labyrinth where we could become lost. Other sections in the palace grounds await those with more time -- such as the Imperial Coach Museum, The Palm House, the Zoo, the Desert House, the Crown Prince Garden and the Garden on the Cellar, once used as a privy garden by the imperial family until the end of the monarchy.

At 5.15 pm Avril and I enjoy a Scotch and Dry in the Lounge while listening to our onboard musician Peter. An academic couple, Jo and Joyce, from Colorado join us, ready for the briefing on tomorrow's visit to Durnstein and arrangements for tonight's Mozart and Strauss concert. Csaba, our jovial Cruise Manager, arrives at 5.30 pm. He says, 'All of you are in for a treat tonight. You must go to the early dinner seating and be ready by 7.15 pm. You can look forward to a delicious goulash when you return from the concert.' Jo and Joyce join us in the restaurant for dinner. We discover that they are from Colorado, recently retired university lecturers in environmental studies. Appropriately, on tonight's dinner menu is Wiener schnitzel.

The concert takes place in the Auersperg Palace and we are one of the last to be seated in a full audience of around 200 people. Speak about luck! Avril and I are ushered to front row seating where we can stretch our legs in front of the grand piano. We are dazzled by the artistry of the Vienna Residence Orchestra which is regarded as one of the finest chamber orchestras in the world. In 1991 it officially represented Austria in the festivities commemorating the bicentenary of Mozart's death. From the solo violinist to the full 40 man orchestra, the musicians prove their professionalism and their flexibility in more than 500 performances a year. The Vienna Residence Orchestra specializes in bringing pieces of classical music down from the ivory tower to a wider audience. Renowned singers and dancers are included to add variety to their performance. At least half of the orchestra, a couple of singers and dancers perform for us tonight.

Part 1 of the concert is devoted to Mozart and includes the *Flute Concerto, Aria of Macadamia, Turkish March, La ci darem la mano and Don Giovanni*. At intermission our tickets entitle us to a glass of champagne. Part 2 is devoted to Johann Strauss and includes *Tritsch Tratsch Polka, Under Thunder and lightning, Fruhlingsstimmen Waltz, Pasman Czardas, Vienna Blood, and The Blue Danube Waltz* which is complimented by ballet dancing. The concert concludes with much stamping of feet and clapping of hands to the lively *Radetzky March*.

At 10.30 pm our Coach takes us on an illumination tour of Vienna via the Ring Road. The crowded day ends with a delicious late night serving of goulash soup in the Lounge. What a day it has been! One could easily spend a week or more here, soaking in the cultural heritage of this historic city.

****

In conclusion, the importance of Austria and its capital Vienna in the cultural and political history of Europe cannot be underestimated. The following is a brief historical outline:

Like so many European countries, Austria has experienced invasions and struggles since time immemorial. There are traces of human occupation since the ice age. The Celts make the first substantial mark on Austria around 450 BC. They are followed by the Romans and the Bavarians.

The origins of modern-day Austria date back to the time of the Hapsburg dynasty which lasts from 1273 until 1918. In 1273 Rudolf 1 comes to power, the first of nineteen emperors from the House of Hapsburg, a noble family of Swiss origin. He defeats King Ottokar II of Bohemia (part of modern day Czech Republic) and later gains significant territorial holdings for the Hapsburgs in Austria, the cornerstone of their empire. Thereafter, until WW 1, Austria's history is largely that of the ruling dynasty, the Hapsburgs.

The vast majority of the Hapsburg Empire formed part of the Holy Roman Empire which owes its origin to Charlemagne. On Christmas Day 800, Pope Leo III crowns Charlemagne as Emperor of the West. This imperial title asserts symbolic authority over all Christendom. The title is revived and continued by the powerful German Emperor Otto, 962-73, who places the old Empire of Charlemagne under German rule. By the thirteenth century this feudal state of central Europe will be known as the Holy Roman Empire. From the time of Otto's coronation, until the dissolution of the Empire in 1806, its titular crown is held almost exclusively by German monarchs elected by a body of princes. From 1273 the Habsburg family comes to dominate the throne of the Holy Roman Empire with its capital in Vienna.

Europe's greatest Ruling Family originates in Switzerland at a time when Count Radbot constructs Habsburg Castle, 1020-1030, on his feudal lands of Aargau. It is believed he names his castle after a hawk seen sitting on its walls (German for hawk is *Habicht*). In 1415 the Habsburgs are forced to relocate their seat of power to Vienna when Aargau joins the Swiss Confederation.

In 1477 Archduke Maximilian 1 marries Mary of Burgundy, bringing her realms of the Low Countries (Netherlands) and parts of France under Habsburg rule. His son, Philip the Handsome, marries into Spain's ruling family in 1496, bringing Castile, Aragon and their Italian possessions under Habsburg control. In 1521 the vast scattered domains of the Habsburgs are amicably split between the dynasty's two eldest brothers, Charles V, ruling Spain, the Low Countries, their Italian territories and briefly Portugal, while his brother, Ferdinand 1, is awarded Austria, their German territories, Bohemia and Hungary. The Austrian branch continues their domination of the Holy Roman Imperial Crown.

Over time tensions arise between the emperors, the electors and the Pope. The three representative groups would hold an imperial diet (parliamentary body) to elect the emperor and to keep his power in check. The culmination of these tensions comes to a head during the sixteenth century following the Protestant Reformation. While the emperor adheres to Roman Catholicism, the electors, German princes, generally support the Reformation. It is the elector, Frederick III (the Wise) of Saxony, who gives refuge to Martin Luther upon his excommunication, on January 3, 1521. By the sixteenth century, the imperial title is long regarded as hereditary, allowing the Habsburg dynasty to expand dramatically over continental Europe, not only through military conquest but also through carefully chosen marriage alliances.

The Christian world, in conflict, also faces danger from the east along the Danube.

Many wars are fought along the Danube to stop the Ottoman advance into Europe: Ottoman-Hungarian Wars (1366-1526) and Ottoman-Hapsburg Wars (1526-1791). The Ottoman advance into Europe is a conflict between the world's two major religions. If Vienna falls the rest of Europe will no longer be safe.

In 1526, in the Battle of Mohacs, the Ottoman forces of Suleiman the Magnificent defeat the forces of King Louis II of Hungary. The victory gives the Ottomans control of southern part of Hungary, while Bohemia and the western part of Hungary come under Austrian rule. King Louis is killed in the battle. The Archduke of Austria, Ferdinand 1 of Hapsburg, brother of the Holy Roman Emperor Charles V, claims the vacant throne of Hungary in the right of his wife, sister of the childless Louis II. Following the Diet of Bratislava on October 26, 1527, Ferdinand is declared King of all Hungary. In 1527-28 Ferdinand enforces his claim by capturing Buda in south-east Hungary.

In 1529 Suleiman musters a great Ottoman army and swiftly negates the gains made by Ferdinand. Suleiman's aim is to assert Ottoman control over the whole of Hungary, including the western part, Royal Hungary, which is still under Habsburg control. Suleiman decides to attack Vienna and arrives in late September, 1529. His army is depleted during the long advance into Austrian Territory. In the defence of Vienna, Charles V has sent to Vienna a variety of European mercenaries, including German pikemen and Spanish musketeers. They set about fortifying the three hundred year old walls surrounding St Stephen's Cathedral. Suleiman's troops are in a poor state of health after the long march and his siege fails. This first siege of Vienna is seen as the end of the Ottoman expansion into central Europe. However, a further 150 years of tension and incursions follow, culminating in the Battle of Vienna in 1683.

The bitter rivalry between the Protestants and the Roman Catholics trigger the Thirty Years' War of 1618-48. In 1617, when it becomes clear that Matthias, the Holy Roman Emperor and King of Bohemia, will die without an heir. His lands will go to his cousin, Archduke Ferdinand II of Austria, the heir apparent and Crown Prince of Bohemia. Ferdinand, the future Holy Roman Emperor, attempts to impose Roman Catholic absolutism on his domains and this makes him highly unpopular, particularly by the Protestant Hussites of Bohemia.

The Protestant nobles of both Bohemia and Austria rise up in rebellion. At a meeting in Prague Castle, Ferdinand's representatives are thrown out of the castle window and are seriously injured. This provokes open revolt in Bohemia which leads to a series of wars known as the Thirty Years' War (1618-48). Apart from religion, the European nations fight for various reasons, including dynastic, territorial and commercial rivalries.

Ferdinand crushes his rivals in Bohemia after a five year struggle. On November 8, 1620, the Battle of White Mountain takes place 8 km west of Prague. Bohemia draws support from the Protestant Union, a military alliance among the Protestant states of Germany. The combined forces of Ferdinand and the German Catholic League route the Protestant alliance. The battle is the first major victory of the Roman Catholic Habsburg over the Protestant

Union allies. The victory enables the Habsburgs to end constitutional rule in Bohemia and its neighbours. Ferdinand has the rebel leaders tried and executed. He confiscates the lands of their supporters, expels all Protestants and abolishes the Constitution.

The Thirty Years' War that is sparked by the religious conflict involves destructive campaigns and battles over most of Europe. As a result, the map of Europe has been irrevocably changed when peace is restored under the Treaty of Westphalia in 1648. The victory enables the House of Habsburg to establish an authoritarian government that survives three centuries until the reconstruction of central Europe following WW 1.

The Austrian branch of Habsburgs continues to strengthen its power base during the long reign of Leopold 1 (1657-1705). The historic defeat of the Ottoman Army outside the gates of Vienna in 1683 marks the decline of the Ottoman Empire's advance into the Christian world. The Chief Commander of the army who rescues Vienna is the Polish King, Jan Sobieski. He brings with him 23,000 soldiers -- without their help the combined forces of the Emperor and the Imperial princes would not have ventured into an open battle outside the city. It is the combination of all three that makes the victory possible. After the battle, Sobieski paraphrases Julia Caesar's quote by saying, 'We came; We saw; God conquered.'

In 1684 a Holy League of contemporary European powers is initiated by Pope Innocent XI to confront the Ottoman Turks. It marks the end of their incursion into Europe. Austria gains most of Hungary, Transylvania, and Slovenia; and Poland recovers Podolia. In the 230 years that follow, the Ottoman Turks lose all of the Christian lands they have conquered in the previous three and a half centuries.

The Habsburgs suffer genetically from inbreeding and in 1700 the Spanish Branch of the family comes to a dramatic end when the last Habsburg, King Charles II of Spain, dies having failed to provide the throne with a male heir. The question of the day is: 'Who will inherit the vast Spanish domains?'

The two most powerful European rulers, Louis XIV of France and the Austrian Emperor Leopold 1 can make almost equal claims on behalf of their descendants. Charles II of Spain dies in November 1700 after changing his will the previous month, leaving everything to Philip, the second grandson of Louis XIV. This decision ignites into the War of Spanish Succession (1702 to 1713). The Austrians prepare for war. Great Britain is alarmed at the prospect of the grandson of the King of France inheriting the Spanish throne, so it aligns with Austria, United Netherlands (Holland) and Brandenburg-Prussia against France.

The war ends in exhaustion and a settlement signed at Utrecht in the United Netherlands. The Treaty of Utrecht recognises Louis XIV's grandson, Philip V, as King of Spain. But it results in the weakening of Spain's power and the end of the Habsburg influence in Spain. Britain and the Habsburg family, now ruling from Vienna in Austria, gain Spanish territory. The Hohenzollern family, which rules Brandenburg-Prussia, also gains international recognition as royalty. The treaty leaves the Hapsburgs with the Spanish Netherlands (Ghent, Antwerp and Brussels), the kingdom of Naples, the Duchy of Milan and Sardinia.

In 1711, Charles, a Habsburg prince in Spain, inherits Habsburg lands, becoming Charles VI. He also becomes ruler of the Holy Roman Empire – by now little more than a titular position. With the Spanish throne passing to Philip V, Charles moves to Vienna in Austria. Charles VI now rules more territory than any other monarch in Europe. After the Treaty of Utrecht, the French view Austria as their nation's main rival on the European continent. The Treaty of Utrecht holds until the next upheaval in the Napoleon period.

On May 13, 1717, the Holy Roman Emperor Charles VI and his wife, Elizabeth, welcome their first daughter, Maria Theresa, into the world. She is born at the Hofburg Palace in Vienna. Maria's father is the last remaining heir to the Habsburg throne. Fearing that he might not produce a son, Charles VI reforms the Salic law, which prevents any female heir from succeeding her father. In 1713 he issues the Pragmatic Sanction to ensure his eldest daughter's right to take over the throne when he dies.

Most of the European powers agree to honour the Pragmatic Sanction. Charles VI allows his daughter to marry for love. In 1736 Maria Theresa marries a relation, her beloved Duke Francis Stephan of Lorraine, France. Over the course of her marriage she gives birth to 16 children: 5 sons and 11 daughters, including the future queen of France, Marie Antoinette.

On October 20, 1740, Charles VI suddenly dies after eating mushrooms. Marie Theresa, then 23, succeeds to the Habsburg throne. She proves to be one of the empire's greatest monarchs. The Austrian duchies and Netherlands, Bohemia and Hungary are quick to accept her as their empress. But Maria Theresa immediately faces resistance to her succession from European powers who previously agreed to the Pragmatic Sanction. Two months later on December 20, 1740, Frederick II of Prussia invades Silesia, a rich Austrian province, and claims it for his kingdom. Bavaria and France followed suit with their own invasions of Habsburg territories, resulting in an eight year war dubbed the War of Austrian Succession. The war ends in 1748 when Austria is forced to let Prussia keep Silesia and to accept the loss of three of its Italian territories to France.

In 1756 Maria Theresa tries to win back her rich province of Silesia. Fredrick once again wages war against Maria Theresa's empire and the conflict spreads into the Seven Years War (1756-63). Europe experiences sieges, arson of towns and open battles involving heavy losses and the deaths of over a million people.

In 1762, Russia, one of Austria's allies, withdraws from the war when Empress Catherine dies. The Habsburgs cannot win without its allies so the war ends in 1763. On February 15, Maria Theresa and Frederick II agree to a peace treaty, the Treaty of Hubertusburg, on condition that Prussia will keep Silesia. On February 10, France, Spain and Britain also negotiate for peace by signing the Treaty of Paris. This is the last major conflict to involve all the great powers of Europe before the French Revolution of 1789.

Maria Theresa's husband, Francis Stephen, dies in 1765 when she is forty-eight. She cuts off her hair and grieves for years. She appoints her eldest son, Joseph II, as emperor and co-regent. Maria Theresa dies on November 29, 1780, at Hofburg Palace in Vienna, where she has reigned for four decades. With her death, Joseph II assumes full responsibility as Holy Roman Emperor. He begins liberalising his government. He allows faiths other than Roman Catholic to construct churches. He abolishes the death penalty and torture for extracting confessions. He allows marriage by civil contract. He frees peasants from feudal dues and allows them to buy land from their former lords at a modest fee.

Following the French Revolution of 1789, Austria becomes engaged in a war with Revolutionary France and suffers defeats at the hands of Napoleon Bonaparte. He inflicts a heavy human toll on Austria which withdraws from its war against France in 1801. Napoleon's victory leads Francis II to dissolve the Holy Roman Empire in 1806. This seriously reduces the influence of the Habsburgs in their traditional German heartland.

In 1810 Marie Louise, the eldest child of Habsburg Emperor Francis II, becomes Napoleon's second wife. This ushers in a brief period of peace and friendship between Austria and the French Empire. In 1812, Napoleon's fortunes change dramatically after his failed invasion of Russia. The European powers, including Austria, resume war towards France, which ends in the abdication of Napoleon and his exile to Elba.

In 1848 liberal ideas in Europe erupt into Revolution throughout the Continent. In 1849, Hungary becomes a hotbed of discontent and Austria requires Russian help to supress the revolt. In 1866 Austria is defeated by Bismarck's Prussia in the Austro-Prussian War and is forced to relinquish its last domains in Germany. In 1867 Austria agrees to share power with Hungary as the Austro-Hungarian Empire. The creation of the Austro-Hungarian Empire diminishes the Hapsburg's influence in Europe. In 1914 the Austro-Hungarian Emperor Franz Josef declares war on Serbia after the assassination of Archduke Franz Ferdinand. The ensuing Great War (WW1) would prove the Hapsburg's downfall. The country is reduced to a small Republic after its defeat in WW 1.

During the 1930s the Nazis begin to influence Austrian politics and, in 1938, invading German troops meet little resistance. Austria's status remains unclear for a decade following its annexation by Nazi Germany in 1938 and subsequent occupation by the victorious Allies in 1945. A state treaty signed in 1955 ends the occupation and recognizes Austria's independence. Austria is heavily bombed during WWII, but the country recovers well. It has maintained a neutral stance since 1955 and in 1999 Austria enters the EU. Nowadays Austria has a well-developed social market economy, making it the 12th richest country in the world.

Monday April 28, 2014,

Durnstein

We snooze until 7.00 am following a busy day yesterday in Vienna. At 7.30 am the *AmaLyra* is beginning to dock at the riverport of Durnstein as we go the breakfast. The weather is fine and sunny with mixed cloud, perfect for viewing the picturesque countryside of Austria. At 9.00 am we step ashore for a guided walk along the banks of the Danube and into the quiet and charming streets of this fairytale village. Our guide says that the Danube overflowed last year and turned the river here into a lake. It flooded the vineyards. 'Look at where the sand (silt) piled up here. We are still cleaning up the beach.' She points to a small river ferry that is used to transport people, especially cyclists to the opposite bank. 'You ring a bell for service.'

At a vineyard we turn right and continue up a narrow road that winds through the cobble stone pavements of the township. The town services tourists with local wines and apricots. At the height of the tourist season, the 300 local inhabitants are overwhelmed by visitors.

On the way I notice a plaque displaying the Babenberg duke, Leopold V, who captures the King of England, Richard the Lionheart. Above the town, the road leads to the ruins of Durnstein Castle, 159 m above the Danube. It is here that Leopold V holds Richard the Lionheart of England prisoner in 1193. Apparently, Richard has insulted the powerful Austrian Duke in Palestine during the Crusades. Unfortunately, Richard's boat flounders on the rocks of the Adriatic when he is trying to return home. He tries to sneak through Austria disguised as a peasant. Somebody snitches on him and the English monarch is swiftly arrested. Leopold V extracts a huge ransom, but he is not able to enjoy his money for too long. The Duke is excommunicated by the Pope as punishment for making King Richard the Crusader his captive. Soon after, Leopold falls from his horse and dies unexpectedly.

Our guide takes us to sample apricot products of the region. Wine has been grown here since the Roman days, but some farmers have switched to apricots when their wine crops are hit by disease. A store owner allows us to taste sweet apricot liquor as we observe his stock of apricot jam, chocolate coated apricots, and apricot soap, among others. Then Avril and I amble into a gift shop where I spy a large novel mug with an interesting picture of a leaping Australian kangaroo. It is a road sign warning: NO KANGAROOS IN AUSTRIA. I must have it.

On board again at 11.00 am we make ourselves a cappuccino and at midday we have a light pasta lunch in the *Lounge*. We prepare ourselves for beautiful scenic sailing through the fantastic Wachau Valley, with commentaries broadcasted. The Wachau is one of the most beautiful and famous regions in Austria. Visitors from all over the world come here to enjoy the picturesque landscape, the cultural heritage and the superb wines that grow in this area. Features not to be missed on this two hour journey are Schonbuhel Castle, the ruins of Aggstein Castle and the villages of Spit and Willendorf. Some of the oldest remains of civilization have been unearthed at Willendorf during the construction of the railway to Vienna.

We see the ruined Burgruine Aggstein Castle perched on a steep cliff 300 m above the river. Burg Aggstein is one of Lower Austria's popular tourist attractions. The castle dates back to the 12th century and is built upon a massive 150 metre long rock. It came into the hands of the Kuenring family, a dynasty of notorious rebels. In 1230 they lead an unsuccessful revolt against Duke Friedrich II who conquers Burg Aggstein. The Kuenring family regain the castle, only to lose it a generation later in a revolt against Duke Albrecht I. In 1295/96, the Kuenringers besiege and retake the castle which remains in their hands until 1355. After that the castle falls into disrepair.

In the 15th century, Duke Albrecht V gives the task of repairing Aggstein Castle to Scheck von Wald. His duties include maintaining the paths by the Danube that are crucial for transportation and to collect tax from passing boats. Scheck von Wald becomes corrupt and turns into a cruel robber. He is the first in a series of robber landlords. In 1477 the Duke conquers the castle in order to stop the looting of ships. A few years later the castle itself is looted by Turkish troops, in the course of the first siege of Vienna in 1529.

The Wachau region produces some of the most revered wines in Austria, including world class Rieslings and some of the best Gruner Veltliner as well as Neuburger and Gelber Muskateller. The countryside is a beautiful mix of apricot trees, steep terraced vineyards and medieval villages, providing a majestic backdrop to the beauty of the region. During our scenic cruise an ice cream party is held on the deck. I enjoy a dip of rum and raisins and pistachio.

A dozen of our passengers have opted to take the Durnstein-Melk bike tour by following a 30 km course of the Danube which is only about 200 m wide here. We wave to them as they are waiting to catch the river crossing at the half way point. They are there waiting for us when the *AmaLyra* arrives at Melk. At dinner tonight we sit with Alan and his wife Elaine who claim that the bike experience was a highlight of their trip.

At 4.00 pm we join the Melk Abbey tour. Melk has been an important spiritual and cultural centre in Austria for over 1000 years. With its sparkling and majestic abbey-fortress, Melk is a highlight of any visit to the Danube Valley. Stift Melk (Melk Abbey) is the most famous of the many abbeys in Austria. Melk was of great importance to the Romans and later to the Babenbergs who built a castle here. In 1089 the Babenberg margrave, Leopold II, donates the castle to Benedictine monks who convert it into a fortified abbey. For over 900 years monks have continually lived and worked at Melk Abbey, following the rules laid down by St Benedict. The tireless monks are active in parishes, the school (currently 750 pupils), the economy, culture, and tourism.

The monastery has been destroyed and rebuilt several times. Today's architecture dates from the beginning of the 18th century. Fire destroys the original edifice which is completely rebuilt between 1702 and 1738, according to plans by Jakob Prandtauer and his disciple, Josef Munggenast. Since 1978, extensive restorations of these splendid Baroque buildings have been carried out and adapted to meet the needs of the school, the guests, and cultural events.

We have two guides to explain the highlights of our visit to Melk. Leslie, who escorted the bike riders, accompanies us on the coach for the short 5 minute drive to the monastery where she introduces us to Anita. She is a well- groomed slim young lady with brown plaited pony tail, good eye contact and pleasant rapport. I guess that she is a product of its church school system. Nowadays about 900 students attend co-ed classes ranging from kindergarten to college. We walk through a tall gateway entry of the abbey and are standing in a large courtyard beside a fountain.

Anita guides us to the grand marble stairway that leads to a second floor containing the Abbey Museum rooms. Down the long Imperial corridor there are many doors. Anita explains, 'Empress Maria Theresa used to visit here with her large entourage and you can imagine that they needed lots of rooms to accommodate all of them. They would arrive in lots of coaches after a day's travel from Vienna.'

Standing in the hallway, Anita carefully explains the history and the daily routine of the abbey, as well as life in the monastery and the Benedict's current duties. We are ushered into the main Museum Rooms and Anita diligently locks each door behind as we proceed. Historic works of art such as the Melk Cross and the St Coloman Monstrance are on display.

St Coloman, according to legend, is a king's son from Ireland on a pilgrimage to Jerusalem. He is martyred in 1012 in Stokerau, near Vienna. In this dangerous border area he comes under suspicion because of his strange language and clothing. He is suspected of espionage and is imprisoned, tortured, and finally hanged from a dead elder tree. The miracles, which then occur, soon cause the local population to venerate Coloman. Heinrich 1 becomes aware of these miracles and has Coloman's corpse brought to Melk in 1014. A ceremonial funeral is held on October 13, 1014, in St Peter's church on the castle cliffs in Melk.

One reason for Coloman's translation to Melk may have been a desire of the Babenbergs to enjoy the mercy of the Saint in life and death. Having a Saint in their castle is seen as a sort of divine confirmation of the rule conferred upon them by the Emperor, and is intended to promote the inner stability of their realm. Next to Coleman's grave the Babenbergs can now establish a burial site worthy of them. The existence of this burial site is probably the reason why Leopold II makes a Benedictine monastery out of Melk Castle in 1089. The Benedictines in Melk have kept the memory of St Coloman alive.

The most important rooms of the Abbey are the Marble Hall, the Library and the huge Baroque church which dominates the complex with its twin spires and high octagonal dome. We follow Anita into the all-important library room. The library comes second only to the church, in order of importance of the rooms in the Benedictine monastery. Anita points out that the library of Melk Abbey consists of a total of twelve rooms containing 1888 historic manuscripts, including 750 prior to fifteenth century.

From the library we follow Anita to the Marble Hall. This room serves as a dining hall for the imperial family and other distinguished guests, as well as a festival hall. The ceiling fresco shows Athena on a chariot drawn by lions as a symbol of wisdom and moderation. Hercules can be seen on her left, symbolical of the force necessary to conquer the three-headed hound of hell, night, and sin. The fresco alludes to Emperor Charles VI, who likes to be celebrated as a successor to the Roman emperors in the Hercules legend.

We are led outside to the terrace, a wide balcony that offers a wonderful view of the Wachau Valley and the town of Melk. The high point of our visit comes as we are taken into the abbey church. It glitters with dazzling gold leaf, seven kilograms of it according to Anita. The interior is Baroque, gone barmy, with endless prancing angels and gold twirls. A ten year long restoration of the abbey church, financed with help from the state and federal government, is completed in 1987. The meaning of Melk Abbey Church is inscribed in Latin on the high altar: *NON CORONABITUR NISI LEGITIME CERTAVERIT* ('Without a legitimate battle there is no victory', taken from 2 Timothy 2, 5). The battle which leads to victory is depicted on the high altar through the martyrdom of the apostles Peter and Paul. This victory is further depicted by that of St Coloman on his altar in the left side transept where his skeleton lies in a sarcophagus. The altar to the right is dedicated to St Benedict, but the sarcophagus is empty.

It is time to leave this highly impressive and enriching world heritage site. Instead of returning to the *AmaLyra* by bus, Avril and I decide to walk from the lofty heights of Melk Abbey. We scramble down the cobbled main street of Melk and cross the bridge of a picturesque canal as a white swan glides under it. We continue through filtered sunlight in a woodland filled with the enchanting melody of song birds dancing to the sunset.

On board we have time for a Scotch and Dry and to be seated in the Lounge ready for a classical performance by *La Strada* at 7.00 pm. The classical trio from Bratislava constitute a violinist, a viola player and a Spanish guitarist. Their magnificent version of *Adagio* by Rossini is musical magic. At 8.00 pm after the performance we dine with Alan from Ontario, his wife Elaine and his 88 year old mother who lives in Nottingham. During their tour of Melk Abbey this afternoon, Alan notices that his mother has lost her watch. By pure luck he sees a German tourist in the group behind them waving it about, wondering who has lost it. Alan suddenly twigs. He only has seconds to claim it and to return to his own group through the security door before it locks him in. Tonight he gently teases his mum about it, but she ignores him. For dinner Avril and I choose turkey for mains. On the dessert menu is the rich chocolate cake, Sasha-Torte, served with cream. We opt for that.

Tuesday April 29, 2014,

Salzburg

This morning the *AmaLyra* docks at Linz to allow some passengers, including Avril and I, to disembark for an optional tour to Salzburg. The *AmaLyra* will cruise to Passau in Germany while we are visiting the breathtaking city of Salzburg, Mozart's birthplace. En route to Salzburg we will drive through the beautiful Austrian Lake District known as Salzkammergut. The Salzkammergut area with a total of 76 lakes is one of the most impressive regions in the heart of Austria. The name literally means: 'The Estate of the Salt Chamber'.

Nowadays, salt is so readily available that it is hard to imagine that it was once traded as 'white gold'. Salt was so important that the Habsburg dynasty monopolised the privilege of salt mining. The imperial salt chambers oversaw salt mining very closely. The Habsburg salt came from three large salt-works at Hall in Tyrol, Aussee and Hallstatt.

In the seventeenth century the production of salt expands considerably in response to increasing demand. Until the reform of the 'Chamber Estates' in 1783, the Salzkammergut has a special status and is administered by a specially appointed 'Salt Officer' (*Salzamtmann*). Eventually, competition for mined salt comes from the south, from Trieste where sea salt can be produced cheaply. Falling production means increasing poverty for people in the salt producing regions.

Today the Salzkammergut region is predominately a tourist destination and has been for over a century. It extends over three Austrian provinces: Upper Austria, Styria and Salzburg. Inner Salzkammergut is home to an especially enchanting landscape such as Bad Ischl, Hallstatt and Bad Aussee. Bad Ischl is where Emperor Franz Joseph loved to spend his summer holidays in the Kaiservilla (Imperial Villa). He describes it as 'Heaven on Earth'. He grants his mistress, Katharina Schratt, a nearby mansion that can be easily reached via a hidden footpath. In the Kaiservilla, on July 28 1914, Franz Joseph signs the declaration of war against the Kingdom of Serbia, signalling the start of World War 1.

Salzburg has a proud past. Once it was an ecclesiastical principality directly accountable to the Holy Roman Emperor. During Mozart's lifetime, Salzburg is ruled by Prince-Archbishops who possess both secular and ecclesiastical powers. The Prince-Archbishop rules as an absolute sovereign of his state. He is elected for life by the Cathedral Chapter. His rule is subject only to the Holy Roman Emperor, his own conscience and Almighty God. Development of his principality depends solely on his skill and resources.

The 18th century goes down as a dark period in Salzburg's history. During the Reformation, Archbishop Leopold Anton von Firmian rules with absolute power and forces over 20,000 Protestants to emigrate.

The principality is marked by political, economic and social decline. Salzburg is drawn into the War of Austrian Succession (1740/48) and the Seven Years War (1756-63). During this troubled time, Wolfgang Amadeus Mozart, Salzburg's greatest son, is born on January 27, 1756 at 8.00 pm in the house on Getreidegasse No 9. A monument is built here in his honour in 1842 in what is today Mozart square.

These wars cost the Archbishops a lot of money. Military spending rises as the salt trade undergoes drastic decline. The aftermath of the Seven Years War sees a shortage of meat between 1764 and 1770 and a shortage of grain from 1770 to 1772. Prices double and millers and bakers are unable to go about their trades. Breweries are forced to cut back their production. As a result, there is a decline in population during the latter half of the 18th century. There are fewer marriages and births in Salzburg and an increase in the mortality rate. Yearly averages recorded from 1761 to 1780 reveal 60 marriages, 246 births and 341 deaths. In 1771 Salzburg has a population of 16,000. At that time some 15 percent of the poverty stricken population lack proper sustenance.

The modern city of Salzburg is located on the site of Roman *Juvavum*, a settlement along one of the major military roads of the ancient world. Centuries after the collapse of the Roman Empire, Bishop Rupert founded the city anew in 696 AD.

The face of contemporary Salzburg is dominated by the Baroque majesty of the old city, created in the 17th and 18th centuries. At that time the Prince-bishops launched their major building programs and left the indelible mark on the architecture of the city. Even today, over one hundred churches, castles and palaces bear witness to the power of Salzburg's archbishops.

Today's skies are overcast and rain falls steadily for most of our day. This is unfortunate, but it does not dampen our spirits. The coach to Salzburg takes nearly two hours to reach the city. The dual lane highway is a breeze to travel, even in the wet conditions. We drive through Linz, a city of almost 200,000 and take a 45 minute break at Mondsee, which means Lake of the Moon because of its shape. It is one of the 78 lakes in the Austrian Lakes District and situated 25 km east of Salzburg. A stop-off at this beautiful lakeside town is regarded as an absolute must for tourists on a discovery tour of the film *The Sound of Music*. The Collegiate Church of St Michael in Mondsee was the film setting for Maria and Georg von Trapp's wedding. The actual marriage however of Maria and her naval husband was in Salzburg's Nonnberg Abbey.

Our guide, Noelene announces, 'Does anyone want to buy the lake? It is privately owned and is up for sale for 4.5 million Euros.' Noelene has dark Spanish complexion and is dressed in traditional colourful clothing, a long dress with an apron tied in front on the left. This denotes that she is married. She was born in Guatemala, in Central America. At the age of 16 she was an exchange student for 3 months in Austria. Her host family assisted her to come back for university studies. During the third year she met her husband to be. After 5 years of married life she gained citizenship. They have two boys, 10 and 12 years of age. She speaks Spanish, German and English and claims she has not lost anyone in her 7 years involvement as a guide.

Noelene says her husband loves fishing and has a fishing licence. She ruefully explains, 'But it costs 14 Euro for one day of fishing, more for fly fishing!'

I ask Noelene, 'Why do you need a fishing licence? In Australia you just go where there is a beach, river or lake and thrown in a line?' She answers, 'Just about everything in Austria is regulated. And you are only allowed 3 fish per day.'

Coaches are restricted to a parking area at the edge of Mondsee town. Heavy mist blots the view of the lake and steady light rain is falling. The Basilica St Michael is situated in the middle of the town, ten minutes from the parking bay. The church is the cultural and spiritual heart of the Mondsee region. Often called the Wedding Church of Mondsee Cathedral, this bright yellow church has high towers, 52m tall, reaching into the sky, making a striking presence. The late Gothic church was constructed in 1487 century under the direction of Abbot Benedikt Eck and is the second biggest church in Upper Austria.

We don our wet weather gear and follow Noelene into the village, a delight for souvenir shopping and traditional Austrian coffee and cake in one of the many cafes. We arrive at the courtyards of the monastery which now belong to a hotel centre. The public is free to walk around them and 'soak' up the atmosphere. With steady rain falling we are more anxious to get inside the monastery buildings than get soaked.

The Collegiate Church of St Michael reached international fame because it was the film setting for the wedding scene of Maria and Georg von Trapp in the film, *The Sound of Music*, starring Julie Andrews and Christopher Plummer. The former monastery has become one of the most photographed churches in the world, with more than 200,000 people visiting here every year. In 2005 Pope John Paul II upgraded the spacious church to a basilica. The church itself is renowned for its seven beautiful side altars carved by Meinrad Guggenbichler, a Swiss sculptor who dedicates his life to beautifying the monastery here in Mondsee as well as the church. The main Baroque altar was made in 1626.

From Mondsee our coach continues to the outskirts Salzburg, arriving around 11.00 am. In Salzburg Noelene provides us with a map and takes us to a meeting point near Mirabell Gardens. 'This is where we need to be at 4.00 pm this afternoon,' she announces. She then guides us on a tour of the inner city highlights before allowing us ample free time to explore.

In 1964 the beloved film *'The Sound of Music'* is made in and around Salzburg. We walk to the wonderful Mirabell Gardens where scenes of the film were shot. The grounds contain the iconic Pegasus Statue Fountain. In *The Sound of Music* the Von Trapp children dance around the Fountain singing *Do Re Mi*. The Gnome Park section features statues that are originally modelled after real life dwarfs. The one with glasses on is the one that the Von Trapp children pat on the head during the film scene.

From the gardens there is a splendid view of Hohensalzburg Fortress towering over Salzburg. Since 1077 AD, this castle-like Salzburg Fortress perched on Monchsberg Hill has provided an ever steady sense of protection. 'It was never taken,' says Noelene, 'Whenever a siege took place the enemy tried to starve them into surrender. Once, the inhabitants were down to one cow. Each day they would paint it a different colour to let it graze. Their enemy were tricked into thinking that they had plenty of food to sustain them, so they left.'

We follow Noelene across the Makartsteg Bridge, Salzburg's most modern pedestrian bridge which spans over the Salzach River in the city centre. It is also known informally as the 'love locks' bridge because it contains a sea of padlocks attached to the fence below the railing. Love locks are the latest craze when it comes to couples declaring their eternal devotion. Lovers now paint or scratch their undying love for each other on padlocks and throw the key ceremoniously into the river. It's more environmentally friendly, instead of carving their initials inside a heart in a tree. Avril and I fall behind our group as they continue across the bridge, unable to tear ourselves away from this public display of affection.

The Makartsteg Bridge is named after the 19th century historicist painter Hans Makart, who is born and raised in Salzburg. He becomes a famous painter of the Viennese Historicism, providing artwork for many of the pompous buildings of the Ringstrabe. The original bridge is built in 1905 and is replaced by another in 1967, which is nicknamed the 'swinging bridge'. By standing in the centre it would swing strongly, causing great delight among children. With some 20,000 pedestrians crossing on the average day, the second bridge is soon in bad shape. The Makartsteg Bridge is once again demolished in 2000. One year later the current bridge is opened to a massive festival with live music along the river banks during a warm June night, accompanied by fireworks and cheering of 25,000 people.

A highlight of our walk is strolling through the crowded Getreidegasse, the main shopping street in Salzburg. This long narrow medieval thoroughfare contains a compact variety of shopping outlets including high fashion Louis Vuitton, traditional clothing, fancy chocolates, jewellery outlets, cafes and even a McDonald's with silverware and outdoor seating. Noelene points out the medieval roots of the street, noted by the signage that hangs above each shop. During the Medieval Ages few people could read, so the shopkeepers would hang an icon denoting their trade or craft. This traditional form of signage continues. Above the shops we see signs for a hat maker, an umbrella shop, a locksmith and even one for McDonald's, in keeping with the tradition.

Getreidegasse No 9 is the most visited Mozart landmark in Salzburg, the birth place of Wolfgang Amadeus Mozart. You simply cannot miss the very bright yellow, historic home where one of the true pioneers of Classical Music was born on January 27, 1756.

Noelene takes us to Salzburg Cathedral where Mozart was baptised. The huge Baroque Dom is finished in 1628, replacing the previous church called Virgil Dom that stood there since 774 before burning down. It is a miracle that the new church is built at all, as most of Austria is caught up in Europe's 30 Years' War in the early 1600's, which pits Catholics against Protestants. Salzburg is able to call upon the resources of its rich salt production to have enough money to remain independent and stay clear of picking sides in the War.

Our guided city walk with Noelene ends near the beautiful St Peter's Church Cemetery where the Von Trapp family hid from the Nazis during the escape scene in *The Sound of Music*. But the actual scene was filmed in Hollywood. St Peter's Cemetery contains a serene setting of pansy-filled gardens, providing a peaceful stopping point with Noelene. She reveals to us her favourite restaurants and special dishes. Another sprinkle of rain begins to fall, so, heeding her advice, Avril and I take lunch in nearby St Peter's Restaurant. It feels great to escape the cool wet conditions outside, for the warm, quiet ambience inside. We order a traditional pork fillet with a delicious gravy and herbal crusty potato. Dessert is a tasty strudel with custard.

The afternoon is spent walking about the heritage town and visiting the museum at Mozart's birthplace. Large groups of tourists mill about the entrance. The birthplace is on the third floor of their rented house at No. 225 on Lochelplatz – today's address is Getreidegasse No 9. Inside there are numerous family portraits and Mozart's first piano.

Mozart's father Leopold arrives in Salzburg in 1737. His studies at the university are unsuccessful, so he enters into the service of Salzburg's Archbishop in 1743 as the fourth violinist in the court orchestra. He eventually advances to the position of court composer and in 1763, to vice-conductor. He marries Anna Maria Pertl on November 27, 1747 in Salzburg's Cathedral. Anna Maria gives birth to six children prior to Wolfgang Amadeus Mozart, of which only one survives past the first year of life. She is Maria Anna Waldburger Ignatia whom Mozart nicknames Nannerl.

One day in 1760, Andreas Schachnter, the court trumpeter and colleague of Leopold, accompanies Leopold to his home. They find the four year old busy with his quill pen. Andreas writes what he observes that day –

"Papa: 'What are you doing?'

Wolfgang: 'Writing a piano concerto!'

"His father took it away from him and showed me the smeared notes mostly written over rubbed out ink stains. We laughed, at first, but then Leopold began to examine the composition, and sat in meditation over it for a long time. Finally, two tears escaped from his eyes. They were the tears of awe and joy.

'Look Herr Schauchtner,' he said, 'how correctly and regularly set this piece is, except that it cannot be used because it is so incredibly difficult that no person would be able to play it.'

"Wolfgang interrupted: 'That is why it is a concerto. It has to be practised until it can be done.' Even at such a young age, his dream was to perform concerts and miracles."

At 3.30 pm it is time to return to the ship which by now has reached Passau, Germany. The rain clears and sunny breaks appear during the afternoon drive, revealing a delightful countryside with quaint Bavarian villages. Our coach takes nearly two hours to reach the riverside port and I hear heavy snoring as the day catches up with some of the travellers.

Germany is one of the most delightful and populous countries in Europe, homeland of the great classical music composers Johann Sebastian Bach, Ludwig van Beethoven, Johannes Brahms and Richard Wagner. Germany was separated into two countries following WW II. Western and Eastern Germany were reunited after the fall of the Berlin Wall in 1989. Today, the country is made up of 16 states called Lander and the capital is Berlin, the largest city in the country. Germany is 357,022 sq km in size with a population of 81.5 million.

At 5.30 pm our coach arrives at Passau which is often called 'City of Three Rivers'. It is ideally located at the confluence of the Danube, the Inn and the Ilz. The old town sits on a narrow peninsula, squeezed in between the Danube and the Inn. Noelene says, 'Much of the city was covered with flood water last year during the big floods. We had a very long cold winter and then the rains came and didn't stop. The potato crops failed. Since then it has been very dry and the city has been cleaned up.'

We find the *AmaLyra* docked on the Danube next to the city centre. Sitting high above the rivers are the majestic fortress *Veste Oberhaus* on the Danube side and the Pilgrimage Church *Mariahilf* on the Inn side. Passau was the largest bishopric in the Holy Roman Empire, a legacy that endures today – there are 52 other churches in town, a large number for a city of only around 50,000 inhabitants. The most imposing of these is St Stephen's Cathedral, which contains the world's largest pipe organ.

Originally founded on the Roman camp, the city has long been an important trading point. Its Baroque appearance was created by Italian architects after the town is destroyed by fire, twice in the 1600s. Napoleon called Passau 'the most Italian looking city north of the Alps'.

Today Passau is a very lively city due to around 10,000 students living here. They attend the University of Passau, renowned for its institutes of Economics, Law, Theology, Computer Sciences and Cultural Studies.

At 6.00 pm Avril and I go to the almost empty Lounge for a Scotch and Dry. The wonderful onboard pianist, Peter, is playing relaxing music. We dine at 7.15 pm and enjoy a Chaine des Rotisseurs Dinner. Confrerie de la Chaine des Rotisseurs is the World's oldest International Gastronomic Society. AMA Waterways are extremely proud to be the only river cruise line inducted into the world's most prestigious culinary organizations. Our French chef really turns on his special delights tonight. The turkey breast and dumplings are superb and the dessert combinations delicious.

At 9.00 pm we are entertained by a wonderful local performance by *The Sound of Austria*, a trio of a brilliant pianist, a tenor and a soprano. They sing a couple of arias from Don Giovanni and other classics. The pianist plays with passion and somehow the piano survives a vigorous workout.

Wednesday April 30, 2014,

Regensburg, Germany

Overnight the *AmaLyra* cruises silently towards Regensburg, a perfectly preserved medieval city on the banks of the Danube River. I sleep in an extra half hour to 6.30 am. The weather has improved and sunny conditions welcome us. Sunrise came at 5.53 am and sunset will be at 8.26 pm, temperature range 8 C – 21 C. At 10.00 am we are part of a small group invited to the wheelhouse by Captain Andreas. He has two radar screens in front of him and small steering stick to the right. He tells us that the life of a captain is, 'Eat, Sleep and Work.' He says, 'It takes 7 years in order to become a fully qualified river captain. You need a licence for everything: the radar, the river, the radio and so on. There is no rudder. You steer the ship with accelerators. There is no turning circle like a car. I can spin the ship a full 360 degrees. At Regensburg the river is not wide enough or deep enough to do this. Our ship has a 1.5 m draft. I will have to go back to the lock because the water is too low.'

I am fascinated by an ordinary handyman's tool, a spirit level, sitting on the bench in front of him. 'Why on earth do you need a spirit level?' I ask.

'Oh! It has an important use. I can tell if the ship is slightly unbalanced. We may have to adjust the ballast to keep it level. It's important to be level especially so in locks.' I suggest that he could call on passengers to move to one side. This ridiculous comment brings a laugh.

At 11.00 am a German 'Fruhschoppen' is available in the lounge – tasty thin sausages, bread rolls, and a glass of beer. Everyone is in a festive mood, enhanced by lively German music played by Peter on the keyboard.

Around 2.00 pm the *AmaLyra* arrives in Regensburg and we disembark for a guided walking tour in the charming Bavarian city of roughly 150,000 inhabitants. Christina, a young tall athletically built woman walks us down the river bank towards the old stone bridge that spans the Danube. She explains, 'The people built this masterpiece way back in the 12th century. Except for pedestrians it is closed for vehicle traffic until 2017 while undergoing renovations.'

Next to the bridge is the *Wurstkuchl*, or sausage kitchen, the oldest restaurant in all of Germany, dating back to 1135. The 900 year-old building is notable for its role in feeding the mason workers who built the stone bridge. Today the kitchen serves 6,000 sausages to guests every day! Sausages are the only item on the menu and come in portions of six, eight or ten, along with sauerkraut and mustard. It is a little green house sitting beside the river. I ask Christina if the city was flooded last year. 'Yes, the flooding in June was the worst since 1893.' She points to a mark just below the roof of the sausage kitchen. 'That is where the flood level reached.'

Across the road from the river, Christina shows us recent diggings to uncover Roman structures. She thinks that a future museum may be built there to showpiece the results. She says, 'This side of the river marked the northern borderline of the Roman Empire. The barbarians on the other side could see the fortifications built by the Romans. Eventually hostilities eased and the inhabitants melded as one.'

Our walk around this well preserved medieval city reveals pleasant squares, peaceful passageways and a number of towers built by wealthy citizens. At the Town Hall Square Christina explains that the wealth of city prospered through trade up until the 1400s. Then there was an economic crisis through loss of trade caused by two significant events: The Ottoman Turks attempted to conquer Europe from the East, cutting off trade. Then the New World, discovered by Columbus in 1492, opened up trading opportunities for Spain and Portugal.

The allure of Regensburg lies in the charming cobblestone streets of its old town, a UNESCO World Heritage Site. Oskar Schindler, the title character of the movie *Schindler's List* lived here, as did the most recent Pope, Pope Benedict XVI. Unlike most German cities, Regensburg suffered little destruction from the bombs of WW II, even though it was home to a Messerschmitt aircraft factory and an oil refinery. Today the BMW factory and university are among Regensburg's largest employers. Christina explains, 'The BMW employs about 9,000 workers. Audi also has a factory nearby at Ingolstadt.' Indeed, a small group from the *AmaLyra* opted to take a tour of the Audi factory this afternoon.

The city of Regensburg has a well-known Christmas store called *Drubba* which also stocks the famous cuckoo clocks from the Black Forest. There is a Museum of Golf and department stores sell fashionable traditional clothing. Avril and I venture inside one, thinking we would like to purchase an ensemble of traditional German clothing. Dressed in leather pants, bracers, and forest green hat, how would people view me back in Oz? Too much money to spend for a fancy dress kit! Besides, there is no spare space left in our luggage. 'Let's move on,' I suggest.

The highlight of the city is Regensburg Cathedral of St Stephen, a most impressive Gothic cathedral, famous for its boys' choir, the *Regensburger Domspatzen*. It contains one of the world's largest pipe organs. Christina explains that the cathedral took 600 years to complete in stages. Building started in 1273 and ceased for a while when money was not available.

Avril and I open the huge door and enter the cavernous cathedral. It echoes to the slightest footstep. But it has a serene feeling as people wander about in awe of the lofty stained glass windows. I wander over to take a picture of the massive pipe organ and, as I do so, as if by magic, the heavens open with the voices of a singing choir. I wonder where it is coming from. Then I see a crowd milling around a dozen students who are singing in harmony, testing the acoustics. The appreciative crowd claps their approval as the students slip away.

There is one more must-do before Avril and I return to the *AmaLyra* and that is to sample the world famous sausages and sauerkraut from the *Wurstkuchl* next to the old stone bridge. Believe me, it's yummy! A glass of German draught beer goes well with that. Dinner this evening is another one of exceptional standard. Avril has the sea bream and I choose pork. At 9.30 pm a singer, Valerie May from Nuremberg gives an amazing performance of well-known European songs, including my all-time favourite from Nanna Mouskouri, *'The White Rose of Athens'*.

Thursday May 1, 2014

Main Canal to Nuremberg

I arise at 6.30 am as the *AmaLyra* cruises smoothly in the upper reaches of the Danube. The weather is mild with mixed cloud, the possibility of an afternoon thunderstorm and a temperature range 9 C – 18 C. This morning we leave the Danube River behind as we enter the monumental Main Danube Canal, linking the North Sea to the Black Sea. Through a series of 16 locks, ships such as ours are now able to cruise from Romania to the Netherlands.

The canal is a commercial waterway located in southern Germany, completed in 1992. The canal, 171 km long, runs from Bamberg on the Main River to Kelheim on the Danube River, permitting traffic to flow between the North Sea and the Black Sea. It creates a 3,540 km long waterway that connects 15 countries and can accommodate barges carrying up to 3,500 tons of bulk cargo.

The canal is one of the largest civil engineering projects ever undertaken, with a total of 16 locks each about 190 m long, 12 m wide and up to 25 m deep. It reaches a height of more than 405 m over the Alps south of Nuremberg.

The idea of such a canal dates back to the year 793, when Charlemagne decides to open a route through Europe for his battle fleet. He has a channel excavated between two rivers in Bavaria: the Altmuhl, a tributary of the Danube and the Frankische Rezat, a tributary of the Main. Heavy rains cause the banks of the channel to collapse and the project is abandoned. In 1837, under Ludwig 1 of Bavaria, work begins on a canal between Bamberg and Kelheim, following much the same route as the modern canal. The Ludwig Canal is not suitable for large vessels such as ours.

At 10.00 am we join Csaba Tamas, our Cruise Director, in the Lounge for a briefing on the Main-Danube Canal. He begins by explaining the difference between a European Heaven and a European Hell:

EUROPEAN HEAVEN

Is where the French are the cooks
The British are the police
The Germans are the mechanics
The Italians are the lovers
And it is all organized by the Swiss.

EUROPEAN HELL

Is where the British are the cooks
The Germans are the police
The French are the mechanics
The Swiss are the lovers
And it is all organised by the Italians.

Csaba shows slides to explain the 3 billion Euro project to replace the Ludwig Canal which is still navigable, but it contains 101 locks compared with only 16 on the new canal. During the morning we reach the highest point of the Main-Danube Canal. We are presented with a certificate signed by the captain and the cruise manager to mark the occasion. In our cabin on our bed is the certificate from AMA Waterways:

CERTIFICATE OF ACHIEVEMENT
FOR Mr Welbourne William

WE THE CAPTAIN &CRUISE MANAGER
OF THE MS AmaLyra HEREBY DECLARE
THAT THE ABOVE MENTIONED PERSON (S), WITHIN
HER/HIS OWN POWER (AND A LOT OF OURS!),
REACHED THE HIGHEST POINT OF THE
MAIN-DANUBE CANAL, THE
"WATERSHED MONUMENT"

WE ALSO STATE THAT HE/SHE, WITH COMBINED EFFORTS,
SUCCESSFULLY STOOD THIS EXTREME TEST
OF HER/HIS PHYSIQUE, AND REGAINED HER/HIS
STRENGTH WITHIN SECONDS,
WE THEREFORE GRANT HIM/HER THE TITLE OF:

"FIRST CLASS SAILOR"

CRUISE MANAGER	FIRST CAPTAIN
Csaba Tamas	Andreas Zarwel

The Ludwig Canal remains in use until WW II, but it is never able to compete with the railways. In 1921 the German government and the State of Bavaria form a company to build a much larger Main-Danube Canal. Most of the construction takes place between 1960 and 1992.

At 2.30 pm the *AmaLyra* arrives in Nuremberg, Bavaria's second largest city. During the 13th century, Nuremberg develops into one of Europe's greatest trade towns. The *Burg* (Citadel) is built in the 11th century and the city's medieval walls are completed in 1452, with a total of 126 towers. From the 16th century onwards, the city's residents make considerable contributions to world culture – geographer Martin Beheim, maker of the first globe, and Albrecht Durer, one of Germany's greatest artists, both lived and worked here.

Most of the city is destroyed in a mere 90 minutes during WW II. The historical buildings are mostly rebuilt using the same stones. The Second World War plays a major role in the city's history, as Adolf Hitler chooses the city as the site for his annual Nazi Party Rallies.

In 1933, Nuremberg is officially designated the *Stadt der Reichsparteitage* (Nazi Party Rallies). The Nazis create a link between the Nazi movement and Nuremberg's Imperial past. The Nazi Party rallies are held every September from 1927 to 1938. The rallies last a week and draw as many as one million people from all over Germany. Later, the city becomes the famous location for the Nuremburg Trials.

Nowadays, Nuremberg is a flourishing metropolis with a population of 500,000. Merchants and craftsmen make the city wealthy and the city is still well-known for its trade fairs, the production of toys, its Christmas market, and its gingerbread, known as *Lebkuchen*.

In 1935 the so-called *Nurnberger Gesetze* (Nuremburg Laws) are passed to justify the arrest and interrogation of Jews. Ten years later, captured Nazi war criminals are tried in *Schwurgerichtssaal 600*. This courtroom, where the most famous trial of Nazi criminals are held, is still a working courtroom. The Allies choose Nuremburg for symbolic and practical reasons.

At 2.30 pm we are taken on a tour of the medieval city. Our guide is Linda, a retired English/ German teacher. She announces, 'More people today are listening to what I say.'

We pass a row of modest housing called Garden City. 'These were built in 1910 for workers. The idea of improving the social conditions for workers came from Manchester. It helps improve productivity. There are about eleven of these Garden Cities in Nuremburg. The houses rent for about 800 Euro per month.'

We pass the expansive shunting yards of the railway. Nuremberg is in the middle of Germany and rail transport continues to play an important role in the city's commerce. Linda explains, 'Nuremburg used to be very industrial in the 19th century. Now it is more pharmaceutical and light industry. A small river runs through the city and people used to dump their rubbish which ended up downstream. People in Furth came up with the saying: *'Nothing good comes from Nuremburg'*. Nuremberg has about 500,000 inhabitants and is the second largest city in Bavaria after Munich.'

She points to where two Aldi brothers start the first of a chain of discount stores, which have spread to other countries. 'The brothers came from modest beginnings and they are now the fifth richest in Germany.'

We pass a huge barracks complex that once was the headquarters for Hitler's elite army. Linda reveals, 'The building covers an area of about 3 soccer fields. After the war they were used as barracks for the USA army and then to house displaced persons. It is now used for asylum seekers.'

Linda continues, 'Nuremburg means *stone hill*: Nurem means *stone* and Burg is *hill*. We can trace the name back to an official document of July 16, 1050. 'Norenberc' was mentioned for the first time on the occasion of the release of the serf Sigena by Emperor Heinrich III.'

'Nuremberg was once part of the huge political unity known as the Holy Roman Empire, which was ruled by an Emperor. Nuremburg became a boom city in the Middle Ages,' notes Linda. 'From 1050 to the mid-16th century the city expanded and rose dramatically due to its location on key trade routes.'

Our coach heads to the Imperial Castle, the historic symbol of Nuremburg located on a sandstone rock in the north of the city. Since the Middle Ages its silhouette has been the city's landmark, representing the power and importance of the Holy Roman Empire of the German nation and the outstanding role of the Imperial City of Nuremburg.

The castle and town become a favourite stopping place for rulers on their journeys through the realm. Court assemblies and Imperial Diets are held here. In 1140, King Conrad III starts building a second castle on the site, to be used as a royal residence. Around 1190 the House of Hohenstaufen build an extended castle complex on the rocky elevation over the remains of older buildings. They install a *burgrave* who resides in the front section of the complex, known as Burgrave's Castle. His job is to maintain order and to administer the imperial property.

In 1219, a Letter of Freedom, granted by Emperor Friedrich II, strengthens the autonomy of the city. By the end of the Hohenstaufen period in 1254, Nuremburg has become an independent imperial city. Nuremburg is often referred to as the unofficial capital of the Holy Roman Empire because the Imperial Diet (Reichstag) and courts meet at Nuremburg Castle. In the late Middle Ages Nuremburg is ranked as the 'most distinguished and best located city in the realm'. In 1356, Emperor Charles IV's Golden Bull names Nuremberg as the place where every newly elected ruler has to hold his first Imperial Diet. Therefore, it becomes one of the three key centres of the empire – in addition to Frankfurt where the kings are elected and Aachen where they are crowned.

Over time the Castle becomes less important. Instead, the Town Hall is completed in 1340 and is used as a place of assembly. From Ludwig the Bavarian on, the emperors prefer the more comfortable accommodation of the patrician houses. Charles V also breaks the tradition of holding the first Imperial Diet in Nuremburg. He does not visit Nuremburg until 1522, after the Diet of Worms. Nuremburg's acceptance of the Reformation in 1524 alienates the Protestant city from the Catholic Emperors. In 1663, after the Thirty Years' War (1618-48), the Imperial Diet is relocated permanently to Regensburg.

Linda escorts us through the castle courtyards to a wall near the Emperor's Chapel which offers a grand view of the city. She holds up a picture of heavy damage to the city by Allied bombing in World War II. The castle is severely damaged in 1944-45, with only the Roman double chapel and the Sinwell Tower, one of three, remaining entirely intact. However, the castle and the city have been restored since then and it is now hard to imagine that practically the entire city once lay in ruins.

We leave the castle and continue our medieval tour by descending a cobblestone road leading into the city. On the way, Linda points out a section of the sandstone rock upon which the castle stands. We come to a popular café located in Albrecht Durer Platz. It is overflowing with patrons. Nearby children are swarming over a large bronze statue of a rabbit in a prone position on a footpath nearby to the famous 'Albrecht Durer Haus'. It was created by Jürgen Goertz in 1984. The figurative sculpture called 'Der Hase' is homage to one of the most famous pictures of Albrecht Durer: Der Feldhase (The rabbit). Albrecht Durer (1471-1528) was born in Nuremberg and was a supremely gifted and versatile German artist of the Renaissance period.

Located in the plaza is the medieval Church of St Sebaldus, one of the most important and oldest churches in the city. The original Romanesque construction begins in 1225 and is completed by 1275. In 1309-1345 changes to the construction are made: the side aisles are widened and the steeples are made higher. In 1358-79, a Gothic Hall Chancel is built and the two towers are added in the 15th century. Galleries are added in the 17th century and the interior is remodelled in Baroque fashion. The church suffers serious damage in World War II and is subsequently restored.

The Church of Saint Sebaldus takes its name from Sebaldus, an 8th century hermit and missionary who is venerated as the patron saint of Nuremburg. Legends abound of his early life. One claims he is a contemporary of Henry III (died in 1056) and is of Franconian origin. He becomes a preacher in Nuremburg after a pilgrimage to Italy. Another legend claims that he is the son of the King of Denmark. Another suggests that he is a student in Paris who marries a French princess, but he abandons her on her wedding night to go on a pilgrimage to Rome. The Pope gives him a mission of evangelising in the forests of Nuremburg.

Linda explains, 'He had a cult following in Nuremburg that can be dated to late eleventh century. It is claimed he performed many miracles. For example, one dark evening he came across a distressed farmer looking for his lost cow. Sebaldus comforted the farmer and then pointed his finger. A light shone forth towards a thicket of bushes where the lost animal grazed contentedly.'

I can imagine the startled farmer's surprise as he muttered, 'Holy cow!'

In 1255, Nuremberg adopts St Sebaldus and St Peter as co-patron saints and the city becomes a place of pilgrimage. The feast day of St Sebaldus is August 19 and many children born here bear the saint's name. In 1397 the relics of the saint are placed in the church and once a year they are carried in a procession. It is customary for kings and emperors of Germany, when in Nuremberg, to pray before his shrine. The celebrated Late Gothic bronze tomb of St Sebaldus is contained in the Church of St Sebaldus and is considered a masterpiece of German renaissance. It was fabricated in 1508-19, by Peter Vischer the Elder and his sons.

The Sebaldus cult following survived the Reformation. Linda explains, 'In 1524, Nuremburg turned Protestant, but the merchants kept the shrine. They were smart enough to realise its commercial importance as a place of pilgrimage. They even count his bones, from time to time, to make sure they are all there.'

We continue our walk and come to Schoner Brunnen which is a beautiful 14th century fountain located on Nuremburg's main market next to the Town Hall. The 19 metres high stone pyramid rises from an octagonal base and has the shape of a Gothic spire. Depicted on the fountain are 40 figures that represent the world view of the Holy Roman Empire: philosophy, the 7 liberal arts, the 4 Evangelists, the 4 Church Fathers, the 7 Prince electors, the 9 Worthies, Moses and 7 Prophets (Hosea, Daniel, Jeremiah, Ezekiel, Isaiah and Joel).

The fountain is erected between 1389 and 1396 by the builder and stone mason, Heinrich Beheim. Surrounding the base is a protective railing, forged in 1587 by Paulus Kuhn from Augsburg. In 1902, it is repaired by Albert Leipold and then embedded with two brass rings on opposite sides that may be turned. We see tourists turning the rings which are supposed to bring good luck to those who spin them. Linda says, "One day a woman tourist made a wish and then complained to me that it didn't work. She told me, 'When I turned around, my husband was still there!'"

We return to the *AmaLyra* for the Captain's farewell. Drinks are on hand for a memorable voyage as we toast a farewell the ship's crew -- Captain: Andreas Zarwel; Cruise manager: Csaba Tamas; Hotel Manager: Viktoria Tuboly; Engineer: Csaba Kiss; Executive Chief: Francis Itoumbou; Maitre'D: Cirpian Has; Purser: Korina Tomprou and 1st Housekeeper: Nicoleta Cercel. It is comical to see the tall Hungarian Hotel Manager, Viktoria, standing beside our rather short Captain Andreas. Tomorrow we begin the land section of this tour by coach to Prague in the Czech Republic.

View of the Danube River from Fisherman's Bastion, Buda.

The Bridge of Slovak Uprising spans the Danube river, Bratislava.

World famous sausages and sauerkraut at Wurstkuchi, Regensburg.

Illuminated Chain Bridge spans the Danube River, Budapest.

Statue of St Stephen, first Christian king of Hungary, Trinity Square, Buda.

View of the Danube River and Pest from Buda, Budapest.

Puszta Ranch horsemen showcase Magyar horsemanship, Great Hungarian Plain.

Russian Memorial, Bratislava.

Statue of St Elizabeth who took a vow of poverty, beyond is Bratislava Castle.

Vienna Court Opera House.

Viennese coffee, Sacher torte and apple strudel.

Schonbrunn Palace, Vienna

Garden area, Schonbrunn Palace.

Durnstein: Richard the Lionheart captured here in 1193.

Wine and apricot region of the Danube at Durnstein.

Burgruine Aggstein
Castle, Lower Austria.

Schonbuhel Castle on the
Danube, Lower Austria.

Melk Abbey,
Lower Austria.

Collegiate Church of St Michael, Mondsee, used for the wedding scene in 'The Sound of Music'.

On a rainy day Mirabell Gardens offer a somber view of Salzburg Fortress.

Makartsteg or 'Lovelocks' Bridge, Salzburg.

Huge pipe organ in Regensburg Cathedral.

Exposed Roman wall foundations, Vienna.

Statue of Emperor Joseph II at National Library in Josefsplatz, Vienna.

Mozart's birthplace in 1756, third floor of Getreidegasse No 9, formerly Locheplatz No 225.

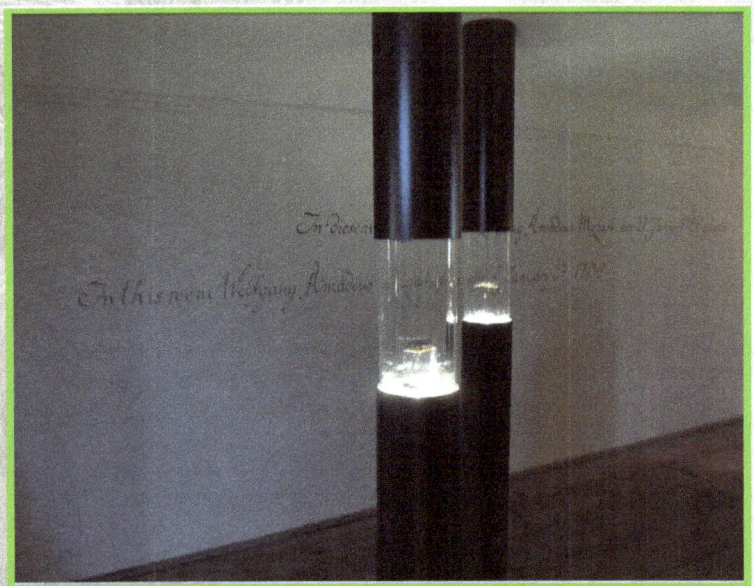

Illuminated lock of Mozart's hair in the room of his birth.

The Getreidegasse, the main shopping street in Salzburg.

Cruising towards Regensburg, Germany, Captain Andreas at the wheelhouse.

German 'Fruhschoppen' on board -- thin sausages, bread rolls and beer.

Roman wall structure used in modern housing, Regensburg.

St Stephen's Cathedral, Vienna.

Gothic Cathedral of St Stephen, Regensburg.

CHAPTER 7

THE CZECH REPUBLIC

Friday May 2, 2014,

Nuremburg to Prague

At 8.30 am we are on board a luxury coach heading down the autobahn from Nuremburg towards the Czech Republic. The skies are grey but it is not raining. The landscape is colourful and picturesque despite the lack of sunshine. In fact the view looks like a scene from an artist's brush, a checkerboard of pine and birch, quaint villages, fields of yellow and green. Our guide is Frankie, a man of solid build, dressed in a red track top. He announces clearly and carefully, 'Here in Germany there is an open speed limit which means you could go 700 km per hour if that is possible. But our coach is limited to 100. Most other members of the EU prefer a maximum speed limit of 130 km per hour and they want Germany to conform. Soon we will reach the western border of the Czech Republic… in about two hours.'

Frankie continues, 'The Czech Republic, Slovakia and Poland entered the EU about 10 years ago. They agreed that there should be open borders with Germany to allow people to move freely. But the Czech Republic still maintains its money, the Czech crown… 1 USD = 20 CZK. So, if you want to get rid of your Euro, you can buy a coffee or something at the border about two hours away. We will stop there for 20 minutes and then go to Karlovy Vary for lunch. The city was founded in 1340 by Charles IV, King of Bohemia and Holy Roman Emperor, after someone discovered hot mineral spring water in the location. There are actually 12 mineral waters here, each slightly different from the other. The hottest one is about 70 C and shoots a continuous spout of water to about 12 m into the air. Actually some say there are 13, referring to a sweet liqueur favoured by the locals.'

We arrive at the rest station on the unmarked border between Germany and the Czech Republic. Avril and I still have 6 Euro between us. We manage to blow it on a kit Kat, 4 AA batteries and a packet of Studenten-futter, which is a nut/fruit mix. 'Wow,' I announce when a one cent Euro coin is returned via the coin change dispenser. The cashier smiles and a couple of fellow passengers in the queue urge me to hang on to it in case I need it.

It begins to rain on the next leg to Karlovy Vary. Frankie speaks about the history of the Czech Republic which is a relatively new country. 'The Czech Republic was formed on January 1, 1993 following the 'Velvet Divorce' with Slovakia. Following the break-up of the Austro-Hungarian Empire in 1918, the Slovaks and the Czechs united as Czechoslovakia and prospered until Hitler came on the scene. Over time many Germans had settled in a strip of land known as the Sudetenland in Bohemia on the western border of Czechoslovakia. Hitler would visit to address the

Germans here. He told them that it was their duty as Germans to be part of Germany. The other European nations were scared of Hitler, so Western Europe signed an agreement to release the Sudetenland to Germany, thinking that it would appease Hitler. But this only whetted his appetite for more power.

'The eventual goal of the German state under Nazi leadership was to eradicate Czech nationality through assimilation, deportation, and extermination of Czech intelligentsia. The intellectual elites and middle class made up a considerable number of the 200,000 people who passed through concentration camps during German occupation. Hitler wanted Czech intellectual elites to be removed not only from Czech territories but from Europe completely. Just like Jews, Poles, Serbs and several other nations, Czechs were considered inferior by the Nazi state.

'The first thing he did was to close down the education system.' Frankie pauses before continuing, 'Over 218,000 Czechs died during the occupation.'

'In May 1945, Russia liberated Czechoslovakia, but it fell to a communist coup in 1948 and became part of the Eastern Bloc. Under a communist system, Czechoslovakia grew increasingly weak relative to Western Europe. In 1968 Alexander Dubcek was appointed to the key post of First Secretary of the Czechoslovak Communist Party. The hopeful 'Prague Spring' of liberalization followed. Censorship was relaxed and political prisoners were released. But he failed to persuade the Czechoslovak leaders to change course. Five other Eastern Bloc members of the Warsaw Pact invaded and Russian tanks rolled in on the night of August 20-21, 1968. The intervention was seen as vital to the preservation of the Soviet, socialist system of government.

'The communist system lasted until the 'Velvet Revolution' of 1989, with the fall of the Berlin Wall. The 'Velvet Divorce' of Czechoslovakia on January 1, 1993 saw a peaceful separation to form the Czech Republic and Slovakia. The Czech Republic joined the EU on May 1, 2004.'

At 12.30 pm we arrive in Karlovy Vary, a small picturesque city sitting snugly in a beautiful forest-clad valley. It is the jewel of the West Bohemian Spa triangle and the second most visited spot in the Czech Republic after Prague. No coaches are allowed in the city, so we transfer to smaller buses to be sent to a drop off point at the edge of town. A statue of its founder, Charles IV, stands proudly in the parkland that bears his name. Legend has it that the 14th century Czech king, who was the Holy Roman Emperor, was hunting in the forest. Suddenly a fleeing stag leapt from a cliff into a pool of unusually warm water fed by a hot mineral spring. Miraculously, the waters helped to heal the king's dodgy leg, so he decided to build a small castle tower on the cliff to mark the spot. Over the centuries, the mineral springs have welcomed famous figures including Goethe, Beethoven, Mozart, Casanova, Gogol, Paganini and dozens of heads of state. Today, Karlovy Vary, meaning 'Charles's boiling water', is one of Europe's most beautiful and popular spas.

Frankie arranges a meeting time at 3.10 pm and we are free to explore the cafes after first visiting the main attraction, the dozen mineral taps that are housed inside a large domed building in the central square. The dozen fountains are in a line and people are filling up brightly coloured water vessels obtained from the souvenir outlets. Parents and small kiddies are all smiles as they partake in a ritual of tasting the mineral enriched water. Frankie says it does wonders for your well-being. I cup my hand and sip the stuff which is not too agreeable, something like dirty water from an old rusty kettle. The water from the end fountain is so hot that you can barely touch it. In a circular room next to it is the main fountain which forces a thick cascade of water 12 metres into the air. I somehow lose Avril in all the bustle and excitement. Ten minutes later I am talking with our Canadian friends, Alan and Elaine, before I am spotted. I hustle her inside the domed building in a belated attempt to get her to smile for a photo beside the big spray.

The rain has gone and the spring sunshine enhances the flowering gardens and shrubs that line the narrow mineral rich river running through the town. A puff of wind causes cherry blossoms to shower pink confetti over passers-by and onto the pathway. It would be nice to sit down to enjoy a coffee and snack, but we have no local currency. We are told to avoid the money exchanges as they are a 'no-commission' trap. Frankie says to use the ATMs to get local currency. Avril and I see money exchanges aplenty, but where are the ATMs? We walk by the café strip and have no luck. We cross the passenger bridge to try the other side, again no luck. We inquire at the Information booth and finally after a long search we find the hole in the wall. Too bad, it is temporarily out of order! I could use my credit card, but not for a light lunch.

We have less than an hour to meet Frankie and the coach to Prague. A roll of thunder announces the arrival of rain. Suddenly I notice an ATM tucked away in a narrow lane near the café strip – as if by magic. Bingo! We are in luck. Avril and I extract 7,500 CZK, about 400 USD. We still have 40 minutes to have a quick bite.

We scramble into a basement of a hotel café to escape the rain and to order our coffee. We enjoy a delicious thin crispy roll filled with prosciutto, soft cheeses, and lettuce as well as some thin slices of rock melon. The rain is bucketing down as we dash to catch up with Frankie's meeting place. In the few minutes, while waiting for the bus to take us to the coach, some of our group are soaked to the skin. Avril and I fare better by sheltering in the doorway of a nearby building. Frankie does a head count and finds two Australians missing, Wenceslas and his wife Joan. 'Wences' was born here and speaks Czech. But to their embarrassment, they become lost in the streets.

The rain accompanies us to Prague where we are checked into the Intercontinental Hotel. At 6.30 pm Csaba is waiting for us in the lobby to join him on a short Orientation Walk into Prague Old Town. It is bitterly cold outside and I am thinking, 'Where is the snow?' Csaba walks us down to the Old Town Square, pointing out the best eating spots and where menfolk should hide their credit cards as we pass the expensive fashion shops.

At 7.40 pm it is time to escape the cold and to find a place to have dinner. Many bars and restaurants are crowded and noisy, but we manage to find one with quiet ambience at Staromacek Restaurant. The waitress lights a candle and straight away I imagine I am sitting in front of a cosy fireplace. I enjoy a scrumptious goulash and Avril has a chicken schnitzel. The local house wines are passable. The day is done, so we return to our hotel for a hot cup of tea.

Saturday May 3, 2014,

Prague

I arise at 6.20 am and take a peek out of the window on the fifth floor of the Intercontinental Hotel. We are situated in the heart of historic Prague with views across the Vltava River to Prague Castle which is the most popular and important tourist sight visited in Prague. This morning Avril and I plan a guided tour of Prague's premier tourist attraction. The weather outlook is for cool and cloudy conditions and fortunately no rain.

Prague Castle is located on a hill in *Hradcany* or the Castle District, one of the five districts included in the historic centre of Prague. Founded around 880 by Prince Borivoj of the Premyslid dynasty, it is the largest ancient castle in the world, 570 m long, on average 128 m wide and covering 7.28 hectares. Over the centuries the castle has transformed itself from a wooden fortress, surrounded by earthen bulwarks, into the imposing form it has today. Several destructive wars and fires and differing political forces have combined to create a mix of intriguing palaces, churches and fortifications. The castle is like a small town with a complex of walls, gardens and buildings in three courtyards. The castle is the ancient seat of Czech kings and has become the symbol of the Czech Republic. Today, Prague Castle serves as the historical and political centre of both city and state and is the official residence of the President of Czech Republic.

The earliest settlement of lands, now known as the Czech Republic and where Prague came to be built, is shrouded in mystery. Ancient trade routes, following the course of the Vltava River, pass through this area, connecting southern and northern Europe. Around 500 BC the Celtic tribe known as Boii gives their name to the region of Bohemia. Various Celtic and Germanic tribes pass this way before the Slavs move in, sometime over the 5th, 6th and 7th centuries.

Around 850 the Great Moravian Empire is established along the Morava River by the Slavic leader, Mojmir. His successors expand the empire to include today's Bohemia, Slovakia, southern Poland and western Hungary. Mojmir's successor, Rostislav, fears the Germanic people in the west. He requests the Byzantine emperor to send two missionaries in order to spread Eastern Christianity into the Great Moravian Empire. Cyril and Methodius of Constantinople come and create the Slavonic script and translate religious texts from Greek and Latin into the Old Slavonic language. This Cyrillic alphabet is still in use in Russia and Bulgaria. When Methodius dies in 885, Roman Catholic religion is adopted and the Cyrillic script is replaced by the Latin alphabet.

The Great Moravian Empire falls with the Hungarian invasion in 907. The Bohemian lands and the city of Prague come under the Premyslid dynasty that dominates Czech rule from the 9th century until 1306. But it is hard to separate the history of the Premyslid dynasty from the myths that surround it. According to legend, the clan is ruled by the prophetess Libuse. Under pressure to find a husband, she goes into a trance and sends a white horse out to find a groom. As predicted, the horse finds a ploughman whose name is Premysl. Libuse marries Premysl and the dynasty bearing his name becomes the first great dynasty on the Czech lands.

Another Libuse legend explains the foundation of Prague. The psychic, standing on top of Vysehrad Hill, fire in her eyes and arms outstretched, proclaims: 'I see a grand city whose glory touches the stars.' She sends her men into the forest to find a wooden hut whose doorway is so small 'that king or pauper must bow in order to enter and look at the threshold.' The word *'prah'*, an old Czech word for threshold, is thought to be the origin of the Czech name for Prague, Praha.

Around 880, Prince Borivoj, the first of the Premyslid princes, founds Prague Castle and the seat of power is moved there. Seventy years after the establishment of Prague Castle, a church and a fortified trading post are built on a clifftop overlooking the Vltava River, on the heights of Vysehrad. In 1085 Vratislav II builds Vysehrad Castle, or the 'Castle on the Heights' which becomes the stronghold of Prague. Forty years later his successors return to Prague Castle where the city has developed around that area instead.

The most celebrated figure in Czech history was a member of the Premyslid dynasty. This is Wenceslas, Duke of Bohemia, (or Vaclav, in Czech language) who was the fourth Premysl leader. In the year 925 he founds a Romanesque rotunda which is the original church built on the site of St Vitus Cathedral in the grounds of Prague Castle. Wenceslas acquires the arm of St Vitus and wants to build a church to hold the holy relic. (St Vitus was a Christian Saint from Sicily who died a martyr in 303 during the persecution of Christians by co-ruling Roman Emperors, Diocletian and Maximian). It is possible that Wenceslas wants the relic to convert his subjects to Christianity more easily. Unfortunately, the ill-fated Wenceslas is hacked to death in a murder plot brought on by an argument with his brother Boleslav. In September 929 or 935 (there is some dispute about the date) three of Boleslav's nobles murder Wenceslas on his way to church to attend the feast of Saints Cosmas and Damian.

Wenceslas's legacy would live on. He is best known through the Christmas carol, *Good king Wenceslas*, although he was not, in fact, a king – merely a prince. The importance of the cathedral grows especially after the establishment of the Prague bishopric in 973 and the founding of the body of canons, the St Vitus chapter. By 1060 the number of worshippers has exceeded the available space in the church. It is then made into a basilica which includes part of the rotunda containing the tomb of Wenceslas, by now a saint. The church serves the needs of the citizens for almost 300 years.

The Czech lands gain significant economic, cultural and political status during the Premyslid rule. Prague grows rapidly, thanks to its position at the crossroads of several trading routes. In 1085 Vratislav II becomes the first Premyslid king. But his crown remains subordinate to Holy Roman Empire and the German king. The royal title is made heredity in 1212 by the Golden Sicilian Bull. The Premyslid dynasty ends with the death of its last member, Wenceslas III in 1306.

The Czech throne is taken by John of Luxembourg who rules from 1310 to 1346 and the kingdom of Bohemia continues to grow. The Czech lands experience a Golden Age in their history under Charles IV, the eldest son of John. Charles IV loves Prague and the city flourishes under his rule. The beloved Czech king is crowned King of Bohemia on September 2, 1347, following the death of his father at the battle of Crecy in August 26, 1346. Charles IV is highly educated; he speaks 5 languages and is an excellent diplomat. He is crowned the Holy Roman Emperor in 1355.

The Prague bishopric is upgraded to an archbishopric in 1344 and Prague's status increases to become the capital of the Holy Roman Empire. Prague is ranked as the cultural capital of central Europe and one of the most prosperous European cities at the time. Charles IV promotes the Czech language to the official language, along with Latin and German. In 1348 Charles IV establishes Central Europe's first university, the Charles University.

Many building projects are started during Charles' reign. He is responsible for building the Charles Bridge to replace the first stone bridge which was built over the Vltava in 1172. It was named the Judith Bridge after the wife of the Premyslid king. The old Romanesque bridge collapses in a flood of 1342. The foundation stone of the Charles Bridge is laid in 1357. Charles IV's favourite architect and builder, Peter Parler, is said to have used egg yolks in the mortar to strengthen the construction of the bridge. In 1378, Charles's remains are taken across the new bridge to Prague Castle to be buried in the Cathedral of St Vitus.

Charles IV is responsible for creating, Prague's New Town in 1348, the youngest and largest of the five independent towns that comprise Prague's historical centre. The five town areas spanning both sides of the Vltava River are connected by the Charles Bridge. They are Lesser Town and Hradcany located on the left (western) bank of the Vltava. On the right (eastern) bank are Old Town, New Town and the Jewish Quarter known as Josefov.

Old Town (Stare Mesto) is established around 1230. This is where our luxury Intercontinental Hotel is located. Early settlements have existed here since the 9th century. It was once fenced by a semi-circular moat and wall connected to the Vltava at both its ends. The moat is now covered up by streets and boulevards. Old Town Square contains the Old Town City Hall, founded in 1338. On its southern wall is the Prague Astronomical Clock, or Orloj. The medieval clock, installed in 1410, is the oldest astronomical clock still working. The clock has three main components – firstly, the astronomical dial displaying various astronomical details and the position of the Sun and the Moon in the sky; secondly, 'The Walk of the Apostles', an hourly show of their moving sculptures and others such as Death, represented by a skeleton, striking the time; and thirdly, a calendar dial with medallions representing the months. This tourist attraction draws a large crowd every hour to watch the performance.

The New Town (Nove Mesto) of Charles IV is founded just outside the city walls to the east and south of the Old Town and encompasses an area of 7.5 sq km, about three times the size of the Old Town. The population of Prague in the 14th century swells to over 40,000 after the New Town is built, making it one of the biggest cities of the time in Europe. The present population of Prague is around 1.2 million out of a total for the Czech Republic of about 10.5 million. New Town's most famous landmark is Wenceslas Square which was originally built as a horse market and now functions as a centre of commerce and tourism.

The Jewish Quarter, known as Josefov, is completely surrounded by the Old Town. It is located between the Old Town Square and the Vltava River and was formerly the Jewish ghetto of the town. Jews settle in Prague as early as the 10th century. They suffer persecution in 1096 and eventually they are concentrated within a walled Ghetto, which, over the centuries, becomes more and more crowded. In 1389, one of the worst persecutions sees around 1,500 Jews massacred on Easter Sunday.

In 1850, the quarter is renamed Josefstadt (Joseph's City) in honour of Joseph II, the Holy Roman Emperor who emancipates the Jews with the Toleration Edict in 1781. Jews are free to settle outside of the city. As a result, the Jewish population of Josefov decreases and only orthodox and poor Jews remain.

The Nazi German occupation does not demolish the old ghetto as one would expect. They preserve the site in order to provide for a planned 'exotic museum of an extinct race'. Since the war Josefov has become crowded with building redevelopment, making it difficult to appreciate what the old quarter was like. Nevertheless, the remaining old Jewish buildings form the best preserved complex of Jewish historical monuments in Europe. Remaining here are six synagogues, the old Jewish Cemetery, and the Old Jewish Town Hall.

The Lesser Town (*Mala Strana* in Czech) and Hradcany or Castle District are the two historical parts of Prague located on the left (western) bank of the Vltava River. The Lesser Town originates from several villages below Prague Castle. It is connected to the Old Town by the Charles Bridge. In 1257 the Premyslid king, Otakar II, formalises the establishment of Lesser Town by merging a number of settlements beneath Prague Castle into a single administrative unit. In 1541 *Mala Strana* is heavily damaged by fire. Today, therefore, most of the architecture is in Baroque style. Palaces of noble families are built on sites of former residential houses.

This morning we will visit Prague Castle in Hradcany located on the hill above Lesser Town. The Castle District originally evolves without any plan. In 1320 the area is granted the status of a Royal town, shortly before the New Town is founded in 1348 by Charles IV. In 1748 the four hitherto independent urban areas of Prague (Hradcany, Lesser Town, Old Town and New Town) are proclaimed a Royal city by Joseph II.

Our coach transports us across the Vltava River which is busy with water craft plying tourists along the scenic waterway. The coach takes a garden route up Petrin Hill towards the Great Strahov Stadium. We stop briefly and our guide, Elena, explains, 'This stadium was once an active sports venue with a capacity of around 250,000, making it the largest stadium in the world. It is no longer used for competitive sports events. It is now used a training centre for Sparta Prague and to host pop concerts. Sparta Prague uses about 8 football pitches for training. It was built by the First Republic after World War 1 and was used to hold massive displays of gymnastics. In 1990 The Rolling Stones performed the first concert to celebrate our freedom from the communists.'

We continue to Prague Castle and Elena urges our group to stick together. Our visit to Prague Castle coincides with one of the few open days of the year. Crowds of people take advantage of the free entry into the castle grounds to explore the individual buildings, museums and galleries. I am busy taking photos and I have difficulty in finding our group in the mix of people as we approach the two guards on duty either side of the front gates. Tourists snap their cameras as the guards, standing stiffly, stare blankly ahead. They face an hour of such torture before the Changing of the Guard.

The Cathedral of St Vitus is the most recognizable part of Prague Castle. Its imposing spires dominate the city skyline. The main South Tower offers excellent views on a clear day. The height of the steeple is 99.3 m and its apex is crowned with a double-tailed lion, the coat-of-arms of the Bohemia Kingdom. A gallery on the tower is accessible via 287 steps. We have no time for that, especially as the outside queue is about 100 metres long. Elena waves her magic wand and we are ushered inside for a peek of the magnificent interior especially of the 20th century Czech stained glass and marvellous pieces of art.

The present day Gothic Cathedral of St Vitus was founded on November 21, 1344, when the Prague bishopric is raised to an archbishopric. King Charles IV and Archbishop Arnost of Pardubice decide to turn the church into a cathedral. The first architect is Matthias of Arras. Eight years later, following his death, Petr Parler takes over and completes much of the structure in late-Gothic style. Over the following centuries, renaissance and Baroque details are added and the job is completed in 1929. The most beautiful of the numerous side chapels, Parler's Chapel of St Wenceslas, houses the crown jewels and the tomb of 'Good King' Wenceslas.

We meet Elena in the crowded outside courtyard where we admire the enormous Gothic landmark. It is time to move on for a short tour of the three castle courtyards. Fortunately, we are equipped with a radio earpiece to hear her commentary as we mingle with the crowd. Next to St Vitus Cathedral is the Old Royal Palace which dates from the 10th century and has been the home of numerous princes and kings. Every president of the Czech Republic has been sworn in here.

In the castle complex stands the Basilica of St George, the oldest church in Prague. It was founded around 920 by Duke Vratislav 1 of Bohemia, the father of St Wenceslas. The church has Romanesque foundations, but the façade is Baroque from modifications of the 17th century and later years. Inside the basilica are the tombs of Premysl royalty. Elena announces, 'There are 120 churches in Prague. Most of them are Roman Catholic. But there are a few Protestant churches and there is one Russian Orthodox Church.'

We continue our walk as Elena points out other features in the three courtyards of Prague castle. In the north east corner is Golden Lane which has a row of tiny colourful houses built right into the arches of the castle walls. The street is created during the construction of the northern fortification at the end of the 15th century. In 1597 the emperor, Rudolf II, gives the area to the castle marksmen who guard the fortification. There are 24 marksmen, so they need to build very small houses for them and their families. By 1641 only 14 houses remain. The castle marksmen are not needed so much, so more people from other occupations come to live there.

Golden Lane gets its name from the stories about alchemists living in the street who try to transform metals into gold. These stories are not based on truth. However, in 1831, the residents of Golden Lane hear a loud explosion coming from the house of an old man named Uhle who spends most of his money on old books about magic. He makes secret experiments in a lab in his house and on this day things go wrong. Firefighters extinguish the fire and they find Uhle dead with a yellow stone in his hand. Later it is proved to be gold on the stone. Believe it or not!

The homes are occupied until World War II. Franz Kafka, a famous writer, lives at No. 22 for a brief time. She is killed by the Gestapo during the war because she foretells the end of Nazism. Today most of the lane is marked by little souvenir shops.

Prague Castle is in an eminent position for visitors to capture fairytale views of the city. Elena leads us to the outer wall where we can capture a magic view of the historic skyline. We now follow her down the main road, engulfed by embassies and swanky shops, through Hradcany and Lesser Town to the famous Charles Bridge. For several centuries the famous landmark was simply called the Stone Bridge until it was officially named Charles Bridge in 1870. The magnificent Gothic structure is one of the city's finest attractions. It is the main pedestrian route linking the two banks of the Vltava River and the two sides of Prague. The bridge is 516 metres long and almost 10 metres wide. It rests on 16 arches shielded by ice guards. The entrances at both ends have towers: Lesser Town Bridge Tower is on the west and Old Town Bridge Tower is on the east. The latter can be climbed for a view of Prague and the bridge from above.

Throngs of people crowd the entrance at Lesser Town Bridge Tower. The thoroughfare to Old Town Bridge Tower is crammed with tourists. There are street artists, musicians and souvenir vendors whose stands line both sides of the bridge. Elena sets a time to allow us to explore and meet at the Statue of Charles IV at the Old Town end of the bridge. In this carnival like atmosphere we slowly proceed to the other end. We need at least half an hour to absorb the attractions and to view the avenue of 30 Baroque statues of saints which adorn the northern and southern balustrades. For many years a simple crucifix is the only decoration on the bridge. Between 1683 and 1714 the Baroque style sculptures are erected above each pillar of the bridge. Prominent Bohemian sculptors take part in adorning the bridge with the sculptures of notable saints venerated at that time. Most of the sculptures are now copies of the originals. Over the centuries, floods and catastrophes have caused damage to the originals which now may be viewed in the National Museum.

During the centuries the bridge has witnessed wild times since Charles IV laid the foundation in 1357. Charles IV was a vocal critic of church corruption, a position shared by his son, Wenceslas IV. But Wenceslas is a weaker ruler and, in the turbulent times ahead, that proves to be a problem.

The trouble begins in 1403 when the rector of Charles University, Jan Hus, begins to preach in Czech rather than Latin, and campaigns against corruption in the Catholic Church. He is declared a heretic and is burned at the stake in 1415 in Constance. His followers, the Hussites, begin a bloody religious struggle against the establishment which lasts till 1434. In 1419, the First Defenestration of Prague takes place when the Hussites throw seven counsellors out of the window of Prague's New Town Hall. (Defenestration is the act of throwing someone or something out of a window). Many historical artefacts and literature are destroyed during the wars and Prague Castle suffers from deterioration. The most famous of the Hussites is the one-eyed military genius, Jan Zizka. He leads a band of peasant farmers to five consecutive military victories over the crusaders sent by Rome to fight him. In 1434, following the Battle of Lipany, the conflicts are ended by an agreement between the Hussites and the Catholic Church.

Relative calm and prosperity is restored in 1458 when George of Podebrady, an elected Czech Protestant king, takes the throne. But peace is short-lived. Hungary's Catholic king, Matthias Corvinus, objects to George's religious beliefs, and declares war. Hostilities continue until George's death in 1471.

The Bohemian crown passes to two successive members of the Polish Jagellon dynasty, Vladislav II and Ludvik. Following Ludvik's death in 1526, the Bohemian nobles elect the Habsburg Duke Ferdinand 1 to be King of Bohemia. Unwittingly, this is the beginning of several centuries of mostly repressive Austrian rule. Over the next 400 years, the Czech language, culture and religious beliefs are suppressed by the Catholic Habsburgs.

In 1555, the Peace of Augsburg has settled religious disputes in the Holy Roman Empire by allowing a prince to determine the religion of his subjects. Ferdinand strengthens the position of the king and firmly reinstates the Catholic religion in the country. He invites the Jesuits to Prague and in 1562 they open an academy which becomes a university in 1616. He moves the seat of power to Vienna and the Prague Castle becomes more of a recreational site for the Habsburgs. Ferdinand's son, the Holy Roman Emperor Maximilian II, continues to frequent Prague, but it is his son, Rudolf II who returns there.

Rudolf II, Holy Roman Emperor, is crowned the Czech king in 1576 and he moves the Imperial Court back to Prague in 1583 (partly in response to the growing Turkish threat to the south), thus promoting Prague to the imperial seat of power again. The eccentric Rudolf is obsessed with art and science, spending little time on his royal duties. He is responsible for building Golden Lane at Prague Castle to house his army of alchemists. His sponsorship of arts, scientists and mystics give Prague the ongoing reputation as a magical city.

Rudolf starts a long and indecisive war with the Ottoman Turks in 1593 which lasts till 1606 and is known as the Long War. By 1604 his Hungarian subjects are exhausted by the war and they revolt. Other members of the Habsburg dynasty view Rudolf as unfit to govern and in 1605 he is forced to cede control of Hungarian affairs to his younger brother, Matthias. This angers Rudolf who prepares to start a new war with the Turks. But Matthias rallies support from the Hungarians and forces Rudolf to give up the Crowns of Hungary, Austria and Moravia to him. The Bohemian Protestants, seeing a moment of royal weakness, demand greater religious liberty which Rudolf grants in the *Letter of Majesty* in 1609. It grants Bohemia's largely Protestant estates the right to freely exercise their religion. This essentially provides for the setting up of a Protestant Bohemian State Church dominated by the towns and rural nobility.

Rudolf dies in 1612, having been stripped of all effective power by his younger brother, except the empty title of Holy Roman Emperor to which Matthias is elected five months later. The Imperial Habsburg court returns to Vienna upon the death of Rudolf. Prague's population then suffers a severe decline following the departure of the court and the effects of the Thirty Years War (1618-1648) that follows. Prague takes another century to retain its cultural prestige as the capital city of the Kingdom of Bohemia, even though its Habsburg king lives in Vienna.

Matthias succeeds in the rule of Bohemia and extends more legal and religious concessions to Bohemia, relying mostly on the advice of his chancellor, Bishop Melchior Klesl.

Matthias's conciliatory policies are opposed by the more intransigent Catholic Habsburgs. Matthias, already aging and childless, makes way for his cousin Ferdinand of Styria as heir to the Czech throne. Ferdinand obtains the support of the Spanish Habsburgs to succeed his childless cousin in exchange for concessions in Alsace and Italy. In 1617 Ferdinand is elected King of Bohemia by the Bohemian Diet. In 1618, he is elected King of Hungary by the Hungarian estates, and in 1619 he succeeds as Holy Roman Emperor following Matthias's death.

Ferdinand II's devout Catholicism causes immediate turmoil in his Protestant subjects, especially in Bohemia. He refuses to uphold the religious liberties granted by the *Letter of Majesty*, signed by Rudolf II, which guarantees the freedom of religion to the nobles and inhabitants of the cities. The king's unpopularity soon causes the Bohemian Revolt. Imperial officials order Protestants to stop erecting churches on lands held by ecclesiastical lords, claiming the lands are not subject to Bohemian Estates. The Protestants claim the lands in question are royal land and therefore available to them by the *Letter of Majesty*.

On May 23, 1618 an assembly of Protestant noblemen storm Prague Castle and take umbrage against the officials for violating the *Letter of Majesty*. They throw two of the governors and a secretary out of the third floor window. They survive a 21 metre fall by landing onto a dung heap. This event is known as the Second Defenestration of Prague and is considered the first step of the Thirty Years' War. Immediately after the Defenestration, the Protestant estates and the Catholic Habsburgs start gathering allies for war. The Bohemian estates depose Ferdinand as King of Bohemia and in 1619 they replace him with Frederick V, Elector of Palatine, a leading Calvinist and son-in-law of James 1, King of England. However, the hopes of the Bohemian Protestants are about to change. Their hopes are crushed in 1620 when Habsburg Emperor Ferdinand and the armies of the Roman Catholic League defeat Frederick's forces at the Battle of White Mountain in what is now Prague's sixth district. There is plundering and pillaging for weeks following the Battle.

Ferdinand takes control, from Vienna, and the suppression of Czech identity becomes even more brutal. 27 Protestant leaders are tortured and executed on the Old Town Square in May 1621. 12 of their heads are impaled on iron hooks and hung on Charles Bridge, making sure the Catholic faith, as well as the Habsburg dominance, prevails. All religions, except Catholic are banned. The Czech language and national conscience are supressed for the next 150 years. This period of Czech history is referred to as the Dark Age. By the middle of the 17th century, German has replaced Czech as the official language of government in Bohemia. For over a century, only peasants speak Czech and the language comes close to dying out.

The situation starts improving with Marie Theresa who rules the Austrian Empire from 1740 to 1780. She and her son and successor Joseph II (1780-1790) make several welcome reforms that include reducing the power of the

Catholic Church, expelling the Jesuits from the country in 1773, and issuing the Edict of Tolerance in 1781. This grants political and religious rights to religious minorities. In 1787, Wolfgang Amadeus Mozart visits Prague as guest of the Duseks, leading Czech musicians, at their villa Bertramka. His opera, Don Giovanni, has its premiere at the Estates Theatre.

A Czech National Revival starts in 1848, beginning with a resurgence of interest in the Czech language led by Josef Dobrovsky and Josef Jungmann. They succeed in introducing the study of the Czech language in schools. Prominent writers include the historian Frantisek Palacky, author of the *History of the Czech People*, and the political columnist, Karel Havlicek Borovsky, and others.

Over time, this cultural revival becomes a political independence movement. (Refer last chapter, April 27) The beginning of the end of the Habsburg dynasty comes with the assassination of Archduke Franz Ferdinand who is shot dead in June 28, 1914 by a Serbian nationalist in Sarajevo, an event that triggers World War 1. Millions of Czech soldiers desert to the Allies, rather than fight under the Austro-Hungarian banner. At the same time, a philosophy professor, Tomas Garrigue Masaryk, and a lawyer, Edvard Benes, lobby abroad for Czech independence.

With the fall of the Austro-Hungarian Empire after World War 1, an independent state of Czechs and Slovaks, called Czechoslovakia, is declared on October 28, 1918. Prague becomes the capital and Prague Castle becomes the seat of the First President of Czechoslovakia, Tomas Garrigue Masaryk. This sovereign state exists through the Nazi occupation of World War II and the Communist Era (1945-1989) until its peaceful separation on January 1, 1993. Czechoslovakia splits into two independent countries, Czech Republic and Slovakia. Vaclav Havel is elected the first president of the Czech Republic.

Compared to most other former Eastern European communist countries, the Czech transformation to Western style has been relatively smooth. Today, more than 20 years after the fall of Communism, the popularity of Prague as one of Europe's premier tourist destinations shows no sign of slowing down.

Avril and I complete our walk across the bridge and descend some steps beside the Old Town Bridge Tower. The view across the Vltava River provides a spectacular scene of river craft against the magical splendour of its historic backdrop, with Prague Castle standing proudly above Lesser Town and Hradcany. A few metres away, our guide, Elena, is waiting for us near the Charles IV statue. She is only too willing to answer questions and explain facts. She explains, 'The Czech Republic joined NATO in 1999 and was approved to become a member of the European Union on May 1, 2004. We continue to use the Czech Crown (Czech koruna) as our currency, but it is not known when the Euro will be introduced. Our average wage in Prague is about 1200 Euro and 800 Euro in the country. The unemployment in Prague is about 4 per cent and about 10 per cent in the country.'

She continues, 'Our population is about 1.2 million in Prague out of about 10.5 million in the Czech Republic. Prague has 22 administrative districts and 57 urban areas. Prague 1 is the historic district and is primarily a tourist zone. The majority of tourists stay here during their visit. Only about 30,000 people live here as permanent inhabitants. If you are in a hurry you can explore the area in a day. The Czech Republic is not very big. It is less than 79,000 sq km in area and from Prague you can visit most centres of Bohemia and Moravia in a day.'

The morning walk continues past Charles University buildings, the *Carolinium* (established in 1366 and named after the king) and the *Clementinum* (established by the Jesuits in 1562). In 1989 students stage several peaceful demonstrations, in the wake of revolutions abroad, that initiate the 'Velvet Revolution' and the fall of communism. Vaclav Havel, a writer, dramatist and philosopher, is recruited from the academic community and appointed President of the Republic in December 1989.

We are about to enter the historic Old Town Square. An old man dressed in a black suit and holding a saxophone is singing 'O Sole Mio' in a loud tenor voice. Elena announces, 'Here is Mathai Loma. He is my favourite musician.' She rushes over to hug him. A small crowd gathers to watch as the well-loved street entertainer continues the song on his saxophone. He has picked an ideal location for his busking.

Located across the crowded square is *The Church of Our Lady before Tyn*, or simply Tyn Church. This dominant Gothic church with towering 80 m twin spires has been the main church of this part of the city since the 14th century. In the 11th century, the site is occupied by a Romanesque church which is built there for foreign merchants coming to the nearby Tyn Courtyard. In 1256 it is replaced by an early Gothic-style Church. The present late-Gothic style construction begins in the 14th century under the influence of Matthias of Arras and later by Peter Parler.

The church is almost complete early in the 15th century except for the towers. The northern tower is completed during the reign of the Protestant king, George of Podebrady (1458-1471). His sculpture is placed on the gable, below a huge golden chalice, the symbol of the Hussites. The southern tower is completed in 1511. In 1620, the Protestant army of Frederick of Palatinate II is defeated by the Habsburg armies of Emperor Ferdinand and the Roman Catholic League at the Battle of White Mountain. Harsh suppression of Czech identity follows. In 1626 the Catholic Habsburgs remove the sculptures of George of Podebrady, regarded as a heretic king, and the chalice of the Hussites. They are replaced by a statue of the Virgin Mary, with a huge halo made from the melted down chalice.

There are many impressive Baroque churches in Prague, but one of the most beautiful is St Nicholas at Old Town Square. It serves as the parish church at Old Town Square until the completion of the nearby Tyn Church. St Nicholas Church is a Romanesque church dating back to the 13th century. The defeat of the Bohemian Protestant army at the Battle of White Mountain in 1620 ends the religious freedom in the city and St Nicholas Church is handed over to the Benedictine order. In the 18th century the Benedictines commission an accomplished Baroque architect, Kilian Ignaz Dientzenhofer, with the design of a new church. Construction commences in 1732 and the new Baroque St Nicholas church is consecrated in 1737. At the time of construction the St Nicholas Church is hidden behind Krenn House. Not until Krenn House is demolished in 1901 that the lovely white façade of St Nicholas becomes visible to the rest of Old Town Square. Hit by the sun during the day and by strong white lights at night, its Baroque façade simple gleams.

In 1781 Emperor Josef II orders the closure of all monasteries without a social function. From 1870 to 1914, St Nicholas is used by the Russian Orthodox congregation. Czech army troops are stationed there during World War II. Today the church is owned and managed by the Hussite Church. It serves as both a church and a magnificent venue for classical concerts.

The Old Town Square is abuzz with tourists, street entertainers and vendors. A stream of blown air bubbles floats by our group as we follow Elena to the statue of Jan Hus in the middle of the square. The religious reformer is burned at the stake in Constance for his beliefs, an event which sparks the Hussite Wars (1419-1436). The Jan Hus Memorial is erected on July 6, 1915 to mark the 500th anniversary of his death.

Elena alerts our attention to another memorial honouring the martyrs beheaded here after the Battle of White Mountain in 1620. Twenty-seven tributary crosses are installed in the pavement in their honour.

The morning with our guide is now complete. Elena recommends we visit the Prague Astronomical Clock at the southern wall of the Old Town Hall in Old Town Square and to explore the souvenir shops on the way through to Wenceslas Square in New Town. Avril and I head towards New Town, to view the displays of the famous Bohemian crystal. I feel like a bull in a china shop as we cautiously enter stores containing quantities of dazzling hand-cut and decorative glassware. On display are enormous chandeliers, champagne flutes, cutglass vases, ornaments and delicate figurines.

Bohemian crystal has a long history of being internationally recognised for its high quality craftsmanship. At home I have several jewellery pieces, including a set of Cortina flutes that I bring out whenever the cork of bubbly is popped. The box is marked 'BOHEMIAN CRYSTAL – FULL LEAD CRYSTAL -- 24% PbO – MADE IN THE CZECH REPUBLIC'. PbO of course means the crystal contains lead oxide. In the Czech Republic the term 'crystal' is used for any exquisite, high quality glass which contains at least 24% lead oxide. The presence of lead in glass adds weight and causes it to diffract light. Additionally lead softens glass, making it more accessible for cutting and engraving.

Excavations of glass-making sites in Bohemia date to around 1250. They are located in the Lusatia Mountains of Northern Bohemia. During the Renaissance, Bohemian glass-workers discover a new technique in glass-making. By combining potash with chalk they create a clear colourless glass that is more stable than the glass in Italy. In the 16th century the term 'Bohemian Crystal' emerges to distinguish its qualities from glass made elsewhere. Czech glassware becomes as prestigious as jewellery. The wealthy and aristocracy seek the highly prized crystal, especially for chandeliers to embellish their palaces, in particular the Imperial palaces of Maria Theresa, Elizabeth of Russia and Louis XV of France.

Avril and I realize that this afternoon is probably our last opportunity to purchase a few small gifts and mementos before we fly home on Thursday. A Bohemian crystal chandelier is out of the question and the intricate figurines seem so expensive. Instead, I settle for a couple of DVDs, fridge magnets and a Prague wall clock. We are so engrossed in shopping for souvenirs that we abandon our plan to continue into New Town and its famous Wenceslas Square. We need to return to our hotel near the river in Old Town and then have a late lunch. Around 2.30 pm we head for an Italian restaurant, the *Pizzera Pepe Neru*, across the road from the Intercontinental. We share a delicious pizza of ham, cheese, tomato and mushroom and some sparkling water. This is sufficient to sustain us until our planned Folklore Dinner evening.

At 6.30 pm we are met in the hotel lobby by Libra, also known as Libby, who is our shapely host for a Dinner and Folklore Evening commencing 7.00 pm. Libra speaks in strong flowing English with a slight German accent. (Rest room becomes 'vest voom'). She outlines the cultural evening as our coach winds its way to *U Marcanu*, a quintessential Czech restaurant in Valeslavinska 25/14, Praha. We are promised three magical hours of live music and folk dancing, where the vibrancy of traditional Czech culture comes alive. Local dancers and musicians will entertain us with the steps and songs passed down through generations.

The folklore program will accompany our traditional dinner of Czech cuisine and unlimited alcoholic and non-alcoholic drinks will be available. Libra announces, 'The Czech Republic has good beer. We hold the world record for beer consumption per capita. So please, don't let us down. We are just ahead of Germany.' The country drinks about 161 litres of beer per person each year, according to figures from *The Economist*. In Prague beer is cheaper than bottled water.

Indeed, the Czech Republic has a strong beer culture and most towns have at least one brewery. The most famous brewing cities in Bohemia are Budweis, Plzen and Prague. The Czechs have been producing beer since 993 AD, at least. Brewing in this early period was largely associated with monasteries. Written documents indicate that Benedictine monks brewed beer in the Brevnov Monastery. The Czech Republic is famous for being the birthplace of pilsner. The most famous Czech beer brands are Pilsner Urquell and Budweiser Budvar. Pilsner Urquell was the first pilsner and pale lager beer produced in Plzen by a Bavarian brewer, Josef Groll, on October 5, 1842. Regarded as a sensation, the clear, golden and light-bodied beer was prepared by combining Plzen's soft water, English malts, and Saaz noble hops from nearby Zatec, and by using Bavarian-style lagering techniques.

The Czech city of Ceske Budejovice was for centuries known by its German name, Budweis. The city has been brewing beer since the 13th century. Budweiser beer, the original Bud, was founded here in 1785. In 1876 the US Company Anheuser-Busch borrowed the name for its now famous Budweiser. In 1895, another brewery in Budweis, now called Budweiser Budvar Brewery, also began selling their Budweiser. Trademark disputes arose when the Czech companies began exporting their Buds to the US. Eventually, the courts allowed Anheuser-Busch to use the Budweiser name, both in North America and Europe, whereas Budvar Budweiser is sold in North America under the label Czechvar.

Libra is in a chatty mood and informs us that car stealing is a major crime in the Czech Republic, many disappearing to Russia. She jokes. "A popular saying here is -- Let's go on a holiday to Russia. Our car is already there.'

Libra announces, 'As part of the food and wine service, you'll be greeted with a small tipple of local liqueur called Becherovka. It's a very aromatic herbal mixture with 38% alcohol content. It looks like honey but tastes nothing like it. Some people say it tastes like a mixture of cinnamon, clove and ginger. Try it… I'll be interested to know what you think. It's supposed to do wonders as a digestive aid. The mixture was formulated in 1807 in Karlovy Vary by a Czech chemist and a British born doctor in their quest to create a healthy 'elixir of life.' The recipe contains a blend of around 32 herbs and spices and is a closely guarded secret, known only by two employees. I am told Becherovka makes a good cocktail when served with double or more of tonic water on ice with a squeeze of lemon. The cocktail is called a *Beton* which means *concrete* in Czech and German.'

Other tour groups are already seated as we arrive in time for the 7.00 pm start. We are seated at long tables that leave room for the band and a dance floor for the entertainment. A chilled nip of the Becherovka is placed on the table. Avril and I say 'Cheers' and sip the powerful aperitif. I say to her, 'I think it tastes like a cough mixture.' The restaurant is soon filled with about 200 tourists from various countries. Our wine waiter dashes from table to table, dispensing your choice of red or white wine. Over his shoulders hangs an ingenious device containing two glass decanters with tubes that extend down to a finger on each hand. The force of gravity squirts wine your glass as he releases his finger.

The small band is led by a mature woman who doubles as MC and plays a zither instrument. Two others are accomplished violinists. She asks the audience from whence they come, 'Who is from Britannia? New Zealand? Greece? Australia? Ireland?', until all nations are covered. The band then plays a representative song of each country. For Australia it is *Waltzing Matilda*. This sets the mood for an evening of song and folk dancing. A woman belts out a Czech song and she is joined by folk dancers in costume, vibrantly whirling and twirling to traditional dance music.

The food and drink come apace with the entertainment: a small salad, meat stew in tasty sauce, spaetzle dumplings and dessert. The MC teaches verses and we are encouraged to sing along. She merrily starts waving a big wooden spoon about and farcically pretends to use it on anyone not singing. She gently plucks people from their tables to take part in traditional dance. It's all good fun and I don't mind, especially when I am paired in a courting dance with one of the young attractive girls from the Lithuanian table. It proves to be an excellent evening with our hospitable hosts, waiters and entertainers.

Sunday May 4, 2014,

Prague

At 6.30 am we arise to a glorious crisp, sunny morning. At breakfast we catch up with a few of the *AmaLyra* tour group. One bemoans the fact that sunny weather has come and they will be travelling home tomorrow. Another from Los Angles cannot believe the picturesque scenery of Prague. 'Is this a scene from a movie set?' she asks herself. The normally cheerful Alan from Canada walks by and complains that he chose a bad restaurant last night and had to complain about the slow service. We are sitting with Wences and Chris from Perth. They had an early night and are looking forward to meeting his cousin today. Wenceslas has dual citizenship. He needed to restore his Czech citizenship in order to claim back a family property confiscated during the communist take-over by Russia in 1948.

Peter's wife, Joan, from Sydney walks by and we swap notes on last night's entertaining Folk Dinner evening. She says, 'Peter joined in the Congo line and I saw you dancing.'

Today is the last day of the Post Extension of our Blue Danube Cruise from Budapest to Prague. We have a choice of two optional tours: a visit to Terezin Memorial or Lobkowicz Palace. Others from the ship will tour the city privately. Alan and Elaine are taking Alan's 87 year old mum, Doris (Dolly) on the open bus tour of Prague. At home in Canada Alan is a day trader on the stock market. Elaine says the break has been good for him. 'He's the most relaxed I have seen him for a long while. He didn't even bring his big computer with him.' Alan met Chris on a visit from England to Canada and he stayed on. It's a second time marriage for both. They will take mum home to Nottingham, England, tomorrow and stay four days before returning to Ontario, Canada.

Most of the *AmaLyra* group choose to visit the Jewish Memorial at Terezin which Avril and I plan to visit tomorrow on a private tour. We join a small group visiting the Lobkowicz Palace which is within the Prague Fortress complex where we visited yesterday. Libra, our guide last night, is with us again today. On the way to the Castle, she points out where once stood the giant granite statue of Stalin, a defiant symbol of communism. It was blown up during the Spring Offensive of 1968. 'They used three small charges rather than a big one in order to protect our important buildings,' says Libra.

Once more we pass two ceremonial sentry guards and enter Prague Castle grounds. This time the courtyard does not have the bustling crowds of people of yesterday and the atmosphere is relaxed and peaceful. This is because yesterday marked one of the three days in the year that many of the buildings contained in the castle grounds are opened free to the public. We pause to view again the magnificent St Vitus Cathedral, so picturesque in the freshness of morning sunlight. The huge Gothic and neo-Gothic edifice is the quintessential symbol of the history of Prague.

Across from the cathedral is Lobkowicz Palace which is the only privately owned building in the Prague Castle complex. The Lobkowicz family museum contains the oldest, largest and most intact private collection in the Czech Republic and offers visitors the opportunity to explore the history of Europe through the unique perspective of the Lobkowicz family. The museum contains 22 beautifully appointed galleries reflecting the cultural, social, political and economic life of Central Europe over six centuries. Additionally the Lobkowicz Palace offers a daily classical music concert in its beautifully restored Concert Hall, with its magnificent seventeenth-century stucco ceilings. Works by famous Czech and international composers (such as Mozart, Vivaldi, Dvorak and Beethoven) are performed.

In 1618 the Lobkowiczes find themselves at the centre of the bitter conflict between the independent-minded, largely Protestant nobility of the Bohemian Estates and the Catholic inner circles of the Habsburg court. At a meeting with representatives of the Estates, three of the Emperor's officials are hurled from a window of Prague Castle (Second Defenestration of Prague). Surviving the fall by landing in a dung heap, they take refuge in the adjacent Lobkowicz Palace. This event is commemorated in a painting depicting Polyxena Pernstejn, Princess Lobkowicz, shielding the bloodied and bandaged men behind her and refusing admission to a crowd of angry Protestants.

Avril and I are attached to audio guides, ushering us through the 22 fascinating galleries that explain the dramatic six-hundred year history of the Lobkowicz family -- how the family lose everything twice and get it back. I study a romantic painting of Polyxena standing bravely and defiantly. Its recreation illustrates a critical juncture in the fortunes of the Lobkowicz family.

Polyxena and her husband Zdenek Vojtech, 1st Prince Lobkowicz are leaders of the Catholic, or Spanish, faction opposing the local Protestants. Zdenek Vojtech, as Chancellor of the Czech Kingdom (under Emperors Rudolf II, Matthias and Ferdinand II), is the ruler's right-hand man. Polyxena is connected to powerful families throughout Europe and is noted for her political and diplomatic skills. Her first husband, William Rozmberk, was once the richest aristocrat in the land. Family connections tie the Lobkowiczes closely to the Spanish diplomats and courtiers trying to protect Habsburg interests in Bohemia. This constant exchange of communication between Prague and Madrid is shown in the religious and decorative paintings, objects and books commissioned from Spanish artists and brought to the Lobkowicz Palace.

Following the outbreak of hostilities in 1618, the Protestants confiscate all of Zdenek Vojtech's and Polyxena's property. But it is short lived victory. In 1620 the Protestants are decisively defeated at the Battle of White Mountain, on the outskirts of Prague. This is the start of the Thirty Year War which will vanquish the Protestant rebels, but confer lasting benefits for the Lobkowicz family who work zealously for the Habsburg faction in Bohemia. The rewards are great, resulting in an increase in the family collections, notably the library, and confiscated land holdings which ensure that the family will play a dominant role in Bohemia for centuries.

In 1740 Frederick the Great of Prussia invades the Habsburg province of Silesia, triggering the War of Austrian Succession (1740-48). This puts the Lobkowicz estate of Sagan in Silesia in danger of being confiscated. It was purchased in 1646 by Vaclav Eusebius, 2nd Prince Lobkowicz, the only child of Polyxena and Zdenek Vojtech. Now, Vaclav Eusebius's 16 year old great grandson, Ferdinand Philip, 6th Prince Lobkowicz (1724-84), in his wisdom, tacitly supports Frederick over the Habsburg Empress, Maria Theresa. This is a provocative and unprecedented step for a family that has long provided staunch support to the Holy Roman Empire. It is no accident that Ferdinand Philip will be one of the only two reigning Lobkowicz princes not to be received into the Order of the Golden Fleece, the highest European Order of Chivalry.

Ferdinand Philip prudently slips away to London during these troubled years following Frederick's successful invasion of the Habsburg's northern province of Silesia. In England the young prince is far removed from the conflicts of Central Europe. His stay provides him with an unusual opportunity to enhance his art collection back home. Among the acquisitions are two of Antonio Canaletto's finest English views, both of London, executed in the late 1740s. Both are on display in Lobkowicz museum. I am awe struck by the scenes. One is entitled *London:*

The Thames on Lord Mayor's Day. River vessels of all shapes and sizes pack either side of the Thames; beyond is the backdrop of London city.

Shortly after Ferdinand Philip's death in 1784, the Sagan estate, that he has so shrewdly protected, is sold to the Duke of Courland for the then staggering sum of one million gulden (German gold coin). Through prudent politics, the Lobkowicz fortunes and family collections increase. The Lobkowicz Palace, Roudnice Castle, in Vienna becomes the focal centre of the Lobkowiczes political and cultural activities. The Emperor, Joseph II, established amicable relations with Ferdinand Philip's son, the 7th Prince Lobkowicz, Joseph Frantisek Maximilian (1772-1816). The Emperor bestows upon him the title of Duke of Roudnice in 1786. The status of the Lobkowiczes rises to become one of the most prominent families in the whole of Europe. Their privileged position remains undisturbed until the upheavals of World War 1 and the disintegration of the Austro-Hungarian Empire.

Maximilian Lobkowicz (1888-1967) is the last heir to occupy Roudnice Castle. Like his ancestors, Maximilian is a politician and diplomat. In the new Czechoslovakia formed after WW 1, aristocratic families with property in the new state chose either German or Austrian nationality. Later in the 1930s, tensions grow between the Czechs and the growing German-speaking minority in Bohemia. With the German Reich threatening on the border, these tensions exacerbate the situation and great strain is placed upon loyalties to the Czechoslovak government.

Anti-aristocratic feelings emanate and the government abolishes hereditary titles. Despite these tense times, Max supports the young Republic and he campaigns abroad for its international recognition. He seeks diplomatic support against German annexation of the Sudetenland, the narrow strip of land at the border of Bohemia, occupied by German settlers. During World War II, all of his holdings are confiscated because he represents the Czechoslovak government in exile. The Lobkowicz family properties are returned in 1945, but are seized again just three years later by the Communist regime upon the foundation of the Czechoslovakian Socialist government in 1948. The Collections remain appropriated until the Velvet Revolution in 1989.

Following the collapse of the Communist rule (1948- 89) it became possible for the Lobkowicz family to reassemble most of their extensive collection of European treasures by the restitution of property laws in the 1990s. Today the restituted Lobkowicz treasures stand open for all to see.

The Lobkowicz Collections feature world famous paintings by Brueghel, Canaletto, Bellotto, Cranach, Rubens, Veronese and many others. Medieval and renaissance works of art and ceramics span five centuries. One the most important art pieces is Pieter Brueghel the Elder's *Haymaking*, painted in 1565 for an Antwerp merchant to hang in a dining room. The painting was originally part of a series of six panels, each presumed to represent two months of the year -- in this case June and July.

The great estates of Bohemia and Moravia once provided some of the best hunting in Europe. As a result the Lobkowicz arms and armour collection is exceptional. The landed elite made hunting a central pursuit. Hunting was a good way that a nobleman could gain the kind of training needed for warfare. At great expense, the hunting landowners planted millions of hardwood trees which provided shelter for deer, wild boar and other game. Without the diverse habitat, the animals they hunted would not have survived. Social aspects of the hunting scene are reflected in the many paintings and graphics by local artists who show their favourite horses, dogs and trophies. The copperplate engravings of Johann Elias Ridinger with his two sons, Martin Elias and Johann Jakub, depict lifelike hunting scenes of the Late Renaissance.

On display is an unparalleled collection of musical instruments, as well as original manuscripts of Wolfgang Amadeus Mozart and Ludwig van Beethoven compositions. The collection includes the valuable manuscript of Beethoven's Opus 55, Symphony No. 3 in E-flat major (*Eroica*), composed in 1803-04. Originally Beethoven had planned to dedicate the symphony to Napoleon Bonaparte, but this would have deprived him of a fee from his loyal supporter, Joseph Frantisek Maximilian, 7th Prince Lobkowicz. He lived in a fertile period for music composition and had a genuine passion for music. Thanks to the prosperity of the family, the young prince made a lasting legacy through his musical patronage. A talented singer, violinist and violoncellist, he was a founding member of the *Friends of Music in Vienna* and a director of the *Court Theatre of Vienna*.

Music was regularly played during evenings spent among aristocrats of the Austro-Hungarian Empire. Concerts were a regular event at Lobkowicz residences in Vienna, Roudnice and Jezeri. Famous artists would be invited to sing, including Luigi Bassi, one of the most celebrated baritones of his time. He performed in *Don Giovanni* at its Prague premiere of 1787.

In keeping to the tradition, concerts are performed every day here at Lobkowicz Palace. Part of our package includes a concert of classic music in the Palace's beautiful Concert Hall, decorated with impressive 17th century painted stucco ceilings.

I have been so absorbed by the museum that I need to hurry to the café for a quick bite before the classic concert at 1.00 pm. In haste, Avril and I share a bowl of soup and a beef sandwich. The hour long concert is provided by two professional musicians from the Czech Philharmonic Orchestra. The 50 or more people attending the concert are in for a treat of superb music. The program includes works from Bach – *Invention*; Eccles -*Sonata for viola and piano*; Mozart – *Turkish March*; Haydn – *Serenade*; Chopin – *Piece for Piano Solo and Piece for Viola*, Beethoven – *Romance, Moonlight Sonata and Fur Elise*; Smetana -- *Vltava (Moldau);* Dvorak – *Humoresque and Piece Romantique*; and Gluck – *Pizzicato*. There are no introductions and none of the artists' names appear on the program. But the sensational music presented by the lady pianist causes the grand piano to rock and the wooden floor to vibrate. She bows to our appreciation and leaves without a word being spoken.

A violinist then appears and plays a very moving number. Strangely, he too bows, quietly smiles, and leaves the room without saying a word. Sometimes they appear together to play a combination. Then they leave the room together after our applause. Hopefully, one of them will return. Fortunately, the program suggests when the recital is finished. We give them an extra-long applause; they bow several times and walk off.

I particularly enjoy their playing of *Fur Elise.* As a youngster I learnt to play a few bars of the Beethoven classic off by heart. Then my elder son, Tony, learnt to play it on a beautiful German steel base piano that I had bought in Port Moresby, PNG. I moved it upon our return to Australia in 1975. I decided it was too heavy and awkward to shift around, so I reluctantly sold it to a young musician studying at a Brisbane School of Music. I requested that she play *Fur Elise* for me before it left. Then I was happy that my piano had found a new home.

On our return to the hotel, the *AmaLyra* group visiting Terezin today begin to arrive. They report how delighted they were of their worthwhile visit there. This is where Avril and I will be heading by private escort tomorrow.

At 5.30 pm we need to find an ATM and to have an evening meal. I plan to ask the concierge for the nearest ATM. As luck would have it, we enter the same lift as our Cruise Director, Csaba. There is no need to see a concierge. Csaba is only too willing to take us outside, where he points to the best locations for dining out as well as the nearest ATM. Within 10 minutes we have extracted 30,000 CRZ, about 1500 USD, enough to cover the final three days of excursions out of Prague by private car.

We head for Baterka Restaurant, one of those recommended by Csaba. A few Americans from the *AmaLyra* have the same idea. Avril orders a spicy goulash and I decide on Papadelle of beef and tomatoes. With two beers it cost only 18 USD. Suddenly Alan, Elaine and Alan's elderly mum walk in and sit beside us. We just keep bumping into one another. It is thumbs up for their open tourist bus ride around Prague today. We offered our farewells to them this morning, so again we have a farewell encore.

Monday May 5, 2014,

Prague

At 6.00 am the morning sky is clear and sunny. From our fifth floor room of the Hotel Intercontinental, Prague looks like a postcard picture as the city awakens. I make a cuppa tea to share with Avril and we take breakfast at 7.10 am. Six months ago I contacted Eva Trkalova, an officially licenced Tour Guide of Prague and the Czech Republic. She arranged for us to meet her colleague, Radek Cizek, who has a deep knowledge of WW II events in the Czech Republic. I book Radek for two days — today we will visit Terezin Small Fortress, Terezin Ghetto and Litomerice, a beautiful little town with a chateau listed on UNESCO heritage sites. Tomorrow we will visit Moravska Trebova a town in the Svitavy District which lies in the Pardubice Region of Moravia in the eastern part of the Czech Republic.

Moravia contains about 30 percent of the territory of the Czech Republic and there are many historic villages. Moravska Trebova is where my uncle, Arthur Dawson, spent 4 years in a POW work camp during WW II. The town was once the largest German linguistic enclave within Bohemia and Moravia and known as Mahrisch Trubau in German. Nearby is the birth place of Oskar Schindler (Schindler's List) and Miretin which has a memorial to an Australian soldier killed on the last day of WW II.

The round-trip to Terezin takes about 7 hours and costs about 400 USD. Radek arrives as arranged at 9.00 am in the hotel lobby. He is a fit young Slavic man originally from Brno in the Moravia area in eastern Czech Republic. He now lives in the capital, Prague and has been a guide for 10 years. He speaks conversational English confidently and has travelled widely, hitch-hiking all over Europe, the UK and Russia. 'But not now,' he says, 'I'm too old for that.'

I ask him how he learnt English. 'I taught myself by listening to English radio and reading books,' he replies.

'What was the motivation?'

'I wanted to travel.'

Radek loves Australia and visited our country two years ago. He has an aunt living in Melbourne. She escaped the Communist rule during the Spring Offensive of 1968 and eventually is accepted into Australia as a refugee. Radek has visited all capital cities on the east coast and Adelaide in South Australia. He swam in the Great Barrier Reef in tropical north Queensland. He loves the Melbourne life style, particularly the coffee houses of Carlton and the wines of Mornington Peninsula. He drinks 5 or 6 cups of coffee a day! He has fond memories of the fairy penguins of Phillip Island, the Australian Open Tennis, the Dandenong's and Wilson Promontory, the southernmost point on Australia's mainland.

'Some of the world's top tennis players came from Czechoslovakia,' announces Radek. 'Have you heard of Ivan Lendl and Martina Navratilova?' he inquires. He rattles off a number of well-known players from here.

'Oh yes,' I reply. He is keen to know that Avril plays twice a week and that my great Uncle Jack played into his 90th year. 'Why is it that the Czechs produce such good tennis players?' I inquire. 'You are a small landlocked country of 10 million people in the middle of Europe.'

Radek answers, 'It was once a means of escape. During the communist rule it was a passport to freedom. No one could leave the country after the communist coup, except for some professional tennis players. The communists wanted their prize money and would tax those players 80 per cent of their winnings. Still they were very rich in comparison because the average worker received only about 100 USD per month.'

Radek speaks about the cruelty introduced by the Nazis. The German Nazis begin the persecution of Jews immediately after their accession to power. Hitler's Nazi Party instigates anti-Semitic passions from the beginning of their existence. Racism, aimed primarily against Jews, is an integral part of Nazi ideology. The Nuremburg Laws, issued in 1935, institute two types of citizenship, which mean the inequality of citizens in the Third Reich. To be a Reich citizen with all political rights is the prerogative of citizens of German blood, and not the Jews. Marriages are forbidden with members of other races. The Laws are designed to create preconditions for their complete extermination.

On March 15, 1935 the German Army occupies Bohemia and Moravia and creates a so called Protectorate. Instead, the inhabitants suffer immense suppression and persecution. The Jews are to suffer the most. A register of the citizens to scrutinize Jews is carried out and their property is impounded and confiscated. Their communications with the non-Jewish population are severely restricted. Jewish children are excluded from schools, and the grown-ups have to leave their jobs. They are prohibited from going to theatres, movie theatres, restaurants, using public transport, entering parks etc. Jews could shop only in specified places and at specified times; many foodstuffs and other products are prohibited from being sold to them. From September, 1941, all Jews in the Protectorate are obliged to wear in public the yellow Star of David. From humiliation, impoverishment, and isolation, their pathway is leading to utter destruction. The Nazi secretly call this 'The Final Solution.'

Our visit to Terezin begins at the Fortress of Terezin. Known as The Terezin Small Fortress, it is completed in 1784. It serves mainly as a military accommodation facility throughout the existence of the Habsburg monarchy and in the time of the First Czechoslovak Republic. In the wars between the Habsburg Empire and Prussia the fortress holds strategic importance. However, it never sees direct military action. The Small Fortress in Terezin serves as a military prison and penitentiary before World War II.

In 1938, Adolf Hitler demands control of the Sudetenland. Britain and France cede control in the 'Appeasement', ignoring the military alliance that Czechoslovakia has with France. On March 15, 1939, Nazi Germany occupies the remainder of the Czech lands and the following day Hitler signs a decree establishing the Protectorate of Bohemia and Moravia, declaring the Czech lands as part of the Greater German Reich. The ultimate goal of the Nazi policy in the Protectorate is the Germanisation of its entire territory. Out of a population of 7.5 million Czechs about half are to be eliminated gradually; the rest are considered capable of Germanisation.

The Terezin Gestapo prison is established following the mass arrests of resistance groups active in the Protectorate of Bohemia and Moravia during the autumn of 1939. The existing prisons, already filled to capacity, force the Gestapo to look for additional suitable places. In 1940, the German occupying power decides to convert the Terezin Small Fortress into a Gestapo prison with barracks to house an SS guard unit. The Small Fortress in Terezin has two advantages for the German police: it is both easy to guard and to access.

Prison Commander, SS-Hauptsturmfuhrer Heinrich Jockel, nicked named 'Shorty' by the inmates, is Commander throughout its existence. He is the main culprit of the brutal treatment of inmates. His assigned wardens, though not all, are equally brutal. Wardens would employ assistants from among the inmates and delegate part of their powers. They are employed in office jobs or as foremen known as *kapos*. Many do this job to the benefit of their fellow inmates, but some abuse their position and bully the inmates. Waffen-SS troops are in charge of guarding the entire complex and to escort the prison transports and work squads.

The Small Fortress is an intermediate prison, not the end of the journey. Inmates arrive for processing and are forwarded to courts and prisons, penitentiaries and concentration camps in Germany. The number of inmates rises from a mere 150 prisoners in 1940 to a peak of 5,500 in the last days of the war (150 in 1940; 600 in 1941; 1,200 in 1942; 2,000 in 1943-44 and 5,500 in last days of 1945).

The main causes of imprisonment are the involvement of men and women partisans in organised resistance groups and sabotage activities against the German occupation. Many are imprisoned for having committed economic or criminal offences, or escaping from forced labour. Wide-ranging swoops of guerrilla-supporting regions bring many villagers to Terezin prison. Foreign nationals and several hundred Soviet and British POWs are interned in the Small Fortress. Jews face the worst treatment. They could be interned for resistance activity, for violation of anti-Semitic regulations, or for offences committed in the adjacent Terezin ghetto. The wardens torture and kill them with particular brutality for their Jewishness.

Radek takes us through the prison to observe the conditions of horror. We observe the Administrative Courtyard and office where the admission procedure takes several hours. Each prisoner has to hand in their personal papers and valuables into the Effects Room (Effektenkammer). Then the storeroom attendants issue a prisoner's outfit (typically an old uniform), a bowl, spoon and blanket. Women prisoners are allowed to keep their civilian clothes. The administration procedure ends with the assignment of new prisoners to their cells.

The cells typically house 60 to 90 prisoners in three-tiered bunk beds, simple cabinets, a washbasin and a flush toilet. At the end of the war the situation is worse in the newly built Fourth Courtyard where several hundred inmates are crammed in each cell in absolutely appalling conditions. Maintaining tidiness is a serious problem. Various parasites, particularly lice and fleas, soon become a rampant enemy. Bed bugs require the prisoners and clothing to be de-loused regularly. The setting up of a delousing facility brings little improvement.

The dreadful standard of prison diet grows worse as management keep reducing the daily rations. By 1945 the prescribed 370 grams of bread per day is reduced to 225 grams, supplemented with a scoop of surrogate coffee twice a day and thin soup for dinner, usually made from bad vegetables.

The combination of overcrowded cells infested with parasites, insufficient hygiene, bad meals and frequent exhaustive labour disastrously weakens the prisoners both physically and mentally. These unbearable living conditions, together with the cruelty of the wardens and the executions by shooting, bring death to hundreds of internees in the Terezin prison in 1940-1945. In all an estimated total of 2,600 deaths occur in this terrible time.

Avril and I come to the Small Fortress shooting range which becomes the site of execution of prisoners in 1943. Execution by firing squad is common. At this chilling site, some 453 men and 13 women are executed by firing squads composed of the SS Guard Company and some of the volunteer wardens. A communist resistance fighter, Frantisek Prokop, shot on May 11, 1943 is believed to be the first victim of execution. The executions are ordered solely by the Gestapo. Arrested prisoners are not given the formal right to a proper trial.

The German occupation of the Czech lands brings the loss of freedom to millions and death to tens of thousands. The Jews suffer the greatest losses, no fewer than 73,000. They are singled out under 'The Final Solution of the Jewish Question'. Most Jews perish after being deported from the Terezin Ghetto to Ghettos and extermination camps in the east.

In Prague on October 10, 1941, a conference is held concerning the Jewish question in the Protectorate and the decision is made to establish a Ghetto in Terezin. The creation of a Jewish Ghetto in Terezin is the brainchild of Reinhard Heydrich, the Deputy Reich Protector. He envisages a plan to isolate the Jews from the remaining population, then concentrating them in a few places and gradually re-locating them into the Eastern reaches for their terminal liquidation. To carry out the plan, Terezin is chosen as the half way camp. Under the direction of Reinhard Heydrich, Terezin is made into a Ghetto way-station for Jewish families.

On February 16, 1942 Heydrich issues an order on the abolition of the community of Terezin. The 3142 original inhabitants of the town are given until June 30 to move out. The mass transports of Jews from various towns in Bohemia and Moravia start arriving. The number of Jews in the Ghetto grows rapidly. Of the 74,000 Jews in the so-called Protectorate, only 26,000 ever manage to evade deportation by emigrating.

On June 4, 1942, Heydrich is killed by Czech partisans as he is driven to work. His open-top Mercedes always uses the same route and the assassins simply wait for him at a point where the car has to slow down. His successor, Kurt Daluege, orders mass arrests and executions and the destruction of the villages of Lidice and Lezaky.

Radek takes us to a movie theatre at the Terezin Small Fortress before we visit the Terezin Ghetto. Here we view a fraudulent film made to serve Nazi propaganda. The Nazi film is made in an effort to hide the truth of the appalling conditions existing within the Ghetto. Reports on the extermination of the Jews are seeping out from the concentration camps. International pressure mounts, especially from the Red Cross, to permit a visit to Terezin, to verify German claims about the character of the Ghetto. In the end the Nazi authorities decide to permit a visit and to use it for propagandist deceit.

Terezin is subjected to improvements and beautification. For example: wooden fences and barriers are removed; the Ghetto is renamed 'Jewish Settlement Area'; a music pavilion is built; shops are remodelled and improved; the Gym is turned into a Community Centre and the housing of prominent prisoners are supplied with brought-in furniture. The extensive adaptation and beautification peaks in spring 1944 when a visit of the ICRC is finally decided. The Nazi are only interested in covering-up the true purpose of the installation. Terezin is presented as a town which 'the Fuhrer has given to the Jews'.

Upon arriving at Terezin Ghetto we walk to the large Central Square and Radek points out the town's buildings surrounding it. Everything looks neat and tidy and it is hard to believe that the town receives 74,000 Protectorate Jews beginning on November 24, 1941. The deportation of its population begins soon after. Terezin is part of the hideous plan for a 'Final solution of the Jewish' question, envisaging the extermination of all European Jews. Less than 10,000 Jews survive to see out the war in Terezin and the various concentration camps.

I query Radek about the terms 'ghetto' and 'concentration camp'. He says, 'Both are used for the same purpose.' He asks me, 'Do you know who first used the term, concentration camp?'

I shake my head. 'The British,' he replies. 'They used these camps during the Boer War in South Africa. But they used them in a good way, in order to protect women and children. Here the term has the negative meaning.'

We visit the Ghetto Museum which contains a comprehensive display of the massive human tragedy. You could spend all day here. To simplify matters, Radek directs our attention to important areas. He points to the Cyklon B toxin sign, the poison that got rid of bed bugs and later was used for the extermination of Jews in the gas chambers. He shows us drawings of life in a Ghetto by 12 year old Helga Weiss. Her parents encourage her to sketch what she saw. At 14 she and her parents are sent to Auschwitz and they suddenly become separated. She inquires of someone who points to the smoke rising from the gas chamber. Fortunately, Helga puts her age up to avoid being labelled a child. She survives and is still alive today.

Another survivor is Zdenka Fantlova who writes a love story, *'Ten Rings'*, about her life in a concentration camp. We also read the heart-wrenching story of a quiet hero, an Englishman, Nicholas Winton. He foresees the catastrophe that is about to befall the Jews, so he organises a rescue mission for over 600 Jewish children. He has to convince Jewish parents to release their children, put them on a train and stay with British families until the grim situation improves. He also has to raise enough money for their return fares before the British government will allow the venture. Of course, the situation worsens and the children never see their parents again. But, thanks to the foresight of Nicholas Winton, the children survive.

At 1.00 pm Radek takes us to the lovely nearby township of Litomerice for lunch. We enter a doorway which leads into a stone arched dungeon and down two flights of steps to a giant cellar where lunch is served. 'You can go down further if you wish,' say Radek. "No, this will do,' I say as we slip into a corner table. We are at the 'RADNK'NI SKLIPER' a cosy underground eating house. Radek tells us that many homes here had a cellar built and many were interconnected by tunnels which could be used to escape from a sudden attack by enemies. For lunch we share a tasty duck liver pate for starters; for mains we have sliced pork with rice and mushrooms. Avril and I have homemade lemonade and Radek has his essential cup of coffee.

At 2.30 pm we emerge from the underground luncheon cellar. Radek points out a couple of features in the town square. Inscribed in plaster above the second floor of a house is an interesting black and white pictorial scene of the ages of man, from birth until his death. Across the road we see the remains of a pillory once used to shame offenders. In another corner is a statue of famous Czech romantic poet, Karel Hynek Macha, who wrote the epic *'May'*. School children study it, but for Radek, at an early age, most of it went over his head. Radek explains that Macha was born in Prague on November 16, 1810 and he died on November 5 1836, just shy of his 26th birthday. The cause of his untimely death is unclear. He was extinguishing a fire at Litomerice and became ill after drinking some water intended for quenching the fire.

Macha is a romantic idealist who loves to wander the Bohemian countryside, visiting castles and making sketches and notes describing the natural beauty of his surroundings. His wanderings take him to Moravia, Slovakia and as far as Venice. He studies law at Prague University and is influenced by Czech intellectuals who are trying to revive the language at the beginning of the nineteenth century. During Habsburg rule, German and Latin are the compulsory languages for education.

At the time of his death Macha is on his way to Prague where he is about to marry the mother of his son three days later. He is buried in a pauper's grave in Litomerice. In March 1939 his remains are exhumed and given a formal state burial at Prague's Slavin Cemetery on Vysehrad, among the great Czech dead. This is the year that Nazi Germany occupies the country. Radek mentions that Macha kept a personal journal where he explicitly describes his sexual encounters with Lori, his wife to-be.

At 4.15 pm we are back in Prague, time to relax with a cuppa tea in our room before a meal later at the *Pizzeria Pepe Nero* across from the hotel. The food is delicious -- Avril has a plate of thick Minestrone soup, more like a stew. I settle for a bowl of mussels cooked in a mix of cherry tomatoes.

Tuesday May 6, 2014,

Prague

At 6.00 am the welcoming morning sunrays herald a wonderful spring day in Prague. After breakfast we meet Radek at 8.30 am in the lobby. Today we're off to Moravia in the eastern part of the Czech Republic. Our driver, Peter, heads east on the long drive towards Litomysl and Moravska Trebova in the Bohemian and Moravia borderland of the Czech Republic. Our mission today is the visit the scene of my Uncle Arthur's POW camp at Moravska Trebova where he spent over 3 years during WW II. Radek says that he has a surprise for us when we arrive. Ahead is a drive of 2 hours before we reach Litomysl on the Bohemian border and then a further 45 minutes to reach Moravska Trebova in the Moravian Province. We kill the time in both trivial and deep conversation.

Radek says the Czechs have a tradition of eating carp and potato salad on Christmas Eve. He laughs because carp are an unwelcome invasive guest introduced into Australian rivers. He says, 'In the Middle Ages fish ponds were developed to grow the carp. I enjoyed my stay in Australia. At Christmas my aunt prepared a beautiful potato dish, but we didn't eat carp.'

Radek's aunt and her fiancé were among the 250,000 refugees who had the foresight and guts to flee the country during the Spring Offensive of 1968. The border into Vienna was open for a short time and they took the window of opportunity. They were accepted into South Africa and in 1988 they moved to Australia.

I talk about the wearing of jeans which was frowned upon by the communists as western culture. 'Yes,' says Radek. 'I was a schoolboy during the Communist reign (1948-89). My aunt sent me a jumper with the word 'Cambridge' written on it. The teacher hauled me in front of the class because it represented western culture. I didn't understand.'

'Life under communism was terrible. There was no incentive to work. It taught people to be lazy and envious. But it was heaven for lazy people. I remember the time I had to do work experience at a canning factory. Mr 'M', the factory boss, just sat in his corner drinking vodka all day.'

'The health standards were poor. A visit to the dentist was painful because they had no money for pain killers. Your teeth were filled with grey fillings. Hospitals were crammed with waiting patients.'

'Everything was dilapidating and falling apart. For example, there was a hole in the ground with a covering around it that needed fixing. It was still there two years later. Workmen would turn up and after half an hour of work they would go to the pub. There was no incentive, the wages were very low. They had to import 60,000 workers from Vietnam. They stayed after the fall of Communism and are doing well.'

Radek continues with the funny story of little Joseph. 'One day the teacher asked the class to bring 5 crowns to help the flood disaster in India. Everyone brought 5 crowns except Joseph. The teacher asked why. My daddy says, 'If it happened in my country no one would help.' Next month there was a famine in Africa, so once again everyone brought 5 crowns except Joseph. Once again the teacher asked why. My daddy said, 'If it happened in my country no one would help.' Next month the teacher asked the children to bring 5 crowns for Communism in Vietnam. Joseph brings 100 crowns! The teacher was nonplussed and asked why. My daddy says, 'Nothing worse could happen to the Vietnamese.'

'The Communists hated the West,' says Radek, 'The Vietnam War was a battle of Communism v Democracy.' Radek directs our attention to some ugly housing-unit blocks that were built during the communist era. In contrast, there are neat office towers and shopping centres on our road journey out of Prague, following the Vltava River. The Vltava is the longest river in the Czech Republic – 430 kilometres from its source in Sumava Mountains on the Czech-Bavarian Border to its confluence with the Elbe at Melnik in central Bohemia.

From Prague the Vltava is crossed by 20 bridges on its 31 kilometre course through the city (11 road, 4 railway, 1 tramway and 2 pedestrian bridges, including the famous medieval Charles Bridge). Radek mentions the great flood of Vltava in August 2002 which killed several people and caused massive damage and disruption. Sections of The Prague metro system became flooded and it took several months to open the damaged stations.

Radek is anxious for us to arrive in the ancient town of Litomysl by 11.00 am in order to join a guided tour of Litomysl Castle. The Renaissance chateau was built between 1568 and 1581 by Vratislav of Pernstejn under the supervision of Italian architects G. B. & U. Aostali. On the rise near the castle once stood the old Mount of Olives Canonry built in 1141. It was torn down to make way for the Renaissance residence of Vratislav. The castle is noted for its unique sgraffito decorations on the façade and gables. (Sgraffito is the painting technique where the artist scratches into the top layer of paint or plaster to reveal the areas of the surface underneath). The castle's inner courtyard employs the same technique for depicting scenes of the Old Testament story of Samson and Delilah. Other scenes feature Rome being conquered by Emperor Constantine and the Battle of the Milvian Bridge. The chateau and its garden were entered into the UNESCO Register of World Cultural Heritage in 1999. The chateau complex attracts thousands of tourists to Litomysl every year.

Radek points out a large neighbouring building that once housed the brewery and stables required for the Renaissance residence. 'That is where our famous Czech composer, Bedrich Smetana was born in 1824. His father, Frantisek Smetana, was the chief brewer at the chateau. Bedrich is regarded as the father of Czech music. He was a gifted pianist and gave his first public performance at the age of six. His music helped to inspire our national movement for an independent homeland.'

Radek introduces us to Carol, a tall young Czech woman of shapely appearance and oozing a bubbly personality. She is about to guide a small group of Czechs through the main castle building. She provides us with a written handout in English and requests us to tag along. We begin by viewing a unique Baroque small theatre established in 1796-97 in the central hall of the ground floor by the then owner, Count Waldstein-Vartenberg. It contains a rare set of scenic backdrops painted by the Viennese court artist Josef Platzer. This magnificent theatre has been maintained almost intact and is the oldest example of this type in Europe.

Our tour of the chateau's interior takes us through representative rooms of historical decorations and furnishings – rare Rococo floral wall decorations, rich stucco ceilings and classical era décor of landscape and geometrical motifs. We are ushered through two floors of parlours, bedrooms, hallways, living and entertainment rooms. Beautiful large paintings displaying Bohemian landscapes, historic scenery and portraits of rulers and nobility enhance the walls.

There is the blue parlour with a picture of an eruption of Mt Vesuvius. The room displays Biedermeier style furniture favoured by the middle class of Germany, Austria, northern Italy and Scandinavia during a period of economic impoverishment between 1815 (Congress of Vienna) following the Napoleonic Wars and the Year of European Revolutions in 1848. Biedermeier style was a transitional period between Neoclassicism and Romanticism. The name Biedermeier was considered a derogatory and comic symbol made in reference to middle class comfort. It was based on the caricature of 'Papa Biedermeier' (He was a humorous character featured in verses by Ludwig Eichrodt published in *Fliegende Blatter*). A piano and a secretary desk were considered important items in emphasising a comfortable family lifestyle in the pursuit of hobbies and private activities, especially letter writing.

Carol leads us into the green parlour and the theme changes to Rococo (late Baroque) furnishings of the early 18th century. The room contains elegant ornate furniture, small sculptures and ornamental mirrors. Unlike the political Baroque, the Rococo style uses light colours and has playful and witty themes. We pass through a voluminous library containing 4000 books and enter the Empire parlour. The furnishings here represent Napoleon Empire style which came to Europe after Napoleon's expedition to Egypt. The legs of chairs are carved lion's paws.

The biggest room is the Grand Dining, set up for festive dinners and banquets. Adorning the walls are oil paintings of horses and country scenes painted by Martin Muckenbrunner who lived here for ten years from 1743. From the stucco ceiling hangs a glimmering chandelier containing over 40 lights. We come to The Battle Hall displaying huge paintings of the victorious battle scenes of Prince Eugene of Savoy, the brilliant famous French military leader of Austria's Imperial Army of the 18th century.

Room after room is a museum showcase: a music parlour for ladies features Baroque furniture and a music parlour for gentlemen contains Chippendale furniture from England and a large music box of twelve melodies; the servants room has a set of Meissen porcelain plates – the first high quality European porcelain outside of the Orient was manufactured in Meissen, Germany, in 1710, from extensive local deposits of china clay; and the horse rider's anteroom has magnificent paintings highlighting their lifestyle and the different breeds of horses.

The Castle of Litomysl is now a national cultural monument, acquired after WWII when it was confiscated from the Thurn-Taxis family whose ancestor Prince Maxmilian bought the estate at auction in 1856.

Carol is keen to chat with us at the end of the tour. She loves the theatre and has recently returned from an acting academy course in Sydney. There she meets an Australian guy and is now torn whether or not to return and follow her heart.

Leaving Litomysl we now drive to the town of Moravska Trebova on the border of Bohemia and Moravia. Of course, the reason I am visiting here is to satisfy my curiosity about this former German enclave where my Uncle Arthur spends 4 long years as a POW during World War II. From his unpublished book, *'A Sapper's Story'* this is how my uncle describes his arrival at Mahrisch Trubau, (the German name for Moravska Trebova):

In due course we arrived at our destination, to find it was a place called Mahrisch Trubau (Pronounced – Mare ish tree bow.). This of course meant absolutely nothing to us. We were too intent on climbing down from the cattle truck, and getting the stiffness out of our bones, to pay anything more than passing interest to the place.

It seemed to be a reasonably compact, small little town, set in undulating country. It was surrounded close by, by heavily timbered hills. Obviously they would be the source of supply for the mills we were to work at. Everything was heavily snowed under, and to an Australian at least, the outlook was bleak and unattractive…

We trudged through the streets, slipping and sliding on the icy roads. The locals, sensibly, kept inside, and there was barely a soul to be seen. After about half an hour, we were led to a medium sized house, the end one in a row, opposite a fairly large timber mill. It was on the outskirts of town, with snow swept open fields behind it.

Following Arthur's recapture in Greece, he is sent initially to Stalag VIII-B (renumbered Stalag-344) near Lamsdorf (now Lambinowice). From there Arthur volunteers to join this working party at Mahrisch Trubau to be with his mates. He sees sawmilling as a safer option than the likelihood of being forced to work in the coal mines to the north in Silesia in Poland. The German war machine urgently needs coal and, combined with the severe winter, there is a desperate shortage of fuel for both domestic and industrial use. This will require a labour force of many more POW's to raise coal production from the nearby Polish mines. Arthur is determined that there is no way he is going down a coal mine if he can avoid it. Born and bred in the NSW coal city of Newcastle, Arthur knows coal mining is a dangerous occupation even under good conditions. His dad and family have been miners and his mother's family too.

Arthur is one of the 54 men who make up the work party sent to Moravska Trebova. A wide range of nationalities are represented, including Australians, New Zealanders, Palestinians, Welsh, Scots and English. They regard themselves as British whereas the Germans regard them as English. Their workforce will man three sawmills, an engineering works and a cement works. For the home timber mill, directly opposite their house, eight men are required. For the large Berg Mill there are twenty. For the small Kollas Mill, where Arthur has elected to go, there are six. For the Koldas Cement Works there are ten. For the Engineering Works there are four. Three men act as cooks and cleaning staff, and another three are administration staff.

I am beginning to wonder about the surprise that Radek mentioned this morning. I know he has done some homework in preparation for our visit. Radek smiled and nodded in approval when I pulled out a copy of Arthur's wartime sketch map of town which was drawn by his mate, Norm Shute. Other thoughts flood my mind. Above all, why was Moravska Trebova a German stronghold? I know that the German inhabitants were kicked out of Czechoslovakia after the war.

And what can I expect when I arrive? In 1987 a protective urban heritage reserve was designated to include the town's historical core and the Castle of Moravska Trebova which is considered one of the most outstanding Renaissance monuments in Central Europe. Unlike the majority of castles and chateaus in the Czech Republic, this one is owned by the town, not the state. The town council completed a ten year expensive reconstruction of the castle in 2005.

The name Moravska Trebova intrigues me and I am yet to discover the mystery. Moravska or Mahrisch in German means Moravia, the name given to the region. The Trebova branch of the Boskovice family brought big changes to the 16th century town. The last member of the Boskovice family to own the castle was Jan Trebovsky, so that may explain the Trebova part of the name.

The Moravian landscape around Moravska Trebova was once crossed by old hunting trails which, throughout the times, became trading channels. Moravska Trebova is founded in 1270 by Bores of Ryzmburk who is the holder of extensive fiefs in northwest Bohemia, southeast Moravia, and as far away as Meissen in Germany. The thickly forested land is given to him by King Vaclav 1 (Wenceslaus I) for his aid in supressing an uprising led by his son, the later Premysl king Otakar II.

Establishing a town in the Middle Ages is an expensive and risky business. Bores is forced to invite German settlers as the area is sparsely settled with a Slavic population. The colonists clear a place to establish wooden houses and they turn to agriculture, crafts and trade. Wooden fortresses protect the trading pathways leading from Bohemia through Svitavy in Moravia to Poland. Bores has the old town built at a strategically convenient place on a slight hill above the river Trebuvka which follows the trading path. Fortifications are built around its extensive main square. To the southeast of the square stands an old castle which at the time is inserted into the fortifications and separated from the town by a deep moat.

Initially, agriculture is the economic basis of the town. Over time families of craftsmen are attracted to the settlement, firstly as spinners and then weavers of flax. The tradition of brewing becomes important until the town's citizens are deprived by law of the right to brew and serve beer in licenced houses.

An important man in the history of Moravska Trebova town and its castle is Ladislav Cernohorsky of Boskovice (c.1455-1520). He belongs to an important aristocratic family and plans a career in the church. His university studies begin in Vienna and continue to Pavia, Padua, and Bologna and then, after 10 years, to Ferrara in 1482. He visits Rome and has the opportunity to meet important personalities of his times and to witness the new fashionable Renaissance art which has not reached any importance yet in Central Europe. With his friend, Jan Stiebnitz, he travels widely through northern Africa, Asia Minor and southern Germany where Gothic churches and fortified castles carry no Renaissance traces at all.

Ladislav gains several church positions at important Moravian centres -- the canon of Olomouc, the provost of St Peter's Church in Brno and the chapter dean in Wroclaw. Then, along with his older brother, Jaroslav, he joins the services of the Hungarian King Matthias Corvinus who awards him his first ecclesiastical sinecure – the post of provost in the Hungarian town of Veszprem. However, the family of Boskovice turns away from King Matthias after he accuses Jaroslav of plotting his murder. Jaroslav is arrested for treason and executed in 1485.

This upset causes the thirty year old Ladislav to resign from his clerical functions and devote his attention to the development of his family estate. He decides to settle permanently in Moravska Trebova. He lays the foundations of today's castle and strives for the town's prosperity. He fortifies the town with walls and supports the burgesses to build their houses of stone. Moravska Trebova emerges as one of the important centres of power on the Czech-Moravian border.

The 'old castle', as it is later called, is built between 1485 and 1497. This small castle occupies the site of an irregular four-sided ground plan and features a mix of medieval and new Renaissance elements. Ladislav surrounds himself and family with numerous servants and a number of works of arts, musical instruments, astronomical devices and a renowned library of over 200 volumes of illuminated manuscripts on parchment, a few of which have been preserved in collections in Brno and Olomouc.

From the works of art, only a large tapestry survives, which is on display in the castle's exhibition of the Treasures of Moravska Trebova. This tapestry picturing *Iphigenia in Taurus* has been miraculously saved. The large tapestry (2.6 x 5.3m) is found packed and not used after spending centuries in the loft. In Greek mythology, Iphigenia is the daughter of Agamemnon who is leader of the Greek forces at Troy. Agamemnon offends Artemis, the virgin goddess of the hunt, by killing one of her sacred animals. Artemis sends a wind which holds the Greek fleet in the Bay of Aulis, where it is assembled before sailing to Troy. The prophet Calchas divines that Agamemnon's daughter would have to be sacrificed to appease Artemis. Agamemnon summons Iphigenia from home under the pretence that she is to be married to Achilles. The sacrifice is about to take place, but Iphigenia is miraculously transported to Taurus, a city on the Black Sea, and an animal is sent in her place.

Jan Trebovsky of Boskovice is the last owner of the castle belonging to the Boskovich family. He dies childless in 1589. He bequeaths the property to his sister's 10 year old son, Ladislav Velen of Zerotin (1579-1638). The young travelling student studies at universities in German Heidelberg, Swiss Geneva and in Italy. He returns to his country and turns to developing his estate. He is so successful in looking after his heritage that he buys more estates. He is self-confident, generous and takes pleasure in precious jewels. He supports various artists, musicians, alchemists and scholars, inviting them to his residential home in Moravska Trebova. The 'old castle' is too small for him so he has the moat, separating the town from the castle, filled in. This provides room for the construction of three wings of the 'new castle' which are built in the style of contemporary Roman architecture.

However, Ladislav Velen's fortunes are about to change as political and religious tensions in the wider regions of Central Europe work against him. Moravian aristocrats agree to pay high taxes to the Habsburg rulers to support the army in battles against the Turks who are regarded as the 'feudal enemy of all Christians'. Moravian inhabitants feel jeopardized by the closeness of the battle field in Hungary. Many of them join soldiers from all over Europe fighting against the Turks in battles at the 'boneyard of Europe'. The danger is overcome when Matthias, with the support of Hungarian, Austrian and Moravian nobility, makes peace with the Turks.

On the other hand religious freedom is of the highest importance for Moravian nobility who hope the high taxes will gain the support of the Habsburg rulers for that freedom. The majority of evangelical aristocrats strive for the equality of their religions.

Ladislav Velen is a member of the Bohemian Brethren. At the time the United Brethren, along with Lutheran and Catholic, are the three main churches of the region. However, only the Catholic Church is legal, though fewer in numbers. In 1619 Ladislav Velen serves as head of government of the Protestant Estates and is elected as regional governor. In the same year he becomes leader of the Moravian rebellion which takes part in the religious struggle against the Catholic Habsburgs.

Revenge comes swiftly following the dethroning of the Habsburgs in Prague and their welcoming of the 'winter king' Friedrich V to the Bohemian throne. In 1620 Ladislav Velen accompanies King Friedrich through his ceremonial tour of Moravia. However, both flee to safety after the Protestant hopes of religious equality are crushed at the Battle of White Mountain, outside of Prague on November 8, 1620. Ladislav evades punishment for treason through emigration to Silesia in the spring of 1621, unlike twenty-seven Czech noblemen who are executed. For the remainder of his life Ladislav leads soldiers on the Protestant side during the Thirty Years' War (1618-48).

Ladislav Velen manages to escape the death penalty, but not the confiscation of all his properties. They are confiscated for the benefit of the Czech Crown, bringing to an end almost a century and a half of the town's flourishing development. The new owner is the ambitious politician Karel of Liechtenstein. He is a distant relative of the House of Zerotin but unlike Ladislav Velen he is a faithful supporter of the imperial cause. In fact he used to be Velen's south Moravian neighbour, friend and a godfather of his sons.

Liechtenstein takes advantage of the fallout. Out of the confiscations of property, he manages to gather large estates all over Moravia. He assumes ownership of Moravska Trebova on March 5, 1622, but by autumn the following year he has to occupy the town with a division of his own cavalry and infantry to quell the rebellious inhabitants. He insists that they join the Catholic Church or face drastic punishment. The town's prosperity suffers by the withdrawal of previous economic privileges – in particular, the right to brew and serve beer.

Prince Liechtenstein only makes brief visits to his new estate. The castle remains untouched by Baroque reconstructions taking place elsewhere, apart from partial improvements for better living. The castle becomes an administrative centre headed by a governor. Its rooms, given over to Liechtenstein's clerks, serve as offices and flats.

A destructive fire affects Moravska Trebova on April 30, 1840. Much of the old castle is destroyed and all the Renaissance houses in the town square have to be rebuilt. Only the tower of the 'old castle' survives. Three wings of the castle have to be pulled down. The eastern wing survives and part of the western wing is rebuilt.

In the final decades of the 19th century and the start of the 20th the overall appearance of the town is significantly changed. Town fortifications across Europe are demolished to allow for the further growth of towns. Most of Moravska Trebova's walls are gone by the 1830's. Electricity is installed in the castle in 1898, but its buildings are slowly collapsing. Restoration of the arcades commences in 1913, but WW1 stops the rebuilding which is finished ten years later.

WWII brings further interference to improvements when the castle loses its aristocratic owner. In 1945 the castle is confiscated and becomes the property of the state. For a time its offices and flats are given to employees engaged in forestry. For decades the courtyard serves as a wood storage and there is hardly any maintenance of its buildings.

Restoration of the castle's former grandeur has to wait until the 1990's when the decrepit monument becomes the property of the town. The extensive reconstruction process takes ten years to complete and in 2005 the chateau opens its gates to visitors in all its original glory. The entire chateau is restored to become the town's cultural centre. It includes a library with a large reading room, halls for short-term exhibitions, a café and a children's playground. Classic exhibitions on offer include *Treasures of Moravska Trebova* and an overview of the town's history. There is the *Hall of Knights* which may be used for weddings and to hold seasonal exhibitions. On offer is a *medieval torture chamber*, the largest of its type in the Czech Republic. A further exhibition with interactive elements is the *alchemy laboratory of Doctor Bonacina* who, during his time at the chateau, tried to discover *liquid gold*, the elixir of eternal youth.

Around midday our car enters T. G. Masaryk Square in the historic core of Moravska Trebova. The huge square is named in honour of Tomas Garrigue Masaryk (Born March 7, 1850, near Goding, Moravia, then part of the Austrian Empire, now Hodonin in the Czech Republic). As the principal founding father of Czechoslovakia, Masaryk is regarded similar to the way George Washington is regarded in the United States. He advocates Czech Independence during World War 1 and becomes the founder and first President of Czechoslovakia on November 14, 1918. He enjoys legendary status and under his watch Czechoslovakia becomes the strongest democracy in Central Europe. He resigns from office on December 14, 1935 on the grounds of old age and poor health. He dies two years later on September 14, 1937. Dying at that time meant he is spared witnessing the Munich Agreement and the Nazi occupation of his country. Today Czechs and Slovaks alike regard him as the symbol of democracy.

Masaryk Square is surrounded by beautiful three storey Burghers' houses, some decorated by stone portals or renaissance alcoves. Dominating the centre of the heritage reserve is a Baroque Plague Column. From August 1715 to January 1716, Moravska Trebova is wracked by the bubonic plague. Latin inscription informs us: *Stand here quietly pilgrim, and learn to keep your promise, such that nemesis shall not once more let fly his poisonous arrows of plague – Those devoted to God and rescued from death have erected this sculpture to the immaculate and pure Mother of God.*

Further Latin inscription announces: *Infection spreads fear through its fury in the ailing citizens; pious sacrifice may drive the pest away. – When here in Trebova there died in seven months four priests, the mayor, the judge, five councillors and of the other god-fearing persons a full 900, this monument was built by the dean, the chief councillor and those people of the town of Trebova who survived the plague.*

Peter, our driver, parks the car in front of the Town Hall which is the most impressive building in the Square. The Town Hall tower and the spire of the Baroque parish *Church of the Assumption of the Virgin Mary* form the distinctive skyline above the main Trebova Square. The original Gothic Town Hall of 1520 is destroyed by fire and then reconstructed in Renaissance style during the 1560's. Its tower is destroyed by fire in 1726. Later in 1764 the tower is completed with an octagonal shape Renaissance base and an onion-dome, topped by a Moravian eagle as a weather vane. The tower, lacking any foundations, is unique.

Radek requests us to wait outside entrance of the Town Hall while he checks inside. My suspicion is aroused that his surprise for us is about to happen. In a short moment he returns all smiles, 'The Mayor would like to see you.' We climb a stairway leading to the first floor where the secretary is waiting to introduce us to the mayor, Milos Izak. He is a friendly and solidly built middle-aged man who invites us to sit at a table in his office. The richly decorated room has beautiful cross-arched and comb-like vaulted ceilings covered with a rich vegetative pattern of vine-leaves, grapes and pomegranates. On the walls are fresco paintings with biblical motives. Milos proudly points to the well-preserved Renaissance fresco, *The Judgement of Solomon* of c. 1560, which should lead the councilmen into making just decisions.

Milos is keen to hear about my uncle's experience as a POW in World War II. There is no hurry despite someone waiting to see him. He orders his secretary to prepare a cup of tea and we spend almost an hour going over the events. Milos does not speak English so Radek translates. He wants to know how the largely German population treated the prisoners and what they were expected to do. Pre-war Czechoslovakia was re-established after World War II. The government confiscated the property of the Germans and expelled about 90 per cent of the ethnic German population, over 2 million people.

We turn our attention to a wartime sketch map that I bring along. It shows Mahrisch Trubau and District as it was known to the German inhabitants. One of Arthur's mates, Norm Shute, was in the same Working Party of 391 and he sketched the map from memory after returning home. It compares remarkably with contemporary maps, displaying the outline of the district's physical features, infrastructure and buildings. Norm's map shows that the historic T G Masaryk Square of Trebova was known then as *A Hitler Platz*.

Milos is keen to show us through the upper floor of the council chambers. A large hall next to his office serves as general meeting place and for functions and even weddings. He explains that the Town Hall underwent structural adjustments in the early 1960's. He shows us the load-bearing pillar that was replaced when the entire building was lifted upward on hydraulic supports. The vaulted ceilings were reinforced with concrete shell-structures and the entire building fortified with steel rods.

Milos hands us a gift package before we leave. It includes three wonderful books of the town which I draw upon for usage in this section. One book explains the architecture and history of its buildings - *The Path from Renaissance to Baroque… Great Buildings of Moravska Trebova*; another tells the story of the castle - *MORAVSKA TREBOVA… Renaissance Pearl of the Czech Republic*; and the final one explains the Moravska Trebova landscape - *The Hrebec Mining Paths*.

We emerge once more into the square, but there is too little time for shopping before moving on. I purchase a couple of post cards at a souvenir outlet and in a restaurant we take a late lunch of Moravian stew. Our tight schedule precludes a visit to the nearby castle. Radek suggests we drive through the town's surrounds and then visit the guard house where Arthur was held for 4 years during the war. The town has less than 12,000 inhabitants and it doesn't take long to reach a row of neat cottages near the outskirts. They face a large saw mill on the opposite side of the road. Radek believes this is the spot where Arthur's work camp was situated. Radek explains, 'There used to be wooden houses here, but they have been replaced with these new ones.'

I nod in agreement. I point to the saw mill opposite and suggest, 'It all makes sense. There is the mill across the road and it's still operating.' It seems likely that the mill is one of the three former mills in operation at the time and the closest to the POW's guarded quarters. Arthur had hoped to be one of the eight POWs chosen to work there instead of trudging to the mills on the other side of town. I feel like a pilgrim visiting a holy shrine. I can only imagine what my uncle may think if he could visit his wartime prison. Gone are the dreary barracks, replaced by pleasant cottages, their springtime gardens flourishing in warm afternoon sunshine.

We now press on to make two more stops on our return to Prague. One is the birthplace of Oskar Schindler, the German industrialist, who is credited with saving as many as 1,200 Jews during the Holocaust. The other is to the memorial site of Lawrence Phillip Saywell, who was the last Australian to be killed in Europe in the Second World War. Both sites are only a short drive from Moravska Trebova - about twelve km to Svitavy and a further 35 km to Miretin.

Our vehicle stops at Zwittau, now Svitavy in Moravia, where Oskar Schindler was born on April 28, 1908. A small monument honouring his bravery is mounted in the parkland opposite a nondescript house, part of the wall to wall housing estate where Oskar grew up. Appropriately, a Star of David is contained on the memorial in recognition by the many Jewish lives he saved. Schindler's story was brought to international acclaim by the 1982 novel *Schindler's Ark* and the 1993 film, *Schindler's List*.

Oskar is from a Catholic German family and lives a privileged life. From an early age he is irresponsible, sinful and opportunistic. On March 6, 1928, aged 19, he marries Emilie Pelzl, daughter of a prosperous German farmer. He is womaniser and loves to drink and gamble. He joins the German Sudeten Party in 1935 and becomes a spy for the Abwehr, the intelligence service of Nazi Germany. In this role he collects information on railways, military installations and troop movements, as well as recruiting spies within Czechoslovakia, in advance of the planned invasion of the country by Nazi Germany. He is arrested for espionage and immediately imprisoned by the Czech government on July 18 1938. His release comes under the terms of the Munich Agreement which allows the annexation of the Czech Sudetenland into Germany on October 1, 1938. His application for membership of the Nazi Party is accepted in the following year.

He sees the opportunity to make money and arrives in Poland on the heels of the SS in October 1939. Diving into the black-market and driven by profit, he soon makes friends with the local Gestapo bigwigs by softening them up with women, money and illicit booze. His connections help him to acquire a factory which he runs using the cheap Jewish labour force. Poland has been a haven for European Jews before the outbreak of war. Krakow's Jewish population numbers over 50,000. Destruction of the Jewish haven begins immediately and is merciless when Germany invades and occupies Poland in December 1939. Jews are herded into crowded Ghettos, randomly beaten and humiliated or killed at whim. Their property and businesses are simply destroyed or appropriated by the SS and sold to Nazi investors, one of whom is the fast talking, womanising, money driven Schindler.

At first Oskar seems like every other usurping German industrialist, unmoved by the means of his profiteering. But then a light-bulb moment causes a change in his thinking, like Saul on the Road to Damascus. 'If you saw a dog going to be crushed under a car, wouldn't you help him?' he says later of his wartime actions.

Schindler acquires his Emalia factory which produces goods and munitions to supply the German front. Soon after, however, the removal of Jews to death camps begins in earnest. Schindler's Jewish accountant puts him in touch with the few Jews with any remaining wealth. They invest in his factory, hoping in return they will be able to work there and be spared. He is persuaded to hire more Jewish workers, designating their skills as essential and paying off the Nazi so they will allow them to stay in Krakow. So Schindler is making money, everyone in his factory is fed and no-one is beaten or killed. His factory becomes an oasis of humanity in a desert storm.

Schindler's protection of his Jewish workers becomes particularly active as the brutality of the Holocaust escalates. In the summer of 1942, he witnesses a Nazi raid on the Jewish Ghetto. He watches innocent Jews being packed onto trains bound for certain death. His humanity empowers him to take revenge. 'Beyond this day, no thinking person could fail to see what would happen,' he says later. 'I was now resolved to do everything in my power to defeat the system.'

By the autumn of 1944, Germany's hold on Poland weakens as the Russian army approaches. The Nazis try desperately to complete their program of liquidation and send all remaining Jews to die. Many of the Jews are sent to the Plaszow concentration camp after the Krakow Ghetto is liquidated. But Schindler remains true to the *Schindlerjuden*, the workers he refers to as 'my children'. He uses his influence to set up a branch of the Plaszow camp for 900 Jewish workers in his factory in Zablocie. He makes his now famous list of the workers he will need for its operation.

The factory operates for a year in its new location, making defective bullets for German guns. Conditions are grim for the Schindlers as well as the workers. However, Schindler saves most of the workers by transferring his factory to Brunnlitz (Sudetenland) in October 1944.

The War ends and Schindler flees to Argentina with his wife and a handful of his workers. They buy a farm, but in 1958 he abandons his land, wife and his mistress to return to Germany. He spends his remaining years dividing his time between Germany and Israel where he is honoured and taken care of by his *Schindlerjuden*. He dies in Hildesheim in 1974. His extraordinary story might have died there with him but for their gratitude.

The final stop on our return journey to Prague is made at the memorial site of the last Australian soldier killed in Europe in the Second World War. Our vehicle leaves a sealed road near Miretin and follows a farming track a few hundred metres along a grassy verge to where Lawrence Phillip Saywell was shot on May 8, 1945, the official date of the end of the war in Europe. His lonely jagged rock memorial lies in a lush green field, far from his homeland, and marks the actual site of his death, almost 69 years ago from our visit. A signpost nearby to the memorial provides a summary of his exploits:

> 'Lawrence Phillip Saywell was born in Sydney, Australia. He was the eldest of three sons and he studied at Scottish boarding school. He is reported to have spoken fluent English, French, German, Russian and Polish.
>
> In 1940 he enlisted to 17th Brigade Company, Australian Service Corps and he subsequently served with the 6th Division in Palestine, Libya, Greece and Crete, where he was taken prisoner in May 1941 by

advancing German forces, and the he was held prisoner in Germany. In January 1945 he escaped with three privates from German Captivity and joined with a local Czech partisan division 'Vpfed'.

One of the inhabitants of Miretin took a photograph of all four Privates and after the end of the war he sent the photograph to Lawrence's mother in Australia. His mother then donated it to the relevant authorities and it was later displayed in the Australian war memorial.

On the 8th May 1945 Lawrence Saywell was killed – shot in the head by a German SS Patrol. Lawrence was buried in the Evangelical Cemetery in Miretin. On the 10th September 1945 a memorial was erected in his honour, which was hosted by the English attaché and a correspondent of The Times G J Mullens. After the war his body was exhumed and transported to the military cemetery in Olsany Prague, where his remains are placed with other deceased soldiers of the Second World War. His grave in Miretin was removed and it is a place of reverence for many of us.

In November 1945 the President of Czechoslovak Republic – Edvard Benes awarded private Lawrence Saywell the Czechoslovak Military cross for his 'brave eminent services to our State in the battle for liberation'.

Lawrence Saywell was the last Australian to be killed in Europe in the Second World War.

The Australian ambassador to Poland and Preston Saywell brother of Lawrence Saywell visited Prosec and Miretin in 2005 and placed the flowers on both the grave and the memorial of private Saywell. In 2012 Petr Vodvarka, on behalf of the Australian consulate in Prague and the consulate for Middle, South and East Europe, honoured the memory of the deceased Australian and New Zealand soldiers who fought so bravely in the Czechoslovak republic, and among these was of course Lawrence Saywell.

What rotten luck for Saywell who survived almost the entire war, only to be shot on the last day! His wartime experience is almost identical to my Uncle Arthur's wartime record, except Arthur made it through. From my uncle's notes he writes, *'Of the 31,000 Australians taken prisoner during the war, some 8,000 did not make it through'.*

Saywell was 20 when he enlists in the Second AIF, in November1939, soon after the outbreak of the Second World War. As he is under the age of 21, his mother signs his attestation papers. Although he has poor eyesight, the examining medical officer apparently overlooks this, and Saywell is assigned to the Australian army service corps, a non-combat unit attached to 17 Infantry Brigade, 6 Division. After initial training in Australia, Saywell embarks for service in the Middle East in January 1940. His unit spends most of the rest of the year training in Palestine before being sent to support the first Libyan campaign. At the end of March 1941 Saywell embarks for Greece with the ill-fated allied expeditionary force. From Greece his unit is withdrawn to Crete in the face of the German advance. Saywell is reported missing on June 5, 1941.

In fact, like my uncle, he has been captured and taken as a prisoner of war on Crete, while attempting evacuation to Egypt. They more than likely may have rubbed shoulders. Saywell and my uncle are then transported by train to Germany. However, my uncle manages his first escape attempt in Northern Greece as the train chugs slowly towards Stalag VIIA at Moosburg. Saywell is transferred to Stalag VIIB (later 344) at Lamsdorf in Poland. This is the same prison where my uncle is sent after his on-the-run experiences in Greece and his subsequent recapture.

Saywell then spends time in the relative freedom of a number of labour camps in central Europe, taking the opportunity to learn to speak German and possibly some Russian. My uncle also learns to speak German during his labour camp time in Moravska Trebova. Saywell teams up with a New Zealander fellow-prisoner, Sydney Mac Kerkham, and makes at least two unsuccessful escape attempts. They are finally successful in January 1945 when the Germans order the evacuation of POW camps in the face of the approaching Soviet Russian forces. In the confusion Saywell and Kerkham escape from a camp at Pardubice, in what is now the Czech Republic. They find refuge with families near the village of Zderaz, which is less than 50 km from my uncle's work camp at Moravska Trebova. Slovenian and Czech partisan groups in the area, supplied and encouraged by Soviet forces, harass the Germans, who in turn conduct anti-partisan operations around Zderaz.

In the first week of May a major uprising against the Germans flares up in Czech lands and the German army retreats west. My uncle writes:

In 1945 Europe was clearly falling apart, although in our sector the Germans were still in control. The Russians, our nearest Allied forces, were advancing very slowly. We could hear their artillery 20 to 30 miles away. We were monitoring the situation on the radio from BBC London. It had tuned into the VE Day celebrations there. We immediately informed our Guards that for us the War was over and that we were moving out. They tried to talk us out of it, but their communications having broken down, they clearly did not know what to do. We told them they could tag along too and it would look as if they were taking us somewhere, but we were going and that was it. Soon we were stretched out in small groups on the march. There were refugees everywhere all making for the West and the Americans.

Saywell and Kerkham come out of hiding and make their way to Miretin, where, on 8 May, the official date of the end of the war in Europe, they encounter a confrontation between a retreating German column and a Soviet-Czech partisan group which has taken about thirty German officers as hostages in the local school. Saywell offers his services as an interpreter and succeeds in getting the officers released and disarmed. For reasons that are not clear, he is shot and killed by an unknown German soldier shortly afterwards. His body lay in state in the village school until 10 May, when he is buried in the local cemetery.

Later in 1945 the villagers erect a headstone on his grave and a stone memorial at the actual site of his death. In November 1945 he is posthumously awarded the Czechoslovakian Military Cross. In 2005 a further posthumous award of the Meritorious Cross is made by the Czech Republic. Lawrence Saywell's remains are transferred to the Prague War cemetery after it had been built in 1949. Even so, his death is still commemorated at Miretin every year when a ceremonial procession takes place between the site of his original grave and his memorial stone.

My uncle eventually meets up with the Americans and freedom. He returns to Australia to marry Jean, his sweetheart and to live a long happy life. In his writings he says, *'I had served some six years during World War II, although four years of them had been on a continental 'Holiday' as a guest of Mr Hitler. I suppose my military achievements were pretty poor, having been involved in mostly disasters. However, I did achieve my main aim which was to survive and come back in one piece. While you never forget the hard spots, what sticks with you the most is the people, the ordinary blokes, and as the ode says: We will always remember them.'*

Wednesday May 7, 2014,

Prague

I forget to set the alarm for 6.00 am and I hear Avril preparing a wake-up cup of tea at 6.30 am. The morning sky is clouding over and I have my fingers crossed that it will stay fine for our full day trip to Cesky Krumlov. The city is not on our original itinerary, but a couple of our friends say it is like a scene out of a fairy tale and you must go there. Radek, our guide yesterday, says it is his second favourite place after Prague. Cesky Krumlov has a picturesque setting above the meandering valley along the upper Vltava River in southern Bohemia. More than three hundred historic buildings, dominated by a huge castle and the Church of St Vitus, bear witness to its rich past.

Daniel, our driver and our guide, arrives in a mini bus at 8.40 am. We are accompanied by three other passengers from our hotel. Seated next to me is a stylish South Korean woman, with gold painted toe nails, accompanied by her 10 year old daughter. She has opted for a two week's break in Budapest and Prague during the school holidays while her workaholic husband, a lawyer, stays home to run his legal practice. The other passenger, an Egyptian citizen, is a businessman who is coordinating his IT contacts In Europe. He has not been home to Cairo for 4 months.

We are out of luck with the weather. I have left my rain gear in our hotel room and ten minutes later steady rain sets in. Thankfully, Avril brings a small fold-up umbrella for us to share. The two and a half hour drive, south from

Prague, takes us through southern Bohemia, almost to the Austrian border. We have a break at Ceske Budejovice which has 100,000 inhabitants, making it the largest city in south of Prague in the Bohemia Region. Daniel informs us that the German name for the city is Budweis. Here in the 14th century the city established the first brewery in the region and it is still operating. The beer was so successful that two Germans took the recipe to Germany and later it was brewed in the USA as Budweiser beer. (Refer May 3, trademark disputes)

Daniel says that German was the official language of the the old Austro Hungarian Empire. Following its collapse in 1918 the Czech and Slovak languages became the official languages of Czechoslovakia.

Continuing through Southern Bohemia we admire a symphony of yellow flowering canola, green forests and pristine ponds, an overture leading to the beauty of Cesky Krumlov. We arrive at 11.30 am and there is a break in the weather. Our friend's advice, 'You must see Cesky Krumlov', proves well founded. What a perfect natural setting for a fairy tale medieval city! Its scenic beauty and grandeur unfolds before you, full of glory and charm of the days gone by. The town is erected on a promenade located inside a meander of the Vltava River, the bed of which cuts deep into the surrounding hills. The town and its castle stand out romantically like a landscape masterpiece of an artist's brush. In 1992 this urban city of 8,000 inhabitants was put on the list of UNESCO World Cultural and Natural Heritage.

Daniel takes us on a walk through the ancient cobbled lanes of the picturesque town. Daniel says, 'The town was very run down when the Communists left in 1989. Our new government offered zero interest loans for two years to help the restoration. Most people took up the offer and in no time the town was one of the first to be restored.'

The name Krumlov is derived from German, *Krumme Aue*, which may be translated as *crooked meadow*. The name aptly describes the natural topography of the town which nestles tightly around a crooked meander in the Vltava River. The word *Cesky* (in use from 1439) simply means Czech, or Bohemian, as opposed to Moravian or Silesian.

The flow of the river has long been a natural transportation route for entrance to this region. Settlements here go back to the Older Stone Age (70,000 – 50,000 BC), followed by mass settlements in the Bronze Age (1,500 BC). Celtic settlements began in the Early Iron Age (around 400 BC) and Slavonic settlements began from 500 AD. The History of Ceske Krumlov begins probably around 6000 BC, given there is evidence of the first permanent settlement in the area of the present day town. From the eighth to the twelfth century early medieval settlements begin in the area. In the 9th century evidence suggests that the area is owned by a noble Czech family of Slavnikovci, who are slaughtered by the rival family of Premyslovci in 995.

In 1253 Krumlov is first mentioned in written documents as the seat of Vitek, a member of the House of Vitek. In 1302 the Krumlov branch of the House of Vitek dies out. Their property is passed on to their relatives, the lords of Rosenberg who make Krumlov their family residence. For the following three centuries the Rosenbergs rank among the most powerful aristocratic families in Bohemia until their family dies out in the 17th century. Thanks to their tutelage, Cesky Krumlov becomes the centre of the economy and culture in the vast Rosenberg dominion in the southern part of Bohemia. Their coat of arms is a red rose in a silver field. This emblem is still used as a decoration around the city.

The gradual building of the Castle of Krumlov begins around the early 1300s. The older building, called the Lower castle, is extended by the newly constructed Upper castle. A settlement arises below the castle, called Latran, and a large inner town square is established. In the early 1400s, Peter 1 of Rosenberg establishes the parish church of St Vitus and a hospital with St Jodock's Chapel. He endows the town with extensive property privileges.

From 1551 until 1592 the ruler of Cesky Krumlov is William of Rosenberg. He attains high offices in the Kingdom of Bohemia and many foreign diplomats refer to him as the 'vice king' of Bohemia. He carries out a Renaissance reconstruction of the Gothic castle. The town changes its appearance too, by remodelling the Gothic houses in the Renaissance style and by constructing new ones. In 1555 he orders the uniting of the formerly independent settlements of Latran with that of the inner town to form a whole. In 1584 he invites the Jesuits to Cesky Krumlov and allows the construction of a Renaissance Jesuit College.

In 1601, Peter Vok, the last ruler of the Rosenberg family, is forced by debts to sell Krumlov to the Emperor King Rudolf II of Habsburg. For a short time, from 1606 to 1609, the Emperor places his mentally deranged bastard,

Don Julius de Austria, in residence there. But his stay at the castle is accompanied by stormy excesses, resulting in the brutal murder of his lover Marketa Pichlerova, daughter of a Krumlov barber, during a fit of madness in 1608.

In 1622 Emperor Ferdinand II of Habsburg vests Cesky Krumlov to Johann Ulrich von Eggenberg in return for their financial support during the Thirty years' War. The Eggenbergs are aristocrats from Styria, Austria, holding a seat of power there since the mid-1400s. They gradually acquire property in Bohemia during the 17th century. The Eggenbergs are in the Emperor's favour at the time and received many honours. In 1623, the family are raised to the estate of imperial princes and in 1625 they are given the palatinate and the right to print coinage. In 1628 the Krumlov dominion becomes a principality, holding the title of Duchy. But neither Johann Ulrich von Eggenberg nor his son, Johann Anton I von Eggenberg, settle into the Czech environment or make their seat in Krumlov.

It was not until 1664, under the rule of Johann Christian von Eggenberg (1641 -1710), Johann Ulrich's grandson, that the Ceske Krumlov Castle becomes the residential seat of the family. From 1664 Cesky Krumlov serves as the Eggenbergs' residential town until 1719. Under their rule, the castle and town houses are remodelled in Baroque style. He and his wife, Marie Ernestine, nee von Schwarzenberg (1649 – 1719), support the arts. Both are fond of theatre and music and take an interest in visual arts and the castle library. At first, plays are performed in the Deer Hall (today's Masquerade Hall) and in 1689 they install a separate theatre building with a permanent ensemble. The male side of the family dies out following the deaths of Johann Christian in 1710 and his widow in 1719.

Without a male heir, their property, the extensive domain of Krumlov, passes through inheritance to Marie Ernestine's nephew, Adam Franz von Schwarzenberg. The Schwarzenbergs come from Germany and start to reside in Bohemia permanently. Adam Franz is a noted Baroque cavalier who is successful at the imperial court and as a generous patron and passionate hunter. In 1732, at the peak of his career he is killed in an 'accident' by a bullet wound from the gun of Emperor Charles VI during a hunt near Brandys nad Labem.

From 1741 until 1782 the Krumlov ruler is Joseph Adam von Schwarzenberg (1722-1782) who continues remodelling the castle in the Baroque style. He has the Masquerade Hall established with wall paintings by Joseph Lederer. In addition Schwarzenberg has the castle chapel rebuilt and the winter riding hall constructed. In 1767 the Baroque chateau's theatre is rebuilt, thereby gaining its present-day appearance.

From the end of the 18th century, the whole region goes through a period of stagnation in economic and cultural development. The events of the French Revolution, the Napoleonic Wars, and the introduction of a new style of art, Classicism, bring substantial changes in attitudes, views and values of human life. The Schwarzenbergs turn their attention towards the castle of Hluboka and Vltavou (35 km towards Prague), where they later move to. Cesky Krumlov then loses its position as a town of the royal residence and becomes a provincial town.

The industrial revolution during the 19th century does not scar this region as much as other regions, because it lacks resources and transport facilities. Heavy industry is not established here; the main manufacturing processes focus on timber and paper mills. Cesky Krumlov is left aside of industrial development and urbanisation. That is why the ancient feel of Cesky Krumlov and the beauty of the surrounding countryside have been maintained. In the course of the World War II, no military operations take place in Cesky Krumlov and no material damage is inflicted upon the town.

In May 1945 Cesky Krumlov is liberated by the American Army. For centuries the town has been bilingual, Czech and German. The expulsion of the German inhabitants after the war results in an interruption of the town's cultural continuity and brings about a prolonged period of cultural stagnation. In 1947, the castle and the chateau in Cesky Krumlov, along with other Schwarzenberg property, are transferred to the Czechoslovak State. In 1963 the town is declared an urban reservation area, among other historical towns in the state.

In 1992 Cesky Krumlov is put on the list of UNESCO World Cultural and Natural Heritage. The town has become a well-known tourist centre noted for its magical charm and a number of important cultural events such as *FIDELIO classic music concerts, the Five-Petalled Rose Celebrations, an International Music Festival, and a Festival of Baroque Art.*

Avril and I are glad we have taken the opportunity to visit this well-preserved medieval enclave tucked away in a relatively unspoiled area of Central Europe. Cesky Krumlov is a pearl of Renaissance architecture. Daniel parks the minibus and we stroll through a labyrinth of delightful cobble stone laneways, showcasing the Renaissance facades of painted houses and their richly decorated coats of arms. We admire the medieval taverns and traditional artisan shops, particularly of those displaying Czech gingerbread. We wander past the gates leading into the sumptuous Cesky Krumlov Castle where we will meet for a guided tour after lunch.

We stop to admire the majestic parish Church of St Vitus established by Peter 1 of Rosenberg in the first half of the 14th century. It is one of the two dominant structures that define the skyline of Cesky Krumlov. The church and the castle share the promontory created by the River Vltava, thus creating the impressive architectural skyline that characterizes the town. The castle once symbolized the secular ruling power and the region of its influence, whereas the church tower of St Vitus personified the might of Holy Christendom. From medieval times the church functioned as a counterpart and complement of the worldly powers.

It's time for lunch and to enjoy one of those famous Czech beers. Daniel takes us to Restaurant Eggenberg, a huge spacious tavern with 200 seats contained in the former brewery rooms of the Eggenberg brewery. The famous Eggenberg brew is now produced by modern technology installed in the Rosenberg armoury building which in 1594 was the widow's residence of Anna Rosenberg, mother of Peter Vok, the last ruler of the Rosenbergs.

In 1611 the male inheritors of the House of Rosenberg die out in and their lucrative dominion is given to the House of Eggenberg. It includes the possession of Cesky Krumlov Castle and the brewery. In 1717 the last male heir to the House of Eggenberg dies at only 13, after which the Eggenberg Bohemian possessions are inherited by the House of Schwarzenberg. In 1719 they modernize the brewery and decorate it in the Baroque style.

In 1945 the brewery comes under state ownership and, together with Budweiser Budvar Brewery (Budejovicky Budvar) in the city of Ceske Budejovice, is incorporated into the national enterprise known as The South Bohemian Breweries (Jihoceske Pivovary). In September 1991 the state sells the breweries at auction to entrepreneurs Jiri Shrbeny and Frantisek Mrazek for CSK 75 million (approx. US 3.5 million). Mysteriously, the infamous Mrazek is shot dead in 2006. The Eggenberg brand quickly becomes well-known and popular, not just within the local region, but on foreign markets too.

Avril and I fly home to Australia tomorrow and it is appropriate that we toast our last luncheon in the Czech Republic with a glass of one of their best beers. Daniel is sitting next to me, but he has to stick to soft drink because he is driving. Raising my glass I taste the silky smooth drop and pronounce, 'Mmm… yummy! It's almost as good as a Heineken.' Daniel pretends to dong me on the head with his umbrella for my derisory comment. We all laugh as we tuck into the tasty Czech cuisine.

My lasting memory of this enchanted town comes with a visit to the castle after lunch. One is greeted by the black bears in the bear moat at the drawbridge of the castle. Within the castle walls are the wonderful picture galleries. But the most spectacular exhibit for me is of Johann Anton von Eggenberg's magnificent golden carriage. It is made in Rome in 1638 by Giuseppe Fiocchini for the Duke of Krumlov who is asked to lead an important political mission to visit Pope Urban VIII. The golden carriage is part of a parade in the streets of Rome and it is pulled by six horses wearing silver horse shoes. The shoes of the Duke's horse are made of gold. The carriage is decorated with carvings and gold stamping of ancient motifs including the Rosenberg roses and the armorial symbol of the Lords of Krumlov. The famous carriage bears gifts for the Pope.

The extravagant golden carriage remains a Kodak moment imprinted on my mind. However, the highlight of the castle tour is the stunning breathtaking vista of Ceske Krumlov from an open tower window of its castle. This pilgrimage of Central Europe to discover my uncle's footsteps in WW II has led Avril and me to this enchanting and marvellous location.

Plaque outside the birthplace of Oskar Schindler at Svitavy, Moravia.

Imperial Castle, Nuremburg, Germany.

Bronze rabbit in Albrecht Durer Platz, Nuremburg.

Church of Saint Sebaldus, Nuremburg.

Karlovy Vary, mineral springs area, Czech Republic.

Fountains of mineral spring water for tasting, Karlovy Vary.

Prague Castle District, Czech Republic.

The Charles Bridge spans the Vltava River connecting the Old Town to the Castle District, Prague.

Dominant Gothic 'Church of Our Lady before Tyn' at Old Town Square, Prague.

Armory room of Loblowicz Palace at Prague Castle.

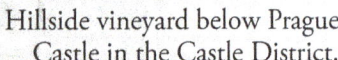

Hillside vineyard below Prague Castle in the Castle District.

Cemetery for Jews at Terezin Gestapo Prison.

Terezin Small Fortress used by the Gestapo as a processing prison 1940-45.

Delousing room at Terezin Gestapo Prison.

Sgraffito example.

Litomysl Castle noted for its sgraffito decorations.

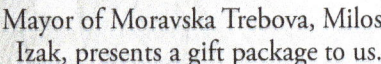

Mayor of Moravska Trebova, Milos Izak, presents a gift package to us.

Arthur's POW barracks once stood on this vacant lot at Moravska Trebova.

Avril and I with guide, Radek Cizek, at the memorial site of Lawrence Saywell, the last Australian killed in Europe in WW II (May 8, 1945 at Miretin, Czech Republic).

Picturesque Cesky Krumlov, Czech Republic.

The Plague Column and Town Hall in T.G. Masaryk Square, Moravska Trebova, Czech Republic.

Astronomical Clock in the wall of Old Town Hall in Old Town Square, Prague.

Jet of hot mineral water, Karlovy Vary, Czech Republic.

Memorial Plaque at the original gravesite of Lawrence Saywell.

Gothic Cathedral of St Vitus in Prague Castle.

MAPS

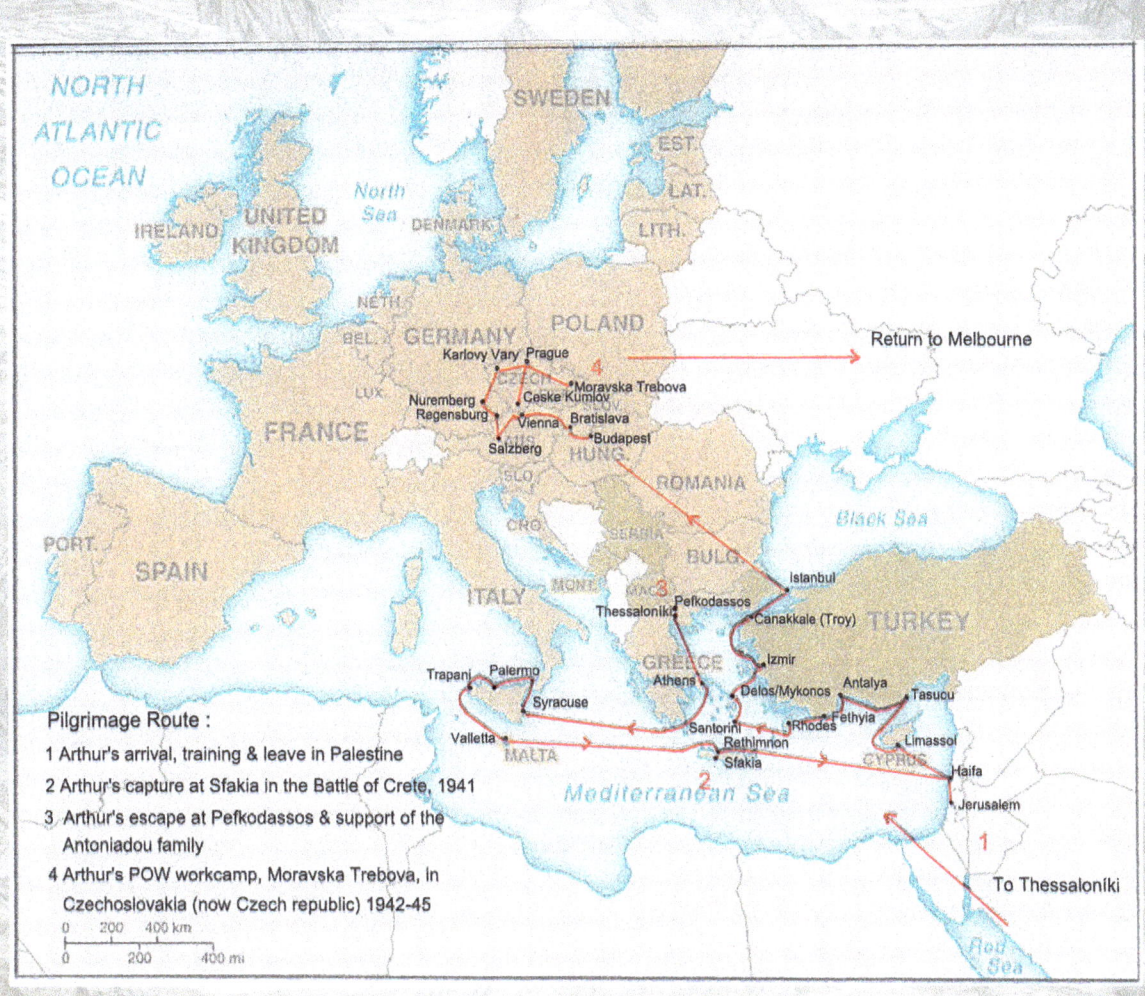

Pilgrimage Route taken in April/May, 2014

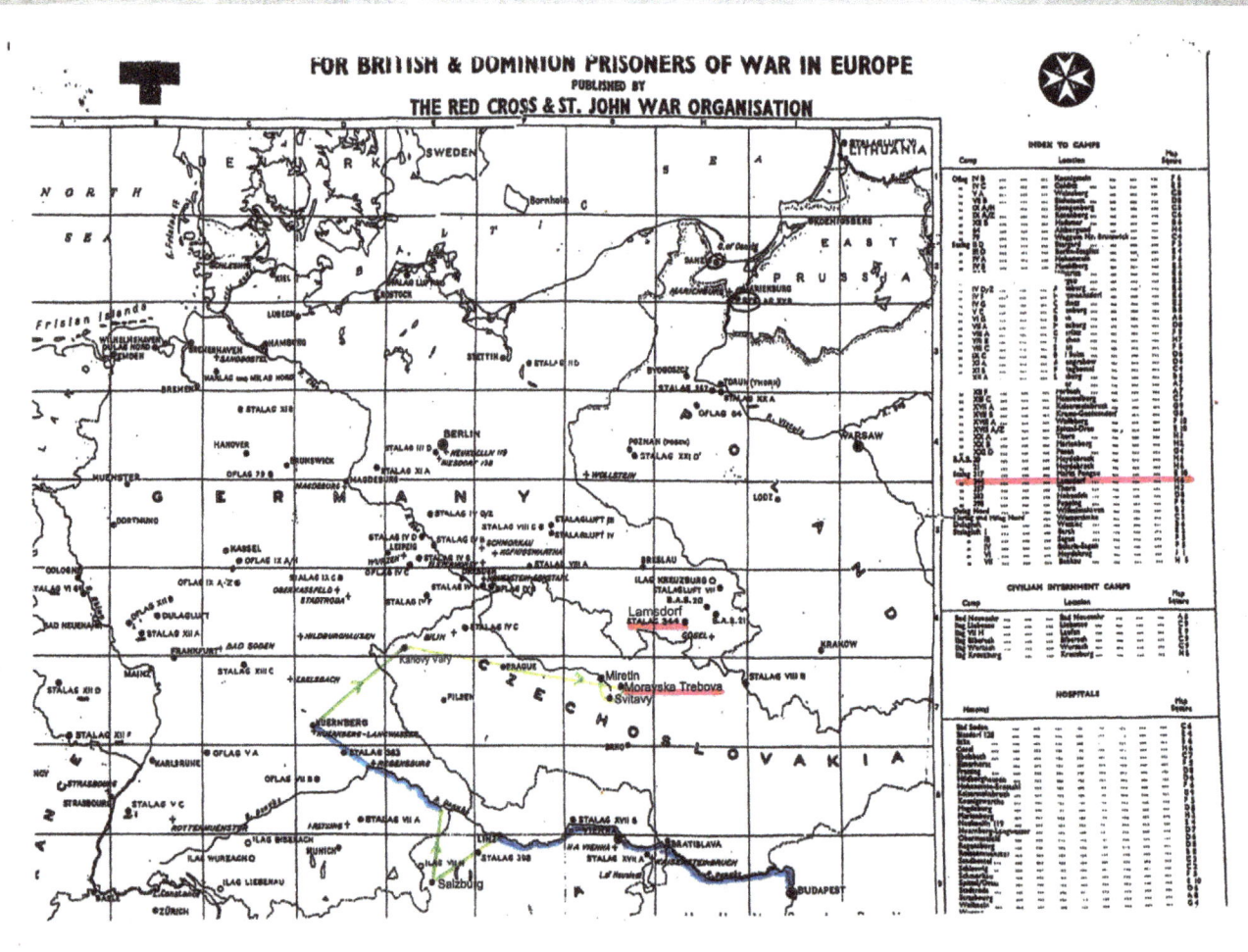

Red Cross Map showing German POW sites and our journey to the Czech Republic

Image Courtesy of: British Red Cross Museums and Archives

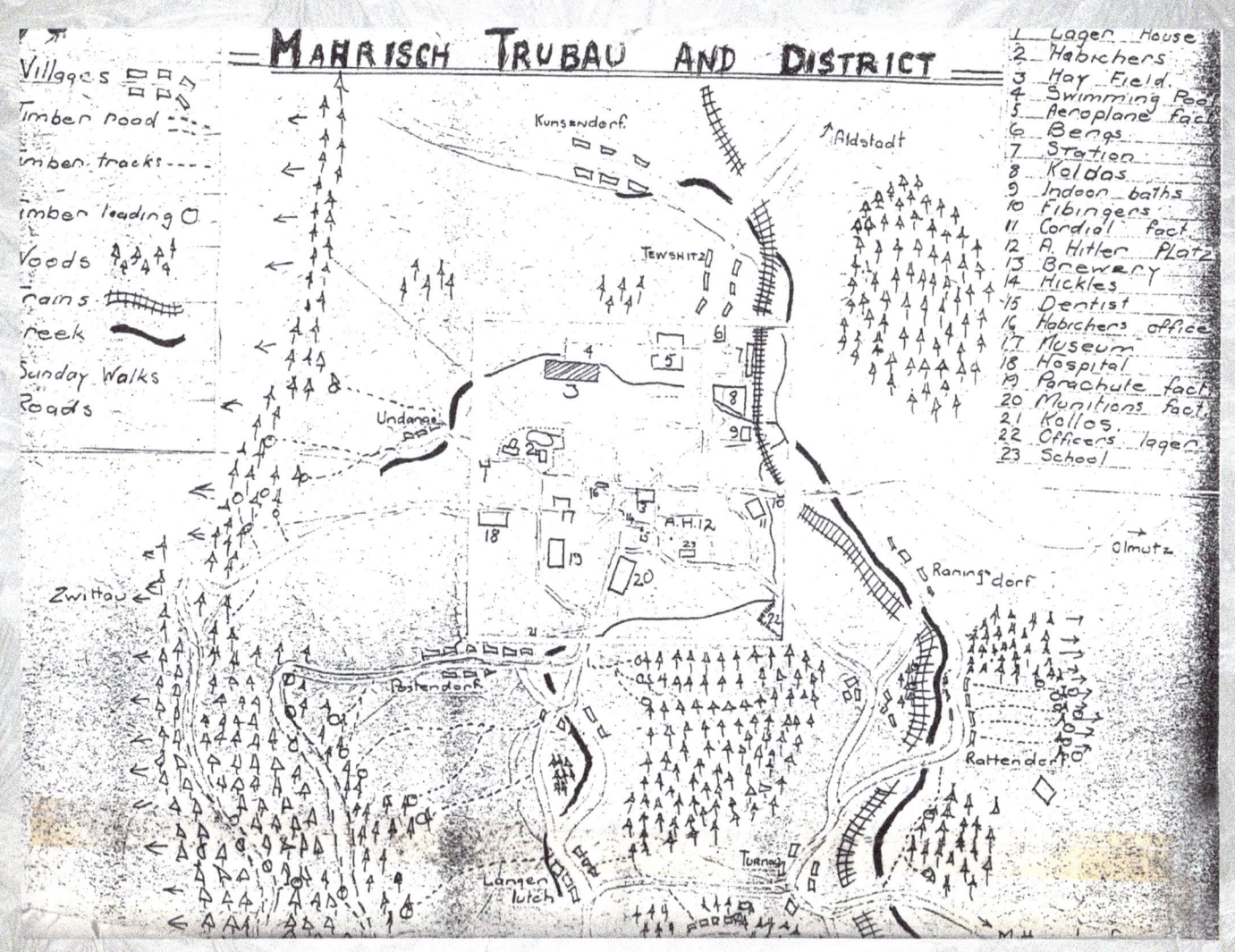

Sketch Map of the Prison Work Camp at Mahrisch Trubau (Moravska Trebova), drawn from memory by Norm Shute after returning home

www.ingramcontent.com/pod-product-compliance
Lightning Source LLC
Chambersburg PA
CBHW061124070526
44584CB00033B/4209